ROUTLEDGE LIBRARY EDITIONS:
SOCIAL THEORY

Volume 74

SOCIOLOGY AND SOCIAL RESEARCH

SOCIOLOGY AND SOCIAL RESEARCH

GEOFF PAYNE, ROBERT DINGWALL, JUDY PAYNE
AND MICK CARTER

Routledge
Taylor & Francis Group

LONDON AND NEW YORK

First published in 1981

This edition first published in 2015
by Routledge
2 Park Square, Milton Park, Abingdon, Oxon, OX14 4RN

and by Routledge
711 Third Avenue, New York, NY 10017

Routledge is an imprint of the Taylor & Francis Group, an informa business

British Library Cataloguing in Publication Data
A catalogue record for this book is available from the British Library

ISBN: 978-0-415-72731-0 (Set)
eISBN: 978-1-315-76997-4 (Set)
ISBN: 978-1-138-78379-9 (Volume 74)
eISBN: 978-1-315-76329-3 (Volume 74)

Publisher's Note
The publisher has gone to great lengths to ensure the quality of this reprint but points out that some imperfections in the original copies may be apparent.

Disclaimer
The publisher has made every effort to trace copyright holders and would welcome correspondence from those they have been unable to trace.

MIX
Paper from
responsible sources
FSC
www.fsc.org   FSC® C013604

Printed and bound by CPI Group (UK) Ltd, Croydon, CR0 4YY

Sociology and social research

**Geoff Payne, Robert Dingwall,
Judy Payne and Mick Carter**

Routledge & Kegan Paul
London, Boston and Henley

First published in 1981
by Routledge & Kegan Paul Ltd
39 Store Street, London WC1E 7DD,
9 Park Street, Boston, Mass. 02108, USA, and
Broadway House, Newtown Road,
Henley-on-Thames, Oxon RG9 1EN
Set in Times by
Saildean Ltd
Walton, Surrey
and printed in Great Britain by
Biddles Ltd
Guildford, Surrey

British Library Cataloguing in Publication Data

Sociology and social research.
1. Sociological research – Great Britain
I. Payne, Geoff
301'.07'2041   HM48   80-41512

ISBN 0-7100-0626-8

To our parents

Contents

Preface

This book has its origins in the period when all four authors were working in various parts of Aberdeen University. Informal conversation about how research is actually done, and the way in which the organisation of academic life helps to determine the intellectual production of the discipline, developed into a more serious look at recent British sociology. During the writing, we each followed separate careers in very different settings and, as a result, the completion of the book took much longer than expected. This underlines our basic view that what one produces as a sociologist depends on the wider social conditions of one's life.

In looking at contemporary British sociology, three themes seem to be paramount. First, the discipline has retreated from *doing* research to *thinking* about sociology. It has become predominantly a theoretical discipline, mainly at home in the library or the study. When it is not concerned with the abstracted realms of generality, it is considering its own navel, lamenting the impossibility of all kinds of empirical research, and demonstrating the intellectual inferiority of all rival schools of thought. Why is this so?

Second, the craft of sociological research is not only being neglected, but is being taught in a totally false way. The neat, precise instructions of the methodology textbooks have little resemblance to our personal experiences of doing research. Despite much talk about the crisis of positivistic science, there is still little attempt in Britain to analyse research *sociologically.*

And third, linking both of these problems, is the position of the sociology profession in the early 1980s. Its rapid post-war development, the relative youth of its practitioners, the current unpopularity of the discipline, among politicians, sixth formers, and other academics alike, are not matters of mere coincidence. Sociology consists of *people,* and what people *do*: these sociologists are enmeshed in complex social processes with other groups and institutions. They exist in a unique historical setting. If we are to understand what we preach as sociology, we must look at the conditions under which sociology is produced and practised.

In the first three chapters, we look at the intellectual origins and recent growth of sociology in this country. With certain exceptions, we concentrate on indigenous, post-war events and ideas, because sociology in this country has combined a radical break with its own roots with a comparative insularity in its outlook. In the third chapter, the emphasis is on ideas: it deals in the wider context of epistemology and a supposed positivist sociology. The previous two chapters are more concerned with the social conditions which produced these ideas.

Part two of the book elaborates on the main 'styles' of research in recent sociology. Chapter 4 is concerned with Grand Theory, the kind of 'research' which can be done from a chair. The following chapters examine the success or failure of ethnography, ethnomethodology, and applied policy research, in each case trying to identify how and why that particular version of sociology came to occupy its present position.

The final section concentrates on sociology as a research activity. Four of the chapters are about what actually happened when sociologists attempted to do research; the political and organisational pressures; the interpersonal, ethical and psychological experiences; and the *normality* of difficulties. We recount several research case studies which involved different methodologies, in an attempt 'to tell it as it is'. Chapter 8 surveys the ill-fated CDP programme, Chapter 9 looks at recent attempts to establish a new methodology based on 'owning-up', Chapter 10 looks at problems of a survey research project, while Chapter 11 deals with the difficulties encountered by ethnographers.

This is followed by a critical discussion of the Social Science Research Council's role in sociological research, and we conclude in Chapter 13 with some suggestions for the future organisation of British sociology and research.

Although this volume was planned as a collective enterprise, its completion has spanned several thousand miles and two continents. It seems appropriate to record that, although the authors subscribe jointly to the contents, Geoff Payne wrote the initial draft of part of Chapter 2, and Chapters 3, 4, 10 and 12; Chapters 5, 6 and 11 were written by Robert Dingwall; part of Chapter 2 and Chapters 7 and 8 by Judy Payne, and Chapter 1 by Mick Carter. Chapters 9 and 13 were written by the first three authors together.

We would like to thank many friends and colleagues for their assistance, not invariably in ways that they would recognise. In

Aberdeen, these included Robert Moore, Fred Twine, Gordon Horobin, Alan Davis, Phil Strong, David May and Mick Bloor. In Oxford, parts of the content were influenced by Max Atkinson and Doreen McBarnet, while among colleagues at Plymouth, David Dunkerley and Adrian Lee listened sympathetically and made helpful suggestions. Pam Watson read and commented on several chapters and the overall structure. We have also benefited greatly from conversations over several years with Eliot Freidson, Anselm Strauss, Julius Roth, J. A. Barnes, Meg Stacey and many others. None of them can be held responsible for any shortcomings in what we have written. Particular thanks are due to Suzanne Tolan in Plymouth, and Angela Palmer and Ginny Rosamond in Oxford for their help in preparing the manuscripts, and to Peter Hopkins of Routledge & Kegan Paul for his patience.

Finally it should be stressed that the ideas expressed are entirely those of private individuals. In no way are our present or past employers to be held responsible for the contents of this book.

part one

1 The development of British sociology

There has been plenty of debate in the last decade or so – indeed, in the last century or so – as to what sociology is. Its antecedents are traced variously in accordance with particular views of its subject matter. While it has been asserted that 'the mere existence of competing sociologies over a long period of time is no grounds for assuming that one of them is not the truest' (Bandyopadhyay, 1971, 27), the intention here is not to debate that issue, least of all to portray the 'one true sociology', but to explore some of the factors which affect the activities which sociologists pursue in their differing ways and with their varying emphases and objectives.

In what ways is sociology a product of society? And how does sociology play back upon the social context in which it is generated? At a certain level, sociology in Britain can be seen as the product of the Enlightenment – an outcome of 'the growth of social thought in the development of philosophical ideas and in the consequential pursuit of certain lines of thought, especially about religion and history' (Mitchell, 1970, 131). On the grand scale, sociological study has its roots in notions of progress and development, Social Darwinism, and economic and technological determinism. The accumulation of knowledge and its re-definition in the light of new modes of scientific enquiry, especially in the nineteenth century, resulted in innovatory ways of perceiving the world – including the social world.

It has been proposed that the development of sociology depends upon turmoil within society and an associated mood of uncertainty among the populace. Questions about the nature of social order are, of course, more likely to occur at times of disruption or when social structures, ideas and values are undergoing rapid change. Whether one looks at the Germany of Max Weber or at contemporary 'underdeveloped' societies factors can be discerned which thrust sociological issues into the forefront of immediate national concerns. But this does not mean that 'sociology' necessarily develops as an instrument or a reflection of particular historical phases or social predicaments. Worsley has reminded us that 'the country which has made the most spectacular and world-historic developmental breakthrough of the post war period' – namely, People's China, has done so without the benefit of institutionalised sociology (never mind Western sociological theory!) (Worsley, 1974, 16).

The evidence suggests that particular social climates may be conducive to the development of sociology as a discipline, may retard it or may render it irrelevant or unremarkable. At one level of explanation, the tardy development of sociology as an academic discipline in Britain – compared, say, with the USA – can be attributed to the (at least erstwhile) dominance of the ancient English universities in decisions on the direction of scholarly studies, and to their antipathy towards, or ignorance of, sociology as a field of knowledge. Yet, as Hawthorn suggests, one can explain the absence of sociology as an 'intellectually and academically distinctive pursuit' prior to 1939 in terms of the fact that it 'was virtually everywhere present as part of the general liberal and liberal-socialist consciousness'. Class and status, class conflict and status difference featured in the everyday conceptions of the people and 'the continuity of English social and political thought through-out the nineteenth century and into the first four decades of the twentieth is most simply understood by the absence of any threat of revolution from the left and of any concerted resistance from the right' (Hawthorn, 1976).

A concern with facts

None the less, throughout the nineteenth century in England, in Europe and in America, there developed an increasingly insistent new concern with 'facts'. This, Glazer has argued, represented the 'origin of contemporary social science':

> it began to be felt that the collection of scattered observations from writers, combined with the casual observation of social life as one saw it in the ordinary course of one's activities, could not possibly tell one what was true and important: it was necessary to collect all the relevant facts, to consider the grounds on which one accepted these as facts, and ... to test knowledge by professionally investigating what had previously been casually observed (Glazer, 1973, 46-7).

Urban, industrial society could not do without facts, without censuses, knowledge of the economic and social condition of the people and of trends in population movements and migration. The 'impersonality' of cities, furthermore, was conducive to regarding men and women as objects – and therefore as susceptible to study as if they were but objects (Easthope, 1974, 10). A 'positive science of society' was given impetus: a 'scientific' study which was attractive in an age in which the pure and applied sciences were making rapid advances and meshed well with notions of 'rational man' derived from the idea of a social contract.

Whether one is inclined to cite the Domesday Book as an example of empiricism as an integral part of the British character or as an early indication of kingly or governmental concern to maximise income from taxes, the accumulation of statistical 'facts' is deeply inlaid in British social history and is associated with a particularly strong element in sociological research. Censuses have been held every ten years since 1801 (1941 excepted, and additionally in 1966). These 'numbers pertaining to the State' are supplemented by a number of other sources of official statistics. Rating lists, reports of the various Departments of State, Registers of Electors and so on at once provide information in their own right and may serve as a basis for sampling in particular research projects. Of course, even statistical facts are not pure and simple: it is salutary to note the subtle differences between the Statistical Society of London (later the Royal Statistical Society) which was founded in 1834 and its somewhat younger sister Society in Manchester. Glazer argues that both societies had 'a deep belief in the saving power of the fact as against the theory'. However, the London Society was strongly influenced by academics, and its prospectus stated that it would 'consider it to be the first and most essential rule of its conduct to exclude carefully all opinions from its transactions and publications – to confine its attention rigorously to facts – and, as far as it may be found possible, to facts which can be stated numerically and arranged in tables.' The Manchester Society was more oriented to reform, its first Annual Report attributing the origin of the Society to 'a strong desire felt by its projectors to assist in promoting the progress of social improvement in the manufacturing population by which they are surrounded' (Glazer, 1973, 51-2).

A concern with reform

Social reform has long been recognised as a significant strand in the story of British sociology. This intellectual 'tradition' includes people such as Chadwick, Booth and Rowntree and in more recent times Titmuss and his colleagues and successors. Despite some reverence paid to grand-scale theorists such as Hobhouse and Spencer, in histories of British social science there is a tendency to give more deference to the line of social surveyors, informed as they were by a social conscience and anxious that their research should pave the way for reforms. Whether it is appropriate to dismiss with Glazer theorists such as Marx and Comte for moving off into the philosophical clouds of human endeavour (Glazer refers to the 'large general ideas, which soon began to lead a life independent of social realities'), it is important to emphasise the 'direct involvement' of reformers such as Beatrice Webb and Charles Booth 'with the human beings who made up the problems' associated with the rise of an industrial proletariat and 'their attempt to ground any general statement about the poor and the working classes on direct acquaintance with them' (Glazer, 1973, 59).

The stalwarts of the social reform element in the development of British sociology were not soft-headed 'do-gooders'. The Simeys, in their biography of Booth, are at pains to point out the significance of their subject's contribution in sheer methodological terms. The sophisticated use of survey and other methods and the careful weighing of evidence by reference to hypotheses were the hallmark of Booth's work: 'if Booth's work means anything at all to the twentieth century, it is because it demonstrates that there is an inseparable relationship between fact and theory which can be established as an essential element in successful social research.' The conclusion is that the work of Booth amounts to a 'watershed in the history of British social policy. . . . a new attitude was created towards the study of the problems of contemporary society.' Hitherto, policy had developed from belief and doctrine: 'Booth's work now provided the nation with a new instrument of government' (Simey and Simey, 1960, 256).

In attempting to comprehend the different (and in some ways contradictory) definitions or styles of sociology which can be discerned in Britain now and in the past, differences in motivation (such as passion for reform or a disinterested pursuit of 'the truth') must be taken into account as well as the contrasting personalities and varying social backgrounds of social researchers. Matters of chance are not to be discounted however. As an example, the Simeys contend that the gulf between Booth and other social reformers on the one hand, and his contemporary Hobhouse and associated academics on the other – a gulf which served to perpetuate a separation of styles of research, in particular the blend of deduction and induction of the former compared with the essentially deductive method of the latter – was, although 'open to speculation', probably a consequence of the fact that 'Hobhouse's attention was diverted ... by the sharp conflicts concerning the nature of sociological studies ... which arose as soon as attempts were made to introduce them into the universities.' It is interesting to speculate on how much more sociological effort has been prejudiced by the exigencies of organising university studies and placating contentious colleagues in the last two decades of British sociology. Yet, as the Simeys say, Hobhouse 'shared with Comte a belief that sociology should, as it matured, render increasingly possible an expansion of the area of conscious control over the trends of human development and this was in full agreement with Booth's view.' The Simeys' conclusion is that 'had Hobhouse attempted to translate this dictum into practice he would have found himself working alongside Booth, and the subsequent history of sociology in England might have been very different.'

Sociologists – anxious for academic acceptance – are perhaps too readily concerned to trace their pedigree to grand theorists and to disown the seemingly more modest contributions of social reformers. Glazer is in no uncertainty on this issue, arguing in 1959 that

> present day sociologists have more in common with the earnest men of the early nineteenth century mainly in England, who painfully built up a picture of social reality, detail by detail, than with those strongminded thinkers, disdainful of such details, who wanted to tear down worlds and build quite new ones.

A squabble over the pedigree – not to say the legitimacy – of one's forebears may be unseemly, but the prospect of an alliance between Hobhouse and Booth is cause for reflection on the scope for mutual enhancement of sociologists of apparently very different persuasion and concern.

Industrial and urban growth, ideological change, new techniques, new concerns and new definitions – these and other factors have contributed to the state of sociology in contemporary Britain. Patterns can be shaped, but no overriding pattern will satisfy. Traditional theoretical concerns with order, change and conflict persist. Number-crunchers (the victims or protagonists of 'quanterphrenia')* still stand proud or dejected; whilst there is an ever-present concern to comprehend social action in terms of the 'meaning' for the actor – though the methodological consequences of this concern are by no means uniformly agreed. T. H. Marshall viewed sociology as being at the 'crossroads' in his inaugural

---

* David Eversley discusses issues associated with Sorokin's term interestingly in *A Question of Numbers?* Runnymede Trust, 1973.

lecture at the LSE in 1946. Which road should sociology take? Not, in Marshall's view, the 'way to the stars' – 'sociologists should not ... expend all their energies climbing in search of vast generalisations, universal laws, and a total comprehension of human society as such.' Marshall did not find an alternative route attractive either – 'the way into the sands of whirling facts which blow into the eyes until nothing can be clearly seen or heard.' There was, Marshall thought, a middle way

> which runs over firm ground [and] ... leads into a country
> whose features are neither Gargantuan nor Lilliputian, where
> sociology can choose units of study of a manageable size – not
> society, progress, morals, and civilization, but specific social
> structures in which the basic processes and functions have
> determined meanings (Marshall, 1963, 20).

Sixteen years later W. J. H. Sprott rejected the notion of a crossroads, carrying as it does the implication of 'a body of men, marching together and faced with a decision as to which way to go'. For Sprott, the sociological terrain approximated more 'the seven dials' – he could see 'several bodies of men converging on an open space where they spend a good deal of time abusing one another' (Sprott, 1962). It was almost as if the sociological profession had come together at Hyde Park corner. Sprott, like Marshall before him, identified the fact gatherers (responsive to what they and administrators see as social problems). Then there are the method-men ('accused of letting their methods dictate the information they will obtain'). The historical sociologists are differentiated from social historians in having a general sociological problem as a base for their studies. The sociological bird watchers can themselves be spied – they, in fact, supply much of the data used in imparting the subject in the university setting. Then Sprott discerns three sorts of theorists – the middle rangers, the analytical theorists and the dynamic theorists.

This variety in scope, interest and approach is attributed by Sprott, at least in part, to the 'odd nature of the subject-matter, its subjectiveness': he refers to Hobhouse's observation that 'there are still many deep divergencies of view as to the nature and province of the inquiries which [sociologists] professedly pursue in common.' Perhaps sociological endeavours are intrinsically and necessarily untidy; this may offend the analytical aspirations of its practitioners, but can be seen as a challenge – Westermark, as Professor of Sociology at the LSE, made the point that

> anyone who takes up the study of sociology must not expect to
> come to an exhibition, where every article may be had ready and

finished. On the contrary, he will find that he has entered a workshop, where everything is in the making – and he will have to take part in the work.

Towards a professional sociology

The springs of sociological inquiry are, clearly, many and varied. There is an interest and an intellectual excitement in understanding society, if only because, like Everest, it is there. There is a concern to change the social world and a concern to control it or at least to contain the rate and direction of change. Increasingly, too, there is an aspiration 'simply' to cope with it. Neustadt has indicated that 'there are many reasons for the growing demand for sociologists in highly industrialised as well as in so-called "underdeveloped" society.' Among them are the social needs and pressures which demand, within a smaller or wider compass, changes guided by a degree of planning. It is becoming less and less possible or desirable to rely on automatic changes pure and simple or on guidance by intuitive illuminations of so-called 'practical common sense'. For the solution of increasingly complex social tasks, a solid basis of scientific sociological teaching and research is as necessary as a similar basis of teaching and research in economics. Hence an increasing demand for sociological skills and approaches amongst social workers, doctors, lawyers, town planners and so on. The 'decline of the traditional trust in amateurishness' is to be seen 'wherever men are concerned with taking decisions over others: [in] factories, government offices, courts of law, homes, schools, hospitals and welfare agencies' (Neustadt, 1965, 5–6). The 'decline of the traditional trust in amateurishness' paves the way for sociological professionalism. Mitchell has alluded, similarly, to 'a realisation of both the possibility and the necessity of deliberately influencing social behaviour through legislation and the creation of new institutions' (Mitchell, 1970, 130). The point was made by John Mack in 1956 that the rapidly increasing prestige and influence of the social sciences over the last decade or so was not a consequence of 'any great theoretical advance or outstanding social invention' – it was simply that the social sciences were becoming more necessary (Mack, 1956).

No doubt there is much in this. Yet the correspondence between the development of a discipline, its sophistication, its influence or relevance, and the 'needs' of society are surely matters which give rise to circumspection in the sociologist. It requires no great insight to document research which is seemingly arbitrary in direction and intent. The US Space Programme provides an example – it gave rise to considerable government support for the study of the extent to which the new technology was transferable to other sectors of technology and industry. Large programmes of research into scientific policy were funded which resulted in the redefinition of relationships between technology, technological innovation and social change. Furthermore, the direction which research takes may reflect opportunity or diplomacy rather than desirability or strategic significance. Thus it has been argued that the principal reason for the first large-scale European studies of leisure under the general direction of Dumazedier may have been the prospect of establishing contact with sociologists in Eastern Europe 'on politically safe grounds' (SSRC, 1967). Whether a specialist area flourishes or not may be as much or more dependent on factors associated with the particular area of study than with the value or significance of the work.

The twentieth century was three years old when Victor Branford obtained support for the foundation of the Sociological Society. Institutionally sociology got off to a slow start, but of particular importance was the inauguration of two Chairs of Sociology at the LSE, the Martin White Professorships, in 1907. The Foundation Professors were L. T. Hobhouse – whose inaugural address was entitled 'The Roots of Modern Sociology' and E. A. Westermarck, whose lecture took the theme of 'Sociology as a University Study' (Westermarck, 1907). (A few years later, in 1912, it may be noted R. M. MacIver, who had been lecturing in Political Science at King's College, Aberdeen, persuaded the Senate of that University to add the words 'and Sociology' to the title of his lectureship. The University of Aberdeen thereby became the first University in Scotland formally to include sociology in its curriculum.) Morris Ginsberg succeeded to Hobhouse's Chair in 1930. Following Hobhouse and Westermarck, Ginsberg imparted a broad philosophical and psychological version of sociology. The strong historical and philosophical tradition of the London syllabus endured for many decades. Even in the years after the Second World War, when there was a stronger concern with social inequalities and differentiation among a new breed of LSE sociologists, it survived. T. H. Marshall took the third Chair in 1946. His injunction to sociologists to pursue a middle way between universal laws and ultimate values on the one hand, and mere fact gathering on the other, was one important reference point for recruits to sociology in the post-war years. It served as the blueprint for London's progeny in Leicester, Hull and Nottingham, as well as Birmingham, Leeds and other colleges, and is still in certain respects evident today.

Post-war sociology

Nevertheless, the development of sociology outpaced the supply of LSE graduates during this period. As good an indicator of this expansion as any is provided by the University of Leicester which had only two teachers in sociology from 1952-7, six by 1961 and nineteen by 1967. At this time, too, the 'new universities' – Kent, Essex, East Anglia, Lancaster, Sussex, Warwick and York – were established, and all included sociology as a major study. Indeed, by the early 1970s it was estimated that 1200 people were employed as teachers of sociology in universities and other institutions of higher education (Smith, 1975, 309).

This expansion modified and contained the LSE influence. Liverpool had been a strong independent force for some years under Simey, and Leeds had grown in strength. Even a cursory perusal of appointments to Headships of Departments in the 1960s and 1970s refutes the often-heard assertion of positivist dominance. There may have been a contrary influence in publications – perhaps positivists were for a while producing more or getting into print. But despite such counter-facts as the appointment of David Glass to the fourth LSE Chair in 1949, sociologists' teaching programmes were not, by and large, positivist if that term is to have any precise and limiting definition.

One very important influence in the development of sociology at this time was that of social anthropology. Social anthropologists (and social psychologists) together with sociologists formed a new Sociology Section of the British Association for the Advancement of Science in 1960 and this at once reflected increasing concourse between anthropologists and sociologists in Britain and gave it impetus: a number of Chairs of Sociology were filled by persons whose background had been primarily in social anthropology departments. Increasingly, anthropological methods and perspectives were being applied to the study of modern societies, and sociological techniques and theories applied to non-literate or under-developed societies. Of course, the tradition of social anthropology in Britain was distinctive as was the social background of its practitioners. Looking at key decision-makers in the early 1960s and 1970s one can discern the very powerful influence of those who were trained in the social anthropological tradition. Also evident are the influences of particular social class, gender, ethnic and religious characteristics on the composition of the academic body of sociologists.

At the same time, a growth in numbers was accompanied by a trend to professionalisation. When, on the initiative of A. M. Carr-Saunders with twelve associates, the British Sociological

Association was founded in 1951, narrow professionalism had been eschewed. The intention was to encourage 'contact and co-operation between workers in all relevant fields of enquiry': the scope of the Association was 'deliberately made very wide, in order to bring together all those who were interested in the sociological aspects of their own special subjects' (Banks, 1967). Banks estimates that when the first Annual General Meeting of the Association was held no more than a quarter of the four hundred people who had joined 'were sociologists in a fairly narrowly defined professional sense' (Banks, 1975). By the time that the Association entered its second decade, however, the momentum towards professionalism and specialisation had accelerated and this found expression in the formation of the Sociology Teachers' Section, recognised as such by the Executive of the British Sociological Association, in 1963. The Teachers' Section had elaborate 'gates' to control entry, its concern was with promoting sociology as a discipline, through conferences on curricula and methods, through arranging summer schools for post-graduate students and through the compilation of a register of professional sociologists. The Teachers' Section soon came to dominate the Association, with particularly strong *de facto* representation on the Executive Committee. The founding of the journal *Sociology* in 1967 is largely attributable to the aspirations and efforts of sociology teachers in the universities working through and with the Teachers' Section. The decision to found the journal was not taken lightly: the major concern was that there would be sufficient articles of merit to ensure the continuance of a high quality professional publication. It soon became clear that the Association could be sanguine in this respect – yet another measure of the rapid growth in sociology and of the quality of work being done in the discipline.

The professionalisation of sociology has obvious implications for the status of teachers and researchers and for the way in which definitions of its subject-matter and objectives are made. The decline of the amateur and the 'generalist' social scientist-cum-social reformer can be traced back to before the major expansion of the 1960s, of course. Simey has lamented the loss of disinterested activists, consequent upon the decline of private means, observing that:

> the amateur of professional status may be elbowed out of our
> social life by the professional who is becoming deeply en-
> trenched in the bureaucracy of our day, which does not seem to
> be able to generate the energy necessary to mount a successful
> attack on the really serious problems of our age (Simey, 1964,
> 29).

Whether or not the demise of the disinterested reformer has had such a markedly deleterious impact on the nature of sociological inquiry as Simey supposes, it is clear that the changing complexion of the practitioners of social research has had a qualitative effect upon the subject.

This is a concomitant also of the significant change which has occurred in the qualifications and experience of those competent to exert a major influence upon the directions which teaching and research take. An appreciable number of the persons appointed to senior teaching and research posts in the late 1950s and early 1960s were 'converts' from neighbouring disciplines and were cast in a very different mould from the succeeding generations of sociologists who graduated throughout the 1960s and 1970s. Persuasive arguments may be adduced as to the benefits and the injuries which have flowed from the earlier influence of historians, economists, geographers and others. The breadth of knowledge brought to bear upon the subject-matter of sociology may be applauded – whilst an 'amateurish' and unsophisticated approach can be deplored. In 1967 the possibility was referred to, for example, 'that the high proportion of recruits from other subjects may be partly responsible for what is generally admitted to be the lack of thorough systematic training in sociological research methodology and techniques in the graduate schools' (SSRC, 1967). It is not necessary to be contentious in making the point that the composition of the professional body of sociologists has an effect upon the subject-matter of the discipline: changes in composition will be manifested in changes in research and teaching orientations.

Banks provides another example of the interplay of the social position and educational experience of the sociologist and the perception which he may derive in regard to his 'calling' – writing in 1971, Banks notes the perceptions of different groups of sociologists: 'the rapid expansion of sociology teaching ... has introduced a large number of junior teachers into university departments, the older members of which have experienced a sort of rapid promotion which is denied to the newcomers.' The former are:

> rather more conscious of the problems facing the individual in the lower ranks in modern organisations than are those sociologists who are near the top. We should not be surprised therefore to find them identifying with the aspirations of students in challenging the system (Banks, 1971, 19).

Whilst in the 1950s academics who were formulating research questions tended to be social problem oriented, by the 1960s many departments of sociology repudiated such studies. Sociologists, by then, would not deign to belittle themselves with a-theoretical public concerns – these were left to departments of Social Administration (there were some outstanding exceptions to this generalisation, of course). Oddly, many of the young radical sociologists soon resorted to the armchair and spent a decade from the mid 1960s to the mid 1970s contemplating whether society, and hence sociology, actually could exist. Others were seduced by interpersonal theories. Worsley's analysis of the preoccupation 'with applying great ingenuity and sophistication to the personally sometimes problematic, but societally insignificant difficulties of managing the first five seconds of conversations, walking down the street, or exchanging "Good Mornings" in a world agonised by infinitely greater social problems', suggests that the proponents of this 'approach' constitute a particular social category of sociologists. For:

> interpersonal sociology ... strikes powerful ... resonant chords
> and sympathetic responses in the psyches of those who often
> intellectually reject the constraining coercive demands made of
> them by society ... who identify with the insulted and the
> injured, with the deviant, the minority, the marginal, the
> oppressed and the unfortunate.... The abjuration of societal
> concerns has bred a new generation of sociologists, who, unlike
> the positivists they scorn, actually know little about society
> because they do not wish to know (Worsley, 1974, 15-16).

The expansion of sociology in the universities was soon followed by developments in polytechnics and colleges of education and in other institutions of higher education. There was also a rapid increase in the number of full-time research workers. Smith's survey showed that in 1973 over 200 organisations employed a total of at least 895 sociologists as research workers. Higher Education institutions, mainly universities, accounted for one-half of these, about a third of that half being employed in research units. One-third of the total worked in government agencies, two-thirds of that number being in local authorities: relatively few worked in industry or commerce (Smith, 1975, 310). There had developed by the early 1970s, then, a significant body of full-time researchers who were not involved in, and in many ways could be said to be divorced from, the teaching of the subject. University teachers were pursuing research, but of a different order and within a different institutional framework from the bulk of full-time research workers. Indeed, it is possible to discern a hierarchy of occupational fields in sociology manifesting different interests and making different contributions to the subject. This gives rise to interesting speculation about the relative capacity of sociologists of different ability and/or qualifications who enter different levels of the hierarchy to make decisions influencing the direction which research will take (Banks, 1974, 297-304).

The organisation and content of British sociology

Jennifer Platt has exposed many of the realities of social research not least those implicit in, or spawned by, the organisational arrangements which provide the framework for the research enterprise (Platt, 1976). University organisation has important effects upon sociological research based therein. The inadequacies and hindrances to research could be dwelt upon at length – duplication and waste through lack of communication with others working in the field; the lack of resources, even of small amounts of money for postage; inadequate funding resulting from lack of experience in the research workers making submissions for grants, or lack of expertise in those adjudicating upon an application. At the time of rapid expansion in the universities in the 1960s over-large teaching loads, constant revision of courses and the devising of new courses, as departments extended their curricula, left little time for research. Most universities, if they had research workers at all, were dependent upon outside fundings for specific projects, and hence could offer only short-term research posts. Liverpool, with several permanent posts of research lecturer, was a significant exception – and the device undoubtedly bore fruit in quantity and quality of research output at that time. Platt summarises the position as follows:

> there are a variety of respects in which the character of the university setting affects projects located there. Teaching commitments complicate research timetables and communication within teams, and for a variety of reasons tend to take priority over research; departmental character can give intellectual support and stimulus to the research team or sap its morale; disciplinary divisions create divergences of intellectual style and reference groups that are hard to overcome; the relatively unworldly pursuit of ideas for their own sake leads to research styles with special strengths and weaknesses (Platt, 1976, 43).

Research workers based in other institutions, of course, have their own battery of factors which facilitate, hinder and in various ways colour the research process. In respects which have important implications for social research, universities and other institutions have features in common, however. The large size and increasing specialisation of disciplines in universities, the separation of place of dwelling and place of work make it 'hardly surprising', as Banks indicates, 'that universities are less communities than they are

15

organisations similar in all major respects to the other large organisations that constitute our type of society' (Banks, 1971, 14).

One aspect of the growth in social research, not least in reference to the SSRC and its mode of operation, is the 'bureaucratisation' of the research grant process. Rex has traced the unfortunate influence of committees in vetting, sponsoring or preventing research, and has argued that the 'institutionalisation of science posits its neutralisation as a means to mastery of the environment' (Rex, 1970, 152). And Brown has suggested that an overemphasis on methodological and technical matters as criteria in making research awards is a direct consequence of the committees' structure, which demands 'statements which can be processed quickly and which confirm text-book standards of scientific proto-col' (Brown, 1973). Alas, however, the academic making the application may be bureaucratised or at least routinised, too – Worsley, following Wright Mills, stresses the distinction between the 'academic' and the intellectual. Whilst the latter 'suffers agonies in wrestling with his soul to make sense of the world' the former 'is a grey man, often as routinised in his pursuit of an occupation as any affluent or black-coated worker, and as orientated to career as any other kind of middle class professional' (Worsley, 1974, 14). Most academics in Worsley's view are wholesalers and retailers rather than producers of ideas. This analysis appropriately gives rise to circumspection since the traditional approach to research by most grant-awarding bodies is indeed individualistic.

It is not necessary here to parade the bureaucratic and administrative obstacles which the research grant applicant – and indeed the recipient – has to contend with. Funding agencies *could* be more flexible, they *do* tend, in their conditions, to apply a straitjacket to the research activity. Then, too, award-giving bodies may wish to affect the outcome of the research, and even withhold support or access to data if the study is taking a direction which they dislike. The research may have been supported, in any case, for the sake of appearances – as a political or industrial manoeuvre, rather than for its own sake. A study of redundancy in Birmingham, substantially financed by the national government in 1957 as a token of the seriousness with which it viewed the problem, fell into difficulties soon after the research got off the ground because most of the men had been taken on again. A new, technological phenomenon of redundancy, it turned out, was really only an old-style lay-off.

Administrative convenience or established procedures may shape the university's approach as well however – in terms of the duration of research associated with a higher degree for example, and difficulties inherent in team research when higher-degree studies are involved.

Julius Roth has reprimanded sociologists for not keeping their own research houses in order. He points out that it is commonly accepted from studies in the sociology of work that restriction of production and deviation from stipulated procedures are *normal* in the work-place:

> it is the expected behaviour of workers in a production organisation ... the only problem for an investigator of work practices is discovering the details of cutting corners, falsifying time sheets, defining work quotas, dodging supervision, and ignoring instructions in a given work setting (Roth, 1966, 190-6).

Why, then, do sociologists blithely assume that their interviewers, coders, analysts and participant observers – or those of the contracting market or other research agency – are not cheating? Or, to put it more subtly, there are surely good grounds for circumspection on the links of the chain between research design and the drawing of sociological conclusions.

The character of sociology in the universities and the research which it gave rise to is in part, then, to be explained in terms of an as yet unaccomplished consideration of the minutes of short-listing processes, choice of referees and external advisers for appointments. The rapidity of expansion in the universities has already given way to a steady state – though not before a similar wave of expansion had occurred in polytechnics and other colleges, which have already put an important stamp upon certain directions in teaching and research in sociology. Patronage and friendship have undoubtedly played a part in the shaping of British sociology, then, as well as disinterested concern for the development of the discipline. Succeeding generations of students already have been socialised into certain modes of thought and certain aspirations, or have reacted against what has been placed before them as the subject-matter of sociology.

The flurry of expansion has not been accompanied by any evident 'breakthrough' in the discipline. It is probably not a discipline of that sort. Of course, technology affects possibility – the computer obviously presents options of an altogether different kind from Hollerith. In matters of technique we may still witness significant developments in statistical procedures analogous to the devising of correlation, which transformed research activity in many areas of study. Rex considers that the impact of the computer was so disturbing that it represented a challenge to sociologists who reacted with 'fierce debates' as to the nature of their discipline: this,

17

the argument goes, presaged a strong anti-positivist phase in British sociology. Conceptually, claims may be made – Max Gluckman, for example, sees the extended case study method as a radically new methodological tool of significance (Gluckman, 1967). But, by and large, the 'paraphernalia of research – the theory, the methodology, the techniques' (Brown, 1973, 13), are much the same at the end of the 1970s as they were at the end of the 1950s. The significant change is in the volume and quality of substantive work.

It may be that distance from the 1950s, 1960s and 1970s will enable the identification of significant and permanent changes in sociological approaches in Britain during those years. At present all that can be discerned clearly are changes in fashion – although one common thread has been the variety of sociologies concurrently practised, and the institutional forces that have maintained such variety. This is especially true in regard to research output. The organisation of research underlined the tension, delineated by Platt, between aiming at a 'neat, rounded research project' (one which sponsors would find satisfying) on the one hand; and on the other feeling subject to an 'arbitrarily delimited part of the continuous stream of interrelated interests and ideas which goes to make up the intellectual career' of the research worker (Platt, 1976, 31-2). In substantive areas, too, fashions have come and gone. The interest in the 1960s took many people by surprise whilst the sociology of law remained largely dormant until the last few years. Socio-linguistics came and went spasmodically. The sociology of gender developed dramatically in the last decade and has been one of the most important features of British sociology. Education has flourished as an interest, while the sociology of work has continued to be a major enterprise in its various forms. This represents, perhaps, a wide dispersion of research interests in British sociology and a necessary span of time between initiating research and writing up conclusions. Not, as the SSRC will testify, that *all* research is written up.

With all the various factors affecting what research is done, it is scarcely surprising that the sociological scene has been described as piecemeal and unco-ordinated. Major gaps blot the map – despite important studies there has been relatively little done on the family, a central institution, for example. Even basic inventory material on population, religious affiliations and so on is modest in scope. Certain vital areas – such as political power – have been neglected, again despite important work. Electors have been studied rather than cabinets, just as trade unions have been studied rather than boards of directors. The desirability of 'studying up' has been asserted and re-asserted, but the task seems to be too large. The signs of building upon the research of others – or of oneself

– save in terms of general intellectual development are few. There have been some replications and some repeat studies – Banbury has been re-visited and the affluent worker set in a composite framework. Social mobility has been measured and examined in Scotland as well as in England and Wales – and, to some extent in Ireland. There are a number of institutions and departments with well-defined strategies of research: but there is no overall strategy, perhaps there cannot be one and probably ought not to be.

Much remains to be done in the sociological workshop, then, and it is work which of its nature is unending. Sociology is the product of society in numerous, varied and often paradoxical ways. Macro-processes are manifested in micro-influences: the link between the two, as between 'fact' and theory, challenges the intellect and often threatens to dismay the heart. The pursuit of knowledge about society for its own sake, or its pursuit in a manner as if it were for its own sake, implies major problems in the sociology of knowledge as well as in philosophical and methodological terms. The aim here has been to depict the range of factors playing upon issues as to the nature of sociology and the status of sociological research, rather than to attempt a definitive history or a contemporary inventory. The subject was, is and always will be untidy.

2 The social context of British sociology

The previous chapter has provided us with an overview of the history and culture of British sociology. In this chapter and the next, we embark on more detailed investigations of the consequences of this tradition for the present state of research and teaching. We begin with a discussion of sociology as an occupation, in keeping with our general stress on the importance of the discipline's social context for an understanding of its production.

Although the study of occupational change is part of the sociologists' stock-in-trade, relatively few sociologists have commented on the significance of the brief history of their own profession in Britain. Sociologists, just as much as car workers, radiologists, computer programmers and nuclear scientists, are the product of an advanced industrial society. They may not owe their existence to some specific technological development, but the explanation of sociology's post-war growth lies in the recent history of the society in which it exists. The frequent comment that sociology is a relatively new discipline is more true than is normally recognised: in Britain the profession has existed for all intents and purposes for a bare thirty or forty years.

British sociology as occupational history

The growth of sociology is quite remarkable. In the last full year before the outbreak of the Second World War there were only 35 professors in *all* of the social sciences in Britain and 177 lecturing staff on other grades (Clapham, 1946). The number of graduating students in sociology, anthropology and social administration combined was just 33 (Heyworth, 1965). In 1955/6 there were only 118 graduating students in the same group of subjects. About two-thirds of them were women who were unlikely to be able to make much professional contribution in an era of discrimination. By 1973, as we have seen, there were around 1,200 sociology teachers in Higher Education, and another 900 sociologists in research work. Indeed, a 1975 survey of only 19 polytechnics found more sociologists than all the Higher Education social scientists in 1938/39 (Nicholas, 1978). By 1970, there were 1,700 graduates a year in sociology and social anthropology, while 5 years later there were over 2,500 social science post-graduates (Smith, 1975; DES, 1975). Over 60 per cent of all social science research organisations in Higher Education institutions were founded between 1965 and 1972 (Cherns and Perry, 1976).

Social science in general expanded in the post-war years, but none more so than sociology. Most of this growth took place in the 1960s, but by the early years of the 1970s this expansion had peaked and was levelling-off. Student numbers doing 'straight' sociology degrees have gone down somewhat, but the number of professional sociologists has remained stable and social science students now make up about one-third of all undergraduates. The staff of sociology teaching departments are very much of one young generation, recruited during those heady days of the explosion of sociology as a discipline in Britain.

Not surprisingly, if the profession of 'sociologist' has not been long in existence, the content of the discipline, its areas of interest, its strengths and its weaknesses, its very nature, are all fresh, fluid, and, in the strict sense of the word, immature. The familiar observation, that the great majority of all natural scientists who ever lived are still alive, is even more true for sociologists. The death of a sociologist in Britain is a rare event. Although the discipline is steadily moving towards the more conventional age profile of an established occupation, its members are still, as a group, much younger than those of the typical academic subject. Their sociology – British sociology – has been a young person's game.

For example, Gerstl and Hutton's study of mechanical engineers as long ago as 1962 showed that 45 per cent were aged between 35 and 44, and 27 per cent were 45 or older (Gerstl and Hutton, 1966, 96). Furthermore, this is a conservative estimate, because it is based on a sample survey which the authors record as under-representing older respondents (22-3). Even with the ageing of the 1960s generation, it is still not the case that more than 7 out of 10 sociologists are older than 35. Visiting American sociologists have expressed their surprise at the youthfulness of participants in BSA conferences: the ASA is still dominated by the pre-war generation who are the counterparts of the present British generation of sociologists as the consolidators of the discipline.

21

Another way of looking at this is to consider the dates of foundation for professional bodies. The Institute of Civil Engineers was founded in 1818; RIBA in 1834; Electrical Engineers in 1868; and even Chartered Auctioneers and Estate Agents by 1886. Of course one could go back to the fourteenth and fifteenth centuries for the Inns of Court, or the seventeenth century for the Apothecaries, but it is the nineteenth century which saw the real growth of the professions (Millerson, 1964, 246-58). In this century alone such illustrious trades as Sewage Purification (1901), Hospital Administrators (1902), Insurance Brokers (1906), Certified Grocers (1909), Marketing and Sales Managers (1911), Medical Laboratory Technicians (1912), Book-Keepers (1916), Advertising Practitioners (1917), Remedial Gymnasts (1935), Chiropodists (1945), Market Researchers (1947) and Public Relations Officers (1948) all predate the BSA's 1951. More seriously, law, medicine, natural science, geology, astronomy, zoology, geography, statistics, botany, chemistry, anthropology, archaeology, meteorology, mathematics, history, economics, psychology, English, and town-planning – not to mention numerous smaller or more specialist parts of other disciplines – all established themselves with national associations for the most part well before the First World War. Having a professional body is not a magical mark that a discipline has finally arrived, or reached a certain size: bodies vary from rigorous gatekeepers through trade promotion organisations to voluntary social clubs. But all academic disciplines have their own professional bodies, and the late emergence of the BSA accurately reflects the late emergence of sociology as a recognised discipline in Britain.

Of course, the BSA was not the first sociological association. Arguably, the National Association for the Promotion of Social Science might lay claim to that title, which takes us back to the middle of the nineteenth century. However, this was a general gathering of socially concerned reformers, whose sociology as 'effective philanthropy' or 'applied Christianity' (Abrams, 1968, 29) would be hardly recognisable to the modern sociologist, despite Abrams's contention that 'the striking thing about the development of British sociology is the continuity of its principal traditions' (Abrams, 1968, 53). It was not until almost fifty years later that the Sociological Society was founded, producing the *Sociological Review* from 1908. This became the Institute of Sociology in 1929 when it joined together with several other groups which were also based in London at Le Play House. All three organisations necessarily attracted persons with a variety of backgrounds; since there were few 'academic' sociologists: a 'profession' as such did not really exist at that time.

Even after the Second World War, there were still tensions

between the amateur tradition and the new professionals. Banks recalls the origins of the BSA:

> The BSA began very much as the Sociological Society had begun in London nearly half a century earlier. Its founders intended it to be a meeting place for scholars in the social sciences who were especially interested in the sociological aspects of their own special subjects. Yet even at its first Annual General meeting its senior members were made aware that some of the latest generation of sociology students, who had come to the LSE after the war, were concerned to push it in the direction of activities of a more professional kind (Banks, 1975, 2).

This pressure group became the Teachers' Section in 1963, and increasingly took over the Association through its control of the Executive Committee, as we saw in Chapter 1.

However, compared with other professional bodies such as the British Psychological Society, the BSA has been something of a light-weight body. Only a minority of sociologists are members, and its activities have generally been open to non-members who were identifiable as sociologists. It has signally failed to be the central point of reference for organisations which are concerned with sociological practice, like the Council for National Academic Awards, the Social Science Research Council, or the School Examination Boards. Even its own leading figures have been critical of its performance: one past President and still active member has written that the BSA

> is unsure whether it is a professional association concerned with maintaining the standards of the subject, a trade union of teachers and researchers, or a kind of ideological pressure group. Moreover, it has swung violently from being governed as a gerontocracy to total and uninhibited democracy (Rex, 1978b, 414).

If the BSA has had little influence on events as an organisation, its members as individuals and small groups have. The same generation of LSE students that Banks spoke of set the tone for the new post-war sociology. Their influence was considerable: without wishing to belittle other institutions, the only significant department of sociology in the country at that time was at LSE. Their revolution against what had passed for sociology before the war was the start of modern British sociology.

The central figures among the 'old guard' at LSE were Marshall, Ginsberg and Mannheim. These men represented continuity with the early years of British sociology, both in their experience and also in terms of what they were teaching. Mannheim taught a theory course, while Ginsberg was centrally concerned with Hobhouse's style of sociology. A student of that period has remarked that, in teaching theory and method together, Ginsberg was strong on methodology at the level of philosophy of science, but less so on techniques of data collection. In most respects this was the final flowering of the old sociology, for there was an abrupt change in the early 1950s. Largely under the influence of Shils, American sociology was introduced to the School. Both Parsonian functionalism and a watered-down version of Lazarsfeldian empiricism were suddenly challengers to Social Darwinism and civic sociology. These new doctrines were taken up by a particular group of graduates and young staff in the early post-war years: among them Asher Tropp, Cyril Smith, Chelly Halsey, Joe and Olive Banks. Others connected with LSE around this time (largely through the David Glass study of social mobility) were Tom Bottomore, Jean Floud, Fred Martin and Keith Kelsall. Many of these were the 'young turks' who were to determine the future direction of the new BSA towards a professional association.

The influence of LSE's version of sociology

These sociologists made successful careers and were influential in setting up new departments in other universities. At one time, LSE could boast that 40 per cent of British sociology Chairs were filled by LSE graduates. One thing that they took with them was the London University model of a social science degree. It was what they had known, either as students or instructors, and some of the new universities had in any case been University Colleges doing the degree externally. In many respects a discipline is what it teaches, particularly in a phase of rapid expansion. Undergraduate teaching therefore merits some attention.

The London degree was a good model, both in its own right, and also in the strategic sense that it allied the teaching of sociology in its first and second years with economics, politics, anthropology and the like – disciplines which were slightly better established. These other social sciences could both help to protect the early growth of the new subject, and also benefit themselves from having an extra cognate subject in the academic battle against the massed ranks of traditionalist disciplines like medicine, classics and engineering.

In Part I of the degree, students took three subjects which were then dropped for the third year: Ethics and Social Philosophy; Economics; and Statistical Methods in Social Investigation. Part II contained more sociology: two papers in the Social Structure of

Modern Britain, and one each in Sociological Theory, Comparative Social Institutions, Social Psychology and two options from Criminology, Political Sociology, Industrial Sociology, Social Policy, and Social Administration, Demography, or Comparative Morals and Religion (other minor variations existed, such as 'option B' in Social Anthropology, or two papers in Graeco-Roman civilisation to replace the modern Britain papers). Strictly speaking, the theory course was 'Theories and Methods of Sociology', but like the 'Comparative Social Institutions' it was essentially a course in general theory. Students came as close to research in substantive areas as anywhere in the options. Thus the hidden curriculum of the degree stressed sociology as a theoretical enterprise. Three of the ten papers were theoretical (Philosophy, Theory, CSI); two at least were in other social sciences (Psychology and Economics, with one of the options possibly in Social Administration or Politics), while the remainder – anything from only two to four papers – were in substantive sociology.

This leaves the Statistical Methods in Social Investigation course, the title of which indicates its emphasis on elementary statistical theory and survey techniques. It was examined in two sections: one was statistics and the other methods of data collection, and both were characterised by a conservative and narrow outlook. Even when electric calculators and computer packages like SPSS were becoming standard tools, students would be asked to undertake the arithmetical calculation of correlation coefficients, t-tests and chi-squareds, rather than display a real understanding of the appropriateness, limitations and usefulness of particular statistical tests or computer techniques. Similarly, the second section of the paper on data collection techniques reflected a lack of concern for any of the rival perspectives which were beginning to influence empirical research. The usual questions covered such topics as sampling and non-sampling error, various sampling techniques, the use of official statistics, interviewing and non-response. Lip service was, however, paid to participant observation and candidates had to display some sociological knowledge by being required to 'illustrate your answer by reference to relevant studies.'

Methodology in its wider sense was supposed to be covered in the 'theory' course, and studies used to illustrate research techniques would also be discussed in terms of their sociological contribution in the other courses. However, the methods course was never regarded as an integral part of the sociological content of the degree. Like economics and philosophy, 'methods' was removed from the 'real' sociology in the course by being examined at the end of the second year, and, whatever the intention of this structure, the

25

implication was that students could forget such non-essentials in order to concentrate on sociology proper in their final year.

Furthermore, because of widespread innumeracy and lack of interest amongst sociology lecturers, the statistics classes were mainly taught by statisticians, who rarely had any interest in, or understanding of, sociological problems. This, compounded by the emphasis on techniques in the syllabus, had little intellectual appeal or relevance for students. Moreover, the students (being drawn predominantly from 'arts' backgrounds) were just as innumerate as the staff and the mere thought of solving what appeared to be extremely difficult algebraic equations created genuine anxiety for many. This mental block against statistics was exacerbated by the statistics lecturers' often unsympathetic approach to non-specialist teaching.

This servicing feature of the course occurred not only in the colleges which offered the external degree but also at its original source – the LSE. In the Calendar for 1964-5, for example, we see four of the five courses for the subject (including the main lecture course) being undertaken by the statistics department. The fifth course consisted of weekly classes (seminars) held for two terms by the sociology department. This central control of the course by statisticians (Moser at LSE and Ilersic at Bedford College) ensured the primacy of formal survey techniques. This still applies, although to a lesser extent, in the present LSE course, where sociologists now give half the lectures (Wakeford, 1979).

Both the syllabus and the predominance of statisticians on the board of examiners for the external degree meant that few innovations could be made. Attempts at introducing more sociologically relevant questions into the external paper in the early 1970s were met with a mixture of hostility, incomprehension, silence and condescension. The suggestion that a question about *limitations* and feasibility of the social indicators approach to measuring 'the quality of life' might be included in the examination paper was initially regarded as approaching heresy, although it was eventually included in a much modified form.

In as far as British sociology had a positivist tradition it was enshrined in this course. Kingsley Amis's fictional sociologist would have been quite at home among these practitioners.

'We're trying to find the social switches', he said.
   'The social switches?' I said.
   'That's right, Now: when you switch on the light,
what happens? The light comes on, doesn't it?'
     'Yes, if the lighting system's in order.'
     'Agreed, yes, agreed, a very fair point. But

if it is in order, then the light must come on,
mustn't it? It's got to, hasn't it? Simple cause
and effect. That's all it is.'
   'Well . . . ' I said.
'Right, well we want to find the social switches,
that's all. We're after the points of contact, if
you like, such that if you do *a* – pressing a switch –
then you get *b* and nothing but *b* – the light comes
on. *B* being in this case the social effect of your policy *a*, got it?
There's nothing very mysterious
about it, is there?'
   'Supposing . . . ' I said.
'Of course, we've got a long way to go yet. But
when we've acquired the requisite knowledge then
society will in fact be an object of scientific
study, got it?' (Amis, 1953, 248-9).

The limitations of the course as a preparation for undertaking sociological research were substantial. Not only were many of the students apathetic towards the approach, but the syllabus also demanded a knowledge of the formal techniques of survey investigation rather than a detailed understanding of the practical and ethical constraints on actually *doing* research. Those sociologists who did teach the course, and who questioned the assumptions on which it was based, were faced with a difficult dilemma – should one provide the conventional survey techniques 'cook book' course, or teach what one believed was a more properly sociological research course which might give students a deeper philosophical and practical understanding of the methodological issues involved? Examination criteria usually took precedence.

The majority of sociology students, therefore, graduated with little understanding of how to undertake research and a one-sided impression of its importance. Those who proceeded to postgraduate study or became employed as research assistants would have had little practical training, and, unless they had a conscientious supervisor, their further progress was through trial and error. Such ignorance might well offer a partial explanation of the large proportion of higher degrees in sociology which remain uncompleted.

The expansion of university sociology was matched in the 1960s by an expansion in the non-university sector of Higher Education. The starting point for the teaching of sociology in the pre-polytechnic colleges was the London University BSc (Hons) Sociology (and Economics) external degree. This did not so much impose a common curriculum from the centre as provide the mechanism for arriving at a consensus within each of the centrally-specified papers. During much of the 1960s subject specialists from each college met once or twice a year to establish the 'shadow syllabus' and the broad content of the examination paper. Subjects varied: Statistical Methods in Social Investigation remained both more centrally-controlled and traditional than, say, Comparative Social Institutions. The balance between college influence and professorial domination depended largely on personality. What happened was that the in-coming young sociologists were socialised into the London system with its heavy emphasis on theory even if they had not served their own apprenticeship at LSE. This process provided a sense of security and a source of advice about what to teach for the novice lecturer, so that graduates from other universities were initiated into the London way.

The third generation of sociologists

With the advent of the polytechnics and the Council for National Academic Awards (CNAA), however, each new institution had in theory the opportunity of designing precisely the degree schemes that they really wanted. In practice, relatively few of the new polytechnic degree submissions deviated far from the beaten track. Why was this?

In the first place, as we have just noted, there had been an effective system for generating and maintaining a national consensus about priorities and content, even if detailed interpretations were accepted as a legitimate local concern. Second, staff had been recruited to teach an existing set of courses, and had been doing so for several years. Such an investment in lecture preparation and specialisation was not to be lightly discarded. The first requirement of a new degree scheme was that it should employ all the current staff and allow them to continue to teach their specialist fields.

The third constraint on innovation was the chronic insecurity of the new polytechnics. This operated both internally and externally. Internally, there was a resistance to change among many sociologists themselves, together with a jockeying for position in the new degree. Offering new third-year options provided a good outlet for the specialist interests of discontented staff, without taking on the greater task of seeking consensus on a new degree structure. Public expressions of disagreement among sociologists were to be avoided if the critics among the technological disciplines were to be kept at bay. An uneasy alliance between disciplines existed at this stage: the technologists from the old technical colleges reluctantly accepted that polytechnic status depended on having something other than the mono-technic disciplines of engineering and science, and that the social sciences could attract students. Nevertheless, they distrusted and disliked the alien beings who taught them; young, university trained, articulate and radical – everything that the technical college teacher was not. If the sociologists could not display a united front, there were plenty of opponents within the polytechnic who would not waste an opportunity to exploit such a weakness. If this sounds like incipient paranoia, then it accurately reflects the atmosphere in most polytechnics at the end of the 1960s. It does not matter whether such a view was realistic: what matters is that it existed.

Nor did the state of insecurity end within the walls of the polytechnics. Lurking just over the horizon was CNAA validation, with its power of life and death over the new-born degree. The 'CNAA Visitation', to inspect facilities, to vet staff, and to dissect syllabus content was regarded as little short of the arrival of the Spanish Inquisition. Indeed those with first-hand experience of both university and CNAA demands have commented on how much higher are CNAA standards of course preparation.

The relationship between CNAA and the polytechnics has been from the start an ambiguous one. Despite the gross imbalance of power between the subject panels which vet the proposals at some length and the department putting forward the degree, there have been continued protestations from CNAA that a case well put will carry the day, that no censorship or single national pattern is being imposed, and that a thousand flowers should bloom (even if not expressed precisely in those words). Given the operation of the system, with a panel who delegate a visiting party, control cannot be too tight. After all, the people concerned in content evaluation are themselves academics sharing some kind of academic ethos, and the inevitable inefficiency of committee work with its rushed reading of papers and turnover of attendance must militate against the detailed application of a consistent policy of control. Many of the leading figures on CNAA visits were men committed to sociological development and to the encouragement of young staff: names like John Rex, John Smith, Cyril Cannon and Stephen Cotgrove come to mind as firm but essentially benevolent chairmen (although this could not be said of all participants). Of course, many of them were themselves products of the London system or the London external degree.

And yet, because of the powers of professional life and death that it wielded, most departments regarded – and still regard – CNAA with distrust and fear. One direct consequence has been that new submissions have been tailored to meet what were imagined to be CNAA preferences. At one level, this is reflected in the temporary popularity of superficial modifications such as

29

continuous assessment, or modular degrees (few of which were in fact modular in anything but name). At another, it is manifested (paradoxically) in conservatism of content and even basic form. Perhaps, with different and more aggressively imaginative CNAA personnel, more experimentation might have been attempted, but this is probably unlikely. In the departments putting up new schemes the fear of failure was a great incentive to conformism. The demands of the visiting panel were no casual constraints: teaching in the universities was never exposed to such a test.

If one looks at the teaching of sociology (which presents one good indicator of the subject's content and style) in the polytechnics, then it is the relative lack of variation that is striking, rather than the reverse. True, there are some interesting experiments in application of skills; in time spent on work experience; and in the combination of sociology with other and often vocational disciplines. But, given the original excitement of educational innovation that the polytechnics embodied, the strength of the new polytechnic ethic of relevance, community-orientation, and interdisciplinary study, and the much vaunted radicalism of sociologists, the outcome has been remarkably static. Nowhere is this more true than in the teaching of methods of sociological research, even after ten years of polytechnic sociology.

Teaching research methods

From the methodology course outlines compiled by John Wakeford for the BSA Methodology Conference in January 1979, it would seem that nearly half of such undergraduate courses in the polytechnic sector were still of the traditional 'London type', and this proportion rises to nearly 90 per cent if we include those courses which, although including some wider aspects of either methodology or practical work, are strongly influenced by the formal techniques approach of the London methods course.* The university sector, on the other hand, showed slightly less of a tendency towards this approach with approximately 25 per cent of the undergraduate courses now offering more integrated and relevant approaches to sociological research methodology. Examples of such 'modern'** approaches range from the plural methodology emphasis of the workshop-seminar course at Keele through

* These figures are based on a self-selected sample of 12 polytechnics covering 24 courses.

**'Modern' is used here to denote a different style of course, integrated into the discipline in contrast to the separate statistics survey approach, rather than an implication of recent development.

the project workshops at Lancaster to the more formal but wide-ranging 'Research Methods II' at Cardiff. Although having no common format, all of these 'modern' courses share a similar emphasis on the methodological and practical issues and problems involved in undertaking sociological research. However, such an approach to sociological methodology is taken in only a minority of courses, and the results of Wakeford's survey suggests that the majority of those graduating in sociology still receive very scant and often biased understanding of the research process*:

> The absence of a reference to the philosophy of the social sciences or to social statistics can only be taken to imply that the respondents to our enquiry chose neither to include them in their courses nor provide reference to any such courses available in their institutions. In the syllabuses received some issues are frequently mentioned – interviewing, questionnaire design, participant observation and sampling procedures.... Teaching methods differ ... some teachers initiating class research projects.... Particularly when the state of method is in such ferment, it is worth asking whether a sociologist with undergraduate and postgraduate degrees should not have a broad knowledge and experience of the research process (Wakeford, 1979, 1-2).

Despite the inherent problems in using formal course outlines (and in the case of polytechnics, often photocopies of relevant sections of CNAA submissions) to discover the nature of 'methods' teaching, there is a clear indication that undergraduates receive a limited understanding of sociological research processes.

Few sociologists have experienced the whole range of methodological techniques and problems which arise in sociological research, and fewer still are sufficiently broadminded, or have the necessary knowledge, to provide adequate accounts of the various perspectives and styles of research. It follows that unless such courses are taught by a number of lecturers (and few sociology departments include staff representing the whole range of perspectives and experience), those responsible for methods teaching must turn to the accounts of others.

Many of the texts available for this purpose are predominantly a formal presentation of the correct procedures for carrying out the various data-gathering techniques. Moser's (1958) text book which is still to be found on many reading lists in its revised form (Moser

---

*Wakeford does not give his definition of 'course'. We identified 77 undergraduate and 10 postgraduate courses from his data whereas Wakeford talks of 55.

and Kalton, 1971) is one of the best examples of this style. After 48 pages of general introduction to social surveys, it proceeds to over 100 pages on sampling, 13 on documentary sources and observation, 11 on mail questionnaires, 25 on interviewing techniques, 36 on questionnaire design, 23 on response errors and 42 on data processing and analysis (13 of which are concerned with analysis and interpretation). Of course, one cannot expect a book concerned, as its title suggests, with survey methods to give a full account of other methods, but with approximately 40 per cent of all of those social science projects covered by an SSRC survey using non-survey methods (Perry, 1975, 79) it is somewhat surprising that the most frequently chosen methods text book devotes only 4 per cent of its coverage to other techniques. Even for those concerned with survey work, the book provides little information about the reality of research and its index makes no reference to ethics, values or 'objectivity'.

The available literature on sociological methodology is still dominated by such formal recipes for research. The reading lists included in Wakeford's survey illustrate the heavy reliance upon such work by those responsible for teaching. Not only Moser and Kalton, but also Goode and Hatt, Madge, Sellitz *et al.*, Festinger and Katz, etc., are as familiar to many current sociology undergraduates as they were to those of fifteen to twenty years ago. Michael Young and Peter Willmott's families are still a popular seminar topic and *Street Corner Society* illustrates participant observation just as often today as it did when the present authors were undergraduates. This is not to suggest that such research examples and texts are in any way poor references; rather we use them to illustrate the timeless quality of methods courses. While sociology and research have developed into a state of what Bell and Newby term 'methodological pluralism' a lot of the undergraduate methods courses appear to have stood still.

To be fair, many of these reading lists (including a proportion of those courses which are classified here as 'traditional') do indicate at least some movement towards the adoption of more up-to-date texts. Although Bell and Newby, Platt, Fletcher, Filstead, Hughes, Phillips, etc., are recommended in only a minority of such lists, Bulmer and other more modern readers seem to be coming into fashion.

However, the extent to which any written account can give students an understanding of doing research is questionable. Such understanding can only be achieved by first-hand experience which in practice means undertaking projects. The tedium of coding or data indexing; the pressures of consuming ever more cups of sweet milky tea; the problem of dealing with children and pets; and the alternate elations and depressions of analysis can only be partially appreciated by those who lack this background. However, Wakeford's survey suggests that less than half of those graduating have any such experience and many of the practical tasks set are often little more than classroom exercises.

Although desirable, it must be acknowledged that teaching by project is problematic. The teacher must have the ability and flexibility to sustain momentum and offer support. The ethical problems are considerable: both the student and the respondent must be considered. There must be protection against an unsuspecting public being used as a training ground for successive years of inexperienced undergraduates, and students should not be merely unpaid interviewers or research assistants for some current project. A solution to these problems is offered in the approach of the programme put forward by Wakeford in 1968. A series of such projects could be designed for first- and second-year students which would not only involve small-scale practical tasks but give time for more detailed theoretical and methodological discussions – and the development of statistical and computer appreciation, if not expertise. Such a course would provide the much-needed grounding for the more detailed investigations and dissertations which are often required of final year students.

This approach to methods teaching is still rare, with possibly 5 per cent of the courses listed by Wakeford taking this form. A few institutions have attempted to provide such experience and training by introducing Research Methods branches into their sociology degrees (e.g., Newcastle, North East London and Birmingham Polytechnics) or have provided Masters courses in Research Methods (e.g., Surrey University). But such developments are rare and are usually specifically geared to careers in central and local government and market research: to social research rather than sociological research.

The expansion of sociology in the 1960s

On the evidence of Wakeford's survey, the polytechnics seem not only to have failed to grasp their opportunities but to be even more conservative than the universities. Sadly, this is reflected across the whole range of their sociology teaching. It is perhaps even more surprising that polytechnic sociology should remain so faithful to its origins when it is set in the wider context of the discipline's growth in the late 1950s and 1960s. As the opening chapter noted, the expansion of sociology in the polytechnics was only part of a fourfold explosion in post-secondary education: the others being the introduction of new departments in old universities, the establishment of new universities, and the growth in teacher training at degree level. The generation of new jobs for sociologists was dramatic: complete new departments were set up from scratch, or where there had been one or two service lecturers buried in liberal studies or management departments, there were now a dozen or more specialists working on their own degrees. And this process was happening in over a hundred Higher Education institutions, quite apart from the teacher training colleges. As Rex observed, 'literally hundreds of the university students of the sixties came to live off sociology by teaching it in polytechnics and colleges, at A and O level in schools, or as the theory of social and community work' (Rex, 1978b, 297). Such a mushrooming necessarily placed a severe demand for good sociologists on the still infant profession.

The post-Robbins policies were part of a drive for national economic growth: highly skilled manpower was an investment in the country's productive capacity. Although all disciplines gained from an expansion of Higher Education some stood to gain more than others. The new universities apart, few institutions needed to designate new departments of science or engineering, or, to a lesser extent, of humanities and arts. These subjects already existed, as in the case of the technologies, or were seen as less important for economic growth, as in the case of the arts in the non-university sector. The social sciences were a different story. The development of sociology in Britain coincided with a uniquely benevolent period for any new subject. Sociology flourished by filling the vacuum created by expansionist policies, and it outpaced more established disciplines which paradoxically were in a better position to supply trained personnel to staff new departments.

From an administrator's point of view, it is easy to see why sociology was a suitable case for expansion. At an ideological level, a concern with social problems, and the application of scientific methods to the study of society, was very much in tune with the popular ideas of the day. Social science could be presented as a 'relevant' sort of activity, well suited to the philosophy of expanding Higher Education in the quest for more economic growth.

At a practical level, sociology was cheap. It required no laboratory space or expensive equipment. Even its library requirements were limited at that time. Furthermore, the older establishments had less of a hold on sociology, because of its novelty as an academic discipline, and so it was relatively quick and easy to set up a department with a good reputation in a new institution. Again, expansion outside of more traditional faculties was easier to achieve than overcoming elitist opposition to the expansion of higher education.

However, despite these attractions, there was one central fact that overrode aspirations and policies: the wishes of the qualified school-leavers. For some time, the 18-year-olds had been voting with their feet. Science and engineering degrees were barely full, or were increasingly filling places with students whose 'A' levels did not match up to the then-held expectations of attainment. The immediate customers, the annual intake of new students, were for the first time choosing social sciences in large numbers.

This shift in consumer preference may be explained by a number of changes in post-war British society. The Second World War had both disrupted the routines of 'normal' social life, and produced a crop of war-service graduates who entered the professions – and not least teaching – with new values and a wider experience than their predecessors. This new generation in turn became the parents of the 1960s intake to Higher Education. The 1950s were also the key decade in the expansion of non-manual employment and the growth of the service sector, which generated new cultural forms quite different from the established society of manual, routine white-collar and professional workers, with its traditional close social control. The return of the 1964 Labour government (preaching the age of white hot technological revolution) and the growth of welfare provision were both a cause and a symptom of a new social awareness and concern. In those days of optimistic liberal socialism, bad housing, poverty, and unemployment once more became public issues. Particularly in the late 1960s, the post-war bulge of children, brought up on a diet of television, were more aware of social problems and working-class life in general. This is not to say that there was a universal rise in social consciousness, or that the largely middle-class members of the sixth form properly understood the range, intensity or causes of these social problems. On the contrary, many of them *wanted* that understanding, and looked to the social sciences for answers. When the schools changed from collecting bottle tops for orphans in India, to home visits for the elderly and direct community service, they were recognising a new era in which 'an interest in people' (that popular and exasperating response in entry-interviews) was a genuine, if ill-considered, expression of concern.

It is still not easy to assess the 1960s, not least for the sociologist. The reality of the period is disguised by the extravagant myths of popular journalism and the nostalgic yearnings of intellectuals now threatened by approaching middle age. *It is in the latter camp that most sociologists find themselves.* For this generation, nothing can ever be the same again, because they lived through both the more traditional, oppressive mores of the 1950s and the new 'liberated' fashions of the 1960s. Their days of youthful exuberance coincided with a major shift in values: phenomena as disparate as the Aldermaston marches and rock and roll were not external or intellectual things, but intense emotional and personal experiences.

During that decade, while the present generation of sociologists was learning its sociology, there was a celebration of youth and social change. They became adult in a glare of publicity as the media cashed in on the titillation value of the new sexual, personal and political freedoms. More importantly, the universities under-went a rapid, if partial, democratisation, spearheaded by student activists. 1968 became the symbol of student power (even if most of the year passed quietly in Britain). Those years in which British society adjusted to a new social order were years with few established rules of conduct, and an openness to new ideas and behaviour. They bred both sixth formers who wanted to read sociology, and the sociologists themselves who became the new lecturers needed to meet the demand.

Educational expansion and the growth of sociology coincided with a period of apparent prosperity. Despite the fluctuations of the economy and recurring balance of payment crises, the late 1950s and 1960s were basically good times in which graduate unemploy-ment seemed an unlikely prospect. For many sixth formers sociology offered something apparently relevant to their own lives. A better understanding of people and society had to be a marketable asset when it came to getting one of the increasing number of new jobs that involved 'working with people'. This optimism has since evaporated in the face of economic depression and rising unemployment. Sixth formers turned to the vocational disciplines of economics, business studies, and even back to technology as safer bets in the post-graduation world of the 1970s.

The legacy of the 1960s

As a result of these trends in consumer taste, sociology has been left isolated as a child of the 1960s. Not only has the subject's popularity declined among sixth formers, but the educational expenditure freeze of the mid-1970s (and now the advent of Rhodes Boyson) has frosted much of the early promise. It is not easy to explain the subject's fall in the ratings among university entrants. There may be a temptation to write it off as a simple change in fashion: one year's trendy image leads to general popularity, while another year sees us back to a hard core of serious users. Hula-hoops, frizbees, kites, skateboards and sociology degrees all had their brief day in the sun. Indeed, the very trendiness of the discipline helped to establish it at a crucial stage of educational expansion. In a new era of little growth (and even with the threat of the demographic downturn only a few years away) a reduction in student demand may in fact not be totally unwelcome.

However, to regard this turnabout as just a random matter of fashion is to overplay what is only one facet of a more complicated process. Just as the 1960s saw one kind of society, so the 1980s are witnessing another, marked by economic stagnation, growing intolerance towards dissent and deviance, and high rates of unemployment. In this world, students must choose subjects which provide a meal ticket, and sadly, that is something which sociology is not too well equipped to provide. This will have a profound effect on the future of the discipline, because without students there is no need for departments of sociology in Higher Education. A climate of opinion which emphasises vocational relevance and security of employment is not one favourable to sociology as it has developed in Britain.

The employment prospects for the sociology graduate are poorer than those for graduates of other disciplines. In certain respects, many of the traditional humanities have a similarly narrow outlet, but sociology is weakened by the restricted school teaching market. It is still not widely accepted as a sixth form subject, let alone in the junior forms. In contrast, languages both modern and classical, history, and even theology are well rooted in the basic secondary school curriculum. In a period of cut-backs in expenditure, it is harder for new disciplines to become established. On top of this, all disciplines have been hit by the closure of the teachers training colleges and the restrictions on numbers of trainees. This affects both staff and students: the former lose posts and the latter lose career opportunities. It is true that many of the former training colleges have managed to survive by introducing new degrees, often with sociology as a large part of them. But the dubious intellectual standards of many of these, combined with their arbitrary amalgamations of subjects and sometimes inexperienced and poorly-qualified staff, have served as much to damage the academic standing of sociology as to maintain employment for sociology lecturers. The insistence that those who train teachers (or do research for social services departments or nursing) must be 'professionally' qualified has been a double handicap. It restricts career opportunities for sociologists, and also often results in sociology teaching and research being done by people who are not first and foremost sociologists.

This closure of an important career line compounds a parallel disadvantage in other occupational spheres. Few of the present generation of senior managers and administrators are social scientists. If they have any educational experience at all, it is still commonly in arts subjects. Not surprisingly, their recruitment policies frequently favour the generalist devil they know, over the unknown risk of the social scientist. In addition, the unenviable reputation of sociologists as radicals, idealists, and troublemakers – however unjustified – militates against their employment. If a degree in sociology does not improve his chances of getting a job, why should the 18-year-old choose it as a subject? Intellectual idealism is not the strongest motive for embarking on three years of Higher Education, when unemployment is running at over 2 million.

It may be that, even for the idealist, and despite the normal cultural lag, time has run out and word has filtered back to the schools that sociology never was the liberating subject that many sixth formers had thought it to be. While recognising the over-ambitious claims of earlier days, sociology has not set itself up as the ultimate revelation of social truth, and so cannot be blamed for this disappointment. Nevertheless, the way sociology has often manifested itself – obsessed with ancient theories, bogged down in abstruse verbiage, endlessly questioning, disputing and yet never answering – has made it a less attractive choice. Without students, there is no need for lecturers; and at present it is lecturing that pays most of the bills for sociology's existence.

This last is a fundamentally important point. Sociology as it has developed in this country has increasingly become an irrelevant and unmarketable commodity. Outside of teaching the subject, there is little that can be directly done with it. It is a relevant subject for welfare or some local government work, or for industrial management – but only one such 'relevant' subject. It is its general frame of reference that is useful, not the skills it imbues. While sociology has an important role in contributing to the professional training of occupations like social work, town planning, teaching, medicine or law, this is essentially a subordinate role. No discipline can survive on such a meagre diet. In a few areas, such as policy research, a sociologist's social survey training may be applied to data collection. For the rest, and despite our protestations that our graduates get jobs in many different walks of life, three years of sociology imparts little more advantage than three years of any other social or management science.

No doubt this view will raise the objection that sociology does not need to be relevant, or useful, or marketable. Sociology exists in its own right, for its own sake. Some sociologists would go further, and argue its role should be precisely the opposite of useful; it should be an exercise in pure understanding and mental skills. Others again argue that it should stimulate true consciousness, challenge the capitalist ideology of universal market value, and work towards the undermining of the capitalist system.

In one sense, much of such an objection is justified. Sociology should not depend for its existence purely on an ethos of vocational training. A degree in sociology is not the same as an apprenticeship in plumbing: it is not a training in specific skills to be applied to the tasks that constitute a particular job. It is an exercise in coming to terms with a body of knowledge that has its own internal rules and logic: it is a process of intellectual stimulation and development, and in this sense perfectly interchangeable with anthropology, Latin, philosophy, theology or pure mathematics as a degree subject – which is of course not a particularly strong argument in favour of sociology or any other discipline. Conversely, sociology should not just be the tool and creation of others in society. Without room for autonomy, no discipline can hope to make progress: the same is true if one style of work is imposed to the exclusion of all others.

In other words, what we are saying is *not* that sociology should have a strictly applied and utilitarian nature (nor for that matter should it be strictly pure and self-indulgent). But the *consequences* of maintaining independence, of stressing critique, of not becoming involved in problem-solution, of concentrating on the theoretical issues and not on its application, of producing graduates who are employed almost despite their degree specialisation – are that sociology will remain attractive to only a limited range of students. And with fewer students, there will ultimately be fewer jobs for the professional sociologist. The subject does not exist in isolation from its practitioners, and the context in which they operate.

One extreme case of this fact is Cuba in the mid-1960s. To judge from the contents of two university libraries there in 1966, sociology flourished for a number of years following the revolution. The book stock was first class, and ranged all the way from radical and conflict theorists, through 'conservatives' like Parsons, to anti-marxist and anti-Russian tracts of a dubious kind. Both in size and range, the Library at Santiago de Cuba put many British university libraries at that time to shame. But the last additions had been in 1962 or perhaps early 1963. And insistent requests by one of the present authors to meet some sociologists led eventually to the admission that, some social psychology apart, sociology was no longer taught and sociologists were not employed in Cuba.

To what extent can it be said that sociology still existed in Cuba? With no practitioners, and no teachers, there could be no proper survival of the discipline, let alone the generation of new knowledge. It is true that the sum of sociological ideas to 1962 had not perished absolutely, and that sociology could be reintroduced from outside at a later date. But for all practical purposes, it is the embodiment of ideas in occupational form which constitutes existence. That requires an organisational base, training programmes, financial arrangements and so on. There is no pure science, free from social context, and it is the occupational part of that context that is paramount.

3   Theory and empiricism

Paradoxically, despite its own short history, British sociology has become very much a subject dominated by the development of theories rather than by empirical research. Indeed, our concern with nineteenth-century writers, the way in which we constantly rediscover new nuances in the classical texts, and the frequency with which we invoke the masters to justify our contemporary speculations suggests more than a simple interest in the evolution of sociological thought. It suggests an almost neurotic desire to legitimate current endeavours by locating them in a long and glorious tradition, and at worst, an attempt to disguise present poverty by hiding in the apparent richness of past contributions.

In this respect, sociology is different from other social sciences. In economics, anthropology, and political science, which share the same nineteenth-century pre-history, and in the slightly younger psychology, there is much less dialogue with the ghosts of the Greats. Each contains the specialisms of Theory and the Historical Development of Ideas, but the citation of Ricardo, Morgan, Bagehot, or Galton is restricted to such sub-fields, and does not intrude in work which deals with contemporary phenomena. In comparison the preambles to many sociology articles and books are spiked with incantations to Marx, Weber, and Durkheim.

We do not make this point in a spirit of philistinism. However, questions must be raised about the apparent need to return to our intellectual forebears, other than as an exercise in the history of ideas. The criterion for a return to the past is its relevance for analysis of the present. It may be that a long debate requires us to return to its origins. An idea may have its clearest exposition in early work. Old ideas may have a renewed relevance as old problems return in fresh guises, like the persistent renaissance of racism noted by Worsley (1974, 2).

In so far as these formulations are not simple and indisputable, there will always be some element of introspection and philosophical argument: 'Sociology will remain as it is and always has been [a] very disorderly and wholly provisional enterprise ... [because] it rests on a philosophical anthropology, upon a view of what men are and may be that is essentially contestable' (Hawthorn, 1976, 259). Theoretical questions, then, must necessarily play their part in our present discussion as we examine the intellectual climate of the discipline and its methodological consequences.

The importance of these questions is linked to their social significance for discipline members. As a result of the explosive growth of British sociology, theory has come to occupy a dominant place in professional activities. It forms an area where the layman's commonsense knowledge cannot readily match the sociologist's scholarship, while being accessible to all competent practitioners. This is not to say that it may not be intellectually demanding, but rather that it requires no more support than a library, a little peace and quiet, a comfortable chair, and no more experience than an undergraduate degree. The data are given in the form of books, articles and, occasionally, manuscripts. The whole may easily be fitted into the interstices of teaching or administration. Since anyone may participate, professional recognition comes freely and speedily, particularly given the anti-empirical climate of the English universities.

In contrast, empirical sociology is both practically and physically demanding. Whether it involves survey research or ethnography, data collection takes time and money. It happens 'out there' and must be co-ordinated with academic commitments; no mean logistical problem. Young staff have heavy teaching loads, their departments are underfunded for research support and their access to external funds is limited. The time-lag between beginning research and publishing results is substantial – commonly four or five years. During the crucial expansion of the 1960s, then, those who took the empirical road had less influence on the development of the discipline and their delayed output left them on the career margins, with reputations limited to specialist fields. Since it is the theorists who have so affected the present state of sociology in this country, our first task must be to inquire into their contribution and its implication for methodology.

What sort of theory?

In his 1959 book, *The Sociological Imagination,* C. Wright Mills identified two great fallacies in American sociology: 'Grand Theory' and 'Abstracted Empiricism'. In so doing he characterised the major stances for much of the debate over sociological practice in the twenty years that were to follow. His was an important critique, powerfully argued, but despite its merits – or perhaps precisely because of them – this often-invoked dichotomy needs to be treated with some caution, particularly in this country. British sociology has never been dominated by these two tendencies in the same way, and any attempt to operate with this model is therefore likely to produce a distorted picture.

Mills tackled head-on the twin gods of American sociology, Parsons and Lazarsfeld. They stood for the evils that others had perpetrated in lesser ways, and not without justification, given the extent of their dual influence over academic sociology since the 1930s. Parsons's complex, technical and language-specific systems theory demands massive effort to master it, before it might even be considered for use in illuminating problems of the external world. His structural functionalism became almost synonymous with sociological theory for American students during the 1950s. Lazarsfeld, on the other hand, had succeeded in selling his colleagues the sample social survey as the method *par excellence* for sociology. Only if a thing could be measured could it be admitted for consideration. Both positions had tremendous advantages in marking out a professional domain for the discipline, a domain, furthermore, that was safe from the very real attacks of right-wing political militants during and, to a lesser extent, after, the McCarthy era. In that context, both styles of sociology could claim to be 'apolitical'.

But none of this sounds much like the post-war Britain in which modern sociology established itself. It is true, as we have already seen, that the dominant conception of 'methods' teaching was statistical analysis, but this was not integrated into the rest of undergraduate training, nor part of the necessary practice of a British sociologist. Numeracy has never been an essential qualification, and developments in survey research technology and statistical analysis have almost without exception occurred in America, or if in Britain, in other disciplines. Even in that key work of survey research, *Social Mobility in Britain* (Glass, 1954) we find a paper by Chambers on voluntary organisations which owes much to observational techniques and another by Martin on the subjective meanings of social class. If there was an empiricist tradition it was a half-hearted and confused one, directed to issues in the external world, not abstraction.

Nor can it be claimed, on the other hand, that Parsonian sociology has been even the one pre-eminent theory in Britain, despite its importance and temporary popularity. It flourished briefly in the early 1950s under the influence of Shils at LSE, when it helped to legitimate a new generation's professional rebellion against pre-war, Ginsbergian models of the sociological enterprise. Thereafter Parsons did maintain a covert theoretical influence through the way in which he had selected and emphasised only certain parts of Weber and Durkheim's work in popularising these figures in the English language. His ideas survived more directly for a while as a disputed perspective on substantive areas; the 'functions of the family' and the Davis/Moore/Tumin debate on stratification. At a different level Parsons's systems theory has become a mandatory part of what we regard as 'sociological theory'. None of this, however, constitutes even the status of *primus inter pares:* Parsons is one contributor, usually ranked perhaps with Goffman, Habermas or Garfinkel, or at best with the founding fathers.

And yet we find that Mills's characterisation of abstracted empiricism and grand theory is still employed in commentaries on the state of the art today, for example in Worsley (1974), Hawthorn (1976) and Rex (1974, 1978a). Rex has presented the troubled development of British sociology as a struggle to escape from Lazarsfeld and Fabianism on the one hand, and functionalism on the other. The first involved a failure to deal with the meanings which men bring to bear on events and settings, with the construction of social realities, with a failure to grasp the complexity of social relationships. Worse still in Rex's eyes was the way in which the Fabians conceived society as

> a world of individuals with problems ... [with] an enlightened
> body of civil servants and local government officials which will
> solve them ... the Webbs took the British status system for
> granted and, in part, imagined themselves as setting up a new
> system of educating bureaucrats (Rex, 1974, 89).

This political naïvety made little sense by the 1970s, if it ever did in an earlier era. Rex argues that functionalism, too, had lost any former appeal by that time. Its political character as a conservative ideology had become manifest to most sociologists: 'the implied conservatism of functionalism, needed little demonstration. We simply wanted to show that the people didn't agree with the powers that be and that, if they appeared to, it was because they were being manipulated' (Rex, 1978a, 295). Worsley in his 1973 BSA Presidential Address also identified Mills's as one of the two major post-war attempts to assess the state of theory in the discipline. He couples Mills with Gouldner, drawing inspiration from the former's interest in the Third World and from the latter's reformulation of the dichotomy into empiricism versus marxism. However, he devotes much of his address to an attack on that post-Millsian newcomer, ethnomethodological sociology in its several forms.

In contrast, Hawthorn has very little to say about ethnomethodo-logy in his pessimistic historical account of social theory. What little he does say refers to American reactions against previous conserva-tive sociological paradigms in an era dominated by Vietnam, the Bay of Pigs, urban riots, Nixon and other great American disasters. Instead he portrays British sociology as a failure of the liberal socialist doctrines (Rex's 'Fabianism') and the rise of a new marxism, largely outside of sociology at first, but then within. Even liberal ideologists agree

> that the events of the 1960s, the lack of change as much as the changes, make Marxism initially more plausible than it seemed in 1955 or 1962. As the liberal socialism which once accompan-ied and indeed defined it comes to seem less like commonsense, sociology in Britain makes more sense, although quite what remains to be seen (Hawthorn, 1976, 252).

It will be clear by now that there is no consensus about the lack of a sociological consensus. This may explain why English writers of different views have turned to predecessors like Mills and Gouldner for some guidance. Certainly Mills provides such a hope if British sociology is seen as overshadowed by our American cousins or if we wish to talk about sociology in a general, world-wide sense. A more important explanation lies in the nature of the debate in which Mills was participating, the debate between positivistic notions of social science and their alternatives. This second strand of the debate about sociological practice has developed in tandem with the political debate about what sociology is for.

Post-war British sociology has consisted of many themes and its struggles have not been so much bi-partisan as many-sided: Sprott's battle of the seven dials. It may help to consider these struggles in terms of two main dimensions. One dimension is concerned with the choice of *what to study*. Thus we have the argument about whether sociology should be about the 'master problems' of modern industrial society, or the more mundane problems of everyday life. In this context 'abstracted empiricism' is at one end of a continuum because, at least consciously, it is apolitical: it is concerned with its own internal logic rather than key issues of social structure and process.

The second dimension is one of methodology. This can be thought of as ranging from 'hard' quantitative styles, drawing on a natural science model (again, 'abstracted empiricism'), through 'soft' qualitative methods, to sociology which contains no empir-ical research whatsoever. At this pole is theoretical introspection, the world of pure rationality. The reader may care to consider

45

where his own brand of sociology comes on these two dimensions.

The point of thinking about sociology in this way – and it obviously involves a crude simplification – is that it separates out different components of the discipline's internal disputes. Similar methodological stances can be in opposition because of the subject chosen for study, while the same phenomenon can often be studied in different ways. Within this framework the present authors are promoting methodological pluralism applied to substantive problems of modern society.

Problems of epistemology

The idea of methodological pluralism has an ambivalent status in any discipline, and nowhere more so than in sociology. When a member of the SSRC Sociology Committee said, at the 1977 BSA Conference in Sheffield, 'Sociology is what sociologists say they do.... "Let a thousand flowers bloom"', he was articulating the usual token democratic tolerance encountered in British sociology's informal interactions. But he was in no way reflecting the continual cut and thrust of the doctrinal disputes in journals and monographs. It was not for nothing that John Rex used the phrase 'wars of religion' in the title to a recent article on current sociology.

In recent years, the methodological battles of this war have been fought over the territory of epistemology and positivism (i.e., about the question of how we can 'know' something to be true, and whether sociology can be 'scientific' – see below). Phrases like 'epistemological crisis' have been employed to describe the intensity of doubt within sociology about the discipline's intellectual status. Put at its simplest, sociologists have become exercised by the problem that, as social beings themselves, they import their previous experiences, socialisation, attitudes and beliefs into the social setting that they are studying. They *interpret* events and create their own version of social reality, which may not be anything like the social reality that the people being studied have. Sociologists cannot be neutral, scientific observers because no person can be. Values and beliefs inevitably get in the way, and 'value-freedom' is a myth. Some critics see sociologists as being politically biased or as having an obligation explicitly to be so, an extreme form of this problem. While there undoubtedly is an epistemological crisis, it is not a crisis that applies uniformly throughout sociology, nor has it arisen at the same time in all branches of the discipline. On the one hand, there has been a reformism within the positivist or neo-positivist camp, which has led to an abandoning of some of the more naïve assumptions about quantification and measurement. But since Britain never suffered from 'Lazarsfeldianism' seriously in the first place, there was less to correct, and less institutionalised resistance to correction, than in the USA. Those sociologists who want to know about macro-sociological issues, at a fairly high level of approximation, have improved their research technology, eliminated wilder excesses by restricting the range of phenomena which they care to study, and taken on board a bastardised version of ethnomethodology as a kind of improved interviewing technique. This, together with a more critical reflexivity, has improved the grounds for justifying their enterprise. Only in a small way has ethnomethodology impinged on them, and marxism has made even less of an impact. A few useful concepts have been taken over and incorporated but these are mainly elaborations of basic issues that interested the British 'positivists' all along, like power, social class, status, inequality, ideology and so on.

So where is the crisis, the paralysing anomie of which Bell and Newby (1977) speak? It arises first from ethnomethodology, for whose adherents the cause of anti-positivism has ideological value in the struggle against a more conventional kind of sociology. That is not to say it is only an ideological weapon, but its importance in marking off boundaries and in providing legitimation for professional enterprise is very important. Most ethnomethodologists see the rest of sociology as having an epistemological problem, one which they themselves have solved (or nearly so). Their 'apathy' is one towards the *political issues* which concern sociologists like Worsley and Rex.

The second area of methodological dispute lies in marxist sociology. This is dealt with at more length in a later chapter, but marxism 'has always had trouble with its own epistemological status, that is to what extent it is a neutral science, and to what extent it is a critical theory linked to the interests of the labour movement' (Giddens, 1976, 718). Later marxists like Althusser have compounded this long-running problem, and the popularity of his work among young sociologists has meant that marxism's epistemological crisis has been exported to sociology. Again, anti-positivism is an ideological weapon against the bourgeois fact-grubbing sociologists, whose entire enterprise can be summarily dismissed without further thought, and better still, without the marxists needing to dirty *their* hands grubbing for their own counter-facts.

Newby and Bell are not quite correct to argue that 'the epistemological disarray in sociology is therefore a feature which transcends theoretical boundaries. It is not *simply* a politico-scientific crisis within positivism or bourgeois sociology' (1979, 11-12). They tend to over-estimate the extent of the disarray, and to attribute it equally to mainstream sociology and to marxism. This does not help us to see where the heart of the problem lies, and how it is being manifested. It is the ethnomethodologists and especially the marxists who have the bigger problem, and it is diffusing into the rest of sociology. As we shall try to show, there is a partial solution to methodology which most sociologists concerned with substantive issues are already taking.

This does not imply that one should ignore the view that there is a 'crisis of positivist science', which has left sociology without any clear cut path to follow. A widespread interpretation of what is happening (following Kuhn, 1962) is that we are experiencing a 'pre-paradigmatic struggle' to re-establish a 'normal social science' which escapes from 'the ruins of positivism'. Whatever the terminology employed, there are real issues of epistemology at stake, and for that reason it is necessary to spend a little more time dealing with basic steps in the debate about sociological knowledge. We can then decide whether they can usefully be applied to recent British sociology.

Epistemology is that part of philosophy which is concerned with a theory of knowledge. It addresses itself to the problems of what can be known with certainty – as against 'known' in the sense of personal opinion or believed as an act of faith – and by what means can we be said to know about something; that is, what is the proper source of knowledge? Its project is to produce a comprehensive statement about the conditions and nature of the possibility of human understanding of reality. Its particular connection with sociology is that 'understanding' depends on the language in which that understanding is achieved, and 'language' in turn is derived from social processes (it must be learned, controlled, corrected, clarified by regular social practices). The philosopher interested in epistemology has become drawn into consideration of the social, that is, the realm of the sociologist. This development has eased the transfer of ideas between the two disciplines, leading to a more rapid realisation of their own fallibility and unjustified presuppositions on the part of the sociologists than in the other social sciences. What had hitherto been regarded as 'evidence', 'theory', and 'concept' was now open to question at a fundamental level.

Positivist sociology

The focus for this questioning has been regarded as positivist social science. Positivism is one position within the field of epistemology. It has been a somewhat abused – and abusive – term, used in a number of ways over the last 150 years (Kolakowski, 1972). Its essential conception is that there is no knowledge without experience of the external world: this experience-based knowing is contrasted with unreliable mental phenomena like opinion or belief. It was Saint-Simon and Comte who set sociology up as a positivistic science, and grafted on several other ideas which make up an extreme form of positivism. Comte proposed sociology as a new moral and political force that would produce a new order in society. The high priests of the new ruling science would be the sociologists. Human society evolved through successive stages (although, as Hawthorn argues, Comte did not see this happening in a simple coherent way): from the theological (or military) through the metaphysical to the positivist society, in which the religion of humanity would replace older religions by means of its rational scientific understanding. This scientific understanding would arise by means of 'the discovery, through reason and observation combined, of the actual laws that govern the succession and similarity of phenomena' (Andreski, 1974, p. 20). Reform of the new industrialising societies would be possible by using this positive science. While social evolutionism, glorification of the scientist, naïve belief in the power of scientific 'truth', and faith in social engineering are not logically essential parts of positivism, Comte grafted them onto the core of his philosophy and echoes of them still occur in some of the more simplistic accounts of science and technical expertise today (e.g., Asimov, 1960).

In its later versions, positivism came to depend more on two other elements of its original formulation. The first was the 'unity of science'. This assumes that the positive method is the only correct method, and that anything claiming the label of science can only do so justifiably if it is based on the positive method. All 'true' knowledge is acquired in the same manner. In practice, that manner is most highly refined in the natural sciences, so that all other sciences must strive to follow their example and emulate their methods. In one version, this means that all phenomena are ultimately reducible to physics, but more usually the emphasis is on uniformity of method (Giddens, 1974, 3-4). Even though it may be recognised that the experimental method is impractical in social science, or that social phenomena are more complex, variable, and autonomous than physical entities, or that social science has developed later than, and is conceptually dependent upon, the natural sciences, these are usually regarded as simple historical accidents or temporary matters of detail to be overcome.

The second element is really a special case of the first. Comte sought to reduce all phenomena to the smallest number of principles or laws of explanation. Thus new facts could ideally be subsumed under previous laws. If not, then the law would be falsified in some respect. The scientific enterprise was a quest for the smallest number of laws, by means (in practice) of setting up *predictions* which would be 'tested' against the external world, and so upheld or rejected. In the modern form of this epistemological position, 'logical positivism', a scientific explanation of an event is one which includes it in a universal law, such that at its simplest, if one kind of event occurs, then another kind of event will also occur. To be more precise, if in the past the first kind of event has always been observed to be followed by the second kind of event, then all future occurrences of the first event will produce the second. This 'covering law' approach combines a specification of what the event to be explained is like with a universal law as a premise: the deduction, on observing the event, is what is predicted to happen.

This conception of explanation seems to have both advantages and disadvantages. Its main advantage is that it is neat and tidy. If a prediction fails, the theory fails. One disobliging exception, and the rule is disproved.

Unfortunately, it is not that simple. All belief systems carry with them auxiliary sets of beliefs about what a 'proper' test or an adequate disproof are like. These supporting beliefs lay down conditions which must be met, and in extreme cases invoke quite other metaphysical justifications for not rejecting a theory. This can be seen in anthropologists' accounts of tribal society, as in Evans-Pritchard's (1937) study of Zande witchcraft, which shows how difficult it is 'to break into the closed circle' of belief (Gluckman, 1963, 104). Rain magicians do not make rain during the dry season, so that no severe test of their abilities is made. If a spell fails to work, then by definition some taboo has been broken, so weakening the efficacy of the magical ritual to prevent disaster. There were always 'excuses' for why something magical failed to materialise and even the individual charlatan still had faith in other witch doctors. In the same way, school experiments in general science classes frequently fail 'to work': this does not lead to the rejection of the lesson, but a criticism of the conduct of the experiment. In principle, there is no reason why these auxiliary belief practices should interfere with positivist science: in practice, they often do. Where they do not, the direction of research is usually to understand *why* an awkward piece of evidence does not fit, rather than a total rejection of the original theory.

The logical (as opposed to the sociological) problems of positivist explanation are several (e.g. see Ayer, 1970, or Popper, 1961), and have increasingly been taken by social scientists as constituting grounds for rejection of the whole apparatus. First, what is the status of causality in this mode of endeavour? If all that positivism can say is that in the past things tended to work this way, this is less than establishing a causal explanation. Perhaps next time, x will not precede y, despite all previous trials. Further, positivism rejects all notions of mystical connections between events: therefore if x always seems to proceed y *something* must connect them. The positivist scientist can only logically assume that some other law, as yet undiscovered, binds the two events together. But that law is no more than another level of the same pattern of explanation: we are faced with an infinite regress of successive levels of explanations. Alternatively, we may be faced with an infinite regress through an endless catalogue of other events which might be supposed to provide cause.

Again, it is possible to be predictive without providing an explanation. When night falls, the Eddystone Light shines out. Night does not *cause* the light to come on, but if we believed that it did, we could reliably predict the event of when the light would shine. More complex scientific schemes have provided successful predictions without being correct for all time. Newtonian physics had a good run for its money, but during its period as a dominant paradigm scientists did not ceaselessly strive to falsify it, or look forward to the day it would be overturned. They operated with its assumptions and treated these as laws which could be employed in particular areas, areas in which for many years their predictive powers were regarded as satisfactory.

That is to say, scientific practice falls short of the canons of positivism. If 'falsification' is not strictly to be employed, it can be replaced by 'confirmation' (Hempel, 1966). A set of correct predictions 'confirms' the explanation, and is taken as acceptable in the absence of demonstrable falsification: it becomes recognised as a weak form of falsification, and so assumes a key position in actual practice.

And what of phenomena which by their nature are unobservable? Later positivists have accepted that things which are in principle unobservable may be included under the scientific rubric, despite not being open to conventional confirmation, always assuming of course that we are capable of knowing what is observable or not. A special case of this is the nature of a universal law. Many of the most accepted physical laws refer to an ideal state, not to what actually happens. Furthermore, physicists know that specific cases do not follow the general rule precisely, but find it convenient to proceed as if that were not so, because a simplification often has heuristic values. Ted Benton's critique of natural science elaborates on these 'dangers' of positivism from a philosophical position, and the reader who wishes to find a more extensive but still introductory treatment would do well to look at his Chapters 3 and 5 (Benton, 1977).

51

These objections to positivism have chiefly come from within the positivist tradition itself, as an attempt, through self-criticism, at self-reform. Ironically, its very success in rigorous self-criticism (at least at a philosophical if not at a practitioner level) has led to its failure as far as sociology is concerned, namely a vigorous rejection of positivism. As we shall see, this rejection is not brought about purely by the criticisms raised from within positivism: other critics have not been slow to graft onto their own objections those proffered by the positivist himself.

Thus, for example, critics of survey methods in America were able to expand their specific objections by virtue of the wider problems being identified by philosophers. What started as an expansion of method and technique – one thinks of Cicourel's *Method and Measurement in Sociology* (1964), Webb *et al.*'s *Unobtrusive Measures* (1966), Denzin's *The Research Act* (1970b), and Phillips's *Knowledge From What* (1971) – rapidly became an attack on what were seen as any and all positivistic tendencies – Filmer *et al.*'s *New Directions in Sociological Theory* (1972), Phillips's *Abandoning Method* (1973), or Fletcher's *Beneath the Surface* (1974). As these last examples show, the rejection was also taking place in this country. Indeed, it soon had reached epidemic proportions, leading Newby and Bell (1979) to talk about an 'epistemological crisis', 'methodological defeatism' and an 'epistemological anomie' in which 'there are no longer any obvious criteria for adequately certifying knowledge, nor for judging the appropriateness of methodological procedures, nor even for what are suitable topics for investigation' (Newby and Bell, 1979, 9; also in Bell and Newby, 1977, 21). Even if positivism took various forms, and had been applied within sociology before in an incoherent form, it had helped to guide and legitimate what kinds of 'facts' could be looked at, and how one sociologist could evaluate the work of another. Positivism 'provided the normative standards by which sociological research was both judged and practised ... it no longer does so, hence sociology's troubles' (Bell and Newby, 1977, 21). Bell and Newby suggest that the absence of normative standards is a species of normlessness, that is, a situation of classical anomie in which no action is possible because there are no social guidelines as to how to act. Is sociology even possible at all?

Normal or normless sociology

One of the more persuasive accounts of the epistemological crisis has been found in the work of T. S. Kuhn. Briefly, in his *Structure of Scientific Revolutions* (1962) he presents an account of science as practised, which disputes the conventional positivist model of steady cumulation of knowledge by trial and error, of progress and refinement by falsification. He argues instead that natural science has in fact progressed through great leaps and bounds at an erratic rate. Periods of calm and consensus are suddenly challenged and replaced by outbreaks of crisis when fundamentally new conceptions of what science is about are formulated. His is a picture of a discontinuous history of science, and it attracted sociologists in search of a model for their own difficulties because, not least, Kuhn's mode of explanation is very sociological in character.

Thus the period of consensus is one in which a 'paradigm' is shared by a 'scientific community'. This paradigm defines what is 'normal science': in other words it specifies what should be examined, how it should be examined, what should constitute findings. In short, it defines what science is and how scientists should go about their tasks. Such a model has an intuitive appeal for sociologists: if we had modified our terms and written in the first two sentences of this paragraph that a 'culture' or sense of social reality is shared by a 'community' and that this 'culture' defines what are the acceptable norms of governing action, then such a statement could be found in many an introductory textbook for sociology students.

Indeed, Kuhn's idea of the process by which this comes about is also sociological. He sees scientific education as an indoctrination of the rules which make up the paradigm. Professional training means learning perspectives and techniques, which eliminate alternative approaches to the science. Deviants are not tolerated: there is no acceptance of their 'findings', there is no career made available for them. They are excluded. The failure to solve a problem specified by the paradigm is a failure of technique or a failure by the individual scientist: it is not taken as a failure of the paradigm. Here we have the sociological notions of socialisation, social control, power, deviancy, and belief system under only slight disguise.

The other obvious attraction of Kuhn was that he seemed directly to reflect sociology in the late 1960s and 1970s. Kuhn argues that despite the pressures to stasis, items within the old paradigm become so difficult to contain that they reach the status of 'anomalies'. Eventually the paradigm is shattered, leaving several competing revisionary positions, from among which emerges a new dominant paradigm, re-establishing a new form of normal science. The assurance of an older sociology had given way under pressure from the critique of positivism, the rise of ethnomethodology and the new marxisms. The senior generation of sociologists was being challenged by its juniors.

Whether Kuhn's account of natural science is valid or not, an

53

over-simplistic version of it was grafted onto sociology. At first sight, it seemed to fit, but more careful consideration has shown that its applicability is limited. Criticisms have been of three major types: those concerned with the nature of social science data and theory; general problems of philosophy and terminology; and problems about the nature of social science organisations.

In the first place, Kuhn was dealing with natural science and clearly excluded social science from his schema. The extension is essentially a 'post-Kuhnian' revisionism, which as Worsley has argued, is not justified because of the mutable nature of sociological theory:

> The thought of even the most systematic of thinkers, moreover, displays internal inconsistencies, and changes over time ... Evidently, it is not just that there is no paradigm articulating the social sciences, not even that we are in a pre-paradigmatic era in which several candidates are contending for eventual supremacy. The social sciences, rather, do not follow the Kuhnian model (Worsley, 1974, 2).

He goes on to argue that social theory is a product of its social setting, so that an 'intellectual' discrediting of an idea or a paradigm is not enough. The intellectually-discredited idea will re-emerge, because its base is in the society itself. So long as society produces racism and inequality, it will also produce ideas and theories to legitimate them. Social science is far more closely bound into the rest of society than is natural science and so less free to indulge in paradigms and paradigm shifts.

A similar point has been made by Urry (1973), who also emphasises the problems for explaining the generation of anomalies from within the same set of knowledge. Even the basic concepts lack the levels of precision normally encountered in philosophical discourse. It is no simple matter to identify exactly what is meant by the key terms of 'paradigm' and 'scientific community'. Benton (1977) locates the key problem as lying in the latter: what are the boundaries of this community? Does Kuhn mean to include *all* scientists as its members, because if he does not, he allows for a rival, if minor, community which vitiates his general argument for the dominance of normal science. The scientific community is defined in terms of those who share the paradigm, but in turn a paradigm is something shared by the community. Other critics have complained of the lack of precision in the concept of the paradigm, and certainly in its popular usage among sociologists it has been reduced to such vagueness that it is synonymous for anything from a specific model to the most general of approaches. It has precisely the same problems as the omnibus concept of culture had for an earlier generation of American sociologists and anthropologists.

In particular it raises the difficulty of how to break into the logical system, and identify its constituent parts. This means a problem of what status is attached to 'scientific theory'. As Hawthorn (1976) argues, if science is socially produced and conditioned, it cannot be regarded as strictly rational in a philosophical sense. Alternatively if science is regarded as rational, then how is it possible for it to be socially produced? This dilemma runs throughout attempts at a sociology of knowledge, and does not just apply to Kuhn.

A more specific problem lies in Hawthorn's alternative view of social science as an institution. The social sciences 'have rarely been as well institutionalised as the natural sciences ... social scientists have seemed much more able to resist the pressures of their peers' (Hawthorn, 1976, 5). In the natural sciences, 'the deviant is ignored and unrewarded', whereas in European sociology the academic deviant has a legitimate place, praised and respected even, rather than merely tolerated. Hawthorn sees it as no coincidence that the most Kuhnian of accounts of sociology, Friedrichs's *A Sociology of Sociology* (1970) is a product of American sociology with its greater professionalisation, and its domination by systems theory and abstracted empiricisms. In the same way, America has less of a tradition of the amateur scholar and the American Sociological Association is a far more powerful and all-embracing force than its British counterpart.

Clearly, Hawthorn's view of European sociology accords with our own understanding of British sociology as consisting of multiple schools, differing from each other in more than one respect. In this light, if we take Kuhn's argument at all, there has been no 'normal science' which could be said to have broken down. Nor, therefore, can we be at a pre-paradigmatic stage awaiting the re-emergence of a new dominant paradigm. We are not even in some prehistoric, pre-paradigmatic state, because there are no signs that any of the competing schools in British sociology is likely to displace all others, thus establishing for the first time the rule of normal science. On the contrary, the different schools have been able to institutionalise their position by means of their control over curricula at both under- and post-graduate levels. Certainly there are 'tendencies' – such as the overgrown respect for grand theory which is one of the instigating forces behind this book – but these are not paradigms in any sense that has value for a Kuhnian analysis.

A rejection of any attempt to apply Kuhn's work to British sociology leaves us without the temptations of his neat historical account or his hope for a tidy paradigmatic future. We are still left in our epistemological wilderness. Is there a way out?

The answer, like many a philosophical paradox, is 'Strictly speaking, no – but we will still get out anyway!' In the first place, adopting methodological pluralism means that much of the apparent contradiction is defined away. If 'soft' methods have the same acceptability as 'hard' methods – used mainly of course on different aspects of sociological problems – then there is no longer any need to demonstrate the obvious fallibility of one method at the expense of another. In this case, 'hard', quantitative methods are taken to mean something quite different from what Mills meant by abstracted empiricism. To take one example, if we wish to work on social mobility, we have a choice of methods. A sample survey with interviewers using questionnaires will be successful if we are concerned to know rates of mobility in the country as a whole. The expression of the 'rates' will naturally be a sociological artefact, and we might equally wish to discover what, if anything, constituted 'mobility' for the individuals whom the sociologist identified as mobile or immobile. A softer method is called for here. Goldthorpe's 1972 and 1974 studies at Nuffield College attempt just this. A national sample of England and Wales has been interviewed, and then smaller sub-samples were reapproached to talk about how they experienced their careers. In fact, Goldthorpe was still using moderately hard techniques like open-ended questions and diary-keeping, but the basic point still holds. Again, it would still be possible in principle to look at the process of how individuals construct and negotiate shared meanings of mobility. Each level of method has its place, provided one knows what to study.

Our earlier introduction of *two* dimensions of difference between schools ('methodological' and 'political') reminds us that, at a fairly low level common denominator, much of sociology remains gently positivist at heart. Several of the classical tenets of positivism have been cleared away: there is no need for a unity of science as detailed practice; there are no naïve assumptions of a Comtean kind about high priests or a rationalist future; and there is no prescription as to what may or may not be studied. There is left a model of sociology which believes in a world external to the sociologist, which needs to be experienced in a systematic way. Even ethnomethodology uses what passes between people as raw material in this way. When a sociologist presents an account of his work, he is usually implicitly saying 'the external world is like this: if you in the audience study it in the same way as I have done you will come to the same conclusions'. This is at base a predictive exercise, and at various levels it is also an exercise in generalising. It may be that this appeal to experience of the world is no more than systematic empiricism (Willer and Willer, 1973), and not strictly to be identified as science or positivism. If so, where were the positivists in post-war British sociology in the first place? The *label* of positivist has been tied around a number of necks, but chiefly as a weapon of illegitimation for a school or individual whose issue-orientation has been the real target. In a strict sense, there are very few positivist sociologists in this country, nor have there ever been, apart perhaps from a few marxists.

The rest of us have more in common than we usually think. If there is one lesson which the latter positivists like Bachelard, Popper and even Feyerabend have taught us, it is to look at what scientists actually do, if we want to understand their methods. Part of these doings and methods involves empirical activity and the production of generalisation. The biggest problem lies in the other part of our activities in which we are so concerned, out of our methodological imperialism, to insist that a major problem of rival methods not only exists, but demands our time. Our method is mutual criticism. In a profession where intellectual rigour is *de rigueur,* everything that is done must be seen to be comprehensive and watertight by standards of logic: other people's different methods are an affront to the glorious purity, refinement and security of one's own chosen method. In a profession numerically dominated by young persons with careers to make, this view is perhaps understandable, but nonetheless undesirable.

It has led, paradoxically, to a very unpositivistic pattern in which new ideas are rejected before they have been developed fully or tested out in the external world. Instead of 'the more modest task of working within one of the variously flawed paradigms' (Atkinson, 1977, 33), sociologists are quick on the draw to attack those they see as rivals. If we do work, as Gouldner (1967) says, within the sound of guns, it is the sound of our fellow professionals opening fire on some new hatched piece of sociology – and on the inglorious 11 August, into the bargain! No sooner has something new appeared, in necessarily incomplete form, than it is dismissed (see Chapter 5 below). This may reflect not just the 'young turk' mentality of an immature discipline, but the very real plight of most sociologists who have been employed as lecturers with heavy teaching loads on new courses, especially in the non-university sector. The continual pressure to codify, simplify and report material for teaching purposes – in the early stages of a career with no great store of experience or lecture notes to draw on – contrasts with the careful, in-depth craft of research. Research for the young academic is always in danger of becoming an activity which takes second place, despite his personal sense of priorities. The 'mass-teaching' mode of thought, because it stresses simplification and pigeon-holing, is one that deals harshly with the incomplete new idea. The research mode of thought is more cautious, caring, and interested in innovation. And if career and reputation can be built by criticism, rather than creativity, this tendency in sociological practice is reinforced.

This in turn encourages the rush to judgment, already indicated in the first part of this chapter, in which new ideals are dealt with in terms of their approach, or ideological position. As Bernstein points out

> where theories and methods are weak ... the weakness of the explanation is likely to be attributed to the approach, which is analysed in terms of its ideological stance. Once the ideological stance is exposed, then all the work may be written off ... so that with every new approach the subject starts almost from scratch (Bernstein, 1974, 154).

The result is that, by the very nature of the social organisation of sociology, communalities of empiricism are denied in favour of methodological imperialism, new theoretical developments are still-born, and a premium is placed on theoretical disputation which operates without recourse to the features of the external world. This latter style of sociological practice sounds not unlike something we have already encountered: it is a version of Mills's grand theory. It particularly resonates with that aspect of Mills's critique which demands that sociological theory should be useful to the sociologist who wishes to understand the external world.

The role of sociological theory

What do we conceive of as the nature and function of theory? From earlier comments it will be apparent that the present authors borrow one central strand from positivism, that 'scientific' theory should be something that goes beyond opinion or faith. This still leaves all the philosophical traps of how that is to be known, what is to constitute a 'test' of a theoretical statement, what is causality, and so on. Nevertheless, however erroneous it may be in philosophical terms, sociological practice does go on. Since we all evidently do agree to that, by virtue of continuing to draw our pay cheques, then we implicitly accept that the philosophical paradoxes can only be coped with by ignoring them in our own practice. If we do take account of the limits of positivism, it is to accept that in the 1980s there is probably no place for 'laws' in the sense that natural science claims them. On the other hand there *is* a place for systematic empiricism and a kind of generalisation and theory which guides sociological analysis of the external world, and which is continuously refined by research, not just by armchair speculation and library critique.

This model of the sociological enterprise is neither confined to quantitative styles, nor intended to account for everything that passes as sociology. Rex is correct to argue first that 'there is a great deal to be said for a specialisation within sociology of those who make it their task to look critically at the meanings which are otherwise uncritically assumed' (Rex, 1974, 24), and second that – of course – not all elements of sociology are equally amenable to verification. Because sociology deals with meanings and meaningful acts, rather than attributes of things, it is not possible to 'test' theoretical statements in a direct and simple way. However, members' meanings are no less 'ideological and mystifying' than the sociologist's, and if there is to be a justification for sociology, it must be that:

> in some degree at least, sociologists' theories have a greater claim to acceptance ... [A sociologist] may point to a number of areas in which falsifiers of his proposition might be sought, and it is in this capacity which gives him the right to claim that his descriptions have greater validity than those either of 'members' actually participating in the social relations described or of other participants for whom such social relations are part of the environment (Rex, 1974, 45, 7).

This does not ignore the charge that the decision about what is taken to constitute 'falsifiers' is dependent on agreements between sociologists over appropriate procedures, and that in turn is no more than replacing one set of meanings by another. While there still has to be some kind of faith-like commitment underpinning any system of thought, the stipulation of falsifiers not only opens up the possibility of debate – new evidence can be produced within the terms set – but also the possibility of conceptual challenge because the terms of reference have been made explicit.

Rex adopts a middle-ground position on the question of knowledge and testability in his discussion of Weber's ideal types and verification. If an ideal type of meaningful action is posited, it can include such inaccessible notions as goals, means, norms and conditions. None the less if the applicability of the ideal type is to be claimed as valid (or at least, shown not to be invalid), certain accessible events should occur.

> For example, if we posit that, to use Weber's example, a man chopping wood is doing so in order to earn money, it should be perfectly possible to check on as yet unascertained facts as to

59

whether in fact he has been observed to receive payment for his work. If we found that he worked just as hard whether paid or not, or if we could simply find no evidence of his being paid, we should say that he was not working for money and that this ideal type was not applicable (Rex, 1974, 41).

In other words, interpretations can be subject to falsification – or strictly confirmation – by indirect means. Compared with psychologists, sociologists have been very slow to adopt this style of work. It involves thinking around a topic, in a series of logical extensions: 'if this is true, then that is likely to be the case.' It is a style of thought which is inherently negative, because it is seeking to construct difficulties for the sociologist's pet argument. On the one hand, it is a tightly disciplined, rigorous and painstaking procedure, and, on the other, it is a creative and imaginative exercise.

A special case of confirmation which is second nature in natural science is replication. Given physical objects and universal physical laws, a given finding should be reproducible in any location. However, human phenomena are more variable and transitory, and there have been few explicit attempts to repeat a sociological study. Journals are reluctant to publish them, or foundations to finance them: newness is all. The one-off finding which is accepted as an absolute statement of truth and the grounds for theoretical generalisation is the norm for empirical work in sociology. Only our inter-doctrinal disputes keep this in check, but challenges consist typically of purely ideological criticisms, whether on methodological or political grounds. No new evidence is adduced, and the original 'experiment' is not repeated.

One classic example is the study of social mobility in this country. This was 'done' by David Glass and the LSE team in 1949 (Glass, 1954). No further national study was made until 1972, a gap of 23 years. Everybody 'knew' about social mobility, so what was the point? But the two studies of England and Wales, and Scotland, run independently in 1972 and 1975, produced figures which were similar to each other, but very different from those of Glass (Payne et al. 1976; and Goldthorpe et al., 1977). Additionally, a reconsideration of the Glass tables showed that the LSE team had wildly improbable data (Payne and Ford, 1977). A replication of Glass's work in the 1950s, or 1960s, might have avoided the repetition of erroneous conclusions in theoretical writings on mobility and social class for over 20 years. The alternative to the practice of replication is not just another 'Social Mobility in Britain', but the continued risk of another Burt. There is no reason to believe that sociologists are any more honourable than their fellow men, deeply damaging though that may seem to the idea of professional ethics.

Of course, not all sociology is about ideas and evidence that can be 'tested'. Many of our essential constructs have a purely abstract character, and serve a valid heuristic function without which the discipline could not operate. Elaboration and refinement of these, and the development of new constructs, is a necessary part of sociology. We distinguish this from sociological theorising which attempts to define how society and human actors operate, theorising that says that the social realm is just so, without being susceptible to empirical challenge. It is the procedures of systematic observation, generation of propositions, recorded data collection, and, above all else, confirmation (and replication) which mark off sociology from other activities, and determine the acceptability and utility of theory.

part two

4 Grand theory and not so grand theory

Too much sociological activity goes into producing theories of society, which have few or no empirical reference points. In America the tendency to abstraction has been dominated by structural functionalism, whereas in Britain it has been manifested in several ways but most prominently by marxist sociology. In this chapter we look at two examples of 'grand' or excessively abstracted theory. The first is convergence theory, which, despite its unpopularity in this country, is well-known. This should mean that arguments about its status as theory need not become too confused with partisan counter-arguments about its plausibility. In the second case, marxist sociology, we are less likely to escape that pitfall, but in both cases we are not so much concerned with the ultimate 'truth' or political superiority of the theories, but with their internal structures of evidence and conclusion.

Both theories are ostensibly about key issues in the external world. They tell us how things are, what things matter, and how changes are taking place. It follows that their purpose as theory is to help us to understand society in a way which is both general and predictive. Part of the sociologist's task is to 'test' that predictive power, which means steady application of testing procedures to theoretical statements, in the name of confirmation or falsification. As we have shown, even self-confident empiricists are not in complete agreement about what falsification should comprise, supposing, indeed, that they can at least agree on the style of methods. Very few theories include a statement of what their creators would accept as disproof. This is usually left to the consumer to derive, and it is the dissatisfied consumer who is expected not only to furnish evidence, but to establish its relevance. In the resulting allegations and defences, protagonists argue past each other, each with total confidence and apparent satisfaction in their own rectitude. Of course, this also happens in *intra*-theoretical debates as well but in the case of empirical sociology, the problem is wider because it includes issues of evidence as well as of rationality.

This arises sharply in areas where a general theory is 'tested' by means of applying evidence to its tenets. In most cases, this involves a prior specification, by the tester, of hypotheses that he derives from another author's more abstract statements, together with the specification of a 'site' in which to test the hypotheses. 'Site' in this usage means a time and a place; a social setting such as an institution, or a society, and this will in practice be determined either by the current location of the researcher, or by the site's particular potential to be destructive to the theory in question. Rarely will it be chosen by 'scientific' techniques, such as random sampling, not least because that in itself introduces added problems, like specifying the 'population' from which the 'sample' is to be drawn. It follows that without clear-cut rules for site selection or hypothesis generation, that is for falsification, sociologists can find themselves in dispute over whether a theory has been falsified or not.

Convergence theory

One example of this is an attempt to falsify 'convergence theory' by use of British census data since the First World War and its subsequent challenge by Jones (1977). There were a number of steps to the argument which were implicit in the original article and only became explicit in a rejoinder to Jones (Payne, 1977a, b). That it took three articles to extract them is an indication of some of the technical difficulties in falsification.

'Convergence theory' is a term used somewhat loosely by most sociologists to refer to a body of work mainly American in origin and dating from the 1950s and early 1960s. It is not a single theory, and it ranges over a number of social changes during the process of industrialisation: social, economic, political, technological and cultural. The terms 'industrialisation', 'modernisation', and 'convergence' have all been employed, with different emphases. Clark Kerr and his colleagues are usually regarded as the key exponents of this doctrine although Aron, Galbraith and Moore are also involved.

The argument concentrates on eight propositions which Payne claims are generally accepted by these authors as applying to both early industrialisation and to advanced industrial societies, but which in fact are based on W. E. Moore:

1 Incorporation of all economic operations – such as the subsistence agricultural sector – into the national market economy

2 The transition of activity from primary to secondary, and secondary to tertiary sectors

3 The creation of new occupations and increasing differentiation between occupations

4 Increasing labour mobility, both within careers and between generations to man the occupational structure

5 A decline in the proportion of agricultural workers

6 An up-grading of minimum and average skill levels with relatively few unskilled workers, and 'the vast majority' of workers in various middle categories

7 A shortage of skilled workers

8 An increase in demand for professionals of all categories, and particularly doctors, engineers, and experts in organisation

These 'propositions' are not to be found in this exact form anywhere in Moore's work, but are based specifically on three pages in Moore's *Social Change* (1974), leaving it to the reader to check whether the representation is legitimate.

Jones makes two objections to this procedure. First, convergence theory is too varied and extensive to be represented by part of one author's work. He appears to believe that a critique should tackle all of the convergence theses, or none at all. Second, Moore's *Social Change* is not the best source, because it is a short, introductory text. The rejoinder is that one can choose to emphasise similarities between writers, or dissimilarities: the original paper does the former, Jones the latter.

> *it is precisely because Moore is so clear and compact in his exposition and coverage of main theories that I chose him to represent a tendency:* the other writers are less succinct (Kerr and colleagues' work, for instance, is less easy to abbreviate into a consistent half page statement) (Payne, 1977b, 411, original emphasis).

It may be that this is essentially only a comment on *part* of *one sociologist's* (W. E. Moore) views, rather than convergence theory as a whole. The reader must evaluate the evidence of similarity for himself, using whatever canons of evaluation he feels entitled to bring to bear. In the absence of 'rules', his evaluation may be influenced by his perception of what alternatives are practically available when attempting to handle an extensive and complex body of theoretical writing.

The second area of dispute arises out of the choice of site and the way the problem is operationalised. The fact that the data dealt with Scotland separately from England and Wales reflected Payne's mobility research in the sociology department of Aberdeen University. In other words, these data pre-existed the attempt to test convergence theory: the article arose out of a simple intellectual juxtaposition of the two elements, data and theory. The data were not collected after the 'experiment' had been set up in the classic natural science model. They were lying around for use in mobility research, and so were available for another use when the idea arose.

Jones makes two objections to the proposed site. He argues that convergence theory referred only to industrialising societies, not industrialised ones, and that the technical difficulties of employing different censuses were too great to permit a time series. The second of these objections is a technical question, but the first can illustrate the hidden assumptions that underpin this sort of activity.

Payne claims that there are three reasons why Britain is a valid site for this exercise. In the first place, the various writers who are mentioned in the article specifically refer to industrial society. Second, Moore in particular is concerned with industrial society, and quotations are presented in evidence of this.

The third reason for Britain being a valid site lies in the logic of the occupational transition argument. Even if all the other writers, including Moore, were not talking about industrial society, and Jones were right, it would still be patently ridiculous to argue that occupational transition did not apply to Britain in this century. If there is some reason for occupational transition, it lies in the nature of a technological system which cannot operate without various kinds of technical expertise. There is not a single uniform way in which this expertise is generated or organised but the process in which the technology is first adopted ('industrialisation') does not end at some arbitrary point when an 'industrial society' has been achieved. One may wish to try to isolate some feature of an advanced form of industrial society, but one is essentially dealing with a process, not with a set of stages. What we call 'industrial society' or 'advanced industrial society' (terms which, following Moore, Payne used to mean societies like Britain between 1921 and 1971) is simply part of a process in which occupational transition continues. The logic of Jones's argument is that occupational transition and industrialisation are something separate: industrial society is in some way so 'post-industrialisation' that there is no occupational transition.

The third area of dispute is on the strength of the changes in the tables of census figures. Part of this reflects misinterpretation, and the remainder, although relevant, is inconclusive. How big is an 'important' change? How long is a piece of string? While Payne can be criticised for not attempting some kind of probabilistic test of significance – provided we accept that as a valid scientific approach – he is able to show that for what he considers evidence (census data) for what he considers a valid time and place (Britain this century) what he thinks the convergence theorists mean (certain changes in occupational structures) did not take place in the ways expected (on his reading of their work). Jones's reply shows that even this highly conditional falsification did not convince everybody. He writes that he would only accept a negation of the occupational tenets of convergence were it demonstrated by 'a case where the transition to a high income economy had been made without the same overall structural changes as have occurred in all previously known cases' (1977, 393). But surely this is to operate on too absolute a scale. The 'law' that the arrival of a high income economy depends on new technological occupations is only of very limited use to us. It is far too general to have any analytical use: what is interesting is the form and production of those changes, and their infinite variety in different societies.

But the level of theory espoused by Jones is precisely the level so beloved of theoretical sociologists. Overwhelmingly the statements deal in truisms, the evidence is weak, the way it is used is inconsistent, and even the logical structure is unclear. In the case of most sociological theories of economic change – and is this not one of the 'master themes' in sociology – there are five common inadequacies. First, the analysis is carried out at too crude a level. For example, changes in occupational structure are described as proportional changes in the 'white-collar' and 'blue-collar' sectors: such a dichotomy would be unacceptable as a characterisation of occupations in any other field of sociology, except as an introductory orientation.

In the second place, the data presented do not adequately cover the time period involved. Most of the generalisations are valid only for gross overall trends. This use of the data ignores the possibility that, during the intervening years, such trends may have been manifest either uniformly or spasmodically: there may even have been a counter-trend for part of the time. If this is so, how does this affect a theory of industrialisation which is both causal and uni-directional?

Furthermore, 'deviant' cases (countries which do not conform to the pattern perceived for most countries) are treated as exceptional cases and not as impugning the generalisation. This is not to say that such cases are ignored or suppressed, but rather that the logical status of deviant cases in the argument is unsatisfactory. Indeed, the overall causal structure of the argument is imprecise. It is often not clear whether changes are being described seriatim or that one item leads to some result for another. Nor is it clear to what extent changes (for all their vagueness and lack of documentation) are inevitable, contingent or fortuitous.

Finally, there is a dearth of systematic empirical treatments and an ambiguity about the relationship between evidence and conclusions. Because there is an excessive emphasis on generalisation, it is hard to tell whether data are to serve as heuristic elaboration, supporting evidence, or demonstrating proof. Many of these specific criticisms of convergence theory also apply to the second example of grand theory, the various forms of contemporary marxism as they appear in British sociology. The basic questions of what is theory for, and what are the limits to the methods implicit in the theory, can be applied once again. Where a difference exists, it is that marxist sociology is an extremely important part of British sociology, indeed a growing part. What is more, it occasions in many of its adherents, and equally among its opponents, an emotional intensity and crusading zeal – *vide* the 'Gould Report' (Gould, 1977) and the furore following its publication.

Marxist sociology

The kinds of questions to be asked of marxist sociology are not ones about ultimate prediction, that is whether in the end the marxist forecast of proletarian revolution will be vindicated. That basic issue of classic positivism will have to wait. Rather, we need to know what is the empirical evidence for the marxists' claims, and what is their kind of sociological practice. To what extent are the varieties of marxism scientific in a positivist sense, and, if it is not a 'science' by non-marxist standards, what are its claims to be 'scientific' in its own right? Not all of these questions are ones which would receive primacy among those identifying themselves as marxists nor will we be able to give a complete answer.

One of the central problems for the non-marxist is the varieties of marxism available, each emphasising its own variant doctrine, and each invoking the name of 'True Marxism' to legitimate itself and discredit its rivals. There is the orthodox conservative marxism of the socialist state, the radical marxism of the pre-revolutionary struggle, and the evolution of the marxism of Eurocommunism. There are marxists who locate the revolution in the peasantry, in the urban proletariat, or in the party (and their intellectual vanguard). There are those who stress the early voluntaristic ideas of the young polemical Marx, as against those who favour the systems and neo-Hegelian writings of the later, more cautious Marx. The struggle against each other is as heavy as the struggle against the bourgeois ideologies they all oppose. It is not possible to do justice to all these varieties all of the time in what must be only part of the present discussion.

We can, however, restrict the compass of the analysis by starting with one of the key paradoxes of marxism. As far as sociology is concerned, there has been a kind of barrier between marxism in its large-scale, political form, and marxism as an academic exercise of intellectual reflection. It may be a cliché to say that salaried, tenured lecturers are not part of the working class, but it is an important observation. The marxist sociologist is typically a force for revolution (which we take to be one of the essential tenets of the faith) only in so far as the revolution requires intellectuals and ideologues. His roots in the proletariat (if he ever had them) have atrophied, and his life-style and political activities differ little from his non-marxist colleagues. Thus the obvious, commonsense version of marxism, accessible to those untrained in the arts of marxist sociology, goes almost unregarded.

That is, the kind of marxism which, like Christianity and Islam, is a key world movement, gets left out of marxist sociology. The lives of millions upon millions of human beings are affected by marxism. Yet, the powerful ideas and practice of marxism in socialist societies in the industrialised and Third Worlds do not form the core of marxist discourse in sociology. This external world of marxism is too popular or vulgar to admit to the professional debate: it is constrained and compromised by the force of events, by the need to get on and run things. Even the writings on theory of Lenin, Mao or Fanon do not figure largely in the literature. The external socialist world does not have the freedom of action that theoretical disputation allows the sociologist. The exclusion of marxism as presently practised in most of the world will continue to be taken by critics as a tacit admission that Russia, Cuba, China, etc. are an embarrassment to the utopian marxist. It constitutes evidence that does not fit the optimistic predictions of libertarian socialists.

Of course, this is not a new observation, but it does indicate a fruitful line to pursue. As we are interested in sociology as a research activity, it is not unreasonable to ask what research has been generated from a marxist perspective. It certainly seems plausible to the present authors that since there are whole societies run on a variety of marxist principles that marxist sociologists should be deeply and actively involved in the study of these societies. If they represent valid outcomes of Marx's thought, that is reason enough. If, on the other hand, they are some kind of perversion of his ideas, then their structures, institutions, practices should be rigorously examined, and exposed for what they are. It is true that such an enterprise is not easy, because totalitarian regimes are not noticeably tolerant of sociology (see the story above about sociology in Cuba). But that in itself is a datum, and, as Lane among others has shown, sociological research can be done despite the nature of communist conceptions of suitable intellectual pursuits.

Where is the sociology of Eastern Europe? Where is the sociology of Cuba? Of China, or even the Third World? There are precious few British accounts, because marxist sociologists have presumably chosen not to produce them.

Is one to conclude, therefore, that marxist sociological research has concentrated instead on this country? Sadly the answer is, only to a small degree. The most notable example is Westergaard and Resler's *Class in a Capitalist Society* (1975) which notes in its introduction that it is not interested in Britain *per se*, but only in so far as it is a concrete example of a capitalist society. This book is widely used on undergraduate courses, and is a very welcome addition to the available literature. Unfortunately, the standards of empirical evidence which it sets are none too high. Not only are whole sections – such as that on mobility – highly suspect in being based on rather ancient research, but its data are presented in an inconsistent and casual way. The reader may care to compare it with Trevor Noble's *Modern Britain: Structure and Change* which appeared at about the same time (1975) as *Class in a Capitalist Society*. Noble's selection of evidence to support his contentions is more precise, his data are more up-to-date (e.g., the use of the most recent census) and the categories and dates of his tables are much more consistent and easy to compare. One could also add that Noble provides a fuller picture of life in Britain, notably in his treatment of regional differences which examines how the economic structure impinges on present social conditions. This may be because he is more interested in the external world of British society than are Westergaard and Resler, for whom it is merely a convenient example.

To borrow Gouldner (and his expressed intention too),

> For example, and to be provocatively invidious about it, it was not the Marxists but Talcott Parsons and other functionalists who early spotted the importance of the emerging 'youth culture', and at least lifted it out as an object for attention. It was the academic sociologists not the marxists, in the United States who helped many to get their first concrete picture of how Blacks and other subjugated groups live ... the ethnography of the conventional academic sociology that has also given us the best picture of the emerging psychedelic and drug cultures (Gouldner, 1970b).

It would be unfair to leave the impression that all marxist sociology is in some way inadequate. Indeed, it is precisely because it has already led to such important insights in key areas that its past and potential contributions have such value for non-marxists. Several examples spring immediately to mind. In the sociology of work, names like Hyman and Allen are prominent as authors of books that have attempted to combine elements of a marxist perspective with the study of the external world. In the sociology of education, our understanding of the curriculum and social control have been greatly enhanced by marxist contributors like M. F. D. Young, while the 'New Criminology' has been one of the driving forces in bringing about advances in the study of deviance. Other areas such as poverty, race relations, the position of women, the social organisation of science and more recently urban problems have received injections of marxist sociology, much of it involving work which is oriented to the study of the external world.

However, the main stimulation from the marxists has been intellectual rather than empirical. New concepts and approaches there have been, but the hard systematic graft of demonstrating their validity has been lacking. Given the number of marxists and 'neo-marxists', the output of work on substantive areas has been small. Perhaps it should be stressed that this is no wild assertion of a 'red takeover' of sociology: the comments about numbers are only made to indicate that the call for a substantial output is not an unfair one.

Worsley's (1974) point that there are no clear-cut boundaries between sociology and marxism (as Gouldner wishes to suggest) is important here. British sociology, unlike the American variety, has always had room for Marx. Even the pre-war Fabians had an acquaintance with his work, if only by virtue of their contacts with the British Labour movement. In the early years after the Second World War, much of Marx's work was readily available, courtesy of the Foreign Languages Publishing House in Moscow: fewer of the writings of Weber and Durkheim were on sale in English, and who read in foreign languages? Hawthorn has presented a contrary view, identifying British sociology as the academic fringe of the Labour Party, never questioning the structure of social inequality in a fundamental way. Even if he is correct that British sociology has been more liberal socialist than marxist, this does not rule out a steady minority voice within the profession, and as Hawthorn himself shows, a vociferous presence on the permeable margins of the subject in manifestations such as the New Left Review. Although he says little about the 1970s, his pessimism about the failure of liberal socialism to deliver the goods, and the resulting search for alternative positions is quite compatible with the rise of the new marxism. Rex has portrayed the rise of both ethno-methodology and marxism in the same terms: sociology in the late 1960s changed, but still

took on the look of dogmatic theology. The new sociology
became what it was, not because of the inherent validity of the
marxist and phenomenological critiques of old paradigms, but
because these critiques fitted well with the aims of new social
movements (Rex, 1978a, 296).

Even non-marxists accepted this. There has been a long-established
tradition of 'No enemies to the Left' (Heady and O'Laughlin,
1978), an unwillingness to criticise those who are closer to one's
own point of view than the 'real enemy' of the political right. As
sociology became more concerned with theory, then it became
easier for marxist sociology to gain acceptance, for it is in abstract
systems and concepts, and esoteric language that marxism excels.

Are there empirical questions in marxist sociology?

Why is it that British marxist sociology has been so little concerned
with substantive research? It is not just the general conditions of
academic employment and career which impinge on all members
of a young profession. It certainly is not that the conceptual
apparatus of marxism does not generate questions which cry out
for investigation, as was indicated above in reference to the
phenomenon of socialist societies. But equally, nearer home,
problems abound.

For example, it always strikes the non-marxist as peculiar that
someone writing in the middle of the last century could be expected
to give a precise analysis of the last part of this century. Certainly
Marx provides a perspective and a set of concepts by which his
followers can analyse present-day society, but the nature of
capitalism has inevitably changed over the last hundred or so years,
and will go on changing (that is not to say anything about whether
it is becoming 'better' or 'worse'). There is therefore a continual
task of learning anew about capitalism in its various forms, in order
to test whether Marx's original conceptual formulations still work,
and if not, to adapt and extend them until they do. At present that
process of updating Marx seems to be operating only as a
theoretical exercise. If it includes reference to external conditions,
these are few in number, highly selective and heavily subordinated
to the theoretical apparatus.

This is true of even major substantive problems, like that of
technology and the occupational structure. Braverman has popu-
larised the concept of 'de-skilling', but where are the systematic
treatments of different British industries and occupations showing
to what extent this has taken place, when it has happened and at
what rate, how this has affected the class consciousness of the

workers involved, how levels of employment and production have been changed, how it related to market conditions, what kinds of capital formation and organisational types are most susceptible, why it is not taking place in socialist societies, where 're-skilling' has happened.... Again, what have been the overall changes in the occupational structure? Burnham (1972) has provided an initial spur, but where are the detailed marxist accounts of what has happened? Is there a new managerial class? If so, what are its boundaries? When has it come into being? Recent studies of occupational change (Bain, 1972; Payne, 1977; Brown, 1978) which might provide some answers have not been the work of marxists. But if manual workers have *decreased* by something like nearly one million, i.e., a fall of 7 per cent, since the First World War while the total labour force has *increased* by five and a half million or up 30 per cent, surely this makes a difference. By examining when and where this has happened, it should be possible to see changes in class consciousness, class organisation, and the revolutionary potential of various strata. Or are these all constants during an era when manual workers have gone from being two-thirds of the labour force to less than a half? It is not enough to argue that these things are unimportant just because many so-called non-manual jobs are really proletarian. That may be – and 'may be' is the operative phrase. It is an empirical question which is bound up with the lack of systematic research into de-skilling.

Even the basic issues of ownership and control owe as much to non-marxists as to members of the faith. Evidence on the distribution of income and wealth, and the mechanisms for translating economic power into action and control, have been of common interest to both camps. Several commentators have been on the fringes of marxism but their contributions have not been presented or taken up in a strictly marxist framework. For example, there is Pahl and Winkler's (1974) work on Boards of Directors, Scott and Hughes (1976) on interlocking directorships or Townsend (1979) on poverty. When one does encounter an attempt at a political economy of organisational control, it is likely to concentrate on the conceptual, and also be heavily dependent on non-British sources (e.g., Dunkerley and Clegg, 1980) precisely because there is a shortage of contemporary substantive scholarship in this country, and theoretical elucidation has become acceptable as an alternative praxis.

This structure also applies to other levels of social problems, such as the sociology of the state, bourgeois hegemony, ideology and consciousness. Recent BSA conferences are cases in point: excellent conceptual papers, literature reviews, critiques, and even papers with occasional references to data – but well-worked empirical research was conspicuous by its absence. The nature of bourgeois ideology (or ideologies?) is not a fixed, known thing. We need to study its production through many forms, the mechanisms of its maintenance, its differential impact on groups in society, and relationships between agents and also components of ideological production. How else can one come to terms with the problems in the notion of 'false consciousness'? How else are we to understand the way the working class is being incorporated under capitalism, or the way in which other groups – ethnic minorities, women, students, intellectuals – are perhaps not? What is the revolutionary potential of such groups – not in terms of speculation or nostalgic reference to the good old days of 1968 – but in terms of studying the lives of members of such groups?

To be fair, there can be no doubt that for many marxists, there has always been a place for empirical study of society. Korsch, for example, has outlined a programme for a marxist sociology in which empirical research has an integral part, suitably combined with current theoretical practice (Korsch, 1971). Lukacs and Gramsci both also allowed for such work, the latter portraying sociology as 'an empirical compilation of practical observations' (Gramsci, 1971, 428). These earlier key writers have a somewhat outmoded view of sociology because of course they were writing about an earlier era when it was characterised by Durkheim, Weber and other commentators on the rapid social changes in Europe in the late nineteenth and early twentieth centuries. Moreover, marxists reared on a diet of the dialectic characteristic of the nineteenth century through which Marx's ideas are expressed, naturally turn back to those early sociologists whose style and interests resembled the master's. Thus we find that many of the pre-war European marxists see sociology as a narrowly empirical enterprise, whose activities can be guided by the more important science of marxism. The latter would be able to make use of the fact-gathering of the sociologists, once they had been pointed in the right direction.

This view has been disappointed, as far as British sociology is concerned, by the later developments of marxism, sociology, and marxist sociology. In the main,

> the sociological researches and themes that had been initiated at the beginning of the century were not systematically pursued … marxist sociology has largely failed to develop empirical studies of particular social phenomena. There have not been significant and extensive marxist contributions to the study of crime and delinquency, bureaucracy, political parties, the family, or to a great number of other specialised fields of inquiry:

and even in the study of social class and stratification
 – which occupies a crucial place in the marxist theory
 – there is a notable absence of the thorough historical and
 sociological investigations which might have been expected
 (Bottomore, 1975, 29 and 73).

While a few steps have been taken to remedy this state of affairs
since 1975, Bottomore's assessment still holds generally true today.

Our earlier brief shopping list of substantive research topics and
Bottomore's view are based on some of the current issues in marxist
discourse. Why is the general picture so empirically bleak? Clearly,
as the list shows, it is not that marxism does not generate issues
that need investigation. Nevertheless, as practised, marxism does
not generate empirical sociology. One would therefore be tempted
to suggest that marxism is by its nature grand theory, so that
external reference points are essentially irrelevant.

In one version of marxism, concern with the present forms of
human society *is* an irrelevance. Since it will pass away by the iron
laws of history, there is little point in worrying about capitalism's
present complexities. After all, if the revolution will arise in
response to the inevitable crisis of capitalism, only the crisis period
itself might be worthy of some study, if at all, and that despite
earlier optimism is not now currently manifest even if imminently
expected. This kind of utopianism has no need of the harsh realities
of an uncomfortable, complex, and disobliging external social
realm.

A variant of this utopianism is a more active one, which while
still ignoring empirical issues, wishes to think about ways of
mobilising revolutionary forces. Thus a student of one of the
authors seriously proposed that the way to tackle an analysis of the
transfer payments element of public spending was to discuss
different theories of worker-student alliance. As he explained, 'we
can spend all day arguing about *statistics*. The real issue is to
discuss the raising of the proletarian consciousness.' It will be noted
that he was not proposing that a priority was to convince his fellow
students, let alone to go out and 'mobilise' some passing workers:
he wished to sit in the seminar room discussing *ideas* about how the
revolution might be brought forward.

A third form of marxism is involved with the world, but not as
academic sociology. This is the direct political action of the party
worker. He at least escapes the charge of bad faith, in that he takes
Marx's metaphor of social change literally, as a guide for action.
His praxis may be simplistic and deemed by some to lie outside of
'proper' sociology (except as 'subject'), but it is concerned in a
direct way with substantive problems. While his academic parallels

77

may seek to 'democratise' university departments, the range of their political marxism is usually restricted to the internal balance of power in their own work place, i.e., the state-financed organisations which not only tolerate their attempts to promote its downfall, but finance them in the meantime.

A fourth approach to marxism as an intellectual enterprise stresses the totality of social events. Because the base and superstructure are inextricably interrelated, and the bourgeois hegemony is so powerful, it is not possible to study a small part of a society in isolation. The action of a group of people, or the features of an institution make no sense alone. To understand them, the sociologist must investigate the total social context. In turn, to be able to do this, he requires a full marxist understanding of society at a theoretical level, which must be brought to bear in the exercise. In fact, the sheer impracticality of carrying out empirical research when at the same time this has to be combined with a total study of all institutions and an exposition of marxist theory means that no empirical work gets done at all. The view of the world that renders substantive sociology impossible also provides an intellectual justification for the practical inaction. The project becomes to be seen as logically impossible.

This kind of intellectual absolutism has a moral counterpart. Many marxists see the world in black and white: their stance is essentially an ethical and political one. They reject all possibility of any interim position between defence of, and attack on, capitalism. To these people, the sociologist and social anthropologist must

> side either with the oppressors or the oppressed. From this it is readily deduced that it is always morally deplorable to serve any established authority and always morally virtuous to side with liberation movements. That sympathies may be divided or solutions elusive does not seem to occur to these writers (Leach, 1974, 34).

The possibility of any study other than a politically committed one is excluded. The outcome is predetermined by the researcher's ethical involvement. Any results which might fail to fit the ethics of the case would not only be distasteful but dangerous. It is easier to abstain.

Marx as theorist and empiricist

In both these passive and active modes, there is no need inherent in marxism itself to study the external world. The fact that Marx and Engels felt enjoined to act empirically, is not stressed. Bell and Newby (1977) have commented that Marx even used a kind of a survey questionnaire. Additionally, careful regard for events marks his writing on the Paris Commune, and there are strong elements of 'grounding' in both his own work and that with Engels (e.g., *Socialism: Utopian and Scientific; the Condition of the Working Class in England; The Class Struggle in France 1848-1850*, and so on, (1962)). What Marx considered to be evidence, what he considered to require some external referent, and what he considered to be 'scientific' theory reveal a catholicity of method, and marxists since have followed suit, even descending into orthodox positivism.

We do not wish to get too embroiled in that supremely marxist enterprise of invoking the Master himself to legitimate our argument. Suffice it to say that there is no *a priori* reason to suppose that Marx would have been opposed to empirical sociology or even satisfied with only the more rarefied brands of his disciples' work. After all, Marx was a writer of his time. The technical and intellectual resources available to him in the middle of the last century were severely limited. In just the same way, commentators in another 20 or 50 years will have different perspectives and techniques with which to evaluate our own work in the 1980s. Marx's writings appear to be predominantly theoretical because there was no alternative model. This is not to say that he was not trying to derive a large-scale theory of history and society: of course he was. He sought a level of scientific theory with all the fervour of a good positivist, and believed that previous styles of history and philosophy had been rendered obsolete by the development of his new approach.

> Where speculation ends – in real life – there real positive science begins: the representation of the practical activity, or the practical process of development of men. Empty talk about consciousness ceases, and real knowledge has to take its place. When reality is depicted, philosophy as an independent branch of knowledge loses its medium of existence.... Viewed apart from real history, these abstractions have in themselves no value whatsoever (1970, 48).

It is the variety of 'methods' that Marx embraced that has given later marxists the foundations on which to build so many variations of his ideas, ranging from pragmatic to the most abstract and structuralist.

The questions and arguments that have been addressed to marxist sociology so far have in fact been concerned with only one part of that broad, if disputatious, religion. In the context of an apparent epistemological crisis in sociology this has been not unfair, because there are two essential themes which require exploration. First, is marxist sociological theory 'scientific' in the sense that certain other sociological enterprises can claim to be (in Rex's sense of being able, within known limits, to demonstrate a relatively more grounded and confirmed version of reality)? On the whole the answer seems to be 'no', because the marxists for various reasons have not committed themselves to the testing of their ideas, and have even shown a lack of interest in analysing British (or any other) society. The second issue has been whether there is anything inherent in marxism which brings this substantive apathy about. Here the answer has again been 'no', but in a qualified way: certainly there are tendencies within marxism which go towards explaining their distaste for the external world of capitalism. We shall return to these reasons at the end of the chapter.

However, it is true that the account up to this point has been a distortion, because we have exaggerated parts of marxist work – the parts in which a book on social research must be most interested – and neglected others. Chief victim of this neglect is the marxism of Louis Althusser and the Althusserians. In a sense, Althusser represents the grandest of grand theory. If British sociology is threatened by abstract theorising in the way that Mills saw American sociology threatened by Parsonian theory, it is through marxism in general, and Althusserian marxism in particular. A proper exposition of Althusser's ideas is probably unnecessary here, because there is little to say about the empirical implications of a position which holds the external world in such a lowly place. Nevertheless, his work has been influential among younger sociologists in this country, and his influence cannot be ignored.

Where Althusser's marxism differs from the other kinds that have been discussed is in basing its ideas on the later work of Karl Marx. His reading of Marx is that the mature work is fundamentally different from that which was written up to the mid-1840s (Althusser, 1969). The young Marx was polemical, involved in political activity, and as an actor involved directly in struggle, his work was essentially ideological, i.e., produced to further an interest. This was a humanistic stage in which Marx was concerned to demonstrate the capacity of man to change his oppressive circumstances. It led to a utopian style in which man as a subject occupies the centre of the stage. His predictions of proletarian dictatorship belong to this period and are fallible. After 1845, and culminating in the later volumes of *Capital* in 1866, Marx began to develop a science of systems, which have their own properties and laws. There is thus an epistemological break, in which Marx turned his back on earlier bourgeois knowledge in the form of history, philosophy, and sociology, all bourgeois ideologies which, in as far as Marx was debating with them, rendered his own work unreliable.

After the break, Marx was producing a science, which was true despite his own or anyone else's ideological stance: he had transcended ideology. His science was one of structures, and the analysis of the complex relationship between structures, not a political history of mankind.

The second characteristic of Althusser's position is the relationship he posits between the components of these 'structures'. Having emphasised the differentiation of politics, ideology and science, and of course the material, he also accepts Marx's view that each of these consists of (or are like) a system of production with an object of labour, means of production, and the product (Althusser, 1970). Within this complex, he sees the material as being the most important, but not in an absolute, continuous fashion. Other elements may dominate for a time, so that the totality is in constant stress. In more conventional terms, the modes of production only indirectly determine the superstructure. Only when 'over-determination' is achieved – when contradictions lead to simultaneous conflicts in more than one structure – does change take place. This is at once more subtle than earlier crude accounts, and yet more crude, for any possible combination of events can be explained away as not fitting the required formula. Only from within the theory can this be discerned, because all theoretical understanding is materially conditioned, (including 'science'), but only Althusserian theory can identify the consequences.

It follows that the theory gives meaning to events, but the events are themselves unimportant. Marxism is regarded as not a branch of science, but an independent correct science which sets and answers its own distinct questions:

> indeed it may almost be conceived of as a 'system of questions' which only it can pose – and can therefore only be criticised from within itself. There is no independently given realm of empirical 'facts' by which theory can be judged, because what we call facts are themselves constituted as parts of the 'theoretical object' which each science makes for itself (Peel, 1978, 350).

The result is that history for Althusser (and sociology for British Althusserians) becomes irrelevant as empirical activity, reduced in Vilar's well-known phrase to a 'mere assemblage of facts, something to be left out of account once its suggestive potential for theory has been utilised' (Vilar, 1973, 71). Further, facts cease to have any utility, because they are deemed not to exist outside of theory (Stedman Jones, 1972). Thus we move into a realm in which there is nothing with which to test a theory, except perhaps other theory: the world of purely theoretical discourse has been achieved. While we would accept the view that what constitutes 'facts' is an arena for debate, and that facts 'are always the product of definite practices, theoretical and ideological, conducted under real conditions' (Hindess and Hirst, 1975, 2-3), this does not mean an end to empirical research: it is only a qualification of it. It is not true that the 'positivist' or the empirical sociologist simply 'measures human reason by the standards of the prevailing social order' (Benton, 1977, 44), because there are several prevailing social orders and standards at any one time. The sociologist can choose his own frame of reference: he is not simply the product of a totally deterministic system. He may be more *interested* as a sociologist in some phenomenon in capitalist society rather than in a hypothetical revolution, but this does not mean, to use Marcuse's phrase, that 'the conceptual interest of the positive sociology is to be apologetic and justificatory' (Marcuse, 1955, 342). It only holds true for those who adopt a simplistic view of life in a capitalist society.

The extreme idealism of Althusser makes the status of Althusserianism in sociology highly problematic. It not only rejects 'social facts' but also implies a more fundamental problem. Is discourse possible without a continual accounting for basic facts such as 'Karl Marx's *Communist Manifesto* was published in 1848'?

The upshot is an elaborate kind of non-communication, only slightly caricatured in the anecdote which Bell and Newby relate against Althusser's more recent follower, Poulantzas:

> He was asked whether there was anything at all that could be discovered about advanced industrial societies that would lead him to modify his theory about the nature of that society under capitalism. His answer was that there was not, nor could not be, anything at all (Bell and Newby, 1977, 25).

While Poulantzas and other Althusserians, then, would not wish to participate in an empirical sociology by virtue of their theoretical stance, this contrasts with other marxists who, as we have seen, have at least *advocated* such a programme. Again, as Bell and Newby instance, there are examples of a methodological pluralism in recent writing from this school. There are techniques which resemble 'the orthodox positivism of "bourgeois" social science' (1979, 11). Westergaard and Resler (1975) employ all manner of data from surveys and official statistics, while marxist-influenced studies of the operation of the legal system have imported ethnographic techniques (Carlen, 1976; Cain, 1979). This in turn resembles Marx's own approach, certainly in his earlier work, where he employed several different types of analysis, and levels of information and reflection to suit his need in 'diverse occasions' (Vilar, 1973, 67). Sadly, these examples remain as examples rather than as the typical activity. Marxism as a whole has failed to produce a sociology of contemporary capitalism that is grounded in the way people lead their lives amid the institutional structure, ideologies, and social relationships of the concrete world.

The social context of marxist sociology

We have already indicated in this chapter that this is not entirely fortuitous. Even the advocates of empiricism, or those within marxism who see no theoretical objection to such an enterprise, have not delivered the goods, for a variety of reasons such as a utopian future-orientation, or a concern for action, or from a different set of priorities for their praxis. A further set of reasons can be adduced from the social and cultural settings in which marxism has developed in British sociology.

It has already been emphasised that the discipline started late and that, unlike its history in most other countries, it can be identified only as a post-war, and even then, predominantly post-1965-phenomenon. Sociologists have been recruited from young men and women whose formative years were the 1960s. As Hawthorn has observed these were ultimately years of disillusion: some of the more obvious failures of liberal socialism, so bound up with British sociology, meant that there was a need for an alternative. Marxism seemed more plausible, not least in 1968, and it existed already in a well developed and articulate form. Unlike ethnomethodology, which had to start from scratch, evolve its own tenets, and struggle for its very existence, marxism was ready-made. It had years of evolution behind it. It was institutionalised in the form of political parties and student societies. Its ideas were available in papers, paperbacks and pamphlets, many at very low cost, thanks to the subsidies made available by organisations such as the Foreign Languages Publishing House. It had party members only too happy to talk about their own convictions at a personal level, let alone campaign as a collective party policy to win converts among the next generation of ideological leaders. Just as the Salvationists grudgingly admitted that the devil seemed to have all the best tunes, so academic sociology – particularly of the functionalist or social survey kind – had nothing to compete with the fire, excitement, camaraderie, and intellectualist flair of the Left during the 1960s. The struggles to liberalise the universities and the campaign against the Vietnam war brought diverse disenchanted groups together in experiences that were not just coldly intellectual. They learned from one another in an atmosphere of infectious animation. Somehow, Harold Wilson did not compare with Che Guevara. This is not to imply that marxism succeeded in establishing its place in British sociology solely because of its emotional appeal or because there was a dedicated 'red-under-every-student's-bed' movement. But marxism had a plausibility, a symbolic importance and a ready-made set of organisations and ideas, all of which helped to fill a vacuum that an older kind of academic sociology had left.

The new sociology students of the 1960s created in their turn a new sociology. The expansion of Higher Education outside of the universities gave them numerical influence. Their older counterparts, having so recently thrown off the shackles both of pre-war sociology, and more established university disciplines, had no moral grounds for challenging this second wave of revolution. Students were soon being taught what the new lecturers had found seminal in their own development – and of course, this was quite justified. After all Marx was one of the Founding Fathers, and current exposure to ideas from continental social thought had an intellectual cachet, particularly when it involved a critique of capitalism. The doctrinal disputes within marxism had the appearance of academic discourse – which of course they are, of a kind – so that a variety of marxist texts began to appear on the undergraduate reading lists. The strength of this tendency led the political scientist Ivor Crewe to observe in the *THES* in 1976 that

> no single political thinker is paid greater attention (nor had his Great Political Thoughts more frequently and uncritically quoted) than Marx. He is stuffed down the students, poor things, until they talk about praxis and 'commodity fetishism' in their sleep (Crewe, 1976).

Now, as one of the major political thought systems of the modern world, marxism rightly has a place in the curriculum of every social science student – but by that token, there are several other systems of thought that should also be included, and are not. However, some of these others have not made such an impact on British academic sociology.

Grand theory

This is not unrelated to a further aspect of sociology – the profession's relative youth. At its simplest, it takes time and great effort to develop a coherent sociological perspective, and once launched on a marxist tack it is hard to divert into another kind of activity, even if one wanted to. The marxist tack is one which has its own style of discourse: language, issues, and orientation. This, as we have seen, is a theoretical discourse *par excellence*, requiring no empirical work. The young marxist can sit comfortably in his office, or in the library, reviewing the contributions of others and adding his own opinions, balancing and synthesising, criticising and evaluating. Once he has mastered the art, the enterprise is intellectually challenging and satisfies the requirements of the contemplative, academic life of the scholar. The inconsistencies and complexities of the world outside of sociology can be left to look after themselves. Indeed, the young academic will already have made one of the great steps forward in his profession by identifying himself as a 'theorist'. As Worsley has commented, in sociology

> theorists occupy an especially prestigious place. They are accorded a kind of respect which even the most experienced or knowledgeable of 'substantive' workers do not receive. It is understandable why this is so, since theorists are concerned with generalisation. Hence their ideas can in principle be applied generally (Worsley, 1974, 5).

In fact, as Worsley goes on to argue, the researcher in the field does not actually use wholesale theories, but borrows eclectically, polishing a concept or appropriating bits and pieces rather than complete schemas. Thus the substantive researcher is ambivalent towards the theorist. He knows that his own interest in a substantive area cannot stand in isolation from theory, and that his own contribution is not necessarily generalised beyond that area. He therefore pays tribute to the theorist, but on the other hand continues to pick and choose only those parts which can be adapted for use in knowing the external world. This pattern is repeated in undergraduate teaching, where courses of theory are largely taught separate from substantive sociology. Teaching sociology is a game of presenting a series of straw men of ideas, particularly in the area of theory. What Cohen and Taylor said about 'intellectualism' in the classroom not standing the test of practical experience in the prison is most apposite. British sociology is too much the study of other sociologists, not the study of society. Sociology has always been a heavily theoretical subject but it is now out of balance.

Grand theory in this country has not been Parsonian but it has had its counterparts. In looking at two kinds, convergence theory and marxism, the same underlying questions have been used to order their presentation. What use are these theoretical systems for learning more about society? Is the basic relationship of evidence and conclusion within each a satisfactory one? What are the technical problems associated with trying to mobilise all, or part of a theoretical schema in sociological analysis of social relations and institutions? The discussion of what constitutes a hypothesis, a site and falsification (in convergence theory) apply directly to marxism.

In criticising theory from the standpoint of the substantive sociologist, this chapter has not been intended as an anti-intellectual plea for 'fact-grubbing' or 'number-crunching' (although no doubt some critics will wish to depict it as such). Rather it has been a plea for a different kind of theory, one which is more directly connected to the external world. Such a theory must still be able to meet rigorous standards. It must have an internal logical consistency. It must be able to provide grounds for identifying what is to be studied, and how these social facts will be organised. It must establish what patterned connections exist between them. It must provide grounds for its own falsification. It must indicate what action in the world is appropriate. In practice this means that sociological theory will be grounded in a context of other theories, and related to other social sciences, particularly in terms of assumptions about how we are to obtain.knowledge, and what is to be done with it. That is to say, it must have a clear epistemological base and also provide a guide for the public role of the sociologist.

Here we return to the dichotomy made in an earlier chapter between method and epistemology on the one hand, and issue-orientation and political stance, on the other. It is inevitable that any theory incorporates some kind of valuation, both in its selection of topic and the way in which it is treated. It is equally inevitable that any sociological enterprise can be attacked for its political stance, whether this takes the form of showing what interest the sociologist represents, or is a more direct attack on the product *per se*. Unfortunately, the criticism of stance has been confused with the criticism of method. It may be, to follow Worsley, that ethnomethodology is neglecting a range of issues which some sociologists (including Worsley himself) consider to be more important. For example, Rex has proposed that sociology should devote itself to 'understanding the social structures within which people live or might have to live out their lives' (Rex, 1974, 7) – social structures meaning capitalist, socialist and ex-colonial societies. But that does not represent a fully sociological criticism of ethnomethodology, as it deals primarily with a statement of preference for the object of sociological analysis. A more sociological criticism would be concerned with whether a context-free sociology is *possible*, and if so, what would it then imply for future sociological practice? The same applies to marxism: its object of study is one thing, its method of study is another. In both cases the extreme forms of these abstract grand theories become so totally de-contextualised as to relate not at all to the external world.

5   The ethnographic tradition

One of the important challenges to abstracted sociology has come from the ethnographic tradition. In Britain this has a complex history of indigenous developments, exported to America and subsequently reimported in isolation from their original roots. The depth of the tradition has been obscured by a mythological version of inter-war sociology. It is seriously misleading to consider the discipline in that period as atheoretical, dominated by empiricist survey work and distracted by Fabian reformism. Westermarck, Hobhouse and Ginsberg were nothing if not theorists. T. H. Marshall, in introducing the 1975 edition of *Methods of Social Study*, reminds us of Beatrice Webb's divergence from her early mentor, Charles Booth, over the importance of developing a theoretical understanding of society rather than a statistical framework of self-persuasive 'facts' (Webb, 1975, xi).

It is often forgotten that the Webbs were notably sympathetic to observational approaches: 'An indispensable part of the study of any social institution, wherever this can be obtained, is deliberate and sustained personal observation of its actual operation' (Webb, 1975, 158). Beatrice Webb herself carried out what was essentially a participant observation study as a seamstress which she describes in *My Apprenticeship* (1926). *Methods of Social Study* includes a chapter, 'Watching the Institution at Work', which still offers useful advice. It is particularly interesting to note their approval of Lincoln Steffens's investigative journalism, which also influenced Robert Park's work at Chicago, and the similarities between their, often-mocked, paper-shuffling system for data analysis and the methods employed by Chicago students (Faris 1967).

Nevertheless, there was little evident impact on academic sociology. As we have already observed, the leaders at this period were preoccupied with defining the scope of sociology and defending its intellectual status. Shils (1970) and Abrams (1968) remark on the difficulties of distinguishing sociology as a discipline from the various 'amateurs, enthusiasts and cranks' (Shils, 1970, 769) using it to propagate a variety of personal ideological positions. This was compounded by the nature of the prestigious British universities. Unlike their German and American counterparts, they gave a low priority to the discovery of new knowledge as opposed to the transmission of a cultural heritage. There was little incentive to engage in research and reflections on issues in social philosophy offered better prospects of recognition.

The anthropological heritage

It is to social anthropology, then, that we must look for the development of a research-led social science in Britain. Here it was rapidly evident that, whether asking evolutionary or comparative questions, the anthropologist could not begin to progress without professionally collected data. The sociologists could reflect on their own society by virtue of their own members' knowledge; the anthropologists had to acquire that competence. Moreover, one of the key posts, the new chair at the LSE, went to a man with a background in the European university tradition, Bronislaw Malinowski.

The empirical revolution transformed anthropology in the first three decades of the present century. Sir James Frazer's generation relied upon returning travellers' tales; Haddon, Rivers, Seligman, Boas and their contemporaries collected their own by visiting and questioning native informants. Malinowski and Radcliffe-Brown introduced ethnography immediately after the First World War and, almost overnight, it became the research method *par excellence* for anthropologists. Its legitimacy has remained essentially untouched ever since.

The most explicit statement of the methodological programme is to be found in Malinowski's (1922) introduction to *Argonauts of the Western Pacific*. In this, he distinguishes three main principles: any researcher must espouse scientific values, must live among the people he is studying and must apply a number of special techniques for collecting, ordering and presenting evidence.

His first injunction is that 'the results of scientific research in any branch of learning ought to be presented in a manner absolutely candid and above board' (ibid., 2). He goes on to note that 'it would be easy to quote works of high repute, and with a scientific hall-mark on them, in which wholesale generalisations are laid down before us, and we are not informed at all by what actual experiences the writers have reached their conclusion' (ibid., 4). He emphasises the need to distinguish clearly between the results of direct observation, native statements and native interpretations, on the one hand, and, on the other, the inferences drawn by the researcher.

An ethnographer should not seek out the company of his own kind but should remain in sustained contact with his subjects. This allows him to become part of the ordinary life of the people he is studying so that his presence ceases to disrupt their routine activities. The ethnographer gathers data through direct observation and spontaneous discussion which he then uses to induce statements about the regularities which constitute his subjects' culture. These statements are, in turn, tested through systematic questioning. Such abstracted statements must, however, remain linked to what Malinowski calls the imponderabilia of everyday life. He contrasts the formal bonds of the social group with the flux of everyday interactions which constitute the strongest and most subjectively real sense of the community in the eyes of its members.

Through direct observation of the daily routine of a society, the part played by particular events like ceremonies, or rituals, can be given its due salience. Here Malinowski is taking issue with the de-contextualised accounts of dramatic events exemplified by Frazer in *The Golden Bough* (1890). His emphasis is on the typical events of a society and the typical ways of thinking and feeling about them. In this enterprise an understanding of the native language, and its use in organising and classifying the world, is essential. He suggests that native-language accounts might be collected for inspection by others as a semi-autonomous verification.

The final goal, in Malinowski's words, is 'to grasp the native's point of view, his relation to life, to realise *his* vision of *his* world' (ibid., 25, original italics).

The degree to which Malinowski actually followed his own programme is an open question. His personal diaries (Malinowski, 1967) suggest that he hungered after European contact, fraternised closely with local expatriates and had little sympathy with his native subjects. On the other hand, the diaries do portray the psychological stress and isolation of fieldwork. One suspects that few ethnographers keeping a similar journal would present a very different picture. Questions have also been raised about the degree to which Radcliffe-Brown's work in the Andaman Islands rested on direct observation as against native informants. In the event though, it was not so much what they *had* done that was to have an enduring influence, so much as what their readers and students *thought* they had done. These arguments were taken at face value and a steady stream of graduate students began travelling to the colonial territories of Africa and Oceania and among the Indians, Negroes and Eskimos of North America.

Some simplistic accounts of the development of social anthropology see it as no more than a tool of colonialism. There may be some truth in this where America is concerned. The US government has a long history of using anthropology as a cover for espionage and the massive recent expansion of anthropological funding has much to do with the sort of considerations Foster (1969, 122) presents in his justification of applied anthropology: 'The major stimulus – has been the postwar awareness of the underdeveloped world now composed of independent countries with tremendous economic, political and social problems to be solved if stable governments are to be established.' One must, however, be wary of generalising this to Britain. The relations between anthropologists, colonial officials and residents are more complex.

Powdermaker (1966, 36) recalls little political discussion in Malinowski's department. Malinowski had, however, been interned as an alien during the First World War and may have been reluctant to compromise his status as a foreign national by encouraging such debate. The department played some part in training colonial officials, but this was seen as a way of increasing their responsiveness to the peoples whom they governed (Powdermaker, 1966, 43). Seligman and then Evans-Pritchard served as Government Anthropologist in the Sudan. The latter claimed to have been completely ignored, while the former was never consulted and only once offered advice, without effect, in fifteen years (Kuper, 1973, 128). Harris (1968) criticises Radcliffe-Brown's cautious pronouncements on the transfer of power to indigenous peoples without conceding the degree to which they constituted a risky position when few even questioned the propriety of British colonial rule.

In looking at British anthropology between the wars the main factor to keep in mind is its institutional weakness. On the eve of the Second World War there were no more than twenty or thirty professional social anthropologists in the entire Commonwealth. The colonial service was suspicious of them and felt that their close relationship with native peoples compromised all whites.

After Malinowski, the anthropologists based their methods upon participant observation which required intimate and free contact with the peoples they studied. They therefore had to break down the barriers of the colour bar, which existed in most colonies, and they had to challenge the assumptions of all colonial regimes. Their individual examples of how sophisticated

Europeans could happily adopt many tribal habits and live on a basis of friendship with illiterate and poor people constituted a constant irritation to settlers and many colonial officers (Kuper, 1973, 149).

The early anthropologists may have been gentlemen, but the British upper classes do have a tradition of producing liberal reformists and they can well be seen as part of that.

A major expansion of British anthropology only occurred during the 1940s, paralleling the other increases in government social science funding which we discuss. The Colonial Development and Welfare Act was passed in 1940 and allocated substantial funds for research in the light of the recommendations in Hailey's *Africa Survey*. The discipline's growth coincides with the withdrawal from Empire. While it might be argued that this merely reflects an alternative strategy for controlling Third World countries, that conclusion is difficult to sustain in considering subsequent developments. Today, the prime sources of anthropological funding are the SSRC and a small number of foundations. The Ministry of Overseas Development has provided funds on occasion but its political weight has been negligible (indeed it has now been abolished) and its budget relatively small. One of the most notable features of British intellectual life is the marginality of work on non-European societies, whether one is talking of economics, sociology or any of the other social sciences.

This decline may, in part, be related to the eclipse of evolutionary theories. With the partial exceptions of People's China, Tanzania and Cuba, the study of the Third World is seen as contributing little to our understanding of ourselves; and in those societies it is their routes to modernisation rather than their indigenous social organisation which attracts interest. One should not, of course, neglect the increasing political and economic concentration on European integration as a contributing factor.

Whatever the cause, however, it seems fair to describe British anthropology as a discipline whose star has waned in recent years. Although it remains more prestigious than sociology as judged, for instance, by its place within Oxbridge, it participated little in the university expansion of the 1960s. Only Sussex, of the new universities took it up on any scale. The Social Anthropology Committee of SSRC disposes of about one-third the number of studentships and rather less than half the budget available to Sociology and Social Administration. (The disparity would be even more marked if it were possible to cost the Research Initiatives Board contribution to the latter disciplines.)

If these political changes have weakened the demand for

anthropology, changes in the respondent nations have had an equal effect. Over the last decade or so, it has become increasingly difficult to gain access for fieldwork in traditional locales and, it seems, life in the field has also become more hazardous. Even if fieldwork can be financed, gaining permission to carry it out and surviving the experience have become such problems as to make the successful return of an ethnographer a triumph in itself. Excessive criticism of the subsequent reports can seem, at best, uncharitable. Ethnographic anthropology has, then, tended to become a rather empiricist enterprise where attention has focused on the descriptions produced rather than the grounds for their production and their wider implications.

This is not to say that post-war British anthropology has not had its radicals or its theorists. One can, for instance, point to the influence of the Manchester department under Max Gluckman. It is, however, equally important to note that for their politics, both Peter Worsley and Ronnie Frankenberg paid the price of being excluded from their chosen research sites and that both have subsequently moved into chairs of sociology. Their careers illustrate some of the constraints on anthropologists. The fieldworker has a difficult task in placating host governments who may feel threatened by his inquiry; if he does discover anything of social significance, he faces the dilemma of publishing and being excluded in future or of censoring himself in favour of continued access. Matters of intellectual significance can thus be displaced. The anthropologist who attempts to work at a more theoretical level rapidly arrives at the boundaries of the discipline. Generalisations about human society must, in these post-evolutionary times, presumably include the anthropologist's own community. At this point the anthropologist is faced with the artificiality of disciplinary boundaries.

There are, however, strong influences vested in these present boundaries. Anthropologists, for instance, seem to have limited contact with sociologists out of a fear of incorporation by a vigorous and expanding discipline.* It is notable how few of them recognise the existence of sociological ethnography. Indeed, the insistence that sociologists only do surveys is so prevalent that it seems to operate as an 'atrocity story' in occupational boundary maintenance (cf. Dingwall, 1977b). Sociologists have shown little inclination to engage in dialogue with anthropology. In part, this is related to their increased professionalisation. Anthropology was one of the targets of the new specialists. It was held to embody a

---

* In the 1980s, the advantages of increasing the distance between their own discipline and one as beset as sociology are likely to be even greater.

nineteenth-century world-view, subservient to colonial interests and unable to handle the complex structures of the modern state. This view was much encouraged by a number of renegade anthropologists who moved into sociology in the early 1960s. But, paradoxically, these same anthropologists were also likely to be seen as part of the problem, along with the various other converts, who were subsequently regarded as usurping the promotion prospects of *real* (i.e., newly graduated, specialist) sociologists. A central irony of this attack, however, was the way it was spearheaded intellectually by an ethnography imported from America which was substantially the creation of British influences and was now stripped of its tradition and experience.

The anthropology of industrial society

Before turning to discuss this transaction, however, two indigenous growths from British anthropology do have some significance for any account of the present state of ethnographic research.

The first of these is Mass-Observation, initiated in 1937 by Tom Harrisson and Charles Madge. They organised a national network of data collection combining professional observers and volunteer informants. The model was basically anthropological and received considerable support from Malinowski (Mass-Observation, 1938), although Harrisson regarded their work as sociology, the anthropology of 'civilised' societies as he later described it (Harrisson, 1947, 10-11). He was a vituperative critic of both Ginsberg's philosophical approach to sociology 'in which great laws of human behaviour are produced without observation' (ibid., 10) and quantitative approaches which sacrificed meaning to mathematical rigour.

'The Future of Sociology'* (1947) is Harrisson's most coherent methodological statement. While conceding a role for survey research, he attacks the obsession of establishment circles with this approach. There are serious problems of validity which have gone unrecognised. The quantitative critics of objective observation betray their limited understanding of the relationship between theory and data in science, particularly in their naïve belief that bias is dissipated by coding. Their preference for questionnaires reflects a distaste for the life of ordinary people and their criticisms of the subjective element of observation indicate their inability to consider their own work objectively. As a result, he contends, sociology has made little progress in the last decade. No reference

---

* This is the heading title for the paper. The volume cover and contents page list it as *What is Sociology?*

is made to verbal behaviour other than in answers to questionnaires, to the direct observation of social behaviour or to the
study of everyday social institutions. Such areas require alternative methods. These include informal interviews, life histories, analyses of popular documents and, although he does not
use the term itself, participant observation. Harrisson's models
include the Lynds' study of Middletown, the urban ethnography of the Chicago School and Lloyd Warner's Yankee City
programme.

Madge and Harrisson conceived of Mass-Observation as a channel for ordinary people to speak for themselves, an alternative to the
elite monopoly of communications media. It began with a strongly
empiricist streak, trusting in the self-sufficiency of facts, although
later work gives a more prominent place to theory. Their radically
democratic ideals led them to aim at a wide readership. *Pilot
Papers*, their journal, was written for a lay audience rather than for
academics, while their books adopted a direct, journalistic style for
a popular sale and were among the earliest paperbacks. Harrisson
seems to have taken the view that British sociology would not be
changed from within but only by the development of alternative,
more successful approaches. He argues, for instance, in contrast to
the Clapham Committee, that sociological research and development should be organised outwith the universities (Harrisson, 1947,
23-4). He had little time for the dominance, as he saw it, of
philosophers, survey researchers and social workers in sociology
departments.

Mass-Observation had, understandably, a limited impact on
British sociology. Harrisson earned himself the reputation, justified
or not, of being a prickly and aggressive person and his work was
dismissed as unscientific and trivial. Although Madge took the
chair of sociology at Birmingham, he seems to have made little
impression. His work on art students in 1967-8 was notable as one
of the early studies to be influenced by American interactionism
and relied on an ethnographic methodology. It was not, however,
published until 1973 (Madge and Weinberger 1973), and its
account of scheduling and analysis suggests considerable inexper-
ience in the practice of fieldwork. The present ethnographic revival
has largely ignored the Mass-Observation archive as a possible
source of comparative data to give greater historical depth to
contemporary work. Nevertheless, Harrisson and Madge's attempt
to found an empirically-led, ethnographic sociology has more
than antiquarian interest in its demonstration that the value of
anthropological techniques for research in the home country was
recognised by some at an early date, and that the initiative could
not survive outside the university system. Nevertheless, their

wartime contribution (Calder, 1971, 542-3) played an important part in the governmental recognition of the value of social scientific research, although the suppression of their more disturbing reports on morale illustrated equally the limitations of such support.

The second and more important area of direct anthropological influence has been through community studies. This work is often presented as if it were a coherent school. One should not exaggerate this; to a large degree the coherence is an artefact of devising lecture courses and of *post hoc* synthesising work like Frankenberg's *Communities in Britain* (1966). A large number of people were involved in different places, with different backgrounds and often in substantial ignorance of each other. Nevertheless, the anthropological origins remain unmistakable and, indeed, such work continues to attract students from that discipline, especially given the difficulties which surround Third World fieldwork.

Whatever the received view, community studies were not a British invention. The standards set were American, although these depended on the prior export of British ethnographic models. Chicago sociologists had been doing urban ethnography since the 1920s. The Lynds' study of Middletown, perhaps the archetypal community study, was published in 1929. Apart from their own study, *Middletown in Transition* (1937), one could list Robert Redfield's work in Tepotzlan, John Dollard's *Caste and Class in a Southern Town*, Lloyd Warner's Yankee City and Old City researches and Whyte's original version of *Street Corner Society*, all of which predated any of the major British products.

Indeed the first British study, the 'pioneer' in Frankenberg's synthesis, was an American enterprise. During 1932 Lloyd Warner and Conrad Arensberg worked together for a while in the West of Ireland, before Warner was replaced by Sol Kimball. Warner was an anthropologist by training, whose original fieldwork was with Australian Aborigines. Both theoretically and methodologically, he was strongly influenced by Radcliffe-Brown and Malinowski. The research in Ireland centred on sharing the everyday life of two small parishes in County Clare, documenting a local social and cultural system in a classically anthropological fashion. While this may have been a pioneering effort by British standards, it was in the mainstream of American work at this period.

The British tradition has been discussed at length by Frankenberg (1966) and Bell and Newby (1972, 1974) and we do not propose to duplicate that work here. Suffice it to say that throughout the late 1940s and early 1950s, a succession of communities ranging from small rural parishes (Gosforth, Westrigg) through market towns (Banbury, Glossop) and industrial towns (Featherstone) to urban areas (Bethnal Green, Woodford) were made the focus of inquiry by a variety of people. They had a range of social and intellectual backgrounds. The anthropologists were probably the most significant but there were also, particularly in the Welsh studies, those concerned to document a disappearing culture from a literary or historical standpoint and those whose interest lay in social reform and the celebration of the under-recognised qualities of traditional working-class cultures. There are elements of this in some of the Institute of Community Studies' work, for instance. Some, however, did have a more explicitly sociological interest. Margaret Stacey's work in Banbury was concerned with the process of social change in a traditional society; A. H. Birch and his colleagues in Glossop were interested in the local workings of a national political system. Neither of these could be seen as predominantly exercises in romantic nostalgia or *ouvrierisme*.

Community studies did not rely solely on anthropological methods: Young and Willmott (1960), for instance, based their Bethnal Green work on interview data, although one of the team did live in the locality. However, the main thrust has been ethnographic: 'On the whole the community sociologist has been a better ethnologist than a theorist and this is probably as it should be' (Stein, 1960, 4). Even in the best community studies, one encounters the same strengths and weaknesses as in other ethnographic accounts. They are much better on description than analysis, although it is difficult to say whether this owes more to the limitations of sociology at that period or the influence of anthropological models. In consequence their contribution to subsequent developments in sociology has been more limited than once seemed likely and, by corollary, their methodological appeal has been restricted, although, as we shall see, not without significance.

We have, then, described something of the legacy of anthropology to sociological ethnography. We have seen how a particular mode of inquiry came to dominate a whole discipline as the 'obvious' way to do research. This stressed detailed and systematic observation, the inductive development of hypotheses and their testing in a search for negative instances or by controlled comparisons. First and foremost, however, anthropology developed as a research-based discipline in reaction to the premature theorising and generalisation of its Victorian and Edwardian progenitors. The armchair ethnology of Frazer, Robertson Smith and their generation was successively replaced by an emphasis, first, on travel and direct inquiry, in the Torres Straits expedition of Haddon and Rivers or in the journeyings of Boas, and latterly on direct experience, in the teachings particularly of Malinowski. Anthropological ethnography must also be seen as a living tradition. The point at which it was disseminated solely by the written word in its Atlantic crossing is now fifty years removed. That removal gave a distinctive slant to the method in some respects, but was rapidly reinforced by personal contacts between a relatively small group of workers. Most Commonwealth anthropologists and many Americans passed through Malinowski's department for part of their professional development. Radcliffe-Brown was a frequent visitor to the USA, particularly Chicago. This network of personal relationships assumes particular significance in the light of some of the recent work in the sociology of science on the inadequacy of published accounts for disseminating new techniques. The results could cut both ways: it is arguable that ethnography was a more radical innovation as a result of misinterpretations of the rigour of Malinowski's own practices. Nevertheless, there seems to have been sufficient cohesion to promote the rapid exchange and consolidation of individual experiences into a collective model.

Only in the USA, however, did this model come 'back home' with any lasting effect. American sociologists were, of course, already beginning to do ethnography in the early 1920s. Everett Hughes (1971, 108-11) stresses the close kinship between sociology and anthropology in the inter-war years. Indeed, some workers, notably Lloyd Warner, were equally at home in both disciplines. The attenuated influence of anthropology on British sociology would seem to have both structural and cultural elements. One of the most important is the assumed homogeneity of British society. Where anthropologists accepted the necessity for empirical inquiry, their sociologist contemporaries could presume that they were competent to make statements about their own society simply by virtue of their membership of it. As Hughes notes, in the essay cited above, the Americans could not make this assumption so readily because of the manifest ethnic diversity of their nation at that time. Together with the elevation of discovery in the remodelled American universities, this gave rise to a climate favourable to an empirically led discipline.

In Britain, anthropology's main impact was in peripheral institutions like Mass-Observation and intellectually aborted fields like community studies. It did, however, play an important role in the development of the American model through which British sociologists rediscovered ethnography. An account of that process illuminates both the social influences which shape sociology and the British misapprehensions which led to premature disillusionment.

The development of sociological ethnography

The ethnographic tradition in American sociology is indelibly marked with the imprint of a single institution and a brilliant group of teachers – the Chicago School. Although they were by no means the only ethnographers around, it is the work and ideas produced by that faculty and its students which have had the most substantial impact in Britain. To appreciate the character of the work, we need to sketch something of the history of the department and its social context.

Chicago saw the foundation of the world's first department of sociology by Albion Small in 1892. Small was a disenchanted historian-cum-political economist. In his view, contemporary historians had little interest in empirical work on matters of social concern or the induction of general laws to help interpret current events. Political economy had lost Adam Smith's broad concern with social processes, becoming a merely technical discipline, 'the mystery of the craft of the capitaliser' (Small, 1907, 77). In reading the work of Herbert Spencer, Auguste Comte and Lester Ward, Small had concluded that sociology was the true heir to Smith's vision of a study of the totality of social relations.

Small's career, until his retirement in 1925, spanned a period of remarkable transformation in American society and its model of the university. Carey (1975, 9-39) summarises these changes. These decades saw America turn from a small town, rural society without large-scale industries or national means of communication, into an urban nation with increasing concentrations of industrial power and communication networks which both facilitated and required nationally integrative groupings of social, economic and occupational interests. A 'new middle class' of professional, managerial and technical workers developed, which gave American capitalism a more liberal and humane face, as they extended their rational bureaucratic regard for honesty and efficiency to a wider civic sphere. Where the universities had previously followed an English model of cultural transmission, they were now asked to provide rationally organised certification programmes for these new occupations. In establishing a knowledge base for these activities, they moved closer to a German model of the university as a centre for research and innovation (See also Shils, 1970, esp. 779-82).

Detailed accounts of the tensions produced by these changes may be found elsewhere. (e.g., Hofstadter and Metzger, 1955; Schwendinger and Schwendinger, 1974; Furner, 1975). The application by social scientists of the new spirit of inquiry to the traditional role of the university as a carrier of moral values proved to be too threatening to powerful interests in the surrounding community. To ensure their institutional survival most academics compromised by abandoning explicit claims to moral leadership in favour of a role as 'objective' and 'disinterested' experts.

The new University of Chicago epitomised the modern American university. Harper picked his men carefully and offered substantial inducements for them to join this new foundation for the training of science-based professionals and liberal bureaucrats. Of the founding fathers of American sociology, Small was the closest to this vision. He did not share the apocalyptic stance of Ward, Ross or Summer, although he took the view, more strongly than most, that sociology was *the* holistic science of social action. Of itself, however, it could achieve little; its social contribution would always be in alliance with a reformist constituency.

Small's own intellectual influence at Chicago was slight (Carey, 1975, 103-4; Faris, 1967, 11-12). This was, however, a response which he encouraged. In his view, sociology was, first and foremost, an empirical discipline based on 'the method of observation and induction' (Small and Vincent, 1894, 15). Direct observation guaranteed both the objective character of the knowledge produced and generated an appropriate moral concern in students:

> There is little likelihood that men who personally observe actual
> social conditions, according to the method we propose, instead
> of speculating about them in their study, will want to fold their
> hands and let social evil work out its own salvation (ibid., 374).

While theory was important, pure theorists like himself had a limited and secondary role in relation to research. They should remain a small group attempting to induce and propose more general syntheses from a developing body of empirical work. Both Faris and Carey lay considerable stress on the openness of Chicago to the empirical testing of social theories and on Small's urging of his graduate students to make what he taught them out of date rather than regarding it as received wisdom. His professional and administrative commitments would, in any case, have made it difficult for him to carry out the kind of research he urged on his department.

Small's particular contribution was as an organisational leader in defining and creating a particular departmental climate. This was imparted to the students by an intermediate generation of gifted teachers – Park, Burgess and Faris. Together, they created a strong intellectual community, with a considerable emphasis on group activity and communal support for individual researchers, through the pooling of fieldwork experiences. While Small and his staff had the smalltown, rural background characteristic of their generation of sociologists, their students were increasingly drawn from the new middle classes, with an urban upbringing, few religious affiliations and liberal political beliefs. It was these ambitious new Americans who produced the classic work of the Chicago School (Carey, 1975, 41-53).

The principal architect of this programme was Robert Park, who joined the department in 1916. He had been a successful investigative journalist during the 1890s but became dissatisfied with the *ad hoc* nature of journalistic inquiries. His desire to develop a more systematic framework for interpreting these data led him to Harvard to study philosophy and then to Europe where he followed Simmel's lectures in Berlin and took his doctorate under Windelband in Heidelberg. On his return to America, he worked at Harvard before joining Booker T. Washington as his secretary. In this capacity, he travelled through the American South and acquired considerable experience of racial problems. A chance meeting with W. I. Thomas led to an invitation to visit Chicago and the subsequent offer of an appointment.

Park had an abiding belief in the importance of direct experience as a foundation for social research. In an interview quoted by Carey (1975, 155), Leonard S. Cottrell recalls:

> Park made a great point of the difference between knowledge about something and acquaintance with the phenomenon. This was one of the great thrusts in Chicago, because people had to get out and if they wanted to study opium addicts they went to the opium dens and even smoked a little opium maybe. They went out and lived with the gangs and the ... hobos and so on.

In the main Chicago introductory text (Park and Burgess, 1921, v-vi) this methodology was put more formally

> The first thing that students in sociology need to learn is to observe and record their own observations; to read and then to select and record the materials which are the fruits of their readings, to organise and use, in short, their own experience.

This methodology was set within a social theory which, at that period, owed most to German influence, particularly Simmel's writing.

In his contribution to a lecture series intended 'to evaluate searchingly the objectives and methods fundamental to research in the social sciences' (Gee, 1929, viii), Park develops his syntheses. Sociology is primarily the study of meaning and action. Societies 'are formed for action and in action. They grow up in the efforts of individuals to act collectively. The structures which societies exhibit are on the whole the incidental effects of collective action' (ibid., 8).

Collective action is formulated through a shared language, whose meaning is not, however, given:

> Local institutions ... are symbolic expressions of the common life ... They have extension and form, but at the same time they have a fourth dimension, namely, meaning. This meaning is not accessible to us. We get the meaning of social institutions as we get the sense of words, by observing the ways in which they are used; by investigating the occasions and incidents of their origins and growth, and by taking account of whatever is unusual or unique in their history.... What is a social object? It is an artefact; something made; or a ceremony, custom, ritual, words; anything which, like a word, has meaning and is not just what it seems. A physical object becomes a social object only when we know its use, its function, its meaning; its different meanings for different persons (ibid., 37-8).

While Park emphasises the consensual basis of social action, this does not preclude a view of societies as marked by struggle and competition. The city of Chicago ethnography is in a constant flux of change and development. Park concludes the lecture by adding the interview and life history to direct observation as valuable research methods. The former is of value for its direct account of the meanings of actions, the latter for what it reveals about attitudes. 'It is things which people take for granted which reveal at once the person and the society in which he lives' (ibid., 42).

Chicago was not actively hostile to quantitative methods. From an early date Small had pressed for the appointment of a statistician and later spoke of the value of survey research (Dibble, 1975, 22, 38). Nevertheless the developments at Columbia, where Franklin Giddings had founded a department in closer alliance with social work and where Charles Booth's surveys formed the research model, passed Chicago by until Ogburn's appointment in 1927. Even then Park remained critical. In the lecture cited above, for instance, he argues that mathematical methods over-simplify social life and should be restricted to phenomena made available in a numerical form like land values.

While much has been made of the philosophical influences on Chicago sociology, particularly from John Dewey and G. H. Mead, the anthropological contribution is less well-recognised, although some of the post-war graduates regard it as more significant.* Sociology and anthropology were not separated organisationally until the late 1940s. We have already quoted Hughes's remarks on

---

* Rock (1979) offers perhaps the most comprehensive account of the philosophy of Chicago sociology and we have not sought to duplicate his discussion here.

the sympathy between the two disciplines. Several informants have suggested that Warner and Redfield were the major forces, at least in the post-war period, in defining an empirical stance (methodology is probably too formal a word) and in actually being able to train students. They recall reading Malinowski and the importance attached to Radcliffe-Brown's visits, which had begun in the 1930s. Erving Goffman, in particular, developed very much as an anthropologist under Warner's supervision.

Until the mid-1930s, Chicago virtually defined American sociology as liberal ethnography and controlled most of the major sources of professional patronage. After that period retirements, ill-health and premature deaths took their toll on the faculty and there were problems of succession, compounded by the tensions between Blumer and Hughes. Chicago produced a variety of intellectual persuasions among its post-war graduates – Becker, Freidson, Goffman, Kornhauser, Wilensky are of this generation – while their contemporaries at, say, Columbia – Gouldner, Lipset, Bell, Blau, Selznick – formed an altogether more homogeneous group. Although ethnographers continued to graduate from Chicago in the early 1950s, the leadership of American sociology after the Second World War passed to the Harvard-Columbia axis of Talcott Parsons, Robert Merton and Paul Lazarsfeld (Shils, 1970, 793-6). Their version of the German tradition inclined towards grand theory on the one hand and quantitative empiricism on the other (Oberschall, 1965). Many felt that a narrow scientism allied to a social and political conservatism engendered by the experience of inter-war Germany had come to dominate the discipline. This conservatism fitted the McCarthy years and the spread of empiricist research styles was aided by the apparent readiness with which they could be bureaucratised and controlled. The university system went into recession after the bulge of returning GIs. Such an intellectual, political and economic climate discouraged heterodoxy. When Charles Hauser was brought in to re-organise the Chicago department, his return to the mainstream effectively terminated the traditional models of theory and research. While the Society for the Study of Social Problems was founded predominantly by Chicago graduates or faculty in 1951 to defend liberal naturalism against the prevailing tendencies in the American Sociological Society leadership, its members were marginal figures until the resurgence of the universities in the 1960s (Skura, 1976; Lee and Lee, 1976).

Nevertheless, throughout the 1950s, the ethnographers, through the SSSP, were the most important organised alternative, both politically and intellectually, to the mainstream of American sociology. With individual exceptions, it can be said that there was no indigenous marxist sociology. Their dissidence, however, left them on the fringe of the discipline, working outwith sociology departments or in non-tenured research posts. This limited their ability to reproduce through graduate training and narrowed their writings to research monographs rather than elaborated theoretical or methodological codifications. In such a situation a degree of intellectual stagnation was inevitable. There was little pressure from students to justify accepted ideas or demand for synthetic works to formalise and disseminate the assumptions and experience of the workers. This latter has been a continuing problem. Ethnography has substantially existed as an oral tradition passed on through apprenticeship. At least in America, however, there was a nucleus of experienced researchers who could act as bearers of this tradition. Although an apprenticeship pattern has much to commend it as a model for research training, such an intellectual formation limited the ability of ethnographers to reflect critically on their practice and to spread their techniques beyond the range of personal contact. In such a situation outside criticism could be dismissed as coming from people who did not share the basic paradigm or lacked relevant experience. Dissensus within a group under pressure was not encouraged.

By the late 1960s, one could argue that ethnographers had been outflanked both intellectually and politically by the radical critiques of the ethnomethodologists and the new marxists. Paradoxically, it was at precisely the same point that their work was being taken up by the younger British sociologists as a stick with which to beat *their* Establishment.

The British ethnographic revival

The major site for the discovery of American ethnography was the sociology of deviance in its split from criminology. The latter was, again, a creation of the years of post-war reconstruction. The recommendations of the Clapham Committee on social science research are discussed elsewhere in this volume. However, criminology was one of the few areas where developments in research organisation took place on any scale with the foundation of the Home Office Research Unit and the university centres at Cambridge and LSE. The subsequent history has been widely documented, most usefully by Wiles (1977, 2-8). The field came to be dominated by a narrow conception of social relevance and constricted analytical perspectives, largely stemming from the conservative and secretive traditions of the British civil service. The

103

range of possible research questions was severely circumscribed by the need to fit answers within given policy models*.

Academic criminology was left rather exposed in the generally sceptical climate of the 1960s. Its inflexible political structure and narrow funding base meant that critics would find easy targets while its proponents would find it difficult to mount an effective intellectual response. The attractiveness of the target was enhanced by its disproportionate funding in relation to the overall support for social science research. Initially, the sociologists of deviance saw themselves as sceptics, drawing on the work of Becker and Lemert to ask questions about the definition of deviance, the meaning of deviant acts and the sources of control agents' legitimacy (Wiles, 1977; Cohen, 1971). Such intellectual questions rapidly became politicised. Wiles (1977, 11) suggests that the response of the criminologists had much to do with this. They were so enmeshed in a scientistic and 'value-free' ideology that they could see no other response to criticism than to attack it as political. The sociologists were radicalised ahead of having any coherent analysis. This account may be a little self-serving. The heyday of the NDC was also the peak of marxist humanism with its general reaction against 'one-dimensional' forms of knowledge.

The differences between these factions culminated in a major confrontation at a conference in Cambridge during 1968 and the deviance group left to convene their own meeting, the National Deviancy Symposium (subsequently Conference). The participants were young academics on the margins of Higher Education, in the polytechnics and newer universities, together with a few graduate students. Unfortunately, the NDC rapidly found that it was united more by what it was against than what it was for. The conferences became preoccupied by a search for an agreed analysis rather than empirical development. In the course of this, there was a process of selective disaffiliation and increased politicisation which is apparent even in the short gap between *Images of Deviance*, often regarded as their manifesto, and its successor, the Taylors' *Politics and Deviance* (1973).

Considering the subsequent legend, the NDC itself sparked off surprisingly little ethnography. Of the papers in *Images of Deviance*, only Maureen Cain's account of police work and, to some degree, Max Atkinson's essay on suicide identifications make

---

* Such constraints are neither a thing of the past nor restricted to criminology. The recent OPCS study of fertility behaviour, for instance, was only allowed to ask about pre-marital sexual and reproductive experience after high-level debate. Its publication was accompanied by careful press management, presumably to avoid headlines about 'government sex snoopers'. Yet, what independent fertility researcher would ever imagine reliable findings could be produced without such data?

systematic use of field data. Cain's research was carried out during 1962-3 and the citations indicate a subsequent American influence. The remaining papers depend on press cuttings, anecdotes and chance life-experiences. Even the historical papers are surprisingly uncritical about their data. When the Taylors list nine books, in *Politics and Deviance*, as representing the new British work, only three prove to have any empirical basis. Stan Cohen's *Folk Devils and Moral Panics* (1972) was basically a study of societal reaction to Mods and Rockers. As such it depends largely on press cuttings as evidence of media responses and interviews and pressure group documents as data on citizen responses. Cohen only spent one bank-holiday weekend on the beaches and some days in a volunteer centre doing anything recognisable as participant observation. Jock Young's *The Drugtakers* (1971) relies mainly on American sociological work, fictional sources and clinical medical literature. There is a passing reference to fieldwork in Notting Hill but no data are given. Stan Cohen and Laurie Taylor's *Psychological Survival* (1972), described by the authors themselves as a 'somewhat journalistic exercise' (p. 11), comes nearest to being based on solid and reasonably specific data, although, of course, the adjustment of long-term prisoners is not a topic particularly well-suited to conventional ethnographic strategies.

The texts listed by the Taylors have a predominantly negative tone and rely on American data. Michael Phillipson (1971), Laurie Taylor (1971) and Paul Rock (1973) all seem much more comfortable dismantling traditional analyses on theoretical grounds than at specifying alternative research strategies. Only Phillipson has much to say about appropriate methodologies and that amounts to 3 pages (50-3) in a volume of 184. Taylor has probably the most comprehensive bibliography but its only methodological element is a short section on critiques of quantitative research.* Max Atkinson's verdict seems incontestable.

> The general change in orientation did not, however, provide any immediate solution to the problem of what kind of empirical research should now be done, which is probably one reason why parts of the positivist legacy survived for so long.... But I also retained doubts about the vagueness and apparent sloppiness which seemed to characterise some of the research strategies adopted by interactionists: a funny story here, an apt quote from

* The other books cited are Carson and Wiles (1970), a collection of classic articles and commissioned literature surveys. Rock and McIntosh (1973), a collection of papers from the 1971 BSA Conference and Taylor, Walton and Young (1973). This latter is notable as the major manifesto of NDC marxism, but its call for a political economy of crime is strangely empty of suggestions on how this is to be implemented.

a 'subject' there, a few extracts from a newspaper or television. Indeed it sometimes seemed that anything one happened to stumble across would do, so long as it seemed relevant in some way to the arguments being presented (Bell and Newby, 1977, 42).

One is drawn towards the conclusion that the founders of the NDC had even less idea about the methodological implications of their position than about the political consequences and that their preoccupation with the latter led to the neglect of the former. This neglect may be partly associated with the rejection of criminology and its empiricist concerns. Methodology is often claimed as, or ascribed to, the province of the quantitative sociologist and dismissed by the ethnographically inclined as an irrelevant distraction. Their products, too, reflect the pressures of the time. Most of the essays in *Images of Deviance* are the part-time production of teachers in an era of rapid personal and professional change. Less than ten years later five of the nine contributors have either Professorial or Reader status and are still under forty. The late 1960s saw a desperate struggle to produce some sort of indigenous literature to meet the explosive demand for knowledge and course materials.

In fairness, one can point out that there was a dearth of literature on sociological ethnography. Much of the American work is surprisingly elliptical about how it got done. Becker's *Outsiders* (1963) which almost counted as the Holy Grail, merely advocates observing people in their natural habitat and remains silent on how these observations are to be converted into usable data and treated as evidence. Nevertheless, not one of the works referred to even cite Becker's (1958) article on 'Problems of Inference and Proof in Participant Observation' let alone Whyte's Appendix to the 1955 edition of *Street Corner Society*. The only acknowledged influences seem to come at the very end of the 1960s with Humphreys's *Tearoom Trade* (1970) and Cicourel's *The Social Organisation of Juvenile Justice* (1968).

The NDC founders were in the position of an American anthropologist reading Malinowski or Radcliffe-Brown in the 1920s and being fired to emulate their work. Unfortunately, they lacked personal contact with an appropriate empirical tradition. Throughout the years of expansion inexperienced post-graduates and hastily retrained graduates from other disciplines were thrust into key development roles. Although many of these recruits were outstandingly able, they inevitably had a limited knowledge of the discipline they were being asked to reproduce and few opportunities to remedy this. Further, their actual experience of the world was often slight and they rapidly succumbed to the insularity of the English university. Their interest in the problems of their society became a secondhand one, filtered through a community of like-minded colleagues. Their writing became increasingly theoretical, conforming to the traditional prestige model of English sociological writing and easily combined with teaching, administration or agitation. Those who retained a serious interest in empirical ethnographic work found themselves painfully re-inventing the wheel. Moreover, their apparently low productivity against standards of output set by more ephemeral writers left them at a severe disadvantage in career terms.

The methodological leadership passed from the NDC to medical sociologists. There were early overlaps in membership but the latter group seemed to have been more interested in deviant meanings than social control and to have found the increasing politicisation of the NDC uncomfortable. Medical sociologists began meeting separately in 1969. Significantly, these meetings also embraced the Establishment social epidemiologists who, unlike criminologists, recognised themselves as radicals. Despite methodological disagreements, then, the group was able to avoid political confrontations. These methodological disputes obliged the ethnographers to consider the justifications for their work more carefully. Importantly, they also linked with the community studies tradition through experienced fieldworkers like Margaret Stacey, Gordon Horobin and Ronnie Frankenberg. Finally, there was sufficient variety in funding sources to inhibit intellectual monopolies and permit a degree of continuity in research employment, allowing individuals to accumulate and share practical experience.

However, the impact of medical sociology on mainstream developments has been limited by comparison with deviance or the recent work in cultural and media research. In part, this reflects the dominance of empirical research. Opportunities for participation are limited, while anyone can work on deviance from a theoretical angle or on culture from a collection of ephemera assembled in the comfort of one's office. Few medical sociologists work under the constraints of tenured lectureships in sociology departments. Their employment on research contracts, though, effectively limits the production of generalisable work or the sort of theoretical or methodological discussion which reaches a wider audience. Indeed, medical sociologists frequently criticise their own lack of independent systematic theory, orienting to the prestige models of the parent discipline. Again, one sees the problems of a tradition which exists only as a craft and trains few students. One might argue that the debates with ethnomethodology and epidemiology give the tradition a greater vigour in Britain, but the long-term problems are not dissimilar.

Ethnography and radicalism

There have been other British developments in ethnography, of course. Studies of industrial settings have employed ethnography (obviously among other methods), a tradition which, as we argued at the beginning of this chapter, could almost include Beatrice Webb. Books like *On the Shop Floor* (Lupton, 1963) or more recently Beynon's *Working for Ford* (1973) owe a great deal to detailed observation of work practices. In some studies, there is a sense of the sociologist as the tool of the management, revealing the real practices of workers in areas such as output restriction. In others, sociologists have demonstrated how workers come to terms with boring work tasks and triumph over them. The familiar distinction between formal and informal organisations draws heavily on ethnographic evidence. Because large organisations involve pockets of events invisible to some of the actors and particularly to the organisation's controllers, they lend themselves to ethnographic analysis. Paradoxically, this can mean that the group, department or process investigated is divorced from its context: in Beynon's work, the reader comes to long for more information about the Ford management's position in order better to appreciate the workers' attitudes.

A more recent area of growth has been the sociology of education, with much of its activity taking place under similar conditions to medical sociology, although the two have seldom been explicitly linked. It has, however, been handicapped by the lack of a powerful American model and, to some degree, by the problematic quality of many workers in the field from the former colleges of education. The professional restrictions on entry again limited the acquaintance of many staff with more than a very small and specialised area of sociology.

There is also a marxist school at the Centre for Contemporary Cultural Studies in Birmingham. Their work is an applied sociology of culture concentrating particularly on socially marginal or 'oppressed' groups. Willis's (1977) study of early leavers is a good example. His central question is: how do working-class kids get working-class jobs? More formally, how is it that some children opt out of an achievement-oriented school system into low-level employment without apparently becoming socially disaffected? Willis looks for the answer in the culture of the school and the workplace, identifying in particular an oppositional version based on masculine chauvinism arising from the raw experience of production. There is a basic continuity between this shop-floor culture and the counter-culture of the lower levels of the secondary school. He produces an interesting celebration of this culture but the discussion is ultimately limited by its determination to impose a class analysis. The material is made to serve a much wider purpose than it will bear. (The data rest on contacts with 12 boys for two years.) For instance, little attention is given to conformist pupils, to girls, or to the fact that the research was carried out in a major conurbation with a strong heavy industrial tradition. An account of a particular and localised segment of the working class is expanded into a general statement. The difficulty the Birmingham group have consistently confronted lies in the tension between ethnographic inductivism and marxist deductivism. Classically, ethnography has adopted rather fluid and only partially coherent theoretical approaches. Bits and pieces are borrowed to help make sense of some data. Those data are collected in orientation to a set of hunches and shared assumptions rather than a coherent prior analysis such as marxist approaches generally require. Of course, having developed this, questions can, as we have already shown, arise about the necessity to do any research at all or about the degree to which research is merely producing illustrative material to present theoretical statements in an attractive form.

In general, however, radical sociologists have become increasingly unsympathetic to ethnography, in part reflecting their general hostility to empirical work. The ethnographic tradition is a liberal and gradualist one in which the complexity of social questions is seen to demand piecemeal and partial answers. To some degree one can argue that the Americans became co-opted as a loyal opposition. The SSP Establishment slid into a comfortable bourgeois liberalism, dissipating their efforts on trivia like marijuana smoking or the chronicles of hedonistic sexual eccentricity which fill the pages of *Urban Life*. The classic organisational studies like *Boys in White* or *Asylums* concentrate on the low-life of students or patients, neglecting the role of higher level staff in constructing the environments in which these groups struggle to make out. The organisations are divorced from a societal context so that we learn little of how wider cultural values are used to shape the medical curriculum or constrain the availability of resources for the use of state mental patients. In his attack at the 1968 ASA Convention, Nicolaus (1969) was able to regard the distinction between ethnographers and other sociologists as a matter only of degree:

Sociologists stand guard in the garrison and report to its masters on the movements of the occupied populace. The more adventurous sociologists don the disguise of the people and go out to mix with the peasants in the 'field', returning with books and articles that break the protective secrecy in which a subjugated population wraps itself and make it more accessible to manipulation and control. The sociologist as researcher in the employ of his employers is precisely a kind of spy. The proper exercise of the profession is all too often different from the proper exercise of espionage only in the relatively greater electronic sophistication of the latter's techniques.

Such criticisms were soon to be parroted by British radicals.

The trouble was that these attacks predated the appearance of British empirical work in any quantity. Atkinson (1978, iv) has remarked on the curious British propensity for talking *about* paradigms rather than working *within* them.

> the synthesising texts can often appear absurdly overambitious when written by persons who are not old enough to have accumulated the depth of knowledge and experience that might make such ventures worthwhile – unless, of course, there is already good evidence for believing that the person in question is possessed of the genius to qualify him or her as a paradigm innovator ... the temptations to aspire to this latter status sometimes seem to be more attractive to contemporary sociologists than the more modest task of working within one of the variously flawed paradigms of normal science. In the sociology of deviance, for example, symbolic interactionism had no sooner arrived in Britain than it was being summarised as one of several perspectives on deviance, modified, criticised and even discarded – all on the basis of minimal empirical research.... (Atkinson, in Bell and Newby, 1977, 33).

Taylor, Walton and Young (1973), for instance, sought to demolish the whole ethnographic edifice on theoretical grounds without being able to point to a single substantial British example.

One of the obvious difficulties from a radical's point of view, for instance, is the long gestation of ethnography. Collecting and analysing data demands substantial input of scarce academic time and cannot satisfactorily be delegated. Instant solutions are in short supply. Moreover, fieldwork is a somewhat amoral enterprise in which the investigator is, as Matza (1969) saw, required to be appreciative of the foibles of the world rather than brimming over with correctional zeal. Silverman's remarks in his discussion of Castaneda seem apposite:

> to speak responsibly is 'to stick to the facts'; conversely, to

wander away from the facts, to be unconsciously deflected by biases, prejudices, oversights, etc. is to be irresponsible. Now, I am not saying that I want to oppose to this a directly contrary view. For instance, to stand this position on its head, to formulate responsibility in terms of the production of a text which is informed by bias, prejudices and so on is, in a sense, to accept its view of the world. For in taking a polar-opposite view, we accept the dichotomy (facts and values) upon which the former view is founded. In a way, then, our disagreement turns out to be a deep agreement. But it is an agreement at the level of what we take to be good, or moral, speech (Silverman, 1975, 93)

While the radical may lock horns with an establishment at one level, both share a common preoccupation with fitting the world to a theory – academic marxism or classical functionalism – on the basis of a scientistic epistemology. Both sustain an essentially determinist view of human action, other than their own, and a Puritan mission to reform the morality of their subjects. The model of a human actor depicted in this version is a solemn and earnest one, whether the loyal, conscientious citizen or the serious and committed revolutionary. The ethnographic hero, by contrast, is a fixer, someone who makes out and gets through, winning daily victories over the hassles of life – too sophisticated and subtle to be easily, or desirably, changed.

This is not to say that changes have not occurred as a result of the radicals' critique. If we take, for example, the recent work of Eliot Freidson, we can see how the classic American liberal interactionist tradition has been renewed in a more explicit dialogue with both marxism and the orthodox grand masters, although the author himself concedes that this is a significant break with his own intellectual past. Chicago sociologists had avoided this kind of theoretical debate, but it was coming to be an urgent necessity. While *Profession of Medicine* (1971) leans towards Max Weber, more recent papers (1976, 1977) address Durkheim and Marx as Freidson develops his account of the division of labour as an everyday activity and examines the consequent problems of social articulation. The control of autonomous professions, whose activities have been carefully described by a series of ethnographic inquiries, is nothing if not a grand topic. At the same time Freidson's programme in the concluding section of *Profession of Medicine* (1971) remains less of a prescription than an elaboration of the criteria which reform would have to meet. The details remain to be determined by a citizenry better informed and better able to decide as a result of such discussions.

Perhaps more importantly, ethnographers have also taken more note of the criticism of a preoccupation with low-life, particularly as the 'societal reaction' thesis has been extended and developed, translating the sociology of deviance into, successively, a sociology of law-enforcement, a sociology of law and, ultimately, one would predict, into a sociology of social regulation. Increasing attempts have been made, within organisational studies, to reflect on the contribution of the powerful to the creation of the problems with which their inferiors grapple. This is a theme which extends beyond those institutions explicitly mandated with social control, like those of the law to areas like medicine and education. A renewed appreciation of the fact that it takes two to make a social problem has been displayed. The convergence on social regulation would, of course, reunite ethnography with the classic question of sociology – how is social order possible?

Nevertheless, the conclusions are not self-evidently going to be radical. The appreciative stance of ethnography directs the investigator's attention to the logic of his subjects' positions. The reasoning of the organisationally powerful may seem peculiar to the liberal mind, but carries its own intrinsic rationality as a response to its bearers' situation. In delineating that, the complexity of social life comes to the fore and the investigator is made forcefully aware of the limited changes which are available in any particular context. Marginal increments to human welfare may be possible but revolution seems far from the agenda. As Albion Small saw, ethnography is a tradition for reformists rather than radicals.

Prospects for ethnography

Unlike anthropology, ethnography has always had a rather precarious and marginal position in sociology. In a time of economic difficulty, it may, therefore, be thought differentially vulnerable to cuts. Intellectually, however, we might well want to argue that it is in a healthier state than for some years.

We have seen how ethnography was revived in Britain through the activities of the National Deviancy Conference in the late 1960s. Their import of an American model did, however, have the unfortunate effect of distancing its development in sociology from its anthropological roots. Although it has today something of the faded grandeur of an Edwardian hotel, British anthropology has traditionally enjoyed a great deal more academic prestige and has considerably greater experience in dealing with the problems of management and training and of setting intellectual standards for fieldwork reports. This is an experience from which British sociologists have signally failed to learn. The price of this is a divided and weakened discipline, where sociological ethnographers have learned little from anthropologists on the methodological front and vice versa on the theoretical side. In many ways the tragedy of ethnography lies in the fact that painful experience has been accumulated over a decade of increasing hostility to sociology *per se*. If we leave aside the cruder political dimensions of this hostility, then we are still faced with a residue of charges which have more than a little justice to them. The discipline has been marked by an over-proliferation of armchair theorising. There has been a great deal of naïve polemic dressed up as science. Research experience of any kind provides some corrective to these sorts of tendencies but ethnography is particularly well-placed to achieve this. It takes the sociologist out of his armchair to rub shoulders with people doing the work of the world and to see the complexity of the problems with which they are struggling. The good fieldworker has an instinctive distrust of pat solutions. If one thing can be said about most ethnographers, it is that they hold their political and moral views as citizens rather than as sociologists. The evangelism of those, conservatives and radicals alike, who would use sociology to promote particular asserted truths, is greeted with profound distaste. While few ethnographers make any particular secret of their predilections, these are generally tempered by an awareness of the grounds of alternative views and the relativity of all judgments of value. Such a stance is deeply embedded in the ethnographic tradition, to the degree to which we might suppose it to be a cultural consequence of the mode of intellectual production.

It seems unlikely, however, that the hard-won experience of the last ten years and the possibilities which it opens up will save it in the general climate of the present. Whatever its failings and whatever the theoretical attachments of its proponents it is at least an empirical version of social science which gives priority to understanding the world rather than evangelising it. It is moreover closely allied to the practical problems of people in a society. Its practitioners are, after all, enjoined firstly to appreciate the lives of their subjects and their organisation and only secondarily to think about correcting them.

If ethnography is to develop, however, clearly certain sorts of change would be needed. First, there are institutional constraints. Substantial fieldwork is incompatible with a teaching position. The ethnographic description of an organisation demands the flexibility to follow its schedules rather than those of a sociology department. This means either the development of more career research posts or the improvement and consolidation of sabbatical arrangements. Good ethnography cannot be done part-time but needs a major block of time when nothing else has to take precedence. This is not to say people in teaching jobs cannot do research, but that this is of a kind which can be fitted in – library work, document work and, indeed, conversational analysis. Ethnography is not well-suited to the man-and-a-boy model of survey practice. A grant for survey research can feasibly be held by a tenured lecturer who is directing assistants engaged in day-to-day supervision of the fieldforce of interviewers and in routine data organisation. Good ethnography is very much a matter of experience. *Ceteris paribus* the more experience, the better the product. The accountable member of staff must be engaged intimately in the fieldwork to manage it effectively and control day-to-day issues of relevance or ethical practice. The present funding arrangements introduce all kinds of curious biases. There is a dearth of good work on middle and senior levels of management in many institutions at least partly because there are few ethnographers of sufficient maturity to move easily among them.

Second, there are constraints within the approach itself. Traditionally, ethnographers have disdained theory. There is the reply of Howard Becker to a graduate student at Manchester, who asked him how to choose a theoretical framework. 'What do you want to worry about that for. You just go out there and do it.' (Quoted by Atkinson, in Bell and Newby, 1977, 32.) The result has been a lack of codification and an inattention to the philosophical justification for the approach. This has meant little genuine cumulation in research, but more importantly it has meant that ethnography has been difficult to disseminate. It has been far more of an oral tradition, a craftsman's *bricolage* of hints, tips and recipes, than a systematic approach. This partly explains why British sociologists found it hard in the early days to puzzle out what the Americans were actually doing, and the limited learning from this. It is noticeable in Britain how much of this work has been produced by a small number of groups who have been able to pool experiences and pass these on to students but who have still been very bad at consolidating these experiences into the sort of texts which could be used elsewhere. The standard qualitative texts like Filstead (1970) or Denzin (1970a) are, in fact, collections of short papers rather than major syntheses. The synthetic works that are available like Denzin (1970b) or Glaser and Strauss (1967) move rapidly to a level of abstraction which renders them unusable. What is needed is something between this and the research autobiography. Of the British figures only Bloor (1978) has made such an attempt, and again in a short paper on a particular topic rather than a sustained volume.

Career contingencies, of course, play their part in this. Research is like a treadmill of one short contract after another with continual pressure to produce work, especially work bound to the subject of the contract. Even research units are not exempt from this, given the continual pressure to justify their existence. A worker is as good as his last project. There is, then, little leisure for reflecting more generally on the whole business and trying to pull one's experience together. One does not, on the whole, get research contracts to write theoretical reflections, nor are researchers thought to need sabbaticals for intellectual consolidation and renewal. This failure to produce more coherent justifications has created complications in funding since granting agencies find it difficult to develop criteria for evaluating proposals. Moreover, the training of recruits has been hindered, as has the creation of employment demand through an appreciation of the potential of the work.

Ethnography badly needs to become less of a craft and more of a science, defining its practice more systematically and rigorously without losing the priority accorded to empirical experience. The British have generally been more fortunate in the degree to which internal debate has tightened the approach, particularly in their willingness to confront ethnomethodology and define a position in respect of it. It is that debate which forms the central theme of our next chapter.

6 The ethnomethodological movement

Few sociologists would argue with the statement that ethnomethodology has been at the centre of some of the discipline's liveliest controversies in recent years. Its radical approach to the study of social life has, however, led as much to ridicule, disdain and even persecution as to a serious re-examination of the premises of traditional sociology. But, if one accepts the ethnomethodologists' basic critique, it is clear that many hitherto orthodox ways of doing sociology become untenable. This chapter is devoted to a discussion of the ethnomethodological movement and its analysis of the limitations of conventional research. As such it returns to a number of themes first identified in our earlier discussion of epistemology. The term 'movement' is deliberately chosen. Although most ethnomethodologists would share a common diagnosis of the failings of much previous and current work, there are important differences in the prescriptions which they draw from it. In our view, three distinct currents can be discerned – ethnomethodological ethnography, conversational analysis and Blumian 'analysis'. We have, however, elected to begin by discussing the origins and development of the movement in order to establish what its adherents have in common before proceeding to examine their internal debates. In this case, we must discuss events in American sociology, because this is one area in which 'foreign' sociology has been imported into the British tradition.

The origins of ethnomethodology

Harold Garfinkel recounted at the Purdue Symposium on Ethnomethodology how he had come to coin the term (Hill and Crittenden, 1968, 8-9). His work as a research assistant on the Chicago jury project had stimulated an interest in how jurors

116

reasoned. This project had access to tapes of jury discussions which were being analysed within a framework derived from R. F. Bales's proposals for the study of small groups. Listening to the tapes, Garfinkel found that the jurors appeared to be concerned with problems recognisable as methodological – the adequacy of data, the logic of argument, the relevance of material, the status of facts. These had long been acknowledged as matters of concern for scientists or philosophers, but here they were clearly practical issues for lay jurors. They seemed to deal with the difficulties by reference to a background of commonsense knowledge which provided them with methods for solving these problems; methods whose correct usage, in the eyes of other parties, also demonstrated the social competence of their user.

While writing up these data, Garfinkel explained, he was also working on the Yale cross-cultural area files and came to a group of headings – ethnobotany, ethnophysiology, ethnophysics.

> 'Ethno' seemed to refer, somehow or other, to the availability to a member of common-sense knowledge of his society as common-sense knowledge of the 'whatever'. If it were 'ethno-botany' then it had to do somehow or other with his knowledge of and his grasp of what were for members adequate methods for dealing with botanical matters. Someone from another society, like an anthropologist in this case, would recognize the matters as botanical matters. The member would employ ethnobotany as adequate grounds of inference and action in the conduct of his own affairs in the company of others like him.... I thought, now there is a cognate feature and that is the availability I had encountered among the jurors in their concerns for what members of the society, particularly in the situation of being jurors, came to hold each other to as what one like them would be expected to know, to deal with and the rest where matters of fact, fancy, hypothesis, conjecture, evidence, demonstration, inquiry, ordered knowledge, and the rest were a matter of practical consideration....

Ethnomethodology, then, addressed the question of how people assembled order in social affairs through the systematic use of methods which were equally available to them to produce actions of their own. These methodic procedures organised, or, in the accepted terminology, constituted a setting. That setting itself was, however, simultaneously made available by those same procedures as data which could be constitutive of the developing action. Participants' talk, for instance, is methodically designed with a view to its intelligibility in a particular context: once produced, though, it immediately becomes data on the nature of that context which are, in turn, used by hearers to find its sense. This dialectical quality is a prominent feature of ethnomethodological thought. The procedures which make some phenomenon available as noticeable or observable are, for example, equally those which make it reportable, something which can be communicated to others. Similarly, the identification of some phenomenon as a resource for use in organising action also makes it available as a potential topic for that action.

The intellectual source of ethnomethodology is a superficially improbable synthesis of four elements. These include strands from anthropology, from the earlier work of Talcott Parsons, from European phenomenology and from linguistic philosophy. The first three of these can all be traced to Garfinkel's graduate work at Harvard under Parsons.

It must be recognised that the Department of Social Relations at Harvard was not just a sociology department, but one which embraced a spectrum of the social sciences. In particular, there was an important contribution from social and cultural anthropology. At the time of Garfinkel's studies, Clyde and Florence Kluckholn were beginning to develop work on value orientations. They had been close to Parsons for a number of years and this formed an integral part of the Harvard attempt to produce general theories of social organisation. The value orientations programme proposed that the conditions of human existence gave rise to a limited number of fundamental problems which required cultural rather than biological solutions. Actors were said to solve these by reference to a repertory of solutions made available by the value choices of a society. It was argued that the whole logical set of choices would be available in any particular society, but that one pattern would dominate. In keeping with the influence of Freudian thought on the Harvard department at this period, the learning process for value orientations was depicted as one of internalisation through socialisation experiences. Garfinkel never seems to have had much time for Freud and ethnomethodological accounts of socialisation are rather different. Nevertheless, there are basic affinities between this work and some of Garfinkel's early writing, particularly in its depiction of culture as an invocable resource to produce appropriate action rather than as a set of programming rules.

Of more enduring importance, perhaps, is the formation of a habit of working alongside anthropologists. Mullins (1973a, 249-50) records that Garfinkel formed a connection with Dell Hymes when he went to UCLA in 1954. Hymes has since played a central role in the development of anthropological linguistics and exerted a considerable influence on the ethnoscientists. These latter can, to some degree, be considered as a parallel group to ethnomethodology within anthropology, although their interest has been directed more to the nature of the knowledge available to members of some social group than to its articulation with everyday use. Garfinkel referred to this work at the Purdue symposium and it is the subject of an extended discussion by Lawrence Wider in the Jack Douglas (1974) collection, *Understanding Everyday Life*. Harvey Sacks's work, too, displays a familiarity with anthropological sources. Garfinkel sat on anthropology dissertation committees, like that for Carlos Casteneda (1970, 11) during the 1960s. Michael Moerman, however, is probably the only anthropologist to be identified closely with ethnomethodology at the present time, although a number of others, like William Labov and his associates, have drawn from its approach at various times.

Given that Parsons supervised Garfinkel at Harvard, it should hardly be surprising that his work be identified as the second major influence. Partly because key manuscripts like *A Parsons Primer* have never been published, this link has received limited critical attention, although Garfinkel (1967, ix) singles out Parsons for acknowledgment in his introduction to *Studies in Ethnomethodology:* 'Parsons' work, particularly, remains awesome for the penetrating depth and unfailing precision of its practical sociological reasoning on the constituent tasks of the problem of social order and its solutions.' In the course of the same discussion, Garfinkel couples together Parsons with Alfred Schutz, Edmund Husserl and Aron Gurwitsch as his intellectual progenitors. These may seem strange bedfellows. Such a view, however, can be taken as a reflection of the poverty of our understanding of Parsons. It is, for instance, interesting to note Parsons's (1968, 733, 750) own references to Husserl in *The Structure of Social Action*. Baumann's (1978) recent analysis of hermeneutics and social science brackets Husserl and Parsons.* Schutz, himself, saw important parallels between his criticisms of Weber's theory of action and Parsons's pre-war writings (Grathoff, 1978). Obviously, it is impossible in an account of this kind to argue a full re-evaluation of Parsons's work. Nevertheless, we can attempt to show how Parsons, particularly in his pre-Freudian period, was developing an approach which was capable of leading to ethnomethodology.

In *The Structure of Social Action*, Parsons traces the emergence of what he calls a 'voluntaristic theory of action' in opposition to the positivistic approach of utilitarian writers in economics, psychology and social biology. Parsons stresses that an act is a process in time; that its development is the outcome of a series of

---

* We are grateful to Phil Strong for drawing our attention to this source.

choices on the part of the actors involved, orienting to social norms; that the frame of reference surrounding an act depends on the subjective organisation of phenomena by the actor whose act is being considered; and that the level of analysis of both actors and observers is practically determined and need not approach any ultimate resolution. The failures of utilitarian thought stem from its disintegration of organised patterns of social action into unique, one-off acts. It has discounted the social nature of norms and the social formation of actors' perceptions. Further, it has accorded priority to a narrow standard of scientific rationality as a basis for identifying commonsense, lay action as rationally deficient.

The social meaning of any phenomenon, in Parsons's view, is not derived from natural scientific accounts but from its social use. 'A chair is, for instance, in a physical context a complex of molecules and atoms; in an action context it is a means, "something to sit on"' (Parsons, 1968, 731). Meaning arises in a phenomenological fashion from the logical framework in which we describe and think about action. Following Husserl, Parsons views action as a 'psychological' event, insofar as it grapples with phenomena having an empirical existence in terms of categories derived from subjective experience. Action is linked to the actor's view of the world as it is made available to him in the light of his socially formed knowledge and his practical purposes.

Such a reading of *The Structure of Social Action* does provide for an alternative line of descent than that of structural functionalism. It also helps us to see how the other major contributions to ethnomethodology have become involved.

Much of Garfinkel's early published work bears a clear and acknowledged debt to the writings of Alfred Schutz. Like Parsons, Schutz developed his early work in debate with the shade of Max Weber. Both were unhappy with Weber's idealist formulation of action and with his account of *verstehen*. In *The Phenomenology of the Social World* (first published 1932), Schutz raises a series of problems with the notion of an ideal type and its relation to action, about the assignment of meaning and about what it takes to say that we have grasped the subjective meaning of an action to its participants. Weber, in his view, has arrived at an external and mechanical analysis which is poorly articulated with the production and comprehension of particular acts. Schutz moves away from the use of scientific rationality as a normative standard to an attempt to give serious and systematic consideration to the commonsense world of actors *as it is experienced* – a partially coherent, imperfectly known and precarious intersubjective construction. Weber's abstracted ideal types give way to typifications, practical generalisations continually being modified with shifts in their users' interests and projects. Taken together, these typifications amount to an actor's commonsense knowledge of social structures, his *vademecum* of typical persons, activities and events including a compendium of practical recipes for developing and recognising appropriate action in the light of the particular data made typically available in any setting.

This approach is obviously close to Garfinkel's interests in the practical reasoning of jurors as he spelt it out at Purdue. His early studies on the violation of 'trust', actors' confidence in the reliability and validity of their commonsense knowledge, were designed to provide empirical evidence for a number of Schutz's arguments about the existence and use of this background information and the disturbance which inevitably resulted when it broke down.

Linguistic philosophy was a later influence, contributing more to the development of conversational analysis through the intermediary of Sacks than to Garfinkel's original programme. While this is often seen as antithetical to the phenomenological tradition, they do share a concern with language and its use to locate meaning in the social world. There are, as we have outlined the arguments of Schutz and Parsons, clear echoes of Wittgenstein's attempt to find meaning in language through an analysis of what people did with it, and his insistence on the adequacy of everyday language for its users' purposes rather than as deficient by comparison with science or philosophy. As Atkinson and Drew (1979, 5n) observe, however, philosophy lacked a tradition of empirical research. Although the concern with the use of language might have led to the assembly and analysis of naturally occurring talk, the ordinary language philosophers based their approach on reflections about invented examples whose relation to everyday practice remained obscure. There is, they suggest, a sense in which conversational analysis, particularly, can be seen as an empirical sequel to linguistic philosophy.

The introduction of this influence is, in part, associated with the development of distinctive types of ethnomethodology. Garfinkel's background had furnished ethnomethodology with a theory derived from Parsons, Schutz and European phenomenology and with a method derived from anthropology, ethnography. The first generation of ethnomethodologists – Bittner, Cicourel, Sudnow, Wieder, Zimmerman among them – primarily conducted research that looked like traditional Chicago ethnography, although we shall argue that there were qualitative differences. Conversational analysis was a later development under Sacks at Berkeley in an attempt, we suggest, to achieve greater rigour than is possible within the inherent limitations of ethnographic data.

The social history of ethnomethodology is harder to document than its intellectual precursors.* It seems important that Garfinkel trained at Harvard at a point where this was becoming the major gateway introducing European writing to American sociology. UCLA, however, was a fairly obscure corner of American sociology in the early 1950s. The expansion in Higher Education and graduate work had not yet begun. When it did come, the Californian system grew quite disproportionately and sucked in students and faculty from the whole country. Many of the Chicago ethnographers secured their first tenured jobs there after a precarious existence in the previous decade. Hence, it is hardly surprising that ethnomethodologists should seem to cluster on the West Coast, given the time of the specialty's development.

This can, of course, be seen equally as a defensive move on the part of a group under intellectual attack and unable to publish in an orthodox fashion or to gain posts in more prestigious departments. The circumstances of all this are quite obscure. It is not clear what attracted students to Garfinkel's ideas in the first place. One might speculate that it had to do with the more rigorous approach to ethnography that it seemed to offer but that would be no more than speculation. Equally, it is not at all clear why so much hostility should have been aroused. For instance, Garfinkel allowed his ASA membership to lapse in 1967 and attempts were made to prevent his reinstatement.** Yet at this time, by Mullins's elastic criteria, there were no more than twenty-five ethnomethodologists of whom a third were graduate students. Both Garfinkel and Cicourel had been critical of conventional sociological practice in their published work, but, with the exception of the American Sociological Review's (1968) Symposium on *Studies in Ethnomethodology*, this received little public acknowledgment. Ethnographers had had a difficult time in the competitive market of the 1950s and early 1960s, but we are now talking about a period when jobs were relatively plentiful. Several American informants have suggested to us that it is still a significant career disadvantage to appear 'soft' on ethnomethodology and that this has contributed to the lack of genuine dialogue, particularly with ethnographers in the Chicago tradition. In a much tighter labour market, this is an important

* The main published account (Mullins 1973a, 1973b) has considerable weaknesses in its reliance on marginal figures for information. This has inevitably given it a somewhat partisan slant on such matters as the Garfinkel/Cicourel quarrel. It is also rather weak in its treatment of the academic labour market as a constraint on social organisation.

** British readers may wonder about the significance of this. The ASA is an altogether more powerful professional association than the BSA. Only recognised Ph.D.s are eligible for full membership and exclusion is a significant career disadvantage. A nearer British parallel would be with the BPS.

constraint on ethnomethodology's ability to inspire new empirical work.

Ethnomethodology arrived in the UK at a time when the expansion of Higher Education reached an abrupt check. It has, consequently, become caught in the general struggle to secure scarce positions. Mullins (1973a, 271) mentions the formation of groups at Manchester and Goldsmiths' College, London. Only Goldsmiths' has survived as a stable unit, partly because the head of department, David Silverman, was an early affiliate to the movement. Manchester has proved a less sympathetic environment and entered a relative decline since the departure of key figures like Max Atkinson and Jeff Coulter. Some 'outsiders' might add a third British group at the Centre for Social Studies in Aberdeen but this was based on research money and has subsequently disintegrated as a result of the normal career contingencies of researchers of these three institutions only Manchester would be regarded as a prestigious location in British terms and that was where the greatest opposition was met. Graduate students, particularly those with a conversational analysis background, have found great difficulty in getting posts because of their lack of established sponsors and the degree to which an appreciable number of recent appointments have rested on intellectual or political orthodoxy or the appropriate set of genitalia. Career prospects have not been helped by the diversity between the centres. Goldsmiths' was initially influenced by Cicourel, and subsequently moved closer to Blum although Silverman's most recent work has returned towards ethnography. Manchester became a centre for conversational analysis while Aberdeen developed as an ethnographic group, sympathetic to ethnomethodology but not professing allegiance to the same degree as either of the other institutions.

Like any chronicle of descent, this account of ethnomethodology inevitably appears to make it seem a less radical movement than either practitioners or critics, with the exception of Denzin (in Douglas, 1974), would generally acknowledge. Concerns with language and meaning were current in American sociology and anthropology before the war. We have already quoted from Park's discussion of the subject matter of sociology and similar themes are well-established in G. H. Mead's work. Sapir had elucidated the arguments on language and culture which were to form the basis of the Sapir-Whorf hypothesis on the ways in which language structured perception. Although the ethnographic strand in ethno-methodology has been largely repudiated by the conversational analysts, it has served as an important bridge for recruitment, especially in the UK. Many of the British ethnomethodological ethnographers began from the sociology of deviance and its inspiration in the Chicago tradition, although a significant minority started out as quantitative sociologists, drawn by the prospect of a more rigorous answer to certain practical problems of language and meaning in their work.

In our view, however, this would be to take the ethnomethodological contribution too lightly. Ethnographies in this tradition are demonstrably different from their interactionist counterparts. While conversational analysis draws on renewed concern with the social use of language in a number of social sciences, it does represent a genuine novelty as far as sociology is concerned. At the very least, it could not have existed before the invention of the tape recorder. The Parsonian influence is quite different from the structural functionalist tradition.

The ethnomethodological critique has led its adherents to a substantive change in their conception of the scope and method of sociology, although they would not necessarily speak with one voice on the precise nature of that change. We turn, then, to consider the development of the current varieties of ethnomethodology, their agreements and their differences.

The ethnomethodological critique

In this section, we have attempted to set out an account of those arguments against conventional practice in sociology on which most ethnomethodologists would agree. Since the ethnomethodological criticisms of quantitative or survey approaches are relatively well known, we have chosen to emphasise the criticisms of orthodox ethnography, in part as an introduction to our later discussion of the character of ethnomethodological ethnography. The present discussion leans considerably on Atkinson and Drew (1979) who offer one of the few reasonably authoritative introductory accounts of this diverse literature.

All traditional sociologists, in their view, share three basic assumptions: sociology is capable of producing descriptions and explanations of social phenomena which correspond to actual events; sociological accounts of the social world are different from, and superior to, those of lay members; and lay members' procedures for making sense of their world are flawed and must either be modified or avoided in doing sociology.

The model of the social world generated by these presuppositions is, to ethnomethodologists, unrecognisable as the world in which we actually live. The so-called 'positivistic' tradition holds that descriptions and explanations of events can be produced independently of the settings in which they occur. If this were so, then the world would be a more certain place since the nature of

124

any setting would not be open to doubt and the facts of the setting could not be disputed. Action would be generated by some de-contextualised set of rules which would specify in advance what was to be counted as correct. Social life would be largely predictable with very restricted possibilities for novelty or change. These would basically arise in a way analogous to natural selection in biology, environmental change. Since sociologists have better procedures for understanding the world and, consequently, better accounts than other members, one would have expected them to come to dominate the world in the manner envisaged by Comte and his caste of sociologist priests.

It should be noted that these considerations apply as forcibly to interpretivist or ethnographic sociologies as to the traditional targets of their criticism. In many ways, they subscribe to the same basic assumptions and their dissent from the stable world of the 'positivist' still takes a form which produces an implausible version of reality. There is, for instance, a strain in ethnography which holds that methodological procedures are available to improve on those of lay members. Denzin's (1970b) proposals for triangulation are a good illustration of this. He argues that, by looking at some sequence of events from a greater variety of data sources than might be available to any individual participant, sociologists can put themselves in a position to adjudicate between the participants' competing versions. This current of argument is tied up with the emphasis already noted on low-life, digging out the dirt on an organisation to detach it from the symbolic system which members use to construct their view of the institution. Finally, ethnographers do tend to see literal description as a practical rather than a philosophical problem. If they only had sufficient space unconstrained by the economics of publishing, then short-cuts would be unnecessary.

The ethnographic model of the world as an intersubjective creation is still unworkable. There are so few restraints on the subjectively created meanings assigned to an otherwise unintelligible world that sufficient agreement to accomplish any joint event, let alone the manifest order of everyday life, seems inconceivable. This difficulty is obscured in practice by the piecemeal inquiries which result from the absurdity of applying the above principles literally. Given the indefinite character of description, limits are set by restricting the analysis to selected topics, derived either from previous literature or the investigator's preferred version which gives a spurious certainty to the whole proceeding.

Atkinson and Drew conclude that the two currents of sociological thought – positivist and interpretivist – have failed as a result of an exclusive concentration on one or other of the two dimensions exhibited by the social world. An adequate theory of social order would have to provide for the way in which

> the social world is comprised of unique circumstances which are nevertheless recognisable as instances of generalised types, and is simultaneously flexible *and* patterned, subjectively experienced *and* externally objective, uncertain *and* certain, indescribable *and* describable. That is, the theory would have to be *neither* so inflexible or rigid that it lacks any sensitivity to the potentially infinite range of contextual variation in the world, *nor* so inflexible or loose that nothing at all is held to be general across different contexts (Atkinson and Drew, 1979, 20).

Ethnomethodology proposed a radical redirection of sociological interest as a way of meeting these criteria. Sociologists were enjoined to abandon unanswerable 'why' questions about social order in favour of the neglected, and answerable, 'how' questions. Any attempt to explain why a collectivity took the form that it did could have at best the character of a sophisticated polemic, since the organisation of that collectivity was used as a resource for the development of a particular critique. It might, however, prove feasible to show how members of that collectivity went about producing sufficient order for their practical purposes. The central sociological topic became the production of order through the joint everyday reasoning of members.

The resulting programme of research developed in a variety of ways. They are all, however, bound by certain methodological injunctions. First, the investigator tries to treat his own society as 'anthropologically strange', that is to say, to look at his fellow-citizens in the way that an anthropologist might study some alien society. A key failing of previous work had been the unexamined use of the investigator's own social competence, to ask how it was possible to 'see' order in a setting. This was an important first step to treating the production of that order as their subject matter.

Second, social actors are depicted as rule-using analysts rather than rule-governed dopes. Traditional sociologists saw actors as following sets of programming rules, a de-contextualised cultural apparatus whose use produced action. Ethnomethodology, however, presents actors as interpreters of rules. While they may be consulted for guidance, the essential indefinite character of rules provides that they will require extension, adaptation and modification to meet each unique situation. Actors are, then, cultural producers rather than cultural products.

These considerations have given rise to two main strands of empirical work – ethnomethodological ethnography and conversational analysis – which form the basis of succeeding sections of this chapter. It is, however, also possible to arrive at almost anti-empirical conclusions as the work of Blum and his associates shows. This form of analysis occupies the third part of our discussions.

Conversational analysis and the rejection of ethnography

As we have already indicated, the first wave of ethnomethodological studies relied on classical ethnographic procedures. Examples of this would include David Sudnow's *Passing On* (1967), Aaron Cicourel's *The Educational Decision-Makers* (1964), and *The Social Organisation of Juvenile Justice* (1968), Egon Bittner's work on policing (1967a, b) and Don Zimmerman's work on social welfare bureaux (1969a, 1969b). Ethnography had developed as a way of resolving the anthropologists' problems in understanding strange societies. Might this not, then, be a relevant starting point for attempts to treat one's own society as a strange phenomenon?*

Atkinson (1978) argues that much of this work is, in practice, indistinguishable from traditional Chicagoan ethnography and equally unsatisfactory by comparison with conversational analysis. To understand why, we need to return to a more detailed consideration of the nature of sociological description. The main issues are summarised in the following six points, derived from Atkinson and Drew (1979, 24).

1 Any description of a phenomenon – an object, person, event, activity, setting or whatever – can always be extended indefinitely and must therefore, at some point, be brought to a close.
2 Nevertheless, a single descriptor (i.e., one word or phrase) *can* be adequate description of a phenomenon, depending on the context.
3 Any phenomenon can invariably be described in more than one way. The analyst, then, is constantly faced with the practical problem of choosing between alternative versions.
4 The appropriateness of choosing one description rather than another varies with the context. An adequate rendering in one setting may not suffice in another.
5 Descriptions may be recognised as appropriate without the hearer of the description having witnessed the phenomenon for himself. It is, then, the case that observational techniques which decontextualise their descriptions from the events cannot provide an independent way of justifying a proposed correspondence between a description of some phenomenon and the phenomenon itself.

---

* One must also allow for the state of technology. Conversational analysis could not have developed without the advent of the cheap, lightweight tape recorder and its evolution has been critically influenced by the available equipment for transcription.

127

6 Descriptions are among the features which organise and make available the phenomena which they purport to describe. They are used by observers to scrutinise the phenomena and to assemble their orderly character.

Any fieldworker's report is the outcome of a series of practical compromises in the face of these problems. His own descriptions can be indefinitely extended, must choose between competing versions, orient to disciplinary (and hence non-contextual) standards of appropriateness and, ultimately, provide an organisation of the events they purport to describe. The reader is presented with a clutch of necessarily selective and incomplete renderings of observed events, renderings which have, moreover, been analytically organised prior to any overt analytic comments. He depends on the ethnographer's competence for what he is to know about the events which form the data and on how he is to analyse them. Any attempts to mitigate this problem, either by extending the presentation of the original data or by describing the investigator's own interpretive procedures, are doomed to founder on the same fundamental obstacles.

It is upon this view of ethnography that the conversational analysts base their rejection of it as a valid enterprise. We shall discuss the ethnographers' counter-arguments later in this chapter. For the moment, however, let us remain with the conversational analysts' attempt to resolve these questions.

Conversational analysis claims to depend upon a democratisation of its original data. Its reliance on the recordings and transcripts which modern technology makes possible allows its audience to have equal access to the material being presented and to compare this with the analyst's account. Both the data and the procedures by which the analyst arrives at some interpretation are rendered publicly available for evaluation. In organising and interpreting his data, the analyst trades on knowledge which he shares with other members of his culture. His subsequent reasoning attempts to make this knowledge visible as he strives to account for the generation of this particular collection of talk. The audience can examine both his proposed reading of the data and the apparatus which is claimed to be capable of generating the transcribed passage. Both the reading and the apparatus are available for challenge.

In practice, this may be less novel than it sounds. Ethnographers have conventionally proclaimed their willingness to open field notes to outside verification, subject to ethical constraints, or to invite replications. The same might well be said of the concept of a Survey Archive for storing original data from that tradition for comparative purposes or subsequent reconsideration. Moreover, it is clear that the availability of reinterpretation is restricted by the hearer's standing. As we noted in an earlier discussion of falsification, alternative readings may simply call the hearer's competence and socialisation into question, rather than challenging the original version. Democratising data does not entail democratising analysis.

Nevertheless, while ethnography depends on the observer's description to freeze the action which forms its topic, conversational analysis does employ data which can be preserved and shared for detailed and repeated scrutiny. In this sense only, it furnishes more solid grounding than 'the sorts of introspective and publicly inaccessible reflections which are all that can be offered when there is no opportunity to check them directly with the data' (Atkinson and Drew, 1979, 28).

Conventionally, ethnographers have argued that it is possible to be socialised into a setting, to see how the participants achieve order in it and then to reproduce this in their fieldwork reports. The problems with such reports have already been outlined and these are compounded by the general difficulty of relating these de-contextualised versions to the observed, situated actions of the setting's participants. It may well not be clear how far the claims for particular orientations may be generalised, but too great a specificity in the conditions under which that generalisation holds rapidly leads to total relativism. Where generalisations are proposed, however, they may be difficult to justify without having done fieldwork in those other settings, given the ethnographers' standard claim to special credence by virtue of 'having been and having seen'. If extensive fieldwork is necessary to describe members' orientations in one setting, though, then such accounts cannot be equally valid in settings where the investigator has not done such fieldwork. If they are valid, then this must cast doubt on the alleged importance of extensive direct experience.

A further limitation on ethnography is the way in which features are selected for presentation. This depends upon some theoretical or polemical framework which yields criteria of relevance. In general, these call attention to the unusual or the exotic and to discount the mundane and everyday. Like a journalist, an ethnographer is concerned to find a story to tell and this places an inherent tendency to dramatise at the centre of the enterprise. Conversational analysis, on the other hand, deliberately selects the most 'obvious' of social phenomena as its topic. It is so obvious that most of the time most people can talk to each other amicably and effectively as to seem utterly uninteresting to sociologists. Part of the achievement of conversational analysis is to dissect the complexity of such an achievement bringing back what, self-parodyingly, they term as 'news' from a neglected corner of the world. It must be said, however, that Atkinson and Drew sustain this argument largely by trading off some rather weak examples of marxist ethnography in the study of law.

Finally, ethnography runs up against the problem of demonstrating that the apparatus which generates some setting is not just an analytic construction but can also be seen to be oriented to by its participants. They seldom give running commentaries on their actions; indeed their competence as participants may well be displayed by virtue of the fact that they do not comment on their actions, although this view is not entirely sustained by published accounts of fieldwork experiences. The ethnographer must trade on his cultural competence in the same way as any other witness to the events. This allows him to produce a practical description, just as any lay observer might, but it cannot pretend to certainty or correctness, although, as Bloor (1978) argues, there might be ways of validating ethnographic accounts against those of members. The conversational analysts' claim to make no more than *a* possible sense of their data is not altogether sustained in practice, as we have already remarked.

Conversational analysis is consistent with the injunction to analyse members' knowledge rather than to trade on it. Atkinson and Drew also argue that it comes to terms with the constraints of sociological description, listed above. By focusing on the contextual choice of descriptions by participants (3), the achieved completeness of the descriptions (1 and 2) and their contextual appropriateness (4) cease to be problematic for the analyst. By assuming that there will always be alternative descriptions (1, 2 and 3) and avoiding any claims as to the correctness of any particular reading, conversational analysis circumvents the problem of justifying an asserted correspondence between some description and the phenomenon to which it applies (5).

This is not the place to engage in an extended description of conversational analysis.* Nevertheless, having dealt with the development of its programme, our account would be less than complete if we were to fail to give at least some indication of the ways in which it has been implemented.

The central concern of the conversational analysts is with the achievement of order in verbal interaction and the examination of those contingent and context-dependent features which enable an appearance of intelligibility to be formulated by competent hearers or participants. One cautionary remark should be made here: although we talk of *conversational* analysis, the programme does, in

---

* Obvious starting points would be Atkinson and Drew (1979), Wootton (1975) and the January 1978 Special Issue of *Sociology* on 'Language and Practical Reasoning'.

fact, aim to address *all* talk, whether in natural conversations or in other settings. The restriction to verbal interaction is a technical one – the required data on paralinguistic features are difficult to obtain with present technology. In principle, the same considerations apply.

By choosing recorded talk for analysis, conversational analysts are selecting what is arguably the 'hardest' data any social scientist has available. Whereas the ethnographer has 'been and seen', his account is mediated through his hand notes. The survey researcher is even further removed in his reliance on the competence of his field staff. The conversational analyst's material is preserved in a form which permits its continual repetition as it is. This does, however, restrict the range of data available to those settings which can be recorded and to the physical limitations on the supply of competent transcribers and the rate at which they can work. The production of a transcript to the full requirements of the Jefferson system is a lengthy and exacting business. Although the total corpus of transcripts is reaching substantial proportions, there is at least a potential problem of generalisability about some of the possible subjects for analysis, in particular those which are most closely bound to the particular context of the talk under examination. Investigators do, then, tend to concentrate on a general level of analysis of the fundamental structures of talk, rather than being very interested in how any particular setting is generated by them.

Sacks, Schegloff and Jefferson (1974, 669) set this out in their programme for the analysis of turn-taking.

> We employ a long-term understanding of 'context' in the social sciences – one which attends the various places, times and identities of parties to interaction. What we mean to note is that major aspects of the organisation of turn-taking are insensitive to parameters of context and are, in that sense, 'context-free'; but it remains the case that examination of any particular materials will display the context-free resources of the turn-taking system to be employed, disposed in ways fitted to particulars of context. *It is the context-free structure which defines how and where context-sensitivity can be displayed; the particularities of context are exhibited in systematically organized ways and places, and those are shaped by the context-free organisaton.* [Our emphasis]

The conversational analysts' task is no less than to describe that context-free structure. Their writings have, apart from turn-taking, addressed questions like opening and closing exchanges, storytelling, topic change and the maintenance of thematic relevance, and the design of question-answer sequences. Together, these attempt to account for certain grossly observable features of human communication, that, for the most part, one person talks at a time, that speaker-change recurs, that participants can sustain a mutual orientation to a joint activity and the like. As Atkinson and Drew (1979, 235, n.15) have it, the concern is with the 95 per cent which is common to all social settings rather than the 5 per cent which is locally peculiar*.

Ethnomethodological ethnography

We have, in the previous chapter, already outlined the basic nature of the ethnographic method. In this section, then, we intend to concentrate on what is special about ethnomethodological ethnography. We particularly want to consider its practitioners' debates with conversational analysis and their defence of the fundamental viability of the approach, despite the concession that important modifications are required.

The central issues to be faced stem from the character of sociological description which we set out at the beginning of the previous section. Either those critical features apply equally to conversational analysis and ethnomethodological ethnography, in which case we are left to fall back on Blum's approach, which we discuss later, or conversational analysis has reached a narrow and tendentious conclusion from them. In the latter case, there may be room for other sorts of enterprise, addressing different questions to those of the conversational analysts. One of those enterprises might be ethnomethodological ethnography.

It will be remembered that Atkinson and Drew (1979, 24) identified 6 features of sociological description. Let us reconsider each of these briefly.

1 Any description of a phenomenon can be extended indefinitely. The fact that it *can* be does not entail that it *has* to be. Indefinite elaboration is not difficult to demonstrate in certain natural or experimental situations. It does not, however, seem to be endemic. Indeed everyday life seems to hinge on the practical determinacy of description. Both sociologists and lay people extend their accounts as far as required by their current project.

2 A single descriptor *can* be an adequate description. This partly concedes the above point, particularly in the further qualification that it depends upon the context.

3 Any phenomenon can be multiply described. If this is the case, how do conversational analysts warrant the claims for their

---

* The authors do stress that these percentages are quoted for illustrative purposes only rather than being statements of fact.

approach? Atkinson and Drew (1979, 32) offer a somewhat weak formulation 'While an analyst may not be able to arrive at *the* sense of what participants were *actually* orienting to in some particular context, his members' competences enable him, like them, to make *a* sense of what was going on. ...' It is not at all clear that this programmatic validity claim is justified by a passage like that quoted from Sacks et al. (1974) above, or indeed, by much of Atkinson and Drew's own empirical account. Furthermore, we again have this point that the fact that a phenomenon *can* be multiply described does not mean that it *has* to be.

4 The appropriateness of choosing one description rather than another varies with the context. On the whole, conversational analysts specifically disregard the contextual features of an occasion in their search for the Philosophers' Stone of a context-free mechanism.

5 Descriptions may be heard as adequate without the hearer having witnessed the events described. Can conversational analysis address this by its concentration on formal mechanisms and its relative inattention to content?

6 Descriptions organise the phenomena they describe. This is true for both members and observers. Is there a real bar to observers' analyses of members' descriptive practices and the way these make settings available to each other?

The basic thrust of the ethnographers' argument is developed in Bloor's (1980) discussion of Zimmerman and Wieder's contribution to the Douglas (1974) collection. Bloor takes up the ethnomethodological theme of the contingency of rules. He points out that while this is so in a theoretical sense, empirically the contingent quality may be sharply limited either by the rule-users' sense of the sameness of the context or by other social constraints. Zimmerman and Wieder cite two studies to back up their model of rule-consulting actors: Zimmerman's own work on intake in a public welfare agency (1974) and Garfinkel's description of coding work on clinic records (1967). Bloor notes that both of these studies emphasise troubles rather than routine. Ordinarily, receptionists and coders manage quite happily, unproblematically recognising the sameness of the questions which arise. It is only when particular sorts of trouble develop that rules must be consulted and visibly elaborated rather than just applied. While these rules may have an unavoidable contingent quality, in practice that contingency is not routinely manifest.

Bloor goes on to discuss social constraints on rule-elaboration through reference to Bittner's (1965) work on organisations. In this paper, Bittner has some rather elliptical remarks on the notion of stylistic unity ' ... an all-pervading sense of piety ... a sure-footed conviction of "what properly goes with what" '. His constraints appear to be substantially aesthetic, although he does also introduce notions of rule infractions and their visibility. Again, we have a neglected corollary of an important insight. The fact that rules may be indefinitely elaborated does not entail that a witness has to accept that this elaboration has brought the observed event within the ambit of the orienting rule. The conversational analysts' world does not encompass lies, but merely remediable mistakes. As far as constraints go, a better example may be found in Zimmerman and West's discussions of sex roles and interaction (1975). Here, they show how women's intervention in conversation is systematically limited. How is this achieved? Can one speak of this just as a rule of speech exchange or must one elaborate it into some notion like commonsense knowledge of social structures? Similarly, Dingwall (1980) argues that there may well be certain kinds of encounter which resolve around the assumed or imputed right of one participant to mediate the formal apparatus of speech-exchange rather than each participant having equal access to it. One member, in other words, is preferentially able to decide the sense of rules or the appropriateness of descriptions. How can we account for this and the grounds on which the choice is made?

It is problems of this kind which conversational analysis has difficulty in handling. They are not the 'why' questions which ethnomethodology has so strongly criticised in asserting that it is possible for sociology to be something other than tarted-up political rhetoric. There seems to be a middle range of issues here. Wieder reprimanded the ethnoscientists with having created a world whose members only existed when they spoke (in Douglas, 1974). Conversational analysis presents a picture of people who both speak and listen but whose dialogue is an empty skeleton of formal procedures. It is the content which attracts the ethnographer's attention.

The way in which it is treated does, however, have much in common with conversational analysis. The ethnomethodological ethnographer starts from the question of how the participants in some event find its character and sustain it, or fail to, as a joint activity. He proceeds by a systematic process of inductive reasoning to specify the actors' models of their everyday social world which can be consulted to generate the observable conduct. It is, as Bloor shows, an approach which lies closer to Schutz and the phenomenological currents in ethnomethodology than to the linguistic philosophy influences. Goodenough's (1964, 36-7) account of the 'new ethnography' in anthropology comes very close:

a society's culture consists of whatever it is one has to know or believe in order to operate in a manner acceptable to its members, and to do so in any role that they accept for any one of themselves ... culture is not a material phenomenon; it does not consist of things, people, behavior or emotions. It is rather an organization of these things. It is the forms of things that people have in mind, their models for perceiving, relating and otherwise interpreting them.... Given such a definition it is impossible to describe a culture properly simply by describing behavior or social, economic and ceremonial events and arrangements as observed material phenomena. What is required is to construct a theory of the conceptual models which they represent and of which they are artifacts. We test the adequacy of such a theory by our ability to interpret and predict what goes on in a community as measured by how its members, our informants, do so. A further test is our ability ourselves to behave in ways which lead to the kind of responses from the community members which our theory would lead us to expect. Thus tested, the theory is a valid statement of what you have to know in order to operate as a member of the society and is, as such, a valid description of its culture... The relation of language to culture is that of part to whole. Theory and method applicable to one must have implications for the other....

It is this stress on actors' models which distinguishes ethnomethodological ethnography from its predecessors.

When one looks at more traditionally-oriented ethnographies, one cannot help but be struck by their descriptive quality. In this, they do indeed share much with good investigative journalism. Uurky goings-on are probed and brought to light for our moral delectation. These descriptions may be coupled with polemics in the way Sharrock (1979) so cogently criticises in his discussion of the analysis of professional domination in doctor/patient encounters. Ethnomethodological ethnographers have tried, with varying degrees of success, to suspend that moral stance and to concentrate on recovering the situated rationality of the events they have observed. This is quite noticeable in the development of the Aberdeen group, for instance. One might contrast the earlier interactionist phase which produced a paper like Bloor's essay on functional autonomy, taken by Sharrock as a prime target, with more recent writings like Strong's (1979b) book on paediatric clinics. The earlier period, rightly or wrongly, earned the group something of a reputation for 'doctor-bashing'. Latterly, papers like Strong's (1979a) critique of the thesis of medical imperialism have tended to result in charges of an inexcusable lack of interest in matters of urgent political concern (or, even worse, crypto-liberalism).

In particular, there is a movement towards a rather different epistemological foundation. This seeks to present a more theoretical account of the woolly notion of ethnographic empathy as a warrant for an observer's knowledge. Briefly, it is contended that understanding of some collectivity is possible only if one can deliberately stand on its margin – treat it as anthropologically strange, in essence. By doing so, the observer sets himself up in a position of consciously interchanging cultural frames, now taking those of a member, now those of a stranger. This internal dialogue, as a reflexive creation, enhances his understanding beyond the unreflexive analysis of collectivity members, or aspirants. Through this acculturation experience, the ethnographer acquires knowledge *of* the traditions he is witnessing, the same knowledge *of* as members rather than knowledge *about*. Where conversational analysis remains at a distance from those studied through its emphasis on the study of reified and de-contextualised data, ethnomethodological ethnography seeks to handle its subject-matter through an explicit process of sharing and understanding experience which is subsequently formalised.

The new approaches take a more firmly analytic stance in presenting data and arguing from them. There are still difficulties. The data are usually hand notes. Audio-typist transcripts of interviews may be used to complement such field data although they are, however, rightly regarded as poor data on everyday reasoning outside the context of the interview. The problem of initial selection is mitigated, to some degree, by an attempt at near-verbatim recording of key exchanges or of contexts in which key exchanges are thought likely to occur. Questions can clearly continue to be asked about the role of the investigator's theoretical and other predilections. These are, however, questions about the whole empirical enterprise. How does the conversational analyst know an interesting fragment when he hears it? How does he treat these fragments as instances of a type which can be depicted as part of some trans-situational context-free apparatus? How does he select which portions of which transcripts will appear in published writings?

The apparent lack of technical refinement in ethnography is a problem only by the standards of the conversational analysts. If one is trying to describe the underlying mechanisms of verbal interaction, then clearly high-quality taped and transcribed data are essential. Where concern is focused on a different level of issues, then other data are appropriate. Obviously, it would be nice to have radio transmitters attached to research participants and their everyday doings taped and transcribed, but, at present, to do this on an ethnographic scale would be very expensive and time-consuming. When sophisticated voice processors can take over transcription this may become possible. Such developments are, however, still in the future. The quality of the data one gathers in social research has always depended on the questions one starts with. Finally, we need to point to the spectre of utilitarianism which Parsons sought to exorcise and which still stalks the corridors of sociology. Parsons argued against its unsocial social theory which elevated a narrow evaluative standard of normative behaviour against which individual acts were measured. The result was the decontextualisation of those acts into the product of deficient actors. Like Durkheim in particular, Parsons was concerned with the moral forces which bound a society together as they entered into the practical reasoning of actors. We might not want to follow their entrepreneurial stance on the nature of that order but the general argument is surely valid. It is clearly one which influenced Garfinkel in his earlier writings and particularly his critique of the 'cultural dope' model of actors presupposed by much conventional sociology. Ethnography and conversational analysis pull in different directions here. On the one hand ethnography can, as Atkinson and Drew (1979, 29-30) argue, easily degenerate into a total relativism which disintegrates social life into a series of one-off utilitarian-type unit acts. On the other, conversational analysis can risk lapsing into a 'cultural dope' model by virtue of its stress on context-free mechanisms, which come to look like programming rules. If we go along, however, with the latter's concession that it is possible to talk of the existence of such mechanisms, then there seem few reasons why we should not extend this to talk of a continuing stock of knowledge of social life, which carries through from one situation to another, although locally modified in the same fashion as conversational organisation. If we can talk about it, then we can describe it with at least as much practical determinacy as is available to members themselves.

Such a statement may even make it possible for sociologists to claim a superior status for their knowledge, as we have hinted. Conversational analysis gives an account of talk which, in principle, any member could give, but which, in practice, they would find difficult to do because of their lack of an adequate metalanguage for the task. Similarly, the ethnomethodological ethnographer's description of the commonsense knowledge of his subjects may very well be one they could individually give for themselves. However, his access to a metalanguage and, where knowledge is socially differentiated, his opportunity to recover the analyses of the various groups bearing parts of that knowledge, may leave him in a superior position to any individual member. This is less of an issue for conversational analysis whose subject-matter does not, superficially at least, appear to be distributed in the same way. The fact that ethnographers do not, self-evidently, rule the world, is neither here nor there. The sort of description we are talking about would be a colossal undertaking for a whole society and would, of course, still come up against the ultimately contingent nature of any event. Within a limited area, a particular organisation, say, there does not, however, seem to be any obvious reason why an ethnographer should not be able to achieve a better average success rate in achieving a particular organisational goal than any ordinary member. This does not necessarily mean that he could take over that member's entire role – technical skills will obviously also be involved and few projects have the leisure for more than a partial analysis of any individual's involvement.

Both conversational analysis and ethnomethodological ethnography share the characteristic of being empirical, and even, at times, empiricist, approaches. One can, however, derive an alternative set of implications from Garfinkel's work which lead in a rather anti-empirical direction. Before concluding this chapter, it is worth giving a brief account of these.

The end of sociology?

Daniel Bell ended the 1950s with his celebrated proclamation of the end of ideology; Alan Blum can be said to have ended the 1960s with the proclamation of the end of sociology. Like many of the writers we have discussed here, his work bears an acknowledged debt to Garfinkel, particularly through his association with Peter McHugh. The argument that Blum and his followers have pursued, however, has led them, in effect, to propose the abandonment of any possibility of doing sociology as an empirical enterprise, even with ethnomethodological refurbishment. They have advocated, instead, a return to theorising in the Aristotelian sense, a mental activity engaged in for its own sake.

Their starting point is a view of sociological knowledge as that body of information which practitioners generally agree to accept as such in a particular historical context (Phillips, 1973, 81-179). It can be thought of as a set of procedural rules which can be used to decide whether to recognise some proposition as amounting to sociological knowledge. These rules are broadly drawn and do, in any case, have a contingent quality. They are not programming rules but the commonsense understandings developed within the scientific community in everyday encounters between sociologists. Objectivity and truth are consensually validated in compliance with the procedural canon rather than having absolute status. The social reality of the sociologist is an artefact of his methods for producing it, regardless of whether those methods are statistical, ethnomethodological or whatever.* The use of these productive methods enables a sociologist's colleagues to gauge his competence.

It is a question with which the sociology of knowledge has struggled unsuccessfully from time to time. Blum and his associates propose a radical attack on it, calling, in effect, for the dissolution of sociology in favour of self-reflection. They have, in particular indicated the need to reconsider contemplative strains in philosophy from the Greeks to Nietzsche and Heidegger.

Blum (in Douglas, 1974) discusses the origins of the notion of theorising in Greek philosophy. The restriction of theorising to scientific theorising is a degeneration of this usage. Theorising involves the spectator in search of himself, beginning in a moment of wonder and culminating in a transcendental self-discovery: 'Through theorising the theorist searches for his self and his achievement in theorising is a recovering of this self' (Blum, 1971, 304). It is a way of examining one's society and its possibilities and of clarifying the potentialities of the theorist himself. The existence of theorising as theorising is conditional upon its persuasiveness to an audience. The audience are spectators to the theorist's explication of possibilities. This contrasts with the deductive theorising of the positivists who seek to unite with their audience, for each to become each other. Theorising attains its analytic character through the methods which create it. We cannot, however, formulate rules for doing theorising. Rules and methods are the products of theoretical activity. Theorising is simply something which one does. One learns how to do it by watching another. It is presented through argument and rhetoric, the clash of opinions and points of view (Phillips 1973, 177-8). Sociology is a moral enterprise with a moral character formed by its subjugation of itself to a rule of practice. Its morality and rationality (Blum seems to equate the two) are unexplored. Yet the only moral activity for the rational man is to think about what it means to think morally (Blum, 1972):

---

* 'Ethnomethodology seeks to "rigorously describe" ordinary usage and despite its significant transformation of standards for conceiving of and describing such usage, it still conducts its inquiries under the auspices of a concrete, positivistic conception of adequacy. Ethnomethodology conceives of such descriptions of usage as analytic "solutions" to their tasks, whereas our interest is in the production of the idea which makes any conception of relevant usage itself possible. Whereas ethnomethodology uses the ordinary world "seriously" (they hope to solve analytic problems by doing naturalistic science on this world) we treat the everyday world as a proximate occasion for initiating inquiry and not as a "fact" to be reproduced. In our respective attitudes toward ordinary language and the everyday world, we have about as much in common with ethnomethodology as Heidegger shares with Austin.' (McHugh *et al.*, 1974, 22-23).

'Theorising is not designed to save worlds, nations, classes; it can only save the imagination by freeing it to acknowledge one more option' (Blum, 1971, 200).

The most readily available example of this approach is probably McHugh, Raffel, Foss and Blum, *On the Beginnings of Social Inquiry* (1974). This volume assembles a number of collaborative essays on a variety of themes from the concepts of 'evaluation' and 'bias' to the nature and experience of 'travel'. The flavour of these essays is difficult to capture in a short space such as this but they are essentially reflections provoked by these topics on the conditions which make those same topics available. What are the presuppositions, for instance, which make the whole concept of 'evaluation' possible? The notion trades on an implicit standard of correctness which is, in turn, made visible by the procedures for invoking assumed-to-be-shared understandings by evaluators and for applying them to specific instances. Although apparently empirical data appear, these are used more in the way that an improvisation returns occasionally to the theme which provoked it, to renew its inspiration, than as evidence in any conventional sense.

This sort of analysis is, perhaps, even more hotly contested than any other part of the ethnomethodological movement. In so far as most sociologists take any notice of it all, it is to regard it as so much obscurantist hog-wash. Such a conclusion would, in our view, be unfair. The work clearly represents one possible evolutionary line from Garfinkel's thought and the vigour of the counter-reaction does suggest that some raw nerves are being probed. Its uncompromising stance on the moral nature of sociology, and the exaggerated claims which this can generate, is a valuable corrective to many recent pretensions. Nevertheless, there do seem to be overstatements in this argument which perhaps leave room for other activities.

In particular, this analysis tends toward a divorce between the sociologist and other members of his society. They become an audience for his reflections rather than active co-participants. Theorising is a spectator sport, which is not to say that the spectators may not become emotionally committed to the spectacle and inspired to reproduce it themselves. However, the attack on the scientific monopoly of theorising presumes that any person may do it.*

* Dingwall (1976, 56) develops this argument, albeit in a misprinted fashion elsewhere:

> The world in which the scientist works is an everyday world that is taken as given. It relies on the same everyday judgements of what is real and reasonable as does the everyday world of any other member [of the scientist's society. This leads me to wonder if Schutz has not] mistaken the character of the province of meaning he purports to analyse as the scientific attitude. It may be better to describe it as a *theoretical* attitude to which anyone can resort.... (words in square brackets omitted in original).

Why then cannot sociologists treat lay members' theorising as resources for their own, theorising directed towards an inductive statement of the conditions of lay theories? If we permit this, then an empirical sociology would seem to remain feasible.

We have already noted the difficulties which ethnomethodologists have encountered in Britain, although their influence has had a vitalising effect in a number of areas, notably in the hybrid ethnomethodological ethnography. The Blumian doctrines have few adherents in a pure form. Both Raffel at Edinburgh and the Goldsmiths' group have moved in more empirical directions, although their work still has a distinctive character. The greatest problems have arisen in respect of conversational analysis which has attracted both talented staff and students in some numbers and set down a clear challenge to all orthodox practice which it has been prepared to back up by painstaking empirical work. Whatever else can be said about conversational analysis, no one can deny its commitment to research and to the implementation of its programmatic statements. As importantly, this commitment has been accompanied by a proclamation of intellectual rigour, which has sent a *frisson* through many critics, and of political independence. This challenge to the moral and academic standards of contemporary British sociology is one with which we have considerable sympathy.

However, conversational analysts have tended to be rather indifferent to the practical implications of their work. The study of courtroom interaction can be seen as making a contribution to the advancement of justice (whatever that might mean) although an improved understanding of interrogation might also have more sinister consequences. It is surprising that some of the commercial work on voice processing has not taken conversational analysis more seriously, in improving the capacity of computers to interact with humans. There would seem to be considerable contributions to be made to any personal service occupation which depends heavily on verbal interchange like teaching, psychiatry, nursing or social work. It would be unfortunate if the reaction against ungrounded utopian polemics led conversational analysis to be prematurely blighted through lack of funding from sources unaware of its possible contribution.

Nevertheless, as we have tried to indicate, there are important and unsolved intellectual problems. These would not undercut the conversational analysts' work as such, but would permit a wider range of inquiry than their strict reading of the ethnomethodological literature allows. A sociology which fails to respond seriously is one which will ultimately be impoverished. The present reaction epitomises many of our criticisms of the discipline in its rejection of a current which is marked by rigorous empirical inquiry and detachment from partisan political activity.

7 Sociology and policy research

One of the abiding myths of British sociology is the central influence of Fabianism. While not denying the powerful stimulus given to the discipline in its early days by the reformist tradition, it is all too easy to over-estimate its influence within the profession. Although a number of important figures in the post-war generation were concerned to apply sociological techniques and insights to the solution of social problems, the last twenty years have seen relatively few sociologists involved in this kind of work. If anything, the dominant mood has been anti-establishment and anti-empirical, and this in a period which saw a clear call for more social research by administrators. The test of the Fabianism myth is the very low level of involvement of sociologists in policy research, even at the level of survey technicians. This chapter explores some of the reasons for this non-involvement.

Government initiatives

In the opening chapter we noted the growth of an interest in 'statistical facts' both within and outside of government circles. The General Register Office had been established as far back as 1837, but with increasing government intervention in social policy, a demand for more detailed and wider-reaching information was created. In 1941 the Government Social Survey was set up and various Ministries were starting their own information units. In 1946 the Government Statistical Service was created. This demand for 'hard facts' about social conditions established the now normative statistical methodology of social policy research. That such a methodology was seen even at the time as having little relationship to academic sociology, with its emphasis on theoretical and analytical work, is not surprising. However, administrators' reluctance to accept anything other than quantifiable findings still persists in the policy research field.

The 1946 Clapham Commission Report recognised the government's need for social science research and its recommendations included not only an increase in the funding of social science in the universities but also the establishment of an Interdepartmental Committee on Social and Economic Research. This Committee was to have a dual purpose: that of advising and scrutinising data collection within government departments, and making such information more easily available and understandable to research workers. The Committee contributed to the publication of more official statistics and a variety of surveys were undertaken by Ministries. A further legacy of the Committee was the series of *Guides to Official Sources*, now more likely to be used as undergraduate teaching aids rather than for their originally intended purpose of assisting research workers.

By the early 1950s any impetus in social science research resulting from Clapham had waned and there were very few central initiatives for such research during the decade. However, the social and political climate of the 1960s was marked by a rapid development in the social sciences and an increased recognition of the need for social science research. Both the impact of the expansion in higher education following the acceptance of the Robbins Report, and the importance placed upon thorough research in the Report itself added to this growth in the social sciences. By 1963 the Heyworth Committee was set up with terms of reference 'To review the research at present being done in the field of social studies in Government Departments, universities and other institutions and to advise whether changes are needed in the arrangements for supporting and co-ordinating this research' (Heyworth, 1965, 1).

This period was marked by an increasing belief in the need for information about the extent and nature of particular social problems in health, education, housing, race, crime and other 'social deprivations' in order that they might be more effectively alleviated. For example, the Seebohm Committee Report, despite neither undertaking nor commissioning any research of its own (Seebohm, 1968, 21, para 43), saw it as 'wasteful and irresponsible' not to monitor the effectiveness of social work. Research in this field was to be concerned with two areas: 'First, the collection and analysis of basic data and, second, the clarification, evaluation and costing of the main options available in tackling the problem' (Seebohm, 1968, 143). The Chronically Sick and Disabled Persons Act, 1970, also demanded that local authorities collect data on the extent of the 'problem'. Social policy research sponsored by local and central government was reaching its heyday. The CDPs were under way by the early 1970s (the CDPs are discussed in more detail in the next chapter) and many of the established research institutes, both inside and outside of the education sector, were carrying out an increasing number of policy-oriented research projects. At the same time, there was a rapid expansion in both the number of research institutes and personnel in both central and local government (Cherns and Perry, 1976).

Sociologists and policy research

The state of sociology and research in sociology, even in the early 1960s, was still one of gradual development handicapped by restrictions in both funds and personnel. Its research effort was primarily concerned with the generation of middle-range theory and the description of specific social institutions, i.e., with the development of academic sociology. It is therefore understandable that the Heyworth Committee was unable to find much evidence of any policy-oriented research undertaken outside of the government sector.

This is not to suggest that no sociologists during this period were concerned with social policy issues. Such work as was being undertaken was not government sponsored and tended to be buried in the universities and the few independent research institutes. (For example, Townsend's study, *The Last Refuge*, 1962, was based at the LSE and funded by the Nuffield Foundation.) However, the social policy of the Conservative administration was based largely upon information generated from within the various government departments or from occasionally commissioned surveys undertaken by market research organisations. Thus sociologists' opportunities for explicit policy-oriented work were limited for political reasons.

Donnison (1978) has argued that sociology's influence upon social policy at this time was by means of the social networks of the predominantly London-based 'liberal left'. The contact that prominent social scientists, for example Titmuss, Abel-Smith, Michael Young, Halsey and Donnison himself, had with the intellectuals in the Labour Party – particularly Richard Crossman and Anthony Crosland – must be recognised as having a significant effect upon subsequent policy debates (see, for example, *The Crossman Diaries*). Further, weeklies like the *New Statesman*, *New Left Review*, and after 1962, *New Society*, were bringing the work of such academics to the attention of a larger audience and stimulating both a wider debate upon policy issues and a greater pressure for change. Obviously, Labour governments were more open to this diffusion of ideas than were the Conservatives.

The changing climate of opinion and increasing awareness of social problems which occurred in the late 1960s led to a greater recognition of the contribution which social science in general could make to the understanding of social conditions. The commissions set up by the 1959-64 Conservative government to investigate such issues as housing (the Holland Committee) and Higher Education (the Robbins Committee) both relied heavily upon information from *social scientists*; the Robbins Report of 1963 being under the chairmanship of a social scientist (Lord Robbins was Professor of Economics at the LSE) and having a social statistician (Claus Moser) as one of its principal investigators. In contrast, *sociologists* played very little direct part in these developments and although their work on community and family life had an influence on planning policy and other social services, it was to key figures in the fields of social administration, social statistics and economics that the new Labour government turned in 1964. (The 1974-9 Labour government also appears to have relied on a similar group, for certain contributors to the *Journal of Social Policy* were kept waiting nearly two years for a decision on publication because the referee was fully occupied in his capacity as Chairman of the Supplementary Benefits Commission!)

This passing of the initiative to other disciplines at that time, despite a willingness of some sociologists to be involved, resulted from three factors. First, the number of sociologists was still very small and few of the sympathetic or committed sociologists had yet gained the academic eminence associated with the social network referred to by Donnison. Second, the majority of sociologists were not particularly interested in policy-specific research *per se* but rather in 'social problems' only in so far as they were relevant to some problems of sociological theory. Third, many experienced sociologists, including those who were interested in social policy, were mainly involved in establishing the growing number of sociology departments in the aftermath of the Robbins and Heyworth Committees. There were some exceptions: Halsey became involved in the EPA experiments (1968) and Michael Young (admittedly never a conventional academic sociologist) was concerned first with a policy-oriented SSRC (from 1965) and then with the promotion of Community Councils following the Redcliffe-Maud Report of 1970.

However, this explanation does not allow for the resistance from policy makers which was encountered by sociologists who did attempt to apply their skills to social problem analysis. A good illustration of this is in social work, which looked a very promising field by the end of the 1960s. In local government, the post-Seebohm social services departments began recruiting sociologists as research officers, and in 1972 a national Social Services Research Group was established to encourage and co-ordinate research in this area and to raise the standards of the research undertaken:

> The first objective must be to establish an organisation which has: (a) strong regional groups with resources to support and stimulate social services research, and (b) is guided by a representative national executive committee. The second objective should be to improve the relevance and quality of statistical information about the activities of social services agencies. The third objective should be to demonstrate the contribution that research can make to development planning in the social services. The fourth objective should be to promote training for social services researchers, particularly those already working in local authorities. The fifth objective should be to encourage a more fruitful dialogue between local authority and 'academic' researchers in the social service field (Byre, 1973).

However, these objectives were not attained for several reasons. First, social services operate on fairly tight budgets and 'service' was regarded as more necessary than research, despite the Seebohm Committee's stress on its importance. Consequently, any cuts in public expenditure necessarily meant that research expenditure was cut back before services (and this has particularly been so since 1974). A second, and very significant, reason for the failure of SSRG was that, as one of the present authors found on being brought into the group as an 'academic' researcher, although the social services directors and many junior staff were eager to develop close liaison in social services research, the middle management personnel within the departments were largely uncommitted. This group, composed of deputy and assistant directors, comprised predominantly middle-aged, old-style social workers who did not accept the Seebohm view of research or even the general findings of Seebohm itself. Their views were overtly anti-academic and they believed in action and developments based on practical experience and 'common sense'.

This view, with its fear of scrutiny and rigorous academic standards, is still prevalent in social work practice and education (even at the highest level). Research continues to be treated as a waste of public money because it constitutes a threat. Third, and clearly evident in the above quotation, was the narrow conception of social research which prevailed. Research was primarily regarded as consisting of surveys and statistical analysis, and it was to the development of techniques in these areas that the SSRG was committed. Research was to be a predominantly atheoretical, fact-collecting activity; generating information on which social

146

service professionals could formulate policy. It was viewed as a separate and subordinate function, with researchers playing no active part in the policy-making process, the latter being the realm of the 'professional' social worker. Even so, sociological researchers were increasingly expected to be 'professionally' qualified in social work itself.

In addition to the employment of in-house teams within social services departments, other local authority departments began recruiting social scientists in research posts, notably in planning and housing, and some of the larger local authorities set up their own central research and intelligence units (Newcastle-upon-Tyne, for example). However, the same limited definition of social research predominated, with surveys providing the 'hard' facts for management decision-making. Few administrators recognised the wider contribution of sociology or accepted any other research techniques as appropriate. This ethos was ironically illustrated by the experience of one of our more anti-positivist students who found difficulty in obtaining a job after graduating. Eventually he accepted a research post in one such local authority department. He was shocked to find that instead of being the consultant and sociological adviser which he had assumed, he was expected to spend his time as a survey technician designing and administering various questionnaires for the collection of data on administratively-defined problems'.

Bulmer has recently commented on this lack of occupational recognition for researchers as sociologists *per se*: 'The role of research is defined as being technical, providing intelligence or doing short-term problem-solving research' (Bulmer, 1978, 37). Sociologists were therefore allocated a technical role and, unlike statisticians, natural scientists and economists, no 'Government Sociologist' posts were created within the Civil Service. Instead sociologists are predominantly found in Research Officer or Social Survey Officer posts. Bulmer sees this servicing role as being compounded by the fragmentation of such posts in central government and hence the lack of development of any distinct caucus of sociological expertise. It is still too early to judge whether the recently formed Social Research Association will take on any significantly sociological character, although it seems unlikely.

The emergence of the Social Research Association reflects the extent of the growth in social research outside of the academic world. As Bulmer has noted:

> In central government, local government, market research and polling organisations, independent research agencies and autonomous research institutes, there are probably more people

employed to do social research than there are staff employed on research in higher education (Bulmer, 1978, vii).

With such a demand for, and recognition of, social science skills in central government, Bulmer finds it 'curious' that the contribution of sociology (amongst others) has remained unrecognised (ibid., viii). As we have seen there are several historical reasons for this, but these do not fully explain current attitudes. As Marsland puts it: 'even to the extent that sociologists have been involved in policy research they have done so, I think, reluctantly, apologetically, as a side line, moonlighting from their real work, less than fully constructively, much less than fully effectively' (Marsland, 1979, 2-3).

Policy research and policy making

Why should this be? Arguments advanced for not doing policy research range from questions of relationships with the state to the essential character of the discipline. One of the most pragmatic of these objections is that it makes no difference to the ultimate form which policy takes.

It remains problematic whether policy research actually influences policy making. This is a question which is seldom analysed in detail by sociologists: it is certainly hard to demonstrate cases where policy research findings appear to have had a direct impact on the formulation of policy. The surveys undertaken as a requirement of the 1970 Chronically Sick and Disabled Persons Act, for example, have had little influence on social policies towards the disabled. (That the DHSS did not press local authorities to comply is an indication of their views on the importance of the surveys.) Indeed, one of the consequences of such surveys was to show how inadequate were the available resources to cope with demand (Harris and Buckle, 1971) – and any changes in social policy towards the disabled have been a result of the act itself.

Following Donnison (1978), the influence of sociology has been largely by diffusion through the various social networks of eminent academics, rather than by the direct influence which one might naively expect to be exerted by commissioned or in-house research. Their comments and advice were sought out and accepted because of their depth of understanding, in addition to their connections with influential social networks. This more covert influence is seen by Donnison to be subject to a similar time-lag as that of the 'mission-oriented' research of science and technology, with diffusion, acceptance and assimilation into policy developing gradually over a period of years. Thus, the Bethnal Green studies and

Halsey's work on social class and education influenced policy only some time after they were undertaken. Pessimistically, Donnison sees this type of influence waning, not only because of the present values expressed within sociology, but also because of the development of research and intelligence units within the bureaucracy itself and in the proliferation of quangos (it will be interesting to see what effect the present Conservative government's policies have on this).

Sharpe provides further evidence of the indirect influence which sociological research has had upon policy formulation in his comparative account of social science and policy in Britain and the USA (Sharpe, 1975). The contrast between the extensive involvement which American social scientists have in policy formulation and the low levels found in Britain is explained by Sharpe by the differences in both traditions and attitudes between the bureaucratic structures of the two countries. In America, there is a tradition of politicians being financed to employ their own teams of experts for the provision of policy relevant information, while in Britain an MP is likely to have limited help in this area; information being provided, in the main, by their own enterprise, civil servants or party headquarters. British politicians are thus more likely to be ignorant of the relevance of academic work and often regard such work with suspicion: 'It gives much greater weight to knowledge as accumulated experience – he who does, knows – and in its extreme form sees practical experience as the only legitimate source of knowledge' (Sharpe, 1975, 11). This attitude towards academics is echoed by the policy-making higher civil servants who are principally 'generalists' rather than specialists and, in contrast to their American counterparts, are 'politically neutral'. Their requirements are not for the detailed analyses of the academic but for clear and concise evidence and recommendations. Unlike the American bureaucracy, there is no tradition of wide scale appointment of academic specialists to the British Civil Service. Those academics (predominantly economists) who have been appointed as 'political advisers' by successive administrations since 1964 were never fully accepted by the permanent civil servants, who regarded them as subversive intruders (Haines, 1977).

Within such an administrative climate, therefore, it is unlikely that much real sociological research would be undertaken within government departments or commissioned by civil servants. Surveys of the kind undertaken by Harris and Buckle (1971) and Woolf (1971) in which any actual policy conclusions and recommendations are subsequently produced by the bureaucracy, are the normal research model. Thus, at best, academic influence operates through summaries of academic publications prepared for senior civil servants by their junior research staff – few of whom are sociologists.

Social research and sociological research

A second kind of objection to policy research is that it is not really sociological research at all. Of course, if one's interest lies in conversational analysis or marxist theory, such an argument is understandable, but what of the empirical sociologist concerned with substantive problems? Certainly, policy research is not identical to academic sociology. The term 'social research' is generally used by non-sociologists to describe the empirical activity which involves the collection and descriptive analysis of data about social facts or, even more limitedly, the term is applied just to the process of data collection, normally by survey methods. As against this view, when sociologists refer to 'social research', they mean the processes by which sociological knowledge is generated, i.e., sociological research, which includes a mix of concepts, hunch, data-gathering, analysis, perspective, interpretation, theorising and so on. Social research, in its general form might therefore be regarded as a sub-specialism of sociological research.

This distinction between sociological and social research helps to explain the low output of sociological policy research. Social research may be categorised into four broad groupings. The first includes work initially undertaken as *purely sociological research*, but which later becomes relevant to some aspect of social policy, either before or after its findings are known. For example, the studies of East London carried out by Willmott and Young in the 1950s had some influence on urban rehousing policy, while subsequent government commissions on education drew on the work of Floud, Halsey and Martin's *Social Class and Educational Opportunity* (1957).

The second category includes research which investigates a *topical social problem* in order to develop a deeper sociological understanding of the problem but which at the outset acknowledges policy implications. Julienne Ford's *Social Class and the Comprehensive School* (1969) was undertaken in an attempt to demonstrate the workings of comprehensive education, and Rex's *Colonial Immigrants in a British City* (1979) is another more recent example.

Third, we have work initiated by those concerned with a social problem and *commissioned* by them either with very firm guidelines or with a more general brief, leaving the formulation of the research to the researcher. The studies of family building patterns undertaken by Woolf for OPCS (1971 and 1976) fall into this

category, as do the more broad based health and health policy
projects financed by SSRC to

> explore the operational implications of different concepts of
> health by examining the social, economic and political mechan-
> isms by which health problems are or fail to be identified and
> tackled – looking particularly to the level at which the clients
> encounter the service providers (Brennan, 1978).

The final grouping consists of work carried out by permanent
research personnel within a particular institution as part of a
continuing need for information relevant to that institution. Little
of this *regular monitoring* type of research is published, except
perhaps in the form of HMSO reports (e.g., *Population Bulletin*) or
as part of county councils' structure plan documents.

Only the first two categories can be classified as 'sociological
research' as defined above: in the third category, research may or
may not be classified as 'sociological', depending upon the freedom
which the researcher is allowed in undertaking the investigation.
The fourth type of activity can not, in itself, be defined as
sociological. Indeed, it is questionable whether this activity is
'research' in the strictest sense, since much of it is purely
fact-gathering and, as the Heyworth Committee recognised in
1965: 'We would not, however, regard as research either routine
fact-finding, or fact-finding for specific administrative purposes,
and we have endeavoured to make this distinction in considering
our problems' (Heyworth, 1965, 2).

It will be recognised that the questionnaires and structured
interview schedules predominantly used in this fact-gathering type
of research are more easily scrutinised, and therefore controlled, by
the sponsoring body than the more intangible sociological activities
occurring in the type of research of the first two categories
(whatever the method of data collection employed) and in the
'softer' techniques of depth interviewing and participant observation. Further, quantitative data are likely to be regarded by
non-sociologists as more 'scientific' than qualitative data or theoretical statements: 'hard' methods count as science and so have
ideological value, as Habermas (1972) has shown.

The recently established Institute of Policy Studies provides not
only an example of this emphasis on survey research but also
illustrates the current popularity (among administrators) of inter-
disciplinary research. The aim of the institute is to establish a
multi-disciplinary team of social scientists working together on
various projects. This team is seen as being composed of:

> intelligent young social scientists who avoided the numbing

experience of university departments and have acquired a methodological 'box of tricks' gleaned from fieldwork and survey agencies. They are survey-minded, keen on immediate problems and tangible results (THES, 24.11.78).

The assumption that these 'keen young social scientists' will advance policy studies is highly questionable. In fact, these have been the dominant type of researchers in the past decade, and that is a poor recommendation. The use of a common methodology, survey research, is a weak basis for drawing together the several social sciences: the differences run deeper than that. Worse, it suggests a crass lack of concern for theory. Good research needs to be bedded in theory, and such theories have for the most part been developed within single disciplines. Multi-disciplinary research divorces the research problem from its intellectual context, one which has taken many years to develop. Some academics may be guilty of insularity, but projects will not benefit if teams consist of mutually incomprehensible experts. This fashionable approach is firmly entrenched at DHSS (Lewis, 1979) and also at the SSRC (described in Chapter 12). That it is unattractive to most social scientists only serves to confirm the gulf between policy and academic research.

Despite this pessimism, we would argue that sociologists should undertake policy research, including commissioned work, as long as they are aware that they are not likely to be doing sociology. The issue for sociology is not the policy research itself but the way in which it is regarded by both the researcher and the funding agency. In those studies in which the problem is clearly defined by the sponsor, the sociologist becomes little more than a technician, which is intellectually unrewarding.

Such studies can, however, be of sociological interest if the researcher extends the basic brief, either by obtaining permission to collect more sociologically-relevant material in addition to the basic policy-relevant data, or by treating the research project itself as of sociological interest. This latter alternative is, although likely to be more fruitful, somewhat dubious on ethical grounds unless the sponsors are aware that their formulations and practices are being examined.

The type of research done by government agencies rarely appears in sociological publications. Usually undertaken as a 'one-off' investigation for a local agency, the results are written up as a predominantly descriptive report. Initially, the researcher might hope either to re-analyse or re-present the findings for a sociological audience, but, either because of the nature of the investigation or the sponsor's veto, such examples are rare in this country.

Policy research undertaken from within the agency itself suffers from similar limitations to these 'one-off' studies. However, in this instance the researcher is even more restricted in the way problems are formulated, and critical or controversial reports usually remain unpublicised. Shipman, although supporting such activity, inadvertently reveals its main weakness when he states: 'The applied social scientist can be found in government, social work, industry and international organisations. Here they not only use knowledge produced inside academic communities but collect much of the data on which academic work rests' (Shipman, 1972, 166-7). Shipman appears to misunderstand the nature of research and also the nature of sociological knowledge. Since 'knowledge' is not static, it is constantly being challenged, re-interpreted and added to, and few sociologists who have left the academic world for applied research posts are able to keep up with the state of such knowledge except in a very narrow field. What is more, data collection is not the same thing as research: data on population, health, education, etc., are based on policy makers' questions and problem-definitions, with all that that implies (Hindess, 1973). They cannot be uncritically employed by the sociologist.

This statistical apparatus is different from the output of a sociological research organisation. Much of the policy-oriented research undertaken by, for example, the Institute of Community Studies, the Institute of Race Relations and the various medical and health studies units, has contributed not only to policy formulation but also to sociological knowledge. The dangers of misinterpretation of sociological finding by non-sociologists are still present – as are the limitations upon the range of research topics – but many of the initial conflicts and misunderstandings concerning problem formulation are overcome.

One of the basic issues in all research is the question of ownership of the findings. Ideally research is undertaken for the furtherance of knowledge, but whether the information so generated belongs to mankind in general, or to those who have collected it initially or to those who financed it, is an ethical question. So far in sociology, no one has attempted to patent their work and the ownership of data is subject to a 'gentleman's agreement'. However, because of the possibility of plagiarism, many sociologists are reticent about discussing their research until they have clearly demonstrated through publication that it is their own work.

However, the extent to which data actually belong to the researchers when they have been externally financed is open to debate. The contractual agreement between researcher and sponsor usually includes a clause relating to the control of findings and any subsequent publications but this rarely receives sufficient attention.

As a minimum control, the sponsor will usually claim a right to scrutinise the findings in some way – for instance, the SSRC requires an annual report from its grant holders (although this requirement is more dictated by public accountability than by a desire to ensure control over results). If the investigation produces information which might be regarded as highly critical of the sponsor it is perhaps understandable that the sponsor might attempt to prevent the researcher from revealing it. Such sanctions can be of various kinds, from withdrawing support and destroying data to more subtle methods of delaying any publications arising from the research. The researcher who publishes critical findings is likely to find that both he and his institution are prevented from undertaking further investigations in the particular site.

An understanding about the control of findings needs to be established at the outset of any policy research. Researchers must attempt to ensure that those who make use of the information obtained realise its limitations and the usually tentative nature of any statements and recommendations. They cannot do this, with any degree of confidence, if the control over the findings is completely in the hands of the sponsor.

There are many sociologists who believe that the undertaking of empirical investigations to assist in the making and implementation of policy decisions is professionally unethical. Such studies can be regarded as providing information for those with power about those with little or none, and the sociologist, in such instances, might be viewed as a bureaucratic spy. The sociologist so commissioned might argue that such accusations are unfounded: rather than being a 'spy', the sociologist becomes a spokesman for the underdog. By providing information about the needs and opinions of a certain group, policy decisions can be reformulated and new policies introduced which have a closer relationship to the requirements of the 'users' than previous ones.

However, both of these arguments are incomplete. On the one hand, by providing information about social life upon which decisions may be made by those who have access to such information, all sociology may be regarded as unethical. Thus, non-commissioned research which has a bearing on policy can be as useful to policy makers as that which has been undertaken specifically as an aid to policy formulation. On the other hand, it might be argued that non-commissioned research has been carried out with different aims and objectives than those of the commissioned type. Further, since control over the results and the publications arising from such research is not subject to administrative scrutiny as is much commissioned research, the information revealed is available to anyone (Barnes, 1979, 154). To accept the argument of universal availability of non-commissioned research is to ignore the simple fact of differential access to research findings. Policy makers, at all levels, are far more likely to read accounts of relevant research than those who may be affected by the policies which have been influenced by such research.

In the preceding sections of this chapter, emphasis has been placed upon the problems of misunderstanding of sociological research by non-sociologists and it is here that the greatest ethical problem arises. However clearly the limitations of a study are stated, parts may be taken out of context, ignored or misinterpreted by the layman. Many of these misinterpretations and misunderstandings arise not only because non-sociologists are unaware of the limitations of sociology but also because sociology is regarded by many as common sense (Wall, 1968). Although sociology has developed its own terminology, it has relied mainly upon everyday language to express many complex and specific concepts and ideas. It therefore lacks the mystique of many other disciplines and much of its discourse can be understood – or misunderstood – by all.

Once the results of a study are available, the sociologist has little control over the readership or actions based upon it. Simply to accept that 'the ball is back in the court of the politicians, administrators and practitioners' (Barker Lunn, 1976), is to avoid one's professional responsibility. For this attitude merely compounds the misinterpretation. When sociologists undertake policy research (both commissioned and non-commissioned) they must acknowledge the possible consequences of their findings. They must also attempt to become actively involved in any decisions based upon them, extremely difficult though this may be in practice, given the power structure. To attempt to do less is unethical both professionally and personally. However, by attempting to become involved in policy making, sociologists may ultimately contribute to a clearer understanding of their discipline by laymen.

Policy sociology – a way forward

It is clear that sociology's impact and influence on social policy innovation has been severely limited and is in fact declining, notwithstanding the expansion in both sociology and policy research in the past twenty years. This state has been brought about by resistance among policy makers and by an increasing anti-policy stance within the discipline. Even those sociologists who have become involved in commissioned policy research have remained little more than technicians and the 'handmaidens of policy' (Greer, 1977). For the most part, sociologists have chosen either completely to ignore the policy dimension or to take a critical stance from the outside. They have justified this position on the grounds of intrinsic moral and political problems rather than facing up to these problems by active involvement. This attitude towards policy studies is found not only in marxism and phenomenology, but also in 'ordinary' everyday sociology.

But what this critical spectator-sociology, with its concern for disciplinary purity, fails to recognise is that however much it concentrates on non-involvement, sociology *is* involved in the policy field. Because of the very nature of the discipline, sociological knowledge will be used in the political arena:

> Almost all the topics that sociologists study, at least those that
> have some relation to the real world around us, are seen by
> society as morality plays and we shall find ourselves, willy-nilly,
> taking part in those plays on one side or the other (Becker, 1967,
> 245).

Given this intrinsic political dimension, it becomes necessary to question the role of sociology in society – sociology for what? Rex offers one possible answer when he states: 'We are sociologists, most of us, because somehow and somewhere we detect that sociology has a morally significant role to play for our personal selves and the world in which we live' (Rex, 1974, 3). For Rex, this role is primarily a 'demystifying' one:

> Sociology is a subject whose insights should be available to the
> great mass of the people in order that they should be able to use
> it to liberate themselves from the mystification of social reality
> which is continuously provided for them by those in our society
> who exercise power and influence (Rex, 1974, ix).

But how do sociologists impart these insights to 'the great mass of the people' if they remain within the confines of the academic world? Certainly not by concentrating on the present dominant activities of teaching, studying, thinking and writing. And, given that this sociological insight is more available to those with power than the powerless because of the differential access to knowledge, current sociology – even marxist sociology – can be seen as unconsciously adding to the manipulative abilities of the ruling classes. One way to correct this imbalance is for sociologists to become actively involved in the policy field.

This involvement does not necessarily mean accepting the values of the powerful, although the dangers of this are real. Whatever political stance is taken, sociologists should attempt to change or modify policies which they, as sociologists and moral actors, believe are wrong. We may not have power, but as sociologists we can have influence through the use and demand for sociological knowledge.

156

Clearly, the use of this influence in the policy field involves taking a political stance, but in sociology this is unavoidable. Such active involvement will force sociologists to clarify their own political and moral values.

The influence and involvement required is not of the kind achieved through the usual policy-oriented research role. For this activity, as we have attempted to demonstrate, is not only likely to assume the values and definitions of the policy makers, but also often reduces the sociologist to a servicing-technician of the bureaucracy. The involvement needed is of the type discussed and experienced by Pahl (1977): sociologist as adviser, with full membership of the particular policy making body. Also, rather than the one-sided 'outsider-understanding' that predominates at present, sociologists might acquire a deeper sociological understanding of how policy is made and implemented through their involvement. For example, Pahl's account of the conflicts, compromise and political debate which took place in the committee of which he was a member provides us with a greater appreciation of some aspects of the policy-making process, and this in itself is an area of worthwhile sociological investigation. As Pahl argues:

> If the everyday worlds with which we are most familiar are
> mainly those of the underdog or, at best, the middle dog, we are
> forced to fall back on accounts of non-sociologists for an
> understanding of the top dogs ... If one argues that our under-
> standing of the powerless has greatly improved sociological
> analysis, surely our understanding of the powerful could also be
> improved (Pahl, 1977, 130-1).

This does not mean that sociologists should become 'spies for the powerless', although this might be a possibility. Rather, we believe that sociology's contribution as we have outlined it could be made more worthwhile by such understanding.

Doubts are likely to be raised about whether sociologists would be allowed to acquire such a role. That our knowledge and contribution are needed is clear from the requests made to Pahl, Donnison, Young, Townsend and many other sociologists at a national and local level. This involvement does not mean that we should not make a 'prior analysis of the actual policies being pursued by the powerful' (Rex, 1974, ix). This can be attempted before involvement, as part of the clarification of personal moral and political values. In this version of policy sociology, more genuine sociological research could be undertaken, based upon those units which have proved most successful in the past: firmly entrenched in the academic sector but developing a different relationship and a greater dialogue with policy makers.

To a large extent this relationship determines the way in which research findings are interpreted and assimilated as policy-relevant information. At present, these channels of communication and information networks appear to be inadequate and few personnel at either end have much knowledge or understanding of the other's requirements or limitations. Administrators require clear-cut conclusions and recommendations, simply stated and devoid, as far as possible, of ambiguities, exceptions and theoretical rendition. In such work there is little time to wade through complex and lengthy reports. The sociologist, on the other hand, is often unable, both because of the constraints of his discipline and his assessment of the tenets of good research, to produce the kind of report required.

If it is accepted as possible and desirable that sociology should have a greater impact upon policy decisions, then the sociologists so involved should attempt to communicate in the language of administrators, rather than criticise the administrators' abuse of what usually appears as a sociological report. Sociologists so involved have perhaps to master two sociologies: the sociology of the academic and the more applied sociology of the administrator. In this respect, sociology itself has a responsibility to come to terms with the different uses to which its body of knowledge is put, and to encourage a more open attitude towards those sociologists outside the academic nest. We must look forward to

> seeing sociologists employed as sociologists in many roles
> besides research roles in all sorts of organisations: seeing such
> sociologists fully involved in the policy process as sociologists:
> seeing sociologists of different persuasions and complexions
> arguing with each other publicly in the formal and informal
> meetings where policy work is done: seeing sociologists looked
> to for authoritative guidance on sociological issues (Marsland,
> 1979, 17).

However, this development cannot be achieved by sociologists alone. The policy maker, if acknowledging that sociologists have a valuable contribution to make, should also become far more aware of the language of sociology and accept the sociologist as part of the policy-making process, rather than as an outsider. Administrators should recognise that many findings which are critical are a necessary part of the policy-making process and not, as often occurs, a direct personal or political attack.

Such a development requires changes in both disciplinary boundaries and in bureaucratic structures. From sociology, it demands an acceptance of policy sociology (as distinct from social administration) as a legitimate area of activity. The knowledge which has been acquired about social life by sociologists is little used by them in practice. The discipline has, perhaps, been too concerned with epistemological problems to the detriment of the development of this knowledge. The consequence of this particular stance has been that sociological knowledge has been used in decision-making without a full understanding or appreciation of its limits. The virtually complete non-involvement of sociologists in policy formulation has been, of course, not only because of the views of sociologists but also because of the particular organisational structure of policy making and implementation. Sociological research and knowledge can become more constructive in policy making only when administrators and their political masters accept sociologists (and other social scientists) as advisers and consultants rather than in the research technician role which is more commonly adopted at present.

Is this possible? It would be wrong to imply that the problem will be solved by a simple change of heart. Nor should it be thought that by doing policy research we will endear ourselves to our political masters by showing the 'relevance' of our discipline. Indeed, the more good sociological policy research that is done, the greater the potential threat that sociology can pose, because it will become more difficult to dismiss unpalatable findings as unscientific or unreliable. There *are* some practical short-term gains to be made by embracing policy research, not least research funds and career opportunities, but these are not sufficient grounds on which to argue for change. The motivation for that must come from a fundamental concern with understanding the world in which we live, which owes more to ethics and general philosophical considerations than to sociology as narrowly conceived.

part three

8 Sociology and action research

Action research is a special case of policy research. It is a form of social experimentation in which a 'problem' is investigated in order to develop an 'action strategy' as a possible solution. The action decided upon is monitored and, on this basis, modifications or changes in strategy are made, with further monitoring and adaptation. Thus, research becomes an integral and continuing activity within the action process, rather than the external, before-and-after, or control group design most commonly associated with research undertaken on social innovation (e.g., Mann and Hoffman, 1960). This approach might be regarded as a possible way of achieving a closer sociological involvement in the policy-making process. However, its use is fraught with serious methodological, ethical and interpersonal problems. These problems can be seen as arising largely from the multi-disciplinary base of the approach and its rather eclectic methodological framework.

A number of different aspects of action research can be emphasised. Duncan Mitchell's view of action research could equally apply to a broad range of policy-oriented work resulting in policy initiatives: 'Action research is investigation of a kind oriented to the ends of altering and improving a social situation or helping people in need' (Mitchell, 1968, 2). This concern with policy change is also underlined by Town when he states that action research is 'the knowledge and research techniques of social science ... combined in practical application to plan and achieve change' (Town, 1973, 573). In contrast, the SSRC definition concentrates upon the service/consultancy role of the researcher: 'Research commissioned to monitor and evaluate the operations of specifically implemented policy schemes so as to enable policy makers and administrators to assess the effectiveness of such schemes' (SSRC, 1970). Clark (1972) appears to bring these two aspects together by stressing the researcher's involvement in the action process, while Lees concentrates on its dynamic aspect:

> A dynamic interaction between the social scientist and the practitioners as part of the ongoing experimental process.... Together they would be trying to solve problems in improving the effectiveness of a particular ... service experiencing real administrative constraints. This process would be adaptive rather than controlled, with changes evolving out of increasing awareness and emerging opportunities (Lees, 1975, 4-5).

Such an approach suggests a philosophy of research which accepts continuous experimentation, which is problem specific and is of limited generalisability. Basically an extension of the casework approach to social problems, its contribution to social policy formulation is therefore limited. Underlying this philosophy is an assumption that social problems can be alleviated by locality specific incremental changes, without the necessity for major structural reform.

The popularity of action research in Britain during the late 1960s was part of the increasing demand for social policy initiatives based on research. Such 'experiments in social administration' were seen as bringing together personnel in central and/or local government agencies, social scientists, and the local population in small-scale projects. These teams were intended to study, initiate and monitor action strategies to alleviate 'social deprivations' at the community level. We can explore the utility of action research by looking at the performance of several examples. The Home Office-sponsored Community Development Project (CDP) was not the first experiment in action research in Britain, although it is now perhaps the best known example. However, the Tavistock Institute utilised this approach from as early as the late 1940s as part of its consultancy activities in industrial organisations (Jacques, 1951) and the LSE Industrial Relations and Work Behaviour Unit began methodological experiments into action research strategies in 1968 (Thurley, 1972).

Action research in organisational innovation

The consultancy work undertaken by the Tavistock Institute employed what are now taken to be action research techniques in attempting to fulfil clients' requirements for improving or changing relationships and structures in particular organisational settings. A variety of social research techniques were used to investigate broad aspects of these organisations and to identify problem areas before instigating improvements and changes. Any changes implemented were then further monitored to evaluate their effectiveness.

Because the approach adopted was based on the traditional client/consultant model, it was extremely problem-specific in perspective and conclusions. This has led both Brown (1967) and Rapoport (1970) to conclude that the Tavistock studies have limited application and relevance to the general body of organisation theory.

In contrast, the LSE experiments were set up to investigate the contribution and applicability of the various action research strategies to particular organisational settings. The approach was thus intrinsically different from the Tavistock studies in that the projects were instigated by the researcher and unspecific in terms of the organisational problems to be investigated. The experiments developed out of a growing dissatisfaction with the more usual social research strategies:

> First of all our experience had shown the ineffectual nature of much university based 'pure' social research.... Secondly, the connection between research and policy change seemed a hit or miss affair.... Social research could easily be attacked as a 'con' game in which academics made half promises in order to get collaboration, promises which were conveniently forgotten as the time taken to prepare the lengthy research report wore on (Thurley, 1972, 19).

Action research was seen as a possible way of overcoming these problems. Instead of one long term project, the team decided to work on a number of smaller projects of short duration which would encourage closer collaboration and co-operation to develop between the researchers and the various personnel involved. In this way it was felt that constant feedback from the researchers would encourage initiatives to develop from within the organisation and, on the other hand, such collaboration would enable a clearer understanding of the research objectives themselves, and a greater insight into the workings of organisations. Hence, it would be of direct relevance to organisation theory.

With these aims, the LSE unit chose two areas for study: management in the ports industry and the organisation of public building maintenance. This choice was determined by the fact that, although both areas were regarded as in need of organisational change, there were no clear ideas or arguments within the organisations about the type of changes needed. Funding was divided between the SSRC and the various national bodies concerned with the particular organisations, and there was, therefore, no clearly defined 'client' in financial terms. Thurley's assessment of the projects shows them to have been of some success in specific areas, particularly in improving research formulation and data understanding by the research team; and discussions within local working parties enabled the various 'clients' to develop both a clearer understanding of the problems and a change in some of their attitudes. The conflicts which emerged, however, led him to regard action strategies as having only limited applicability:

> We conclude at the moment that action research strategies have validity in limited circumstances where four criteria are met:
> (a) Where the team is allowed to investigate and think around a specific problem area and where the boundaries of this area are continually renegotiated in an explicit fashion.
> (b) Where there is a general consensus that there is a 'problem' (although there will be different views as to its nature).
> (c) Where a research team contained a variety of skills in the social science *and* technical knowledge.
> (d) Where the conflict level between the parties is neither too low or too high (so that political 'warfare' is taking place) (Thurley, 1972, 21).

However, although these studies were early examples of action research in Britain, neither of them has become as deeply ingrained in the social policy consciousness as the Community Development Project (CDP) and the Educational Priority Area (EPA) programmes. These were the first major attempts at social experimentation using action research. Because of the greater number of agencies involved in implementing policy decisions in the social welfare field, the particular kinds of action research strategies adopted, and the problems that developed, the outcome was very different from the earlier organisation-based examples.

The EPA experiments

The EPA programme was established in 1968 to discover and evaluate methods of implementing the recommendations for 'positive discrimination' towards the primary and pre-school education of children in areas with high levels of poverty. The programme was funded by a three year joint grant from the SSRC and DES and co-ordinated by Halsey at Oxford. It was undertaken in five selected areas: three in inner-urban locations (Deptford, Birmingham and Liverpool), a mining area in the West Riding of Yorkshire, and Dundee. The Scottish research was conducted under separate direction and sponsored by the SED and the SSRC. Each team, although under central direction, operated with a considerable degree of autonomy within the original guidelines.

The first tasks for all five teams were the collection of base line data from the 1966 10 per cent Sample Census and from school records; a survey of teachers' career histories, attitudes and job satisfaction; interviews with a sample of mothers, and the administration of a number of educational ability and attitude tests to all children in the schools (Halsey and Payne, 1972). Because of the particular settings of the local teams and, to some extent, the need to test out a number of different action strategies, each local team then developed its own series of initiatives. For example, the Birmingham project began a literacy drive, a pre-school group and introduced the idea of 'home-school liaison teachers', who worked partly as teachers and partly as social workers. In addition to pre-school groups and language programmes, the West Riding team established a community centre.

It is interesting to compare the accounts and assessments of the EPA by Town (1973), Halsey (1972, 1978) and Halsey and Payne (1972). All stress the locality-specific nature of the action programmes but, whereas Halsey and Payne concentrated on the formal descriptions of the various achievements of the local teams (probably because of the restrictions imposed in reports to sponsors), Town emphasised the lack of any genuine action research in the programmes. This he sees as arising not only from the initial brief, which required teams to pursue a 'wide range of loosely formulated objectives', but also from the problems of negotiating action strategies at a local level, which effectively meant obtaining agreement about both the problems and necessary courses of action with each school. Thus, a formal evaluation design was virtually impossible, and the research undertaken concentrated upon descriptions of the action strategies and their implementation (Town, 1973, 586-688).

The account by Halsey and Payne indicates a possible reason for this lack of evaluative work. In all of the areas except the West Riding, the pupil turnover was extremely high, thus making long-term monitoring very difficult. However, despite these problems, some evaluative research was undertaken. The Birmingham literacy drive was assessed by the use of educational tests, and a marked improvement in the test scores of pupils after the introduction of the literacy programme was found. Again, the Birmingham team used control group techniques to measure the effect of introducing pre-school groups. Town, however, sees such evaluation as having little connection with the action strategy:

> while the report of the projects advocates the idea and suggests ways in which it can be organised, it does so on the basis of distilled experience reinforced by the findings of other studies, rather than on the basis of any independent assessment of the value of the work (Town, 1973, 587).

167

Consequently, Town sees the main weakness of the EPA programme as that of the manner in which these local 'case studies' were used to formulate national policy recommendations, without recourse to any systematic evaluative research.

In contrast to this anxiety, Halsey is more concerned with the basic philosophy of the EPA programme:

> A basic assumption of the EPA programme is that the most advantageous point at which to break into the vicious poverty circle is in early childhood ... and this approach tends to lead to considerable emphasis on working with families, thus raising fundamentally the question of limits to the rights of the State, through its agencies, to intervene in the relation between parents and children (Halsey, 1978, 153).

If one has doubts about both the role of the state and the fundamental causes of poverty, such action programmes can only be regarded as having a minor (and short term) impact on the state's definition of 'poverty'. If, as Halsey suggests, structural changes are the only means of combating social deprivations, then it is with the illustration of such weaknesses that research and action in the social policy field should be concerned. And local educational initiatives, alone, cannot achieve this.

On the basis of this brief assessment of the EPA programme, the limitations of action research in social policy seem to lie in inevitable practical difficulties, and the problem of generalising from local studies. The results of such small-scale experiments are able to indicate possible locality-based initiatives but it is only by systematic macro-sociological research that the structural dimension of inequality can be tackled. If we apply Thurley's four criteria we can see that the teams did contain the necessary sociological and educational skills, and the conflict level was acceptable (discussion with teaching staff took up a considerable amount of time but there is little evidence of open hostility or complete agreement). However, the first two criteria could not be met because of the broad nature of the problem and the need to generate national policy recommendations.

The establishment of the CDPs

In 1969 the Home Office announced the creation of an experimental community development programme as part of the government's 'Poverty Programme'.

In setting up the CDP, the Home Office recognised not only the limitations of national policies but also the organisational changes which had occurred during the previous few years. The initiative was to bring together central and local government, voluntary agencies and academics in an attempt to develop new ways of solving a wide range of social problems and deprivations.

> In the past, official efforts to analyse and meet social needs in the interlinking fields of employment, income security, housing ... and so on, were largely compartmentalised. Nowadays, however, the number of compartments is gradually diminishing ... and their degree of separation is also lessening. The CDP seeks to identify and demonstrate, by reference to the problems of selected small local communities, some practical ways of taking this trend further, through consultation and action among the separate departments of central and local government and voluntary organisations and the people of the local communities themselves (Home Office, 1971).

In each of twelve selected urban areas with high levels of social need, a project and a research team were to be established. These teams would work closely with each other, the local authority, and the central research and action teams, based at the Home Office. Each project team was to be appointed by the local authority concerned, 75 per cent of the cost being financed by an Exchequer grant. The primary tasks of the action team were to be the identification and assessment of need, and the production and promotion of local schemes. There was also to be a continuous feed-back to the central team and notification of problems unable to be remedied at the local level. The research teams, fully financed by the Home Office, were to be based at appropriate universities or polytechnics. Their tasks were to assist with the assessment of need and to continuously monitor and finally evaluate the project.

In this version of action research, the researchers were defined as playing an advisory role, providing the necessary 'facts' for the separate action teams to evolve action strategies at the community level – and monitoring the resulting activities. This separation, together with the high level of flexibility allowed the local teams and the lack of clear direction from the centre, led to many of the now familiar problems associated with the CDPs, as the following examples will show.

The CDPs in operation

The first illustrations of action research in community development are taken from work undertaken by the Batley CDP which was established in November 1971. The information used here was drawn from Lees (1975), Lees and Smith (1975) and relevant papers from the Papers in Community Studies Series, University of

York.

One of the initial investigations of the Batley CDP was to identify the 'Immigrant Situation', i.e., the social needs of the immigrant population, and to promote involvement and self help within this community. The first step was to gain as much background information as possible from existing statistical information and from discussions with various local officials, social workers, etc. The two bodies most closely involved with immigrants were the Community Relations Council (CRC) and the Muslim Welfare Society (MWS) but each, because of various conflicts, worked completely independently of each other; the CRC concentrated on inter-racial relationships and the teaching of English, and the MWS concerning itself with preserving the traditional culture through religous teaching.

The main aim was to assess both 'normative' and 'felt' need (McGrath, 1975) and to establish methods by which such needs might be met through self-help and understanding. From discussions with local officials, the team was able to identify the 'normative' needs of the immigrant population as being primarily concerned with language, health, housing and education. The 'felt' needs (i.e., those perceived by the individual or group in need) were more difficult to assess since no obvious contact agency could be identified.

Eventually, the team decided that contact via the CRC was likely to have adverse effects upon the project because of the rift between the CRC and the MWS. The team hired a student who was fluent in both English and the two most common immigrant languages. She conducted interviews with the leaders of the MWS and undertook more informal discussions with other members of the community. Meetings were then arranged between the MWS and the CDP members.

From such meetings it became clear that the MWS were almost totally concerned with the religious and cultural needs of the immigrant community. Since these were seen as likely to be only part of the 'felt' needs of the immigrants themselves, it was thought that a survey of such needs amongst the immigrants themselves would be necessary. With the help of the MWS a questionnaire was designed and interviews were carried out with 43 households. The results of this study suggested that language problems were seen as the most important area of difficulty, followed by housing and education. However, racial discrimination was not explored in any depth because of the reluctance of the MWS and the reticence of the respondents.

The project was a limited success. First, useful information was obtained on the structure and leadership of an immigrant organisation. Second, local officials were made aware of some aspects of the needs of the immigrant community. And third, during the undertaking of their investigations, informal help and advice were given by the team and, by concentrating the work of the groups involved upon the problem of immigrant need, some degree of self-help was probably initiated and the project team itself established playgroups, etc.

However, several problems were not overcome. The MWS leadership showed little interest in the results of the 'felt' needs survey and continued to pursue its own particular goals. The long-held beliefs, values and ideas held by the local officials were not changed by the findings of the survey or by any of the actions of the team. Finally, and of most concern, was the hostile reaction of the CRC, whose membership would have been expected to have held similar values and goals to those of the project team, and to have been the most likely vehicle for the continuation of action at the local level. However, because of the non co-operation between the CRC and the MWS, the team had decided to use the MWS as its main contact with immigrants and only indirectly involved the CRC. This decision resulted in the understandable reaction of the CRC – namely, that the project team were usurping the role of the CRC. Over the period of the project, the CRC became increasingly critical of the work of the team and continued its own activities and aims. This highlights one key problem, that of operating in the local political system. With which group – if any – should one align oneself for an optimal outcome?

Further, the quality of the research undertaken must be questioned. Any action based upon the results of a survey which was conducted in only 43 households, and which did not explore discrimination in any depth, must be treated with some scepticism. Even though there were problems in asking direct questions about discrimination, a technical knowledge of questionnaire design should have made it possible to ask indirect questions. In addition, given that a large proportion of the research was of a non-directive nature, this area could have been explored in depth using such techniques.

The second part of Batley's CDP was closer to the formal definition of action research than the previous case. From initial investigations, Batley had been classified as a low income area with a high proportion of the population likely to be eligible for various welfare benefits. It was therefore decided to mount a welfare rights campaign in order to attempt to increase the uptake of such benefits. This campaign took the form of various types of action: working with local voluntary organisations to increase the awareness of benefits and to encourage pressure for improvements;

working with staff in the local agencies in an attempt to educate them about the needs of their clients; and initiating various publicity campaigns on benefits to discover the most effective methods of providing information on welfare rights. Research was planned to be undertaken on a before/during/after basis to monitor the effects of the campaign. Concurrently, it was planned to compare the uptake rates in Batley with those of six towns in which no campaign had been undertaken.

These then were the objectives of the campaign. What happened in practice stems largely from the personalities involved, and the fact that the CDP was neither an official agency nor a voluntary group. Events were further influenced by the different objectives of the research and action teams.

The members of the action team were initially not happy to work within the current benefits framework; they would have preferred to encourage community action to press for improvements in provision. However, they did eventually agree to the campaign but spent little effort on those aspects with which they had no sympathy. This attitude meant that the cost/benefit evaluative work could not be undertaken on means tested benefits in Batley, since the cost side became virtually impossible to assess. Further, work with the local officials had little success because of the conflicting value-orientations of the two groups. More success was achieved in the evaluation of the information literature on rent rebates and the help given by the action team in explaining the system to the claimants. Over half of the rent rebate claims in 1974 occurred in the six weeks after the leafleting and publicity campaign and the biggest take-up group were those in the private rented sector.

A further partial success was the action team's involvement in a tenants advice centre. This centre had been set up by a group of local residents before the project team arrived. With help and encouragement from the action team, the centre proved highly successful. However, because of its success, the centre applied for a grant from the CDP to extend its services and employ a full-time worker. After considerable pressure and argument, the centre was finally awarded a grant of over twice the amount for which they had applied, but with certain conditions: the management committee was expanded to include local councillors and members of the action team. These developments resulted in the centre being moved to new premises and the resignation of the original members. Despite these moves to incorporate the advice centre, the evaluative research into these developments found that the majority of clients approved of it, even if they had not been helped.

What is clear from Bradshaw's (1975) paper is that the particular values and ideals of the action team had an adverse effect on not only relationships with the research team and the local officials but, more importantly, on the success of the action research programme. His suggestions for successful action research are primarily concerned with achieving a balance between action and research. To achieve this, Bradshaw believes that the director of the team should be an experienced researcher with a commitment to evaluative research rather than to action. He further maintains that such teams should be joint action/research rather than discrete groups. Research in this area can only be fully successful if a carefully planned programme of action can be maintained. If action programmes are in a continual state of flux, research strategies cannot be fulfilled and only very simple before/after designs accommodated.

A South Wales mining valley is the setting of our final example of the CDP programmes. In contrast to the majority of other project locations, the Glyncorrwg CDP was located amongst a group of mining villages in the upper Afan valley. Also unlike many of the other CDPs, the Glyncorrwg project has been primarily concerned with the alleviation of social deprivation by investigating and advancing ideas for changing the economic infrastructure. The decline in the coal mining industry throughout the 1960s had had a dramatic effect upon the employment structure of the area: all three pits in the area had closed by 1970 and unemployment was around 8 per cent. The poor employment opportunities within the district were further aggravated by the lack of efficient public transport. These factors all tended to encourage a high migration.

The research programme concentrated on an economic analysis of the area: statistics for unemployment, vacancy, activity and migration rates were compiled from available sources. These data demonstrated the depressed condition of the local economy compared with those available for Great Britain. Further research by the team showed that one family in three was wholly or partly dependent upon social security benefits: this support was costing £23,000 per week.

Rather than encourage greater take-up of welfare benefits or fighting for an improvement in such services, as did the Batley team, the Glyncorrwg team suggested that action should be undertaken to alleviate the social and economic deprivations on three levels to increase financial self support:
(a) Action to improve the 'job-getting and job-holding capacity' of the population by better information services, education and training.
(b) Action to improve the physical accessibility of the employment

173

centres in the coastal area by an improved and subsidised public transport system.

(c) Action to increase the range of job opportunities within the area by promoting industrial relocation and incentives.

In undertaking its research programme the team recognised that action at local level would have only a limited success. Consequently, they put forward various courses of action to be taken at regional and national level in line with the three action strategies. In addition to these suggestions they promoted local initiatives. With the aid of the National Council for Educational Technology the project team established a community resources centre at the project headquarters. This centre, although primarily for schools, was extended to cater for the wider social and cultural needs of the community. Other local initiatives were encouraged, for example a mining museum scheme.

The team's main contribution to the alleviation of need in Glyncorrwg might be regarded as being primarily that of thorough research and clear and concise recommendations. In investigating the basic economic structure of the area, they were able to ascertain the more fundamental reasons for social deprivation: those of an economically declining area with few job opportunities and a poor transport network which prevented the population from seeking employment in the more prosperous coastal belt. From their analysis, they were able to conclude that action at the local level could only be of limited success in alleviating deprivation in an area of industrial decline. They therefore made their recommendations for action at regional and national level.

Locally they selected those projects which might help to alleviate some of the problems. Further, by putting forward a cost/benefit analysis argument, the team was able to persuade the local authority to subsidise a private bus service, which was in danger of being withdrawn and which provided the only public transport service between Glyncorrwg and one of the centres of employment for its population.

The CDPs: an assessment

In reading accounts of the various CDP programmes, one has an overwhelming impression of the inability of such small-scale projects to tackle the widespread problems of social inequality. The poor performance of the CDPs can only partially be blamed on the individual members of the project teams. More of the blame must rest with the naïve initial belief that certain needs could be met by action within a resistant official administrative structure.

Even the successful projects illustrate the failure of official agencies to deal with the administration of existing policy. The success of the welfare rights campaign in Batley clearly demonstrates how changes in information leaflets and publicity can result in an increased uptake of benefit entitlement. And the work with immigrants in the same area highlights the difficulties in changing long held beliefs and values – both of officials and of immigrants.

The same project illustrates how tenuous the relationship between teams and agencies could be: the Batley CDP succeeded in antagonising the local CRC, local authority officials and councillors and the founding members of the local housing advice centre. Clearly, any approach to alleviating deprivation at a community level must take into account the importance of the local power structure. This was acknowledged by the EPAs, who gained the sympathy of the local education authorities and committed much of their time to discussions with all teachers concerned. The CDPs for the most part ignored or did not understand the importance of establishing dialogue with powerful groups within the local community. Instead, they attempted to mobilise community action *against* the various local agencies without concern for the power, both financial and political, of such agencies. They were slow to develop community initiatives through community work and a proper community study (which was the implied intention of the original formulation).

This arises from two related factors. First, the very nature and aims of the CDPs attracted personnel who saw such projects as a chance of achieving structural change by motivating the community to question and to overthrow the system at a local level. Second, within the academic institutions approached, scepticism about the basic philosophy of the CDPs frequently resulted in those who were finally persuaded to take part being under-committed to the programme. Those who were recruited to the research teams were, in the main, young sociologists committed more to action than to research, with limited experience of the problems of the 'real' world and even less understanding of the life-styles and ideologies of the communities to which they were posted. Not surprisingly, they showed little desire to negotiate or to establish alliances with those influential sectors within the local community.

A second source of difficulties was the schedule of setting up the projects, for it was not until five years after the initial announcement of the CDP programme that all twelve teams were established. In that time not only had there been two changes of government, but also changes in the organisation of social services, local authority re-organisation, a different economic situation and marked changes in governmental beliefs and values concerning inequality. It is perhaps not surprising that such changes had important effects on the projects, and that conflicts arose.

Within individual projects, operational problems created further difficulties. There were changes in personnel and, more important, teams were established at different times. In the Coventry, Liverpool, Newham and Benwell CDPs, action teams were in post for two years before research teams were appointed, and in Paisley and Southwark research teams were working before the action teams were operational (CDP Project, 1974). The success of the Glyncorrwg project depended on detailed and thorough social analysis, but such detailed analyses are probably only possible with fully operational and co-operating teams, and in few of the selected areas was this achieved. Lack of synchronisation exacerbated basic ideological conflicts and generated a lack of understanding of the different roles of action and research staff.

Both from the inter-project Report (CDP Project, 1974) and from Mayo's (1975) account of the historical development of the CDP Programme, it appears that many of the problems which arose were a direct result of the lack of firm guidelines, or even advice, issuing from the central unit and the various internal problems and conflicts within the Home Office at the time. Initially the project was established with an extremely flexible structure, the original aim being that social scientists would have freedom to produce reports and recommendations for action based upon empirical research. These recommendations would be taken up by administrators from the various services working closely together, who would then be in a position to tackle the whole problem rather than the partial solutions which were currently being offered by discrete service agencies. The central team's functions were to act as a channel for these recommendations at national level and to give advice to the local projects.

This plan was not fulfilled for several reasons. First, the central team personnel, which was drawn from the range of departments concerned, was constantly changing; second, (and more significant), within this team conflicts developed over the goals and strategy of both the project as a whole and their own role in it. By 1971, relationships within the central team had become so strained that regular meetings were abandoned.

> This was partly the result of diversity of interests involved and the consequent failure to agree on goals strategies or tactics. It also reflected the centre's limitation in a broader context, particularly its increasing difficulty in responding to pressure and demands from local projects (Mayo, 1975, 12).

At this time, only four of the twelve local teams had been

established and, along with a change in government, a gradual change had taken place in the philosophy of social inequality. Instead of social need being regarded as pathological, with self-help as a partial solution to the problem, it was now regarded as a structural problem. This view was reflected in the findings of the local teams, who moved outside the original brief and became concerned with more fundamental issues (unemployment, education, housing, etc.). With no firm guidance from the centre, many teams became disillusioned and conflicts emerged between the various parties concerned. By 1974 the central team had been reduced to a small number of staff and its research unit disbanded. However, all twelve teams had become fully operational and were working largely independently of the centre.

From the CDP experiment it is possible to identify five main problem areas which contributed to the minimal achievements of the project. First, because of the comparatively large number of groups involved (the Home Office, various other central government departments, the local authorities, universities, various voluntary agencies and the project teams themselves) it is not surprising that conflicts over values, goals and definitions emerged. Such conflicts can be regarded as being further compounded by the obvious lack of any real control over the project as a whole.

Second, a commitment to the philosophy of experimental action in social policy is, as Smith confesses, difficult to put into practice: 'The promise is of dramatic change: the assumption that experimental action and the "superior vision" of research will somehow identify the magic ingredient' (Smith, 1975, 191). And this demand for 'dramatic change' leads inevitably, according to Smith, to a sense of failure, thus creating a third main problem: a sense of frustration by those actively involved, many of whom were utopian marxists.

The fourth main problem area was the lack of continuity in either the central or local teams. No clear pattern emerged and the resulting somewhat haphazard actions in many of the local projects fail to convince the observer of any real programme of community development. On the contrary, the impression given in many accounts is that of actions 'being a good idea at the time'. What was the real aim of the immigrant project in Batley, for example?

Finally, the philosophy of action research in community development itself creates problems, not only in the belief in incremental rather than structural change, but also in the concept of evaluative research. In many of the local projects, the research team became closely associated with action strategies and was, therefore, only marginally concerned with evaluation. Further, because of the way in which actions were instigated and implemented, little systematic evaluative work was possible. Again, while it might be possible to assess the actions of a separate, but closely related, team, evaluating the work of local officials is fraught with problems.

Action research in social policy

The translation of action research strategies from the problems of single organisations to the wider, and more overtly political, sphere of social policy has been of only limited success, both in problem solving and in methodology. For action research to be successful in the social policy field, a more systematic and limited approach than those of the EPA and CDP experiments needs to be adopted. This approach must relate to a specific problem or set of problems in a specific social setting for, as Cherns (1969) recognises, action research is probably the technique least able to produce generalisations.

Those projects which have been most successful have been concerned with solving clearly defined problems in specific industrial organisations. Although the Tavistock studies have made little contribution to theory, they were reasonably successful within the limited terms of reference which applied. In these studies, the action researchers adopted the consultant role and accepted the values of the sponsor. Further, action research was undertaken as an holistic method rather than in the dichotomised form adopted in the CDP. In addition, such projects were conducted within single organisational settings, and although competing interest groups were encountered, the range of agencies and influential groups which have to be negotiated within the wider field of community action is far greater. Such negotiations were accepted by the EPA as an essential part of the project. However, the dominant pattern in the CDPs was largely to ignore and, in many cases, antagonise local power groups.

The underlying factor which limited the contribution of these projects to social policy was, however, the basic problem of *level of intervention*. This, we would suggest, is a specifically sociological problem. Certain problems can be tackled at the community level, others only on a national, or international, level. If there is to be any hope of success, the key issue is identifying which is which. As Halsey had suspected, such problems as those which the CDP attempted to tackle were, and are, determined by wider structural factors, which could not be changed significantly by purely local action. The majority of CDP local teams recognised this failing early in the programme and some became disillusioned by their inability to encourage or initiate dramatic change, and consequently developed into little more than well informed pressure groups or

178

political activists. Others responded by either concentrating on very local problems or by switching their programmes to fairly detailed analyses of those structural conditions which were seen as basic causes of inequality.

At a far more fundamental level, it is doubtful that the approach adopted by either the CDP or the EPA can be defined strictly as 'action research'. As part of any problem solving exercise, a fully trained professional social worker or administrator should investigate the specific circumstances surrounding and impinging upon the 'problem' before deciding upon the course of action to adopt. The utilisation of some of the methods of investigation used in social research does not automatically define the process as anything more than good professional practice.

What appears to have happened in these experiments, particularly in the CDP, was an attempt to separate action from research. That failed in the first place because the actions initiated were undertaken without an accompanying research strategy being formulated, and, in the second place, because the actions were modified before research had been undertaken or could be adjusted to the changes. Also the research teams became involved in action to the exclusion of the application of sociological knowledge or the undertaking of specific research. Further, the later practice of undertaking more detailed analyses in order that recommendations might be advanced, cannot be regarded as a different research approach in policy studies.

In its strictest sense, action research is a process which utilises sociological ideas and research techniques to formulate and, subsequently, continuously to monitor, evaluate and modify actions to solve a specific problem. The separation of research from action and the reduction of research to a subsidiary role, which was evident in the CDP programme, is not action research. As such, the CDP approach to research is no different from many other examples of policy-oriented research, and one encounters again the familiar danger of the researcher as technician.

Action research in particular and policy research in general represents a specific type of empirical sociology, in which there is not just an opportunity for the sociologist, but also a call for assistance, the offer of financial inducement (as we shall see in the chapter on the SSRC) and even an institutional framework in which to operate. Policy research is by no means the only kind of empirical research, and it will be abundantly clear that it is fraught with difficulties. Each sociologist must make up his or her own mind as to whether these difficulties are just part of the game, or whether they are so completely insurmountable as to constitute sheer impossibility. Obviously, from their first hand experience, the

179

present authors do not see the enterprise as totally impracticable, although whether such research is really 'doing sociology' remains an open question.

What these last two chapters have graphically illustrated is that research is neither straightforward, tidy, or free from the political constraints that impinge on the rest of our lives. Policy research may be more overtly political, but it is only a matter of degree. All sociological research harbours such problems, as the following chapters try to show.

9 The new methodology

In the past, there has been relatively little written about the practice of social research. Of course, a multiplicity of prescriptive textbooks has been published, laying out the techniques of research in the same way that workshop manuals for car maintenance or Mrs Beeton's *Book of Household Management* provide technical procedures for the amateur car mechanic or the acolyte cook. These textbooks will continue to familiarise successive generations of new sociologists with the basic technology of data collection and analysis, but the genre has little to offer on the subject of the practice, as separate from the mechanics, of research. Other earlier accounts of research have tended either to be mainly concerned with problems of abstract theory, or have operated at the level of rather crude imputations of attributes to researchers and their subjects. Examples of the theoretical approach include Denzin (1970b) or Glaser and Strauss (1967), while some of the work cited by Friedman (1967) in his examination of research effects in social psychological experiments provides an example of attribute imputation.

An alternative to this approach is the autobiographical description of completed work, which has its modern origin in the USA with Whyte's (1955) appendix to the second edition of *Street Corner Society*, and has a growing number of American exemplars (e.g., Vidich, Bensman and Stein 1964; Hammond, 1964; Habenstein, 1970; Wax, 1971; Johnson, 1975). In Britain this approach is relatively underdeveloped, except for occasional manifestations in seminar papers, although one could refer to Beatrice Webb's *My Apprenticeship* (1926) with its account of her experiences working in the garment trades to gather data for a study of the social conditions of employees.

However, there has been a growing self-consciousness about

research, and a number of British writers have recently begun to extend the more traditional approach with commentaries on the interaction of theoretical perspectives and data collection. Fletcher's (1974) intellectual autobiography was probably the first contribution in this field, together with Platt's critique of the 'Bethnal Green Studies' and her more recent *Realities of Social Research* (1976). Several collections of commentaries have since become available: Bell and Newby's *Doing Sociological Research* (1977), Shipman's *Organisation and Impact of Social Research* (1976), and Brown *et al.*'s *Access Casebook* (1976), and (on Australian experiences) Bell and Encel's *Inside the Whale* (1978).

In this chapter, we concentrate more on Fletcher and Platt than on the others, partly for the very pragmatic reason that it is easier to discuss monographs than accounts written by several authors. A second reason is that many of the ideas contained in the collections echo those of the present authors and have been dealt with elsewhere in this book whereas the work of Fletcher and Platt raises wider issues. It will probably seem to the reader that we are excessively critical of what they have to say, but the books in question represent a new venture. Since there are no fully established conventions for this kind of work, each author is attempting to impose his own version of the ground rules for debate: the sociology of social research is 'Frontier Country'. By the same token, it is important that shortcomings in this new area of study are recognised by those of us also working in the same fields. If the *aims* of, say, Fletcher and Platt are generally rejected because the *style and approach* they adopt are less than perfect, then there is a danger that the systematic study of research (and hence sociology) as a social process will be generally impugned. These are important books: however critical we appear to be, we wish to build on many of their insights.

One further reason for criticism is inherent in this kind of work. When a sociologist comes to recognise that his research is a social process, that he himself is part of that process, and that the uncertainties, the mistakes, the rows, the constant crises are all an integral part of the outcome of that process, he is faced with a moral dilemma. As a 'scientist' he is bound to make available all information bearing on his results; but not only would this be embarrassing and often humiliating, it could be professional suicide. The norms of professional sociology militate against self-criticism: any expression of 'doubts' about the conduct of a project tend to raise doubts about the validity of the findings through a kind of 'guilt by association'. The ideology of scientism is responsible for this narrow view of research, by which, in the absence of any *reported* difficulties, each research report confers on itself the badge of respectability. A conspiracy of silence about organisational or interpersonal difficulties (which, by the dominant paradigm of what constitutes social science, defines away the processual problems as not relevant or indeed even any part of scientific activity) makes intellectual self-exposure almost as dramatic as sexual self-exposure, in that not all sociologists are equally willing to doff the fig-leaf of respectability which scientism lends them. Can an aspirant research worker admit to a view of his research which is reflexive and which stresses uncertainty and 'un-scientific' features, if he wants his findings to be publicly accepted and his own immediate and future career to be assured? Research assistants must care more for their immediate prospects of employment, while a research director must look to the maintenance of his reputation: both are structurally-constrained to mystify the research process. When writers like Fletcher or Platt present a fuller account of their experiences, they must by definition draw attention to those aspects of their own work which call for comment and criticism, but which other sociologists have avoided by being less forthcoming. This is not an accusation of dishonesty against such latter sociologists: what is being called into question is the contemporary social definition of what constitutes the legitimate boundary of research. The logical outcome of a wider redefinition of research as social process includes paying a higher price in mutual criticism than under the rules of scientism. In criticising Fletcher and Platt then, we are only carrying through the logic of their intellectual stance, as indicated in their written work.

Fletcher's *Beneath the Surface*

Fletcher's *Account of Three Styles of Sociological Research* is concerned with the relationship between styles of research and theoretical perspectives. His book is self-consciously an account of his own 'intellectual pilgrimage' in a personal quest for a satisfying relationship with his research which took him, over the best part of a decade, through the whole gamut of sociological practice from 'hard-nosed quantification' to 'empathic observation' to 'committed social criticism' – the three styles of research identified in his sub-title. The spiritual metaphors of 'pilgrimage' and 'quest' are intentional. We have tried to retain something of the flavour of Fletcher's enterprise in our own account, since he himself accords the *style* of his work equal status with its content (Fletcher, 1974).

The book begins in a methodologically orthodox fashion with Fletcher's account of two studies which he carried out using structured questionnaires to elicit data on various kinds of attitudes, values and behaviour. One of the studies examined the position of industrial supervisors and their exposure of the conflicting demands of shop-floor and management. The other examined the cosmopolitan/local orientations of lecturers at a technological university. Having presented us with these reports, Fletcher turns to ask what is actually involved in executing this type of research. He provides an illuminating (and more readable) example of Cicourel's (1964) theoretical criticisms of this approach as he chronicles the *ad hoc* reasoning which lies beneath the polished surface of the finished papers. Even a method which purports to be objective depends upon a constant and undocumented process of subjective interpretations and judgments. In more orthodox language, the 'quantitative researcher'* has the problems of fitting operational to theoretical definitions of concepts, of assembling questions into valid scales and of selecting the most plausible path analysis. These steps comprise the structure of the research, but the problem remains of fitting this logical structure to the series of events which it is intended to organise. Are the theoretical concepts linked in any sense to the everyday concepts which actors use to organise the world? Are the scale questions intelligibly linked for respondents as well as researchers? How are events to be matched to the categories available to describe them? In Fletcher's perspective, all research, in any field of study, is seen to depend upon the subjective reasoning of the researcher to link the social and natural world to the description given to it by his discipline. Whatever the practitioners may claim, there are no external criteria for the truth of their account, merely that of plausibility, the intuitive feeling that it looks all right. Although this argument is not carried to its logical conclusion the reader is pointed towards the view that scientific truth is a matter of social convention. Science cannot make any legitimate claim to objective, disinterested and impersonal knowledge.

Yet such claims have been made, and very successfully: why is it that such a philosophically unsound position has been so influential and why does it enjoy a continuing influence? Fletcher explains this in terms of two political processes, an academic intellectual crusade on the one hand, and the intentions of research financiers on the other: the two processes are mutually supporting. 'Quantification' has been vigorously propagandised across five continents and its supremacy upheld by fairly ruthless intellectual persecution. Fletcher mentions in passing some of the conflicts in American

---

* In this section, both the terms 'quantitative' and 'qualitative' are used in Fletcher's sense which, as we note below, tends to caricature the styles of research that he is discussing.

sociology in the 1950s between interactionist ethnographers and the Columbia/Harvard establishment (which we discussed in chapter 5). These conflicts did not arise from any deliberate malice: the quantifiers were as sincere as the Spanish Inquisition in their desire to eliminate error and to enforce a system of belief founded on divine certainty. Rather than attacking the personal integrity of the quantitative sociologist, Fletcher is more concerned with drawing attention to their worship at the altar of Certainty. Science tirelessly attempts to substitute its own rationality, which is identified with Absolute Reason, for the rationalities (in Science's terminology 'irrationalities') of human actors. The uncertainties of human conduct are to be replaced by the certainties of scientific prediction.

It is this element which has attracted the research financiers: the style of quantification is the imposition of a simplifying order on events, which is precisely what many people who utilise social research require. Because quantitative sociology is deeply concerned with enhancing the control of its social environment by its practitioners, it provides the means of control for its paymasters:

> Some situations *suit* quantitative sociology. Studies of so-called organizations and their inmates do. Studies which involve extrapolations of having been 'in' organizations do. Wherever there is a pressure for conformity, for uniformity, for mediocrity, for concealment in the grey mass, there is an opportunity for good quantitative sociology (Fletcher, 1974, 67-8).

It is in this way that quantitative sociology serves a political interest.

Yet this is not the core of Fletcher's criticisms. Quantitative methods may enhance the control of subject populations by elite groups. They may mock our everyday experience of the processual nature of life by claiming that this can be studied by means of sections frozen on some glass slide. They may be basically unable to fulfil their ambition of rendering human life certain and predictable. But for Fletcher, the crucial deficiency is that quantitative research has replaced scepticism by error. Since the quantitative researcher neglects the social nature of the research process, he does not know what is the status of his data or conclusions, nor how he came to arrive at them. His rock-like certainty is set on quicksand. There is a blinding contradiction between the ordered phantasms produced by the quantifier's inquiries and the chaotic reality onto which they are projected. In Fletcher's eyes, a person of integrity cannot simply slide through this contradiction but must embrace it and follow it where it leads.

In his case it leads to 'qualitative' methods. The second section of the book opens with an account of Fletcher's observations in a general practitioner's surgery in South Wales. He attempts to analyse doctor/patient interaction to demonstrate how the parties bring off a class-based relationship of domination and subordination. Fletcher regards qualitative research as a movement embracing three distinct tendencies; symbolic interactionism (deriving from Mead), phenomenology, and ethnomethodology (both deriving from Schutz via Berger and Luckman, and Garfinkel respectively). These tendencies are bound together by the central place they accord to the individual, by their view of society as an evolving process, by their attention to the microcosm of individual occasions of social interaction rather than the macrocosm of social structures, and by the intimate dialectic between theory and method.

From this starting-point, Fletcher reviews the key products of the movement and their antecedents. In the context of sociology as a whole, 'despite the years of laborious effort to make Marx a sociologist he is now put out again. Durkheim is in for his work on the "conscience collective". Simmel is a borderline case' (Fletcher, 1974, 112). In general, Schutz can be discounted as a thinker because he was a merchant banker and only a dilettante social theorist whose world-view must be suspect. Mead is a pragmatic liberal reformist, Goffman a play-acting jester and Garfinkel a schoolboy prankster.

It is only in between these personal attacks that Fletcher occasionally faces intellectual issues. He notes the increasingly shadowy character of macrosocial phenomena as analysis moves away from the level of individual relationships. Families and institutions are more sharply defined than classes or societies. He is critical of those qualitative researchers, notably Becker (1958) and Glaser and Strauss (1967), whom he sees as dangerously close to the error of scientism, although he does not do them the justice of setting this against the prevailing intellectual climate. He also condemns Denzin's (1970b) notion of methodological triangulation as being the idea that if one uses all conceivable methods of looking at a question one can arrive at some Grand Synthetic Truth. Eclecticism is substituted for rigour since all methods become equally valid, regardless of their logical status.

But such criticisms are secondary to the political ones. Fletcher presents qualitative research as a liberal aesthetic (which makes it conservative by his own standards). Its liberalism lies in its separation of sociology from politics, and its aestheticism in the appreciative and contemplative attitude which qualitative researchers take towards the world. Their first commitment is to the truth of the phenomena being studied. Their reports may have critical implications but these are mere by-products; where all events are relative, what can a sociologist say which has any privileged status? Most qualitative researchers concede that no privilege over any other citizen can be derived from being a sociologist, except for that privilege which might stem from having more information at hand: but this answer does not satisfy Fletcher.

Instead he advocates what he christens the 'method of social criticism', the third of his 'three styles' of research. He offers us two illustrations of this in practice in studies of comedians and of class in contemporary sociology. The former is based on data derived from press cuttings and biographies and the latter from a reanalysis of data from Margaret Stacey's restudy of Banbury (Stacey *et al.*, 1975). In Fletcher's view both qualitative and quantitative methods presuppose their data and, hence, their problem. Social criticism starts with its problem. This is not just any old problem or what the passing fancy of the sociologist alights on – it is a *real* problem. It is not at all clear what 'a real problem' is, but Fletcher appears to know one when he sees it. Studying society can only go on as an accompaniment to struggling to change it and to raising one's own consciousness.

This may appear a somewhat cavalier account, but Fletcher has written a very cavalier book, the tone of which we have tried to reflect in this summary: one only wishes that the dividing line between intellectual account and autobiographical self-indulgence had been more cautiously trodden. In the end, Fletcher offers us too many cruel parodies, even in his own examples, to carry conviction. Would any 'quantifier' take seriously a study of the role of foremen based on twenty-two respondents from one factory or a study of lecturers at a technological university where a postal questionnaire brought a 36 per cent response rate? Would a 'qualitative' researcher really give much credence to three weeks' observation in one doctor's surgery? As for 'social criticism', we are offered an article on comedians based on eight magazine articles, one autobiography and a chat with a friendly semi-professional, and a piece on class based on a quick re-analysis of someone else's data. Even if these 'studies' are meant to be mere illustrations, the same sense of exaggeration and simplification runs through the rest of the book.

This applies to its basic structure. Fletcher identifies two types of sociological method: quantitative and qualitative. He presents them as clear-cut alternatives, but things are never quite as simple as that. These terms are convenient shorthands, but it is important to remember what they obscure. Workers in each tradition have always been concerned with issues identified by Fletcher as belonging exclusively to one or the other. 'Quantifiers' are often acutely aware of the limitations that operationalisations impose, and by the nature of the research style continually confront the unpredictability of human life. Similarly, qualitative researchers have always made quantitative statements. Admittedly, these have usually been at a nominal or an ordinal, rather than an interval, level of measurement, but are no less quantitative for that. Both traditions have always sheltered behind scientism to cover the nakedness of their particular interests, at least until the influence of the ethnomethodologists came to be felt in some qualitative research. Both traditions have always been deeply positivist in a philosophical sense.

Then there are the specific misrepresentations. It is plainly absurd to suggest that qualitative research kicks Marx back into the cold whence he has just crept. As Dingwall has noted elsewhere (Dingwall, 1975) there is no necessary contradiction between recent Hegelian marxist writing and anything written by recent ethnographers. It could be argued that if anyone has become marginal it is surely Durkheim. That in itself is revealing: one of the distinctive features of Durkheim's writing is his own inner moral certainty. Durkheim knows what the world ought to look like and is searching for ways of remodelling the reality he sees around him. It is particularly illuminating to contrast his views on moral education with those of Mead or Piaget. He sees morality as something to be coercively imposed on children by those who know best, while both Mead and Piaget stress the emergence of morality from children's co-operative interaction. This imposition of morality by the wise is also what Fletcher wants to invoke from the rival legitimacy of Marx and to claim for himself. His criticisms of the quantifiers are largely based on envy of their ability to impose one particular kind of order on the social world. Obviously, all research has elements of ordering disordered events but there is a fundamental difference between bringing order *to* events and drawing order *from* events, between fitting events to theories or deriving theories from events. For all his existential anguish, Fletcher is not questioning the legislative imposition of certainty, but merely questioning the credentials of those who are doing it. His remedy is not that of abdicating the right to define social events in favour of seeking to recover the definitions of those involved in them. He merely wishes to legislate from a different set of premises. His vision remains essentially self-righteously totalitarian rather than libertarian.

This is not to say that there are not features on which Fletcher is strong. For example, his account does bring us into confrontation with some of the pressures that affect all researchers: pressure from sponsors, from colleagues, or from bureaucratic superiors. His remarks on the internal contradictions of research teams find many echoes in our own experience, and also in Platt's account of the interpersonal relations of researchers. Again, he neatly captures the personal and individualistic character of ethnography, even if he does present this solely as a weakness without recognising that it may also be a strength. Unfortunately, his manic style and ultimate self-righteousness tend to obscure the importance of the questions he wishes to tackle, questions which previously have received too little attention in British sociology. It would be unfortunate if his insistence on social criticism (as currently defined by Fletcher and his fellow critics) as the sole 'correct way' for sociological research masked the fact that all styles of research are not equally wedded to a particular ideological standpoint, and that the problems of doing research extend to very different contexts.

Platt's research into social research

Whereas Fletcher's book is both personal and self-conscious in its account of his own intellectual conversion, Jennifer Platt's two studies (1971, 1976) are more orthodox and less explicitly self-revealing, despite dealing with much the same sort of individual evolution in a philosophy of research. In her earlier book she is expressing many of the sentiments which typify Fletcher's view of 'quantification', and which draw heavily on the positivist tradition. Thus we find her applying 'absolute standards' to the work of the Institute of Community Studies: in view of the substantial output, she feels that:

> it seems proper to apply the highest standards. Nor, however, do
> I think that the standards suggested are ideals which are
> impossible to achieve in practice, and belong only in textbooks;
> they all specify procedures which working sociologists have used
> with a reasonable degree of success. Most of these sociologists
> have been American; once again it is a great pity that the
> Institute's researchers have taken so long to show signs of
> familiarity with the best American work in their field (Platt,
> 1971, 97).

While one can share with Platt her concern that the evidence on which conclusions are based should 'not only be had but be seen to be had' (Platt, 1971, 94), this does not involve support for her call for a 'Lazarsfeldianisation' of Willmott and Young. Those authors' commitment to policy formulation, to popularisation, and to observation in depth offer compensations for their lack of rigour: would the 'Bethnal Green Studies' have made an *even greater* impact on British social science, let alone their actual *continued* impact, had their research design been more precise and their methodology (and quantification) intruded further into their books?

But in contrast and perhaps surprisingly, Platt's second contribution to the sociology of social research, *Realities of Social Research* (Platt, 1976), shows no signs of incorporating the American armoury of technical and statistical expertise in its account of the experiences of 121 research workers on 55 British projects. Indeed, quite the reverse, since she has moved some way from the language of scientism when she writes of her book:

> I have lived with it so much that the theoretical implications seemed obvious to me, and I felt that it would be crude and almost insulting to my readers to spell out what was self-evident.... The sample has no formal claim to representativeness of any defined population, and I have attempted in the analysis not to make claims to generality of a kind that it cannot support (Platt, 1976, 186 and 12).

The absolute standards of the critic of *Social Research in Bethnal Green* do not seem to have survived the intervening five years, so that the sense of a developing perspective is similar to that found in Fletcher's work. It is worth speculating whether some kind of intellectual dislocation is a necessary precursor of critical writing on established practices of research – a point taken up below.

At the same time, Platt's two books tell us (sometimes perhaps unintentionally) a great deal about the standards – that is, the normal rules for procedure – in research at different stages in British sociology. But there is no indication of how she intends her readers to evaluate this, because her review of organisational and interpersonal factors in research projects is not situated in a proper historical or theoretical framework. As a result there is an absence of any developmental sense and each project tends to be chronologically isolated from its original intellectual climate. It follows from this that the reader must impose his own ordering on her presentation, particularly so in the light of her own shift of research styles between the two books. Again, Platt (like ourselves) does not make much use of work on collegial networks, citations, analysis or the growth of 'schools' of special interest, so that while her general comments about, for instance, the influence of research publications on the career prospects of researchers, are interesting, they are incomplete. Had she emphasised the sociology of social research frame of reference in her studies, she might have been able to expand her theoretical contribution, particularly in her second book. Despite these objections, Platt's work does provide a great deal more information about the relationship between 'research' and 'sociology' than would otherwise be available, as well as allowing the present authors an opportunity to develop a number of points in relationship to earlier studies.

The first book, *Social Research in Bethnal Green* (Platt, 1971), sets out to be an evaluation of the contribution to British sociology made by the work of the Institute of Community Studies. Platt excludes from this evaluation such work as that done by Jackson and Marsden (1962) and Runciman (1966), because, although published in the Institute series, the authors were not closely associated with the Institute. Instead, she concentrates on the published results of the best known work carried out under the Institute's auspices, specifically on *Family and Kinship in East London* (Young and Willmott, 1957), and on Willmott, Young, Marris and Cartwright as the most prominent researchers at the Institute.

Each chapter is concerned with a particular aspect of the work and, within each, the publications are dealt with in chronological order: the value judgments, the ways in which policy recommendations are derived, research methods, theoretical contribution and use made of existing theory are thoroughly and critically examined. Platt's main conclusion in evaluating the Institute's contribution is that it has been an effective pressure group and has had more influence on disciplines outside of mainstream sociology than within it.

Platt regards the value judgments underlying most of the work carried out by the Institute as detrimental both to the work produced and to the policy recommendations made on the basis of such work. Willmott, Young, *et al.* are criticised for idealising the working-class way of life and thus recommending policies to preserve it, rather than studying both sides of social service provision and putting forward policies based on an objective and thorough investigation of 'the problem'. In such recommendations their value judgments are usually implicit. Platt finds no systematic discussion of a full range of policy alternatives, and costs were rarely discussed.

The research methodology employed in the studies is subdivided by Platt into the 'Old Tradition' and 'Newer Models'. The 'Old Tradition' (i.e., the sample survey and series of intensive interviews usually carried out in Bethnal Green) is severely criticised on various technical and theoretical grounds. Few hypotheses were tested and the resulting descriptive accounts made little use of the survey data. Such material was usually presented in tabular form and often placed in an appendix. The main body of the work was based on information obtained from unstructured interviews, presented in numerous quotations taken out of context and bound together in a loose manner. Description was in terms of an ideal type rather than classification and little or no analysis of deviant cases was attempted. Platt correctly describes the analysis as crude, with little use made of the multivariate techniques developed in America, and doubts the generality of findings and the early exclusive use of Bethnal Green as an appropriate 'field'.

Platt's major criticisms of the 'Old Tradition' are mainly levelled at Willmott and Young for, although Townsend (1957), Marris (1958) and Mills (1962) used similar techniques and analysis, Platt appears to be less critical and more ready to offer excuses, thus on Townsend: 'This shows that it is possible, though admittedly on a more limited subject, to adopt a humanistic and individualistic approach without losing the advantages of rigour and precision of method' (Platt, 1971, 66); and on Marris: 'One may have slight doubts about the accuracy of answers to questions retrospective to before widowhood about familiar contacts, but obviously there was little practical alternative' (Platt, 1971, 67).

The methodology of the 'Newer Models' is seen by Platt as reflecting the Institute's broadening interests in the diversity of topics studied and methods employed. In these studies more sophisticated statistical techniques and questionnaire design are used and Platt is generally less critical although, conversely, Ann Cartwright's work (1964, 1967) is criticised for presenting figures too dense for readers to comprehend.

Platt's evaluation of the theoretical orientation and contribution of the Institute is, for the most part, centred on its conceptions of 'The Family' and 'Class' and she suggests that these ideas have been generally inadequate. Explanations put forward to account for either the extended family or the working-class life-style tend to be tautological: for example, the close mother–daughter tie. The operational definitions used are usually vaguely stated; for instance, 'Class' is defined in occupational terms but is taken to mean far more than this in terms of life-style, values, subculture, etc. Few hypotheses have been formulated in advance and thus explanations are in terms of what data the researchers happen to have collected. The 'ideal type' accounts lead to partial explanations of the discovered patterns: if deviants had been examined in more detail more adequate theoretical explanations might have been proposed.

This lack of theoretical rigour also applies to the way in which the Bethnal Green studies draw on previous sociological writing. Apart from a general lack of attention to the theoretical implications of other work in sociology, Platt argues that even when these ideas are referred to, they are usually employed as confirmation of a description given, rather than as guidelines in hypothesis formulation. Here she compares unfavourably the work of the Institute with that of Bott (1957), Dennis *et al.* (1956) and Mogey (1956) amongst others. Platt suggests that these weaknesses in the theoretical contribution may be the result of the Institute's particularly close involvement with, and commitment to, the working-class way of life, their orientation to policy-related research and a broad general appeal, and the consequent preference for a generally descriptive presentation with little room for formal hypothesis formulation and testing.

The influence of the Institute's work within the social sciences is seen by Platt as being relatively small. It has served more as a catalyst (encouraging people to study sociology and do research) than as a major contribution in itself and its influence has been stronger in other areas:

> Our total evaluation of the work of the Institute of Community Studies as a whole, then, must be one which rates its contribution to thought about planning, and social welfare and to effective political pressure very highly, but which regards its direct contribution to sociology with considerable reservations. (Platt, 1971, 143)

Platt's substantive criticisms of the research undertaken at the Institute of Community Studies, and in particular that carried out by Michael Young and Peter Willmott, are justified. For the most part their methods were weak, their research design questionable and their analysis and theoretical background inadequate, but this is a judgment made on the basis of *current* knowledge and standards of research. Platt's lack of attention to the social and historical contexts of the work (except for one page in the conclusion) is equivalent to criticising a Comet airliner for not being a Concorde.

It must be remembered that the technical side of British sociology in the late 1950s was weak. As we showed in Chapters 1 and 2, earlier traditions drawing on Booth had been forgotten, Lazarsfeld had not made a real impact, and anthropological techniques were only gradually gaining ground. More typically, the 'community studies' date from this period: our knowledge of Ship Street, Gosforth, Glynceiriog and Featherstone is the product of the late 1950s. *Tradition and Change* appeared in 1960 (greatly influenced by the then-recent translation of Weber), the village studies of Ashworthy and Westrigg were published in 1963 and 1964, while 'locality studies' such as Jackson and Marsden's *Education and the Working Class* or Rosser and Harris's study of kinship in Swansea are of a similar vintage.

Again, these were the pre-Robbins days of few separate sociology departments. The discipline was still unestablished, and its basic techniques undeveloped. Even the first 'social class' and 'socio-economic group' classification were not included in the Census until 1951. There were few sociologists in this country and fewer still had read Lazarsfeld (1955) or Hyman (1954), let alone incorporated their work into normal British practice in the way that Platt suggests Willmott and Young should have done with *Family and Kinship in East London*.

By the same token, it is necessary to have regard for the state of knowledge about the working class and family life generally in the mid-1950s. Among sociologists, the dominant view of the family was the Parsonian (1949) doctrine of the isolated nuclear family: among policy makers, the brave new world of post-war slum clearance and rapid construction of new council estates was the prime orientation. If the workers at the Institute have made a contribution, it was to challenge the assumptions of the dominant views held in their time. It is true that like some of their contemporaries (and indeed their successors) they can also be charged with a reification of community, with romanticising working-class life and with over-simplification in their conclusions: but the blame for this cannot be entirely laid on Willmott and Young, even if their work did provide a stimulus for a re-orientation of ideas. It may be the case that their influence has survived with too little criticism for too long: if so, then the complaint should be levelled against other sociologists and policy makers – not against Willmott and Young. It seems the reverse of common sense if their contribution is to be condemned because it has been so long lasting.

How many sociological contributions of the 1950s have had a comparable effect on subsequent sociological thought? By the acid test of undergraduate reading lists, there are only a handful of other 1950s studies to match *Family and Kinship*: Dennis *et al.'s Coal is our Life* – which shares all the 'faults' of Willmott and Young; Bott's *Family and Social Network* – which even in its 1971 second edition pays no heed to American empiricism; Lockwood's *Black Coated Worker* – in so far as it is an empirical study – survives any methodological limitations; and finally Glass's *Social Mobility in Britain*, published in 1954. Presumably this last is closest to Platt's ideal, and yet, as recent work has shown, its basic fieldwork is so flawed that it has seriously misled at least one entire generation of sociologists about class in Great Britain (Payne *et al.*, 1977). In short, methodological expertise is a desirable but not an indispensable requirement of good sociology, and none of us can ever fully escape the constraints that our historical milieu imposes upon us.

It is also a little unfair to evaluate the Institute's work in terms of its contribution to sociology alone. The main aim of the Institute (quoted by Platt) was: 'to undertake research which will both add to basic knowledge about society and illuminate practical questions of social policy, and to publish the findings in a form which will interest the layman as well as the specialist' (Platt, 1971, 1). Its original purpose was: 'to study the relationship between social services and working-class life. The assumption was that the policy-makers [were] insufficiently aware of the needs ... and we hoped that social research might help provide a more realistic basis for policy' (Platt, 1971, 1-2). Thus the Institute did not define itself in a narrow 'academic sociology' way. It wanted to influence policy makers and Platt recognises its success in this area. If sociologists and others have taken the findings produced as more widely generalisable, as Platt seems to think – or fear – that they have, then it is they who should be criticised for not recognising the limitations of the research – or not reading the appendices – not Willmott and Young. Had more sociology degrees over the last twenty years included a sophisticated course in research methods, any over-generous attachment to the findings of the Bethnal Green studies might have been avoided.

Platt's lack of allowance for the historical and social setting in which the research took place might have been avoided had she drawn on the techniques used in her later study. Although she did have contact with members of the Institute, no attempt was made to interview them about the social history of the research projects she examines and no mention is made of the social and organisational constraints imposed by sponsors, colleagues, and domestic and personal factors. While the non-sociological background of the researchers is mentioned, little allowance is made for this lack of training and Platt is a little unfair to expect them immediately to become brilliant methodologists *and* social theorists *and* policy formulators.

Realities of Social Research

Jennifer Platt's second contribution to the field of social research would appear to take into account the area which she previously neglected. *Realities of Social Research* (Platt, 1976) is the results of her study into the social aspects of the social research process. Again, this study was commissioned to fill a gap in the literature and was originally intended to be a British version of Hammond's *Sociologists at Work* (Hammond, 1964) – a gap which has now been partly filled by Bell and Newby (1977). However, because of the poor response she received from various sociologists approached, her fear of refusals, and a development of her own ideas, she decided to carry out a series of depth interviews with people involved (or recently involved) in empirical social research projects in Britain in order to investigate the social processes and organisational constraints to which research projects are subjected, and to evaluate the consequences of these for the outcome of the project. Her aims were not just to 'satisfy a simply ethnographic curiosity' (Platt, 1976, 10) but also to suggest realistic prescriptions for successful research outcomes and to make a more general contribution to the sociology of work and education.

To achieve this, Platt describes how the system of research grants, the university organisation and ethos, the interests of sponsors, the division of labour within research teams and the research workers' own personal lives, values, expectations and perspectives all affect the eventual outcome of research projects. Unfortunately, the result turns out to be rather descriptive and indeed somewhat journalistic; there is little attempt at detailed explanation, although the topics on which she concentrates are centrally important to the understanding of the research process. This is largely due to the absence of an adequate theoretical framework, as clearly neither the sociology of work nor of education provide her with any coherent structure for her analysis, whereas a more direct application of a sociology of social research might have achieved just this.

In part, this problem with the level of detail arises from Platt's concern with anonymity. Because she is dealing with events in the lives of people who are likely to be known to much of her readership, she allows herself no systematic description of any one project. The result is that her conclusions, although generally consistent with our own, are not grounded in sufficient data to carry full conviction and take on a plausible 'reality', let alone grounded in the detailed evidence which a sceptic would demand.

The main impression which the reader is given is of a fragmented account of selected aspects of the organisational constraints imposed on and arising from empirical research projects in sociology. We are shown how the bureaucratic structure of grant giving bodies, with their rigid timetables and internal divisions and politics, create problems for initiating and conducting well thought out research, and how the secrecy and rumours surrounding the system of grant allocation (particularly the SSRC) create professional myths, anxieties and fears. Because of these constraints potential grant holders tend not to apply for enough money to carry out the project satisfactorily and either have to apply for a further extension, or cut costs on fieldwork and analysis, or both. These strict time limits and the doubts about obtaining extensions create uncertainties in which junior research workers are forced to look for jobs before the end of projects, which causes further delays and is detrimental to the successful completion of projects.

Platt suggests that SSRC is too often blamed for project failure: 'it will always be easy and comfortable for researchers to blame shortage of funds for their own delays and inadequacies' (Platt, 1976, 16). She argues that timetabling is an inherent structural problem for these projects which are university based. Within the university ethos, the general academic norms of the pursuit of knowledge and intellectual career development are the major factors in the comparative inability of university projects to meet deadlines. In universities the research director is usually a member of faculty with other academic commitments; his research role being one of entrepreneur and his involvement spasmodic. Research workers, on the other hand, are seen as academically marginal. They have lower status than teaching staff and are often physically and intellectually isolated.

Platt seems somewhat surprised to find that many researchers were not attracted to their jobs solely by the topic area. Many researchers had only a marginal interest in the particular topic and were more concerned with their general career development. But given the insecurity of research posts – a point mentioned by many of the researchers – is it really unexpected that research jobs are generally seen to be a preliminary to a more permanent academic teaching career and, consequently, that full-time researchers tended to be recent graduates?

When researchers were doing higher degrees and had also taken on teaching commitments (usually for the first time) for their personal career development, the project suffered. Platt feels that a change in academic values and a more secure research career structure might eliminate these two problems. But she also reports that wives are often 'unpaid researchers' in participant observation studies, and they may also help with analysis. Husbands were less helpful, so that personal and domestic factors are central to the progress of many research projects. The methods of data colletion often created difficulties for the private lives of researchers, especially those using intensive techniques, while at another level, when colleagues became too friendly, research often became secondary in discussion to other interests. In cases where the team did not 'get on' personally, intellectual differences tended to be highlighted.

The problems arising from the need to gain access to organisations, groups, etc., are discussed along with these various personal factors which create problems for the project, such as gender of researcher, political and religious views, and life-style imposed by the topic under investigation. The most important external constraint, however, is that of the expectations and involvement of sponsors. The effect of sponsors' motives, censorship and control is illustrated in numerous examples and Platt shows how the personalities and career interests of researchers often conflict with the major goals of sponsors. Thus Platt reports how, in one project, the sponsors attempted to terminate their contract when information which they thought damaging to them, arose from pilot interviews. Since the researcher had registered the proposed research for a Ph. D., he attempted to modify the study. However, the veto on publication was exercised and no publication has yet appeared. Again, when another anonymous Ph. D. researcher discovered certain staffing practices, he was confronted with a letter from the sponsors which not only libelled him, but also asked him to destroy all the material he had collected and to modify his study.

Having earlier taken the internal organisation of the research team as being of major importance to the project outcome, Platt suggests several types of projects, based on their size, the role of the director, resources, relationship with sponsors and nature of the topic. However, since her projects ranged from individual Ph. D.s to 'complex projects' with teams of six or more members, and since certain topics can only be tackled by particular scales of manpower, these types do not contribute very much by way of structure or explanation. Nevertheless, her account of 'team styles' is interesting: tasks are allocated on some generally held notion of intellectual demands and skill; standardised and mechanical tasks are allocated to junior researchers while the more senior team members are more involved in design, analysis and write up. More important sources of tension are those created by the system of decision-taking within the team. Where no clear power structure was seen, uncertainties and conflicts emerged. This was especially common when the research director was only marginally involved in the running of the project and important decisions were delayed. But Platt has little to say on the internal power structure of teams, and does not develop the sponsor–professional relationship along these lines.

Platt concludes by giving an ideal typical account of the social research project, pointing to the main problem-causing areas and attempting some broad theoretical conclusions drawn from the sociology of work and formal organisations. She questions how far social research can be regarded as *work* given the academic norms of research as 'freely-undertaken intellectual exploration' (Platt, 1976, 176). Unfortunately she does not go on to deal with the dimension of power, patronage, and structural constraint which permeates so much of research activity, particularly in long-term research units, where a director's position as feudal overlord dominates not merely the conduct of research but the entire work situation and staff, and hence their subsequent market situation.

The overall impression given by Platt's study is one of a lot of data presented in an atheoretical manner. Although she maintains that one of her main aims is to make a contribution to the sociology of work, Platt makes little attempt to relate her findings to the main body of theory in this area; reference is made to only twelve sociological publications, five of which are methodological. Instead, the reader is offered a series of quotations from her interviews loosely linked together, for the most part, by a rather general discussion. This style of presentation gives the impression of an account of conversations she has had with others in her profession rather than a serious contribution to the sociology of social research. Because her readers are likely to be sociologists, she tends to leave the theoretical conclusions to them, as remarked above (Platt, 1976, 186). Although her reluctance to spell out the theoretical implications was modified after discussions with readers of previous drafts, it seems to have determined her approach and this therefore limits her contribution. The reader must constantly resist the temptation to treat the book merely as an exercise in social detective work, as he or she seeks to identify each successively quoted researcher. The danger is that the element of gossip will supplant discussion of basic issues.

The information presented to the reader in her methodological appendix is just as interesting and useful as the main body of the book. Here Platt shows how initial plans were modified, how her ideas and techniques took shape and how external and personal circumstances affected the final outcome. In some ways the reader is given a greater insight into the sociology of social research from the appendix than in the previous 174 pages.

From her discussion of the analytical techniques used (Platt, 1976, 185; 197-203), it would seem that she has not drawn on the available methodological texts and case studies on the handling of qualitative data (for example, Denzin, 1970a and b; Merton, Fiske and Kendall, 1956; Zelditch, 1962; Hyman, 1954; Becker et al., 1961; Whyte, 1955; Gavron, 1966, etc.). Given her demands for scientific rigour and reference to the then-current methodological advances in the handling of quantifiable data in the Bethnal Green studies, it might be expected that she would demonstrate a thorough knowledge of contemporary (1974) techniques for handling qualitative data. This is not the case, since she appears to have been torn between the systematic coding of 'factual' information and a far less systematic coding of significant 'themes' arising in the interviews. The problems of coding which she raises – differences in modes of speech, non-verbal information, unstandardised data – are such integral features of qualitative research that, had she consulted any of the qualitative texts cited above, some of the difficulties she experienced (Platt, 1976, 198-9) would have largely been overcome.

Her method of recording these interviews also seems to have been undertaken without an adequate review of the various techniques available. Platt used her own 'private shorthand' rather than a tape recorder because, 'it did not occur to me. I had never used one before and did not trust my own technical competence, anyway I did not want to carry any extra weight around when pregnant' (Platt, 1976, 183). This seems a little unfair on the cheap, light-weight, almost foolproof, Japanese cassette recorders which had come on to the market in the late 1960s. While tape-recorders are not appropriate to every situation it is unlikely that the use of one for the interviews which Platt carried out would have raised any problems. It would certainly have relieved the burden of dictating from notes which she raises as a problem. However, even allowing that suitably planned and efficient note-taking is usually a fairly reliable method of recording such interviews, Platt seems to have made some errors at the beginning of her fieldwork, and her own 'private shorthand' was not efficient enough to enable her to record verbatim:

> I was not initially worried about the accuracy of my recording because I was thinking of it as a pilot; after I had got it into practice my own method appeared reliable enough.... For most people I could record almost everything that I wished ... the kind of recording error – most likely – is in the tense of verbs, which seldom had substantive importance; in other cases of ambiguity the context almost always makes the necessary word clear.... (Platt, 1976, 183, 184).

Platt's playing-down of such possible errors is somewhat surprising after reading her first book. Given the general problems of memory error and interviewer interpretation, the dangers of data contamination would seem an obvious problem from her above description. It is also clear from her later account of coding problems that she did not know at the interview stage 'everything that [she] wished' (184) and thus, especially during the early interviews, she is likely to have overlooked at least some topics in her note-taking, particularly as her pilot study was later incorporated into the main data. Had she used a tape-recorder throughout, or perfected her note-taking earlier (a more difficult task than using a cassette recorder), this danger would not have arisen.

Platt would seem to have fallen into the trap which many

researchers from the 'survey' tradition make on first experiencing qualitative research when she says:

> I was so fascinated by the data in all its detail that I could not bear to leave anything out, and the task of imposing an analytical framework on it kept getting postponed. Clearly the fascination with every corner of one's data, which can easily become intellectually almost pathological, is a product of a degree of involvement with it which is uncommon except in participant observation (Platt, 1976, 186).

Both in these specific quotations, and in the general tenor of her book, Platt appears to have become so intensely involved in her data that their 'reality' and overwhelming clarity (for her) have diverted her from attempting any detailed sociological analysis.

Her wish for the data to 'tell the story' might possibly have been achieved had she been less concerned with protecting the anonymity of her respondents (or at least the projects they were involved in). This so fragmented her presentation that the important social factors in the research process are difficult to discover since the context of the reported quotations is usually omitted. The reader cannot judge the success or otherwise of the projects since, because of anonymity, no results can be examined. Platt does not see this as a difficulty since she maintains that she is looking at the process of social research. But the resulting publications are an essential part of that process since they form the basis for professional judgments and, hence, much of that research process is geared towards them.

Indeed, if Platt is correct in stressing organisational and interpersonal effects (as we believe her to be) then the publications which are the product of research are absolutely central. It is a commonplace among social scientists that authorship is a point of conflict in research teams: who has the right to write up which parts of the data – and who is credited as the major author when a research director has been peripheral to the project – are not merely questions about responsibility or censorship. They are the questions which make or break careers. And as such they are considerations which contribute to the collective anticipatory performance of all research teams. Eleven of the fifty-five projects studied are listed in the appendix and those involved do not appear to place such great importance on anonymity as Platt does. If she had examined these projects in greater detail, discussed their output, and related their degree of 'professional success' to the major variables highlighted, the reader would have learned even more about the sociology of social research.

The problems which Platt has raised – and the particular problems created by preserving anonymity – would not have occurred if she had carried out the study as originally conceived: a collection of personal accounts about doing research by named sociologists. Because her initial approaches requesting structured accounts of research experiences received a poor response, she reformulated the nature of the study. But had she examined the reasons for such a poor response to this original design she might well have concluded that it was the *type* of approach that was wrong rather than the basic aims:

> I prepared an elaborate and detailed list of questions to be answered in these accounts, and took the opportunity of a conference to show it to a number of people and ask for comments on the idea. *I found this embarrassing, and felt it was gauche and impertinent* to ask people to write to my orders, especially if they were senior to me or not personal friends. These doubts seemed justified by the reception, which was cool; no one overtly criticised, but everyone somehow thought that it would be better for me to talk to someone else about their research (Platt, 1976, 182, our emphasis).

It does not seem unreasonable to conclude from this that while her aims were acceptable, her manner of approach was seriously at fault. Had she made personal contact with, or even written to, selected individuals, explaining her aims and ideas clearly to them, and giving them a list of broad areas which she thought might be included but leaving the structure of the accounts to the writers, she might well have obtained a similar kind of data to that which she finally presented. Although this information would probably have been in a more identifiable form, it would have had the advantage that the social context of the described research would have been known.

This critical assessment of *Realities of Social Research* can be compared with Platt's own criticism of the Bethnal Green studies. By 1971, when she began her study, a number of texts were generally available which dealt with the problems and techniques of qualitative research. Had she been able to achieve in her second book the standards which she had applied earlier, or better still, had she achieved a compromise of approach in both studies, her two books would have been even greater contributions to the study of social research.

Doing sociological research

As we noted at the beginning of this chapter, we do not intend to deal extensively with the several collections of reflexive accounts that have appeared in the last few years. Some of the lessons to be learnt from them are dealt with in the next two chapters, and others we have already covered. For example, Shipman (1976) is concerned with the sociology of education, which has largely been subsumed under the heading of policy research, while the issues of power and politics in research which predominate in Bell and Encel's reader (1978) parallel the problems of action research and the cases discussed in Chapters 10 and 11. Additionally, the latter is concerned with Australian examples, which although interesting, are less directly relevant to the development of British sociology.

We do however need to ask what the achievements of these books are, because a number of lessons are buried in the fifty or so accounts contained therein. Brown *et al.* and Bell and Newby concentrate their editorial comments on providing a context in which their contributors can be understood. They spend relatively little time trying to codify what conclusions are to be drawn. It is of course still necessary to make the case that sociological research must be seen as a social process in its own right, that the sociologist must be reflexive about his work, and that the social context of the enterprise conditions the eventual product. But this does not automatically provide the budding sociologist with improved skills with which to handle the research events he will encounter, or give him a fuller understanding of sociological production among the profession as a whole.

To take a key example, *The Access-Casebook* is at no time precise about what 'access' is. The term is used to indicate various ways in which a researcher achieves some kind of understanding of a social reality. At times this means access in the practical sense of negotiating permission with organisational gatekeepers to collect data in a particular site, or provide the financial backing to run a project (e.g., Cherns's article). At other times, 'access is a matter of the interpretation of the meaning of data … and meaning is intimately related to values' (Brown *et al.*, 1976, 19). Despite the use of summaries and the stated intention of providing the student with an understanding of how researchers construe their role in knowledge production, the guidance given is still only general: 'In understanding the broad notion of access the research student should refer to literature, and his personal experience as a professional and citizen, rather than the reconstructed reality of research reports' (Brown *et al.* 1976, 18). This is obviously a position with which we have much sympathy, but there is a danger in embracing such a line with too much enthusiasm. A balance has to be struck between the traditional view and this more radical one, otherwise the baby will be thrown out with the bath water. Because the research act is accountable in sociological terms, it does not mean that technical procedures can be ignored, or that canons of logic, evidence, ethics all disappear in a welter of subjective meanings.

It is also necessary to consider whether the researcher is the best guide to a re-analysis of his own fieldwork. As an actor in a past social drama, he has no automatic claim to a vision of events superior to those of the other actors or of the subjects caught up in his project. To achieve that, he must be able to demonstrate the greater extent of his knowledge, and the superiority of his vision, by the very canons of traditional research methods which paradoxically he is challenging. The example of Wallis's article and the reply of his aggrieved scientologist in Bell and Newby – or the unpublished exchange between Bell and his former colleagues on the Banbury study concerning his own contribution to *Doing Sociological Research* – shows how much at variance are the interpretations of events which two sides of a dispute can present. Perhaps there is an opening for a new sociological genre: the sociologist not as researcher, but as *researched*. After all, this is one logical extension of sociology's concern with the position of the underdog.

Faute de mieux, the researcher *is* usually the best guide in a reflexive re-analysis. He is the only one with access to most of the key processes, the only one in a position to have the knowledge on which to base an account. It is what he makes of this knowledge that remains problematic.

Early in this chapter, it was pointed out that no rules exist for writing such accounts of research. Given that self-exposure is a traumatic experience at the best of times, how reliable are these reflexive analyses? One of the lessons of anti-positivism is that knowledge is conditioned by social rules which define what can be included, how it is presented, what tests of plausibility are applied and so on. Therefore reflexive analysis must construct a rival social context of rules in which it takes on meaning; that is, it must establish a methodology, 'without method there is no reliable way of resolving competing claims to truth' (Gouldner, 1967, 337). A new kind of research reality is being promoted which must acquire an audience on whose members it is dependent for its acceptance as a legitimate activity. At the present stage, some doubt must remain about the reliability of these accounts. This is not to pretend that some kind of perfectly neutral and objective stance is possible, but rather to stress the need to know what standards of reportage are to be set. If the researcher is the person with most knowledge, he is the person with most power over the selection and presentation of evidence. As he is usually the person with the most to gain or lose, how can his reader be satisfied about the picture which is being presented? There is no complete answer to this dilemma.

Professional ethics are available as a guideline, but there is no reason to believe that the Burts of this world are confined to psychology.

If there is a lesson to be learned from reflexive post-mortems, it is currently one about the conduct of research, rather than the presentation of research findings. A 'successful' piece of research (i.e., one in which the researcher and his audience can have some confidence that fieldwork was completed, data analysed, and the results written up in a form which is open to further testing) will still not be presented with its reflexivity as an integral part of the final product. It is no coincidence that all of the accounts are retrospective and published quite separately from the main works. To do otherwise would, as we have argued above, be tantamount to professional suicide. At present, almost by definition, 'successful' research is the sort which appears to have had no difficulties. No one, not even the contributors to these para-methodological readers, seems to be advocating integration of the two activities, although perhaps this will come in time. Instead, our recipes for the future are in terms of organisational reform within sociology and technical modification in the practice of sociological research.

There is a further reason for restrospective reflexivity. Before the recognition of the 'black side' of research, only the practitioner who had gone through the fire had acquired the first hand experience of what it was really like. In just this way, the research experiences of the present authors provided the motivation for this book. Having satisfied the prior demands of higher degree committees, clients, and funding agencies – to say nothing of satisfying one's own career needs – it is then possible to return to the less tidy and more perplexing world of research that we previously inhabited but could not describe at the time.

The Access-Casebook is an explicit attempt to by-pass this block by providing a manual for research students and young researchers. Its thirty or so chapters, predominantly drawn from organisational sociology and grouped mainly by topic of research, each concludes with 'suggestions for case discussion starters', i.e., as a teaching aid. The editors note that

> there are obvious limitations of the accounts in that they all show the relatively successful research worker's point of view, they are not a statistical representative sample of any clear population, and they focus exclusively upon the individual researcher rather than for instance the host organisation or the funding body.... [However] they could be used by research students to attain insights into the practical conduct of research (Brown *et al.* 1976, 48).

Sadly (and particularly so with the above in mind) the authors are 'reluctant to draw final conclusions for an analytical research methodology or to derive any general strategies for obtaining access or managing a successful project' (ibid., 48). The reader is left to do this himself.

The same slight sense of let-down also applies to *Doing Sociological Research*. The whole is not greater then the sum of the parts, perhaps because there is no concluding attempt to pull together the lesson of the disparate contributions. Having said that, we would wish to make a great deal of common cause with Bell and Newby. The principal aim of their book is to show that sociological research does not bear much resemblance to the picture presented in methods text books, and this they succeed in doing, not least because their co-authors include several leading sociologists who lend the certification of their reputations to that project. One of the main discrepancies between the 'traditional' and 'new' versions of research methodology is the dimension of power and influence. Their intention is to display 'openly and centrally that politics, defined thus widely, pervades all social research' (Bell and Newby, 1977, 10).

A second, and in some ways the major, strand of their introduction is the general problem of epistemology in sociology. Although one can see that dealing with the 'black side' of research is predicated on a rejection of a crude positivist model of science, the rest of the book is curiously quiet on this theme. Bell and Newby draw heavily on Gouldner's *Enter Plato* to criticise any tendency to become obsessed with method, but as argued above, British sociology has in fact not suffered greatly from this heresy. Sociologists may be given to epistemological introspection, but it has not come about from an excessive positivism, unless one sees this as sociology reacting against the positivism of other disciplines. If there is an 'epistemological crisis' its sources lie in the different *theoretical* positions, not just methodological ones – as indeed they seem to recognise in their section on Cicourel and Coulter.

While we would not wish to quarrel with their espousal of 'a decent methodological pluralism' (1977, 10), their orientation is different from our own. Bell and Newby see research as a sociological process of which politics is an integral part, but when they discuss the context of research – i.e., the sociological enterprise as a whole – they fall back on an intellectual explanation. In other words they rely on discussions of disembodied ideas and the de-contextualised writings of key figures (Gouldner, Kuhn, Mills, Althusser etc.). That is to say, they do not see the rest of sociology in the same terms as social research, i.e., as a sociological process of which politics is an integral part. This seems unnecessarily inconsistent.

In contrast, we have tried in this book to show that the whole of sociology needs to be understood in sociological terms, as a process complete with political and social context. Research is only one subset of that totality, and the conditions operating on the various parts of the sociological enterprise interpenetrate and impinge on the final product.

Ironically this is demonstrated in Bell's own contribution to the book, on the second Banbury study. This is probably the best known of the chapters, since it held up publication and became something of a *cause célèbre*. This notoriety may obscure what we see as the real message of the piece, viz. that research is contained within wider sociological operations which can work against it. Bell concentrates so much on the interpersonal level that he does not see the real structural problems that under-pin the study:

> Banbury was always going to be threatened by the fact of an adequate research career structure and security of employment in research. Its history epitomises the consequence – major responsibilities given to inexperienced and ill-prepared team leaders, conflicts between personal interests, particularly establishing a sufficient personal reputation to get one's next job, and team interests, the seductions of tenured posts and the lack of ground rules for collaborative activities (Dingwall, 1978, 21).

The working conditions of the academic are singularly important for understanding the kind of sociology he will profess, but the sociologist most closely involved – like Bell – may be too close to perceive their significance. Two things that emerge from these various accounts are the *intensity* and the *complexity* of the researcher's experience. Doing research really does 'get to' the sociologist: it features as a key part of his life which drains him emotionally and changes him intellectually. Not every researcher will be caught in a house fire and nearly killed, or trapped in a battle between West Indians and tinkers as was Robert Moore (1977a, 87). Not every sociologist will be faced with threats of litigation as were Bell and Wallis, or dragged into struggles with civil servants like Cohen and Taylor. But anyone who has been in the field will recognise Moore's feelings when he writes:

> full time research is not a job; it is a way of life, and so one's life becomes woven into the research just as much as the research becomes part of one's life.... In a twelve-year retrospect it is these personal experiences that stand out and the technicalities of research that are most obscured (Moore, 1977a, 87).

207

Research often has all the intensity of a love affair, and the greater the 'difficulties' encountered, the more the researcher becomes involved with the other people who are part of the activity (whether co-workers or subjects of the research) and committed to the goal of vindicating his own involvement. Where in the traditional text books is there any recognition of this emotional experience?

It is this element of passionate caring that vitiates any lingering notions of the godlike research scientist who stands aloof, neutrally observing events and presenting them in a tidy research report without the slightest hint of value judgment. It is certainly possible for the fieldworker to operate at several levels simultaneously – watching and recording while at the same time caring and helping – so that 'technical' work is perfectly possible. But it goes hand in hand with the personal and emotional life that the researcher must lead during his fieldwork.

Some researchers will become totally involved in their site, as was Norman Dennis for example. Dennis moved from being Sunderland's housing research officer (in part hired to legitimate and celebrate the town's urban renewal programme) to being its critic at public meetings, and finally to a seat on the local council representing householders in a ward threatened by slum clearance. Others, like Newby, working in what he called an Edwardian public school atmosphere, will have to keep quiet under provocation: 'I found their demeanour condescending in the extreme and deeply offensive and only with difficulty refrained from commenting' (Newby, 1977, 125). Suffering in silence may be the only way forward, as the alternative can be complete disaster; the CDP examples above showed how difficult it is to contain these emotional and political pressures.

As well as an emotional intensity, fieldwork also provides an intellectual stimulation of an almost revelatory character. Moore sees his Sparkbrook experiences as having changed his political life: 1965 marked the 'quick death' of his earlier liberal optimism (1977a, 89). Bell writes that, 'Banbury will forever be the social system with which I compare all else; it is my Nuerland and my Tikopia' (1977, 61). Doing research involves the sociologist in discovering new things about himself, as well as about others. This changes the way in which he thinks, and there is an interaction between this new perspective and the original design of the project. Research is inevitably an evolutionary process.

The second main theme that emerges from these accounts is that doing research involves one in a complex, chaotic world where nothing is as easy as it seemed back at the sociology department. Bell remarks in a footnote 'that it was not until I started the Banbury fieldwork that I found it necessary to keep a personal appointments diary: my life for the first time became closely inter-related with that of others' (1977, 62). Another example is Brown *et al.*'s view of the research project. They focus on a research project's imprecise beginnings, its later rationalisations, its need to be justified and legitimated, and the way in which there must be continual dealings with potentially antipathetic forces (1976, 36). Much of this has a naïve ring to it: they could be talking about any 'project' in life that has to be carried out in an organisational framework. Of course, being a student or a lecturer is child's play compared with this, so that the young sociologist is usually protected from the cold wind of a less organised and predictable world until he steps out of the tower and into the field. Again, his education from books is even today still likely to have given him an 'over-socialised' model of man and too structured a view of the political process.

Even the relatively experienced sociologist cannot escape this dilemma. As Pahl points out on the basis of his own experiences:

> Unless one does adopt a 'realistic' attitude one soon loses one's credibility, being seen as a waffler with no practical *alternatives*. Criticising greedy developers, incompetent professionals, self-interested politicians and muddled headed thinkers everywhere is not really so helpful. 'After the Revolution' I fear there will still be muddled thinkers (some might argue that there will be more). The time must come when one is asked: 'Well, what would *you* do?' (Pahl, 1977, 144-5).

Choices confront the researcher at all times: his reactions condition his work.

The world of other independent, self-motivated and downright cussed human beings does not easily lend itself to codification and sociological understanding. It is simply less structured than academic life. The outbreak of research immediately thrusts the sociologist into a vulnerable position in which he must make split-second decisions on how to respond: 'The police arrived in force, and I was moved on. What does the eager researcher do when moved on? I ran around the block, took my coat off and strolled innocently into the middle of the battle again' (Moore, 1977a, 87). Again, how does one cope with the less dramatic but more common problem of interpersonal relationships and casual social intercourse, such as hospitality? Many researchers find themselves 'drawn into establishing dynamic and meaningful personal relationships with their informants – working, playing, drinking with them, giving them political advice ... the optimum level of intimacy and the degree of inebriation seem to have presented dilemmas on occasions' (Wakeford, 1978, 13). The complexity of the field consists of a multitude of small problems, which together tax the researcher to the limit.

It would of course be wrong to depict research 'out there' as being something totally different and separate from the quiet of university world. Different it may be, but separate it is not. Researchers are tied by their employers or their higher-degree regulations and this is not merely a link but rather an interconnecting pipeline through which one part impinges on the other. It is only by talking about how others have experienced this in their research that we can know what it is like. Methodology is how it is practised in its totality, not how it is preached.

With this in mind, we have tried to show that more recent contributions to methodology writing have been something more than horror stories. To be sure, there is nothing wrong in horror stories as a warning to the young sociologist, but morality melodrama does have its limits. It is still too early for a codification of these accounts to be satisfactory. While we can generalise in a simplistic way – like stressing the power dimension – we are not yet at a stage where a more systematic formulation is possible, even in terms of a 'rule of thumb' guide. These early attempts have not been without their flaws – none the less the move towards a sociological approach to the research act is one of the most promising developments of recent years. Because this is so central to our argument, the next two chapters deal with case studies that the authors have followed closely, and that provide further detailed examples of how, although methods may differ, the problems of completing research remain the same.

10 Who runs research? A case study

An account of the status of sociological research in contemporary British sociology would be incomplete without at least one detailed case study. The example chosen is a project which encountered 'technical' difficulties of a sort covered by few – even at a post-graduate level – courses. It also highlights the 'political' difficulties arising from the wider social setting of the research, most notably the sponsors. In itself, the case is much like those in the para-methodology texts discussed in the previous chapter. One of its purposes is to convey some feeling of how sociologists actually practise their craft, rather than how they present the final glossy package. It is further evidence that the research act is normally a complete one, and that a sociological interpretation is a very useful way of making sense out of its component events. If empirical research is to be rediscovered it must be in sociological terms, and not those of idealisations or crude positivism.

In the late 1970s a research-funding organisation provided a grant for a large project to be carried out by Professor A and Ms B.* Part of the budget was allocated for a contract with a market research company to carry out a social survey. The events which followed, and the lessons to be drawn from them, form the basis of this chapter and are taken from extensive discussions with the participants.

Setting up the fieldwork

The decision to use a market research company was based on three

---

* Because the purpose of this chapter is to illustrate certain tendencies, rather than to criticise individuals, all names, dates and locations have been changed to maintain conventional sociological canons of anonymity (despite our comments on Platt in the previous chapter!).

main assumptions. In the first place, a company would have a national fieldforce of interviewers and regional supervisors ready-made. Second, a large part of the administration, such as work allocation, postal checking, and payments, would be taken off the academics' shoulders. And finally, the market researchers would have a store of experience and practical wisdom on which to draw. Another large study had recently been completed in this way, and the funding agency seemed to be encouraging a move in this direction.

The two academics had, at that time, certain clear expectations of what a market research company was. Influenced by other colleagues, and by the self-presentation of firms which had been invited to tender for the contract, they saw the firms as efficient and business-like, sharing at least some elementary concerns for 'scientific ethics', and having the key resource of a fieldforce of interviewers. There was no illusion that a firm would be as strongly committed to the end product, or to attaining the very highest standards of research work, as were the academics, but it was expected that the profit motive would ensure a speedy completion of the job, tempered by a genuine concern about technical standards, if only in the firm's self-interest of opening up an academic market through having at least one satisfied customer in the Higher Education sector.

In addition to these perhaps simplistic notions of the business ethic, the academics also thought that, because they were buying expertise, they were dealing with 'professionals' in a sociological sense. That is to say, dealing with people who were client-oriented, concerned with standards of performance, and having a professional body which followed a code of conduct. It followed that rates of pay, allocation of work loads, and day-to-day supervision could be treated as solely the company's business, providing sufficient interviews of the required quality arrived through the post. Although the research team were to be more involved in briefing and editing than in many surveys, the basic position was seen as one of a sharp division of labour.

The preliminary negotiations took place in a period of rapid inflation, and the original costing of the survey work was too low. The Chairman of the relevant sub-committee at the funding organisation used his discretion to extend the budget to the maximum he could allow. Any higher figure would have necessitated referral to the full committee – a move obviously not to the liking of the sub-committee, to judge from their tone of voice and facial expressions of distaste. It would also have delayed the project by six months, which was not to the liking of the academics. Accordingly, both sub-committee and researchers agreed to get the job started as cheaply as possible.

Advised by the organisation's expert in survey research that a tender by the company of MRF Ltd was 'low but not ridiculously so' Professor A began cautious negotiations. As his letter to the organisation at the time showed, he was persuaded by the reputation of MRF's Chief Executive (who had published on research methodology) that the work could and would be done properly for this sum. Even so, the details of the contract – on which so much was to turn – showed the care that was taken before the final decision was made.

In the contract, MRF Ltd agreed to carry out the main fieldwork of achieving interviews with 80 per cent of the sample in May, June and August, with July excluded as the peak holiday season. Sixty-five regular interviewers plus thirty-five extra recruits trained to a high specification were to be employed. A bonus of 6 per cent of the original fee was offered for obtaining an 85 per cent response rate. An equal penalty per percentage point would be imposed for failing to reach the 80 per cent overall response rate, or 70 per cent in any one constituency. The contract was based on the one used by the Office of Population Censuses and Surveys which reserves considerable rights to the client, such as absolute discretion to determine whether work has been correctly completed, and whether money has been wisely spent. It also provides for monthly progress payments of 90 per cent of costs expended.

In some ways, the arrangement with MRF Ltd was a little unusual. First, the inclusions of penalty clauses on response rates is not a popular measure, but it is one that a company keen to secure a job can hardly refuse without appearing to lack confidence in its own abilities. Second, a binding contract, particularly one such as the OPCS model, is less common than a letter of conditions. MRF were not reluctant to enter into a contract, although they did hint that the academics were perhaps lacking in gentlemanly trust. Both the idea of a contract and penalty clauses came from the organisation.

The third unusual arrangement in the study was that all work was sent direct to the place of Higher Education by the interviewers, instead of going first to the supervisors for a basic edit. The advantage of this was that time was saved, and that direct contact was established between the research team and the interviewers. As it turned out, MRF Ltd were unable to keep adequate records of progress, in part due to this system.

At first, all went well, although only about half of the interviewers arrived for briefing. The Chief Executive of MRF Ltd explained that another major survey was running late, and so had interfered with recruitment, and that the advance briefing pack had put some interviewers off because of its size and the amount of preparation needed. There was, however, no need to worry, since extra recruitment and training would provide the answer.

Each interviewer had to do one dummy interview before the briefing and two more dummy interviews after the briefing, and send them in for checking before starting the address list proper. The first three 'live' interviews had also to be checked before a final go-ahead was given: this double check made sure that the interviewers knew exactly what they were doing, and it served to eliminate any who were not up to scratch. This procedure had been discussed in the previous autumn and was part of the contract: it did mean a delay in starting of perhaps a week to allow for postal deliveries and turn-round, but since the briefings had been held a week earlier than planned at the firm's request, it was not an unforeseen or serious delay.

To the researchers' surprise, there was no flood of trial questionnaires, and there was no difficulty in dealing with them, despite the firm's earlier warning that the academics might be slow in handling them. The month of May failed to produce the expected 1,500 interviews from 100 interviewers, despite numerous phone calls to supervisors and to London. Instead, *seventy-one interviews arrived from sixteen interviewers.*

The fieldwork dispute

Obviously, such a shortfall could not be tolerated, but the tone of the letters and phone calls about it was polite. This low profile was deliberate: a working relationship had to be maintained: the schedule had been revised to work during July in addition to the original three months; the academics were planning (although not admitting this to MRF Ltd) to work through into October; and further recruitment and briefings were taking place. Any changes or improvements required at least two weeks to show an effect, and so the phone calls and flow of letters were carried on in a firm but co-operative tone. They wanted the work done, and still believed in the firm's ability to carry it out.

The central development that occurred in these first weeks of the fieldwork was a dramatic change in the pay rate for the job. It was discovered that the pay rate for each interview was only two-thirds of that of comparable work. For doing 3 dummy interviews, each lasting one hour, there was no payment at all. The failure to recruit even the regular interviewers for the job was not surprising: having agreed provisionally to do the work, they were then asked to donate at least two or three evenings' work free of charge for the privilege of working further evenings at well below the normal rate.

The supervisor, under the impression that there was no more money available, had tried to do the impossible.

The London office reluctantly raised the pay to the going rate for the interviews, but the mileage rate remained pegged at two-thirds the normal, and the trial interviews were paid at less than half-price. No further expenditure was possible as this increase would inevitably result in a loss being made by the company, it was claimed. This first 'loss-making' increase in payments was conceded in the third week in May, and its effects took about three weeks to work through the process of advertising and recruiting, planning briefings, carrying them out, and then vetting the early work. In the meantime, the flow of phone calls went on as before with the company keen to blame the academics, and *vice versa.*

The academics argued that the fieldforce was too small, that the agency had lost potential interviewers by the original low pay rate, that the supervisors were ineffective and too few (out of four, one had resigned for reasons unconnected with the survey, and one was immobilised due to an injury). In July, further progress payments were withheld. The company continued to argue by quoting single cases of difficulty, and ignoring the broader issues. Despite two meetings, a further replanned schedule, and almost daily phone calls, the fieldwork fell more and more behind.

This culminated in a mid-August meeting which involved for the first time the Manager of the parent company of MRF Ltd and Professor A (who although involved in the previous proceedings had not attended a whole meeting before). The two representatives of MRF Ltd, who had been summoned from London, started by first moving the furniture to achieve a strategic psychological advantage, and then claiming it was MRF Ltd who had called the meeting. Their list of pitfalls which had caused the delays did not include a single mention of the low original rate of pay, the lack of supervisors, the absence of their records, or the failure to provide interviewers. In short, there was a straightforward and clumsy attempt to shift the blame for the delay onto the research team. MRF Ltd's explanation for the delay was slowness in vetting, excess criticism of interviews, the Olympics, the petrol prices, the size of the briefing pack, and the length of the interviews.

Professor A indicated the shortfall of nearly 3,000 interviews on the revised targets, and questioned whether the delays of a few interviewers, for which the academics admitted responsibility, could explain such a large deficit.

Four other highlights of the meeting are relevant. MRF Ltd denied promising 500 interviews per week at the July meeting; instead they insisted that their promise was to *attempt* 500 interviews per week. This was indeed what they had *said,* but the impression that they had created was that 500 interviews was the genuine target that would be achieved. Needless to say, this did nothing to increase confidence in the company's honesty.

The second highlight was that the senior supervisor had to ask how to use the copies of the records which had been sent to her. Since she had obviously not understood them, she had not been using them and the survey had effectively run for three-and-a-half months without the firm having any records at all. She was still making enquiries about what another part of the records meant as late as the second week of September, which suggests a certain lack of organisation and supervision of the fieldforce.

Third, it was emphatically repeated at several points in the meeting that there could be no increases made to payments. A large, but unspecified, loss was already being made on the contract, and so even a token improvement to the mileage rage was out of the question. MRF Ltd could sympathise with the delays and consequent extra costs involved for the study, but they were only asking for a short extension to the schedule of about two or three months.

The fourth peculiarity of the meeting was the number of interviewers which MRF Ltd were claiming to be involved in the survey. A list sent from them on 6 August had 102 names on it as 'interviewers working at present'. Of these only fifty-three were known to the academics (some of these interviewers had already completed their quota of work) while nine others were still being vetted for suitability. The remainder could have been trained interviewers, or raw recruits, or anyone. But the research team also had seven names of interviewers already working – but not on the MRF list – plus three more being vetted. At the meeting, a second list of 237 people was referred to, but not presented for inspection. These 237 had been 'contacted' but no details of their qualifications or of their reasons for not doing the survey were presented for inspection.

Despite the fact that the 'summit meeting' turned out to be fractious and inconclusive, Professor A and Ms B had approached it with every intention of getting the survey finished. Consequently, yet another re-scheduling was proposed, together with a bonus scheme to motivate the interviewers. The details of this were subsequently thrashed out in phone calls and letters, but were, as it happened, largely irrelevant except for two memoranda, one from each side. These and all subsequent quotations are verbatim (subject only to changes to preserve anonymity). The memoranda are reproduced in full out of fairness to both parties. The reader will get a good impression of the state of play from both the tone and the contents, which are typical of the relationships during that late summer.

Memo (30 August, Chief Executive of MRF Ltd to Professor A)
'There are three possible factors which have resulted in fieldwork being delayed:
1   MRF's handling of the project
It might be argued that MRF should have reacted more efficiently or more quickly to the situation. But we have continually recruited and briefed (190 to date) for a current pool of 54 'active' on the survey and 18 now being vetted. The previous (23 May) and now the proposed increases in interviewer remuneration were not implemented earlier because the budget was already being exceeded. We have long since accepted a loss on the survey and are now ready to accept further loss in order to complete the survey. We too are highly experienced in social and commercial research and have never previously secured such a slow response from our interviewers on a project. We therefore contend that other factors have contributed to the current situation. These are, in no particular order of magnitude,
2   Extraneous factors
The contract was first discussed in June last year and then accepted in an exchange of letters in October. Neither party at that time could have anticipated the (political situation), the effect on petrol prices (which is a high cost component of the survey) and raging inflation.
   Other extraneous factors during the period of fieldwork were:
   – difficulty in interviewing during the Olympics period;
   – petrol prices;
   – a boom in other activity, for example, we are competing for
   our interviewers with other (better paid) research projects.
We might argue that we did not request an inflatory clause. Whatever the legalities, it has made the price allowed for interviewers on this survey inadequate for what they are asked to do. This is a major cause of the unpopularity of the survey but not the sole one.
   We believe that these extraneous factors alone warrant sympathetic consideration of the extra time requested, namely three further months out of your three-year programme.
3   (The) Academics' handling of the project
Then there are other factors relating to your handling of the project which we contend have contributed in part to the delay and unpopularity
(a)   Your letter to interviewers: 're briefing packs' 'This pile of
         papers must seem terribly daunting. I hope that you won't
         be too put off by it – actually it is quite straightforward
         when you come to look at it.'
         Apart from the psychological effect of such an introduction,

217

the pile *is* daunting and interviewers *were* put off by it.

(b) The vetting stages (by the academics) caused some delay in starting interviewers on the job. There are recent instances of interviewers being held up, sometimes several days, after having sent in their dummy interviews.

(c) Some interviewers have been, and still are being, discouraged by comments made direct to them by your staff following inspection of the completed questionnaires. For example 'wrong as usual' is not likely to encourage interviewer cooperation.

(d) The questionnaire is arguably longer than stipulated in the contract, i e, 'the duration of the interview will not be substantially longer than that experienced by the (previous relevant study), which we understood was calculated at 50-60 minutes. This point should be checked by establishing the average (arithmetic mean) time taken on all the completed questionnaires.

Note: Your letter of the 18th January: 'It is in fact about five pages longer than the (previous) questionnaire. Between the prepilot and the main survey, I shall be eliminating some of the less successful questions'. In fact, after the pilot, two sections were added and only about three questions deleted.

Generally, we have no complaint whatsoever about the cooperation we have received from you on this study. We feel that some factors at your end have contributed in part to the delay but the main explanation for the current situation in our opinion lies in the extraneous factors.

I believe we mutually would have happily agreed to fieldwork ending in September, making allowances for the points mentioned in (3) above. Our request is a further two months above that due to the other points mentioned in this memo.'

Memo (16 September, Ms B to Chief Executive, MRF Limited)
'The points of section 3 of (your) Memo are dealt with in the same order in this memorandum.

(a) *The Briefing Pack*

The 'Briefing Pack' for the survey was based on that used for the pilot study, but enlarged by a test-paper (covering questions connected with the briefing) and a set of notes on the education system. The purpose of these additions was to save time on the day of the briefing. The recommendation that these items should be included came directly from the MRF Chief Executive: we accepted (your) professional advice. The covering letter (from which the quotation is taken – somewhat out of context) was also prepared on the Chief Executive's advice.

The reason that some interviewers were 'put off' by the briefing pack was not simply its size. In our opinion these interviewers were put off when they realised from the pack that they were being asked to carry out a serious social research interview for a rate of pay that was not sufficient reward for the effort needed on their part.

It is also important to note that after the initial three briefings, we gave considerable discussion to changes in the packs, and that for subsequent briefings we have not used the original packs, instead experimenting with different methods including the use of no packs at all for the second (city) briefing. Since the drop-out rate from later briefings was similar to that for the first three, this suggests that the pack *per se* is not the significant feature.

(b) *Delays in Vetting*

We are concerned that this has happened, but we are unsure of the dimensions of the problem. Delay as we understand it refers to any unnecessary time wasted (in our office) between receipt and despatch of questionnaires for vetting. Our normal work rate (as we have informed you) is to clear all questionnaires, which arrive in the noon post, by the end of the day, or the next day, if a large number of questionnaires are received at one time. Since the first week of July we have telephoned interviewers direct where possible to give them clearance.

As far as we can tell, a delay has occurred in only a few cases. In at least three alleged cases (Mrs C, Mrs D, and Miss E) we have found that there was no delay whatsoever.

In order to clear up this problem, may we suggest that you send us the names of all those interviewers affected, together with their recorded delivery slips to show posting dates. We will compare these with our records of receipt, and our recorded delivery slips. If you wish, you could also check independently with the post office for dates of delivery to us, which can then be compared with our records of receipt.

When this has been done, we will know the number of days delay per interviewer. By calculating the average daily output of interviews for that interviewer, a simple multiplication of 'days delay' by 'daily output' will yield a reasonable estimate of how far the total shortfall of interviews is due to delays in (our office).

(c) *Comments Causing Offence*

Naturally, if we have caused offence it is something to be regretted, and should not be repeated. We have discovered, however, that certain cases are not quite as simple as they may appear. Comments made to supervisors are not meant for the eyes of interviewers: if supervisors then fail to respect confidentiality, the blame for the offence is not ours. Secondly, certain 'offended' interviewers are themselves offensive to us as clients; up to now we have not complained of this because we see this as a matter of personality, and we do not want to pursue the matter. It should be remembered, however, that what offends one person may not offend another. Certainly, a comment of 'wrong again' can be made simply as a brief neutral statement of a repeated error, and yet a recipient might read into it condemnation or sarcasm.

At times we have also told interviewers that the answers they have obtained on factual questions are 'unusual', 'unlikely', or 'not possibly true'. But we have briefed interviewers to *probe* in cases where the respondent is suspected of being wrong, as well as recording the verbatim statement. On a largely 'factual' questionnaire, answers which are plainly wrong do show up, and we must take all possible steps to safeguard the quality of our data.

However, it is clear that whatever our intentions we have in a few cases given some offence. To avoid repetition, may I suggest the following procedure? As you have a complete set of our correspondence with the interviewers, please prepare for us a list of relevant names and dates. We will then look through these communications for phrases liable to cause offence, so that they are not used in future. Secondly, we can make some estimate of the effects on output by considering average daily output ·before and after incidents of offence and comparing average daily output of 'offended interviewers' with 'unoffended interviewers'. As in section (b) above, we can then quantify the contribution of this problem to the overall situation.

(d)   *The time of the Interview*

The average time for routine interviews is about 62.66 minutes.* May we refer you to our letter of 5th February, section (5), in which typical times of 55 minutes to 65 minutes are specifically described as not being 'substantial' increases in time taken, compared with the (previous) Study?

Your comments on the physical size and content of the questionnaire are inaccurate mainly because it is not possible to make a valid comparison of the questionnaires (of 50 pages each) in a few lines. However, the physical length of the questionnaire has surely never been a central issue? In our opinion the crucial question is how much *time* an interview takes, and whether the output of interviews per evening's work has been significantly affected by any changes to the time suggested in the contract. We feel that the time taken to complete the interview has no bearing on the failure to complete the fieldwork.'

The memoranda were only part of deteriorating communi-

---

* Based on 800 consecutive interviews received between 24 July and 19th August. If 'trial' interviews are included, the average time is 63.66 minutes.

cations. In a series of phone calls and letters, the chief executive

- (a) claimed an agreement to pay 90 per cent of expenses on completion of 3,000 interviews had been reached – it had not.
- (b) denied that there was a time clause in the written contract – there was *in black and white.*
- (c) accused the academics of not sending copies of the progress records for two weeks – the office held Recorded Delivery slips for the two dispatches.
- (d) said that none of the interviewers had used an appointments letter system instead of making initial personal contact – the office had a copy of a printed letter asking for an appointment (which incidentally included the academic Institution's name without sanction).
- (e) asked the Institution's Registrar to intervene on behalf of MRF Ltd so that payments could be made, without mentioning that less than half the fieldwork was completed, or the criticism the academics had made of MRF Ltd – the Registrar read the entire correspondence before informing Professor A that he was entirely happy with his actions.
- (f) increased the interviewers' pay rate, despite earlier protestations that this was absolutely impossible.

In late September, the manager of MRF Ltd's parent company took over the affair, and for the first time in a letter dated 20 September conceded that MRF Ltd were 'later than contracted in completing the survey'. This followed soon after MRF Ltd had taken legal advice.

But it was too late. The final plans being offered did not seem to provide an answer. On 4 October, on the advice of the Institution's Legal Advisor, the contract with MRF Ltd was terminated. The penalty clauses amounted to stoppages of well in excess of £500,000. It was decided to make no further payments to MRF.

Some lessons from other people's misfortunes

This account of the misadventure of one survey has been written with two purposes in mind. In the first place, it points to some of the things which can go wrong, even when experience, hard work, expertise, and goodwill are in abundance. In the second place, it is a prologue to what followed, which will be even more instructive for the student of sociological method.

What are the lessons to be drawn from what went wrong? First, market research firms are neither groups of altruistic co-professionals with ready-made fieldforces, nor capitalist agents hell-bent on profit. There are elements of both; at the top most market research firms are just like any other London-based small business with secretaries servicing a management structure. This organisation enters into formal relationships to supply services in return for cash rewards, it has a legal existence and bureaucratic structure, it may even be quoted on the stock exchange. But behind this front office, the actual fieldwork world is only partly controlled by the cash nexus. While the interviewers receive rewards in cash, the dominant relationship is not one of employer and employee. It would not be exaggerating much to claim that a better model for this part of market research would be a feudal one in which personal loyalties and interpersonal influence are the principles of organisation. Each interviewer attaches herself to an area supervisor who in turn is retained on a part-time basis by a company or rather, although the supervisor is paid by the company, her attachment is the company's fieldwork supervisor or managing director. So if a fieldwork supervisor changes companies, she often takes her area supervisors, and they take their interviewers, along with her to the new company.

This feudal pyramid is complicated by 'plurality of homages', that is, most interviewers are attached to several companies. This is a sensible arrangement since no one company has enough clients to provide a consistent flow of work for its interviewers. As a result, there are competing loyalties pulling an interviewer in different directions, as she may have periods in which too much work from too many companies is being thrust at her. In addition, not all work is equally attractive, and so she may want to decline one piece of work in such a way that it does not offend her supervisor and interrupt her long-term prospects of more work. One study by the present authors occasioned an epidemic of pregnancy, broken limbs, ailing relations and other 'women's diseases' too delicate for the supervisors to report to us. In her turn, the supervisor will attempt to bribe the interviewer by offering the most convenient set of addresses, or a share in some future, more attractive study.

In practice, the client is likely to get many of the same interviewers (and even supervisors) whichever agency he employs. The conduct of his survey depends on this concealed structure of interdependent personal loyalties in which the interviewers operate. The success or failure of any study is in the hands of the middle-aged housewives who, whatever their skills as interviewers, are not employees of the agencies, have no training in administration and little experience of formal employment, and who do not accept work that they do not like. At times when there is plenty of work, the interviewer is in a powerful situation. When there is little work the power swings back to the companies. Part of the company's stock in trade is judging this balance of power and nursing the personal relationships which underpin the situation.

This has to been seen in the context of a research budget. There are no 'special offers' of cheap research to academics. A tight budget will put pressure on the amount paid to the interviewers, and they will then need greater persuasion by their supervisors to take on the work. Equally, operating expenses will need to be restricted, which will impair efficient operations. Thus we have a simple connection which, to a degree, also works for the researcher who runs his own fieldforce:

Restricted Budget $\rightarrow$ Fieldwork Problems $\rightarrow$ Poor Quality Research

This is, however, most acutely true where a market research company is used, because extra agents with an acute interest in saving money – i.e., the market researchers – enter into the conduct of the research. They are in a powerful position to disguise the corners they want to cut. Only under crisis conditions do these elements become apparent, as we have seen in the preceding pages.

Furthermore, the use of a market research firm fragments the research effort. The researcher loses the tight control he would otherwise have over his own team. He has no way of knowing what is going on in the field work, unless he involves himself directly in it – which defeats the object of hiring a firm in the first place. One can think of a number of major contributions to sociology where the senior academics in teams have not had this kind of close involvement. An absence of detailed knowledge of one's data is a dangerous thing, quite apart from the research career/'hired hand' syndrome drawbacks which were discussed above.

Fragmentation also occurs when things go wrong *as inevitably they do.* Of course, most projects do not suffer to the extent of the one that has been discussed in this chapter, but *all* projects have their difficulties. With a market research company involved, all the parties no longer share the same interest in one optimum solution. Even in a research team, different interests exist: in the market research game, those different interests often cannot co-exist without at least one party being covert about its actions and intentions. It may be over a matter of detail, or a matter of major importance. It is very difficult, if not impossible, for the academic to know which is the case. It is likely to be only from direct dealings with the rank and file interviewers that he is able, if at all, to prise open the door. But only a full recognition of the clash of interests will make the researcher aware of the problems involved.

At the start of this section, we indicated that a second function of the fieldwork account was as a prologue to the events which followed the fieldwork crisis. The present authors have reported their understanding of what took place with a strict regard for accuracy and honesty. They believe that their account is true and valid, and have spent much time and effort researching the 'story'. Naturally, they do not pretend to the Olympian detachment of value neutrality. They believe that Professor A and Ms B were fully justified in the actions which they took, and that MRF Ltd were the victims of their own misfortunes. In certain minor respects, the research team can be blamed, but not for the massive shortfall of completed interviews: the essential causes were the company's miscalculation of the initial pay rates, and their handling of the fieldforce organisation. MRF Ltd felt very harshly treated by the termination of the contract, and the reader may agree that being paid (as was the case) a few hundred pounds for doing between a third and a half of the work on a scheme running into tens of thousands of pounds was unfair. But the contract was freely entered into by both parties, properly enforced, and in the light of the performance of MRF Ltd, severe sanctions were called for.

It will help if the reader shares this view as he will appreciate more fully what follows. Again the story is told from the point of view of Professor A and Ms B, with whom, as fellow academics, the present authors sympathise. As before, identities have been protected, because our only aim is to demonstrate how easily social research can fall prey to political pressures, even when the subject of research is not itself in any way 'sensitive' or controversial.

The second half of the fieldwork

The prime concern of Professor A and Ms B was to complete the fieldwork: this explains their early tolerance towards MRF Ltd during the summer, and also their later determination not to pay over money which, in their eyes, had not been earned. The funds in question were needed to finish the interviewing: a completely new fieldforce had to be set up, and precious months for the research team, who were on short contracts, had to be spent doing the job the market researchers had been hired to do in the first place. It was only possible to complete this work (which was ultimately done with a response rate of over 80 per cent) by using the money safeguarded by the penalty clauses in the original contract.

In August, Professor A had notified the research funding organisation that problems were developing. The sub-committee's permanent secretary replied:

> My initial reaction is to urge you to sort this out with the help of your legal officer as there is a clearly defined contract on which to base your grievances.... [You] do seem to have spent a lot of effort over recent weeks in chasing up MRF and it must be very disappointing for you to be let down in this way.

The sub-committee's Chairman also wrote:

> I am very upset by the position in which you find yourself. It
> seems to me that behind all the smokescreen put up by MRF
> really the problem arises from bad management of their
> interviewers. I think this is a fundamental weakness of any
> fieldwork organisation. They are either good at it or bad. If they
> are bad no amount of monkeying about with the contract can
> overcome the weakness. I am sorry we imposed MRF upon you.
> I shall await to hear what your Legal Officer has to say.

Despite this, the Secretary telephoned the academics in mid-
September to summon Professor A to a meeting of the special
group appointed by the sub-committee to oversee the project. The
Chief Executive of MRF Ltd would not only be present, but the
meeting's timing could not in any way be varied because of his
schedule. When pressed by Ms B (who took the call) the Secretary
began to repeat the familiar list of unsubstantiated MRF Ltd
complaints. He declined to listen to any rebuttal, insisting that the
meeting must take place.

Professor A then returned the call. At first, the Secretary said
that *he* had contacted *MRF Ltd*, but under pressure admitted that
this was really in reply to an initial approach from the firm to the
Secretary's superior. He declined to give his superior's name, until
Professor A made it clear that he wanted to know, or to receive a
formal refusal of the information.

The Secretary seemed unable to grasp the three important issues
of principle involved. First, a contract existed between the academics' Institution and MRF Ltd: the funding organisation was not a
party to that contract. Second, it was improper for MRF Ltd to
attempt to involve the organisation on the firm's behalf – and
certainly the firm had no right to attend a meeting of academic
colleagues to discuss the project. And third, the organisation *had*
been persuaded to interfere in the conduct of a research project:
this was not just a breach of academic freedom but was acting on
behalf of a commercial undertaking to bring pressure to bear in the
interest of its profits.

The main argument of the Secretary was that the organisation
was entitled to see that research was properly carried out (which he
clearly doubted). He declined to change the time of the meeting
because it would inconvenience the Chief Executive: the latter had
to travel into Central London from the suburbs: the academics had
a round-trip of well over a hundred miles. It was only by
approaching a much more senior member of the organisation's staff
that this meeting was cancelled, and prompt action was promised

to restore the correct relationship between MRF Ltd, the organisation, and the academics.

Despite this promise, the Secretary's letter (a copy of which went to Professor A) notifying MRF Ltd that there would be no meeting was very ambiguously worded. For example, it still spoke of MRF Ltd's 'grievances with (the Institution),' and offered advice to the firm to prepare their case as quickly as possible. Even a further phone call to the senior member of staff at the organisation could not allay the academics' anxiety. They began to suspect – without any hard evidence at all – that several members of the organisation's staff who had previously worked in market research were doing their best to cushion MRF Ltd from the consequences of its failure.

This state of distrust and tension was not helped by the Secretary's selection of papers to go to the next meeting of the sub-committee. He proposed that only two letters should be considered: the four-page MRF letter and memorandum quoted above, with its lengthy and detailed allegations – and Professor A's initial letter containing a single paragraph which reported in the most general sense that there had been some difficulties. Professor A and Ms B still believe that this was a deliberate attempt to influence the meeting, either in justification of the Secretary's own actions, or to get both MRF Ltd and himself off the hook. It was necessary to insist most forcibly that the meeting saw the whole correspondence.

Throughout this period – September – Professor A and Ms B were (as we have seen) still trying to find a compromise with MRF Ltd. But as so little progress was being made, and being faced with these manoeuvres in London, it was decided to terminate MRF Ltd's contract. When the sub-committee meeting was told that the contract had already been ended two days before, it served to bring proceedings to rather an abrupt end.

But neither party to the dispute was willing to leave the matter there. Professor A wrote to the Chairman of the organisation, stressing the issues of principle as he saw them. The Chairman replied in a conciliatory tone:

> It does not seem to me there is really much to discuss. We acknowledge that a mistake was made here by the Secretary..., a very able but inexperienced officer. He should not have intervened formally or informally in a contract between an ...[Institution] and a fieldwork agency. His motive in doing so was however entirely laudable. It is always the aim of the organisation's officers to smooth over disagreements. This had happened in an earlier case which was somewhat similar but

differed in the vital particular that a formal contract had not yet been agreed. The Secretary ... recognises that he was mistaken in being guided by this precedent.

However, from a later conversation with the Chairman at a scientific meeting, Professor A felt that the latter's main concern was having good relationships with market research organisations, not promoting good sociological research and further, that he was misinformed about events. The Professor therefore wrote a long letter to the Chairman, which attempted to rectify this.

The letter pointed out that, on the Chairman's own admission, he had not read the relevant papers, and therefore to repeat some of the familiar MRF Ltd complaints was not satisfactory from the academics' point of view. The same applied to the Chairman's suggestion that they were 'making use of interviews which have not been paid for' particularly when the contract had been adhered to, the organisation kept informed and advice taken.

One other item from the conversation that had also occasioned disquiet was dealt with in Professor A's letter:

> You also suggested that you did not like the idea of litigation. As I indicated to the sub-committee, *we* had no intention of initiating litigation; indeed, I wonder what you have in mind in referring to the possibility of litigation? Am I to infer that there has been further contact between the organisation and MRF subsequent to the meeting of the subcommitee?
>
> At that meeting I stressed the importance of there being no further contact between the organisation and MRF pending the resolution of the legal situation and the winding up of the contract. I emphasised that our ability to round off relationships with MRF was dependent upon appropriate exchanges at the legal level and would be severely jeopardised if there were any further contact, formal or otherwise, between the organisation and MRF. (They) appreciated the position and gave clear assurances to me on this point. We are, in fact, having difficulty in securing the co-operation of MRF in winding up the contract and I cannot but wonder whether this is in part attributable to MRF inferring from the actions of the organisation that they may yet receive further moral or financial support from you.

The question of litigation is an interesting one. As this letter states, there had never been any mention of litigation on the part of the academics, so where did the suggestion arise? The solicitor acting for the academics' Institution *had* received a letter from MRF Ltd's solicitor which was written in a somewhat threatening style. However, once it was pointed out that there was a time clause in

227

the contract – a fact which MRF Ltd had omitted to tell their solicitor – nothing more was heard from him. As this was a fairly recent event, it had at that time not been reported to the organisation by the academics. It did not seem unreasonable to conclude that MRF Ltd had told someone at the organisation about the possibility of an action.

The Chairman's reply denied this: 'there has been no contact "formally or otherwise"' between (the organisation and MRF Ltd) since mid-September. The Chairman's reply was brief and dealt only with the issues of contacts and the implied criticism of Professor A's handling of the dispute – from both of which he dissociated his organisation. There was no attempt to discuss the basic issues of funding organisation/researcher relationships, or the conduct of his staff in the handling dispute; or his own ignorance of the facts of the case.

By this stage, it was late November. From time to time, rumblings were heard from MRF Ltd. The firm retained materials and some completed questionnaires belonging to the Institution, despite repeated requests for their return. On the grapevine, it was reported that MRF Ltd's Senior Supervisor had given up market research and opened a dress shop. The research team got on with the task of finishing the fieldwork.

Then, in the new year, two more attempts were made to force Professor A to settle with MRF Ltd on more favourable terms. In the first – for which no documentary evidence is available, unlike the preceding events – the Chairman of the organisation personally invited one of the Institution's senior academics to intervene in the affair. This person was told only part of the story, and, thinking that he would be doing something to save the good relationship between his Institution and an important source of research funds, he agreed to help. Without telling Professor A – and with the best intentions – he approached the Institution's Registrar in a behind-the-scenes move. He was somewhat taken aback when the Registrar advised him that, as the matter was the subject of formal correspondence between the legal advisers of the Institution and the firm, he should not involve himself further in a matter about which he was under-informed. The only result of this clumsy attempt to isolate Professor A from his Institution's support was to jeopardise the relationship between colleagues that had previously existed.

The second attempt to bring pressure to bear on Professor A came from one of the country's older but still well-regarded academics, Sir F. He wrote to Professor A's Vice-Chancellor, explaining how, probably unbeknown to the latter, two of his academics were behaving unreasonably and so damaging the good name of the Institution. Sir F explained, as one Oxbridge man to another, that when a student he had shared digs with the husband of someone now connected with MRF Ltd, and he knew this married couple personally. He was sure that they could be trusted, and therefore fault must lie with the Vice-Chancellor's two members of staff. Sir F had no intention of interfering in the internal affairs of another institution but there was a question of reputation involved.

The Vice-Chancellor called for the papers and read them. He then replied to Sir F that he had investigated the matter, that the points of detail in Sir F's letter were factually incorrect, and enquired if Sir F took the Vice-Chancellor's own view that the Institution was capable of looking after its own affairs. To judge from Sir F's subsequent silence, he did.

The reader may wonder why the two academics did not just ignore these manoeuvres and get on with their research. Professor A and Ms B felt that their professional reputations were being damaged by gossip, and were worried that a few people with both academic and market research contacts in the south-east of England might at any time launch yet another move to help MRF Ltd. These fears may have been unjustified, but given the earlier chronicle of 'dirty tricks', such fears were not to be unexpected.

Nor were the fears completely unjustified, as one example shows. A former employee of the organisation was addressing a scientific meeting in London on problems of survey research, when he began to talk about the need for precision in defining the fieldwork to be done. He gave as an amusing off-the-cuff example the case of a 'paranoid' Professor who had been 'excessively legalistic' in dealing with a market research firm. His audience was suitably amused, until Ms B, who by chance was present, pressed him to go into further details.

He was forced to admit in public that he had not read all of the relevant papers.* Worse, he said that further meetings between MRF Ltd and members of the organisation had taken place, at which attempts had been made to persuade the organisation to help secure payments from the Institution. These meetings had happened after the sub-committee had collectively agreed that no further meetings were to take place, and despite the Chairman's written assurance that there had 'been no contact "formally or otherwise" '. Clearly the organisation had been willing to pat the academics on the head and make reassuring noises about recognising the issues of principle, while at the same time holding secret

---

* This public exposure still did not stop him repeating completely untrue remarks about the MRF Ltd affair at at least one other conference, which showed that even a year later he still had not studied the facts of the case.

meetings to discuss ways of fixing it for the sake of commercial profit.

In an attempt to forestall any further difficulties, Professor A and Ms B decided that the wider the audience who knew the full story, the safer they would be from casual talk and misguided involvement. They therefore notified their professional body; asked their local MP to become involved, talked to several journalists who worked for national newspapers (when one journalist sought open access to the files, the academics gave their consent), and attended a national symposium on funding research to raise the general issues of principle involved. The MP made discreet inquiries, but could find no evidence of any illegalities. He did, however, keep a watching brief throughout the period, and, through writing one or two letters, was a useful source of background information and support. One paper carried a long and accurate account of the dispute in a feature just before the symposium, but the indisposition of the organisation's Chairman meant that this passed off more quietly than Professor A had hoped.

The complaints from Professor A and Ms B to their professional body over the conduct of the Secretary at the organisation dragged on for many months. The Secretary made counter-accusations, such as that of 'quite improper attempts to exercise public pressure' on the sub-committee, and senior officials of the body were frankly embarrassed by the whole business. The latter's final dismissal of the accusations, and recommendation for restoring better relationships, was based in part on factual errors, and showed a somewhat optimistic view of the state of the profession.

Other difficulties with the organisation were encountered over the application for an extension to the grant and other routine business, but a change of staff at the headquarters helped to restore more normal relationships. Once the two academics had given a public airing to their troubles, and demonstrated their competence by completing the fieldwork with a response rate of over 80 per cent, there were no new pressures, at least as far as they knew. The grant of the extension and the successful completion of the project were outcomes which at one stage had looked most unlikely.

The chronicle of woes that beset this one project are almost a caricature of what can go wrong. It is not even a comprehensive list, because for reasons of brevity some details and even whole episodes have been left out, hopefully without distorting the story. Nevertheless, there are some important lessons to be learned about how research just is not the way the standard introductory text books tell it. We say 'research' here because not only did the events arise out of an attempt to do research, but because the research act is carried out by people with full social identities and relationships which extend beyond the obvious day-to-day tasks of editing, coding, or analysing. The morale of the research team, its worries and concerns, turned for a long time on the progress of the dispute. And a great deal of manpower had to be diverted from the core research work to writing memos, checking files, and attending meetings when the team really had much better ways of spending their time. But without this, not just two professional reputations but the survival of the project itself would have been imperilled. We are dealing with the social context of which sociological research is part and parcel.

Perhaps the first moral to be drawn is how to fight battles when a researcher and his funding body come into conflict. The academics made two tactical errors which curiously enough stemmed directly from their ideas of professional conduct. Until almost the end of the troubles, Professor A and Ms B worked on the principle that full disclosure and complete honesty was the only way to proceed. Therefore, as each actor became involved, they sent off yet another copy of a rapidly-growing file. They believed that, just by reading the details of the correspondence, the newcomer would be convinced of their rectitude. This was in quite conscious contrast to the edited, one-sided and misleading version of events which MRF Ltd were presenting.

But busy people do not have the time to plough through lengthy papers. Time and again, it was admitted to Professor A that the correspondence had not been read. The MRF Ltd account was influential because it was short and accessible, and often presented in person over the phone. In trying to be absolutely fair – or to put it another way, by following through those normal canons of scientific practice, full and rigorous disclosure of evidence in all its complexity and documentation of argument – the two academics unwittingly weakened their case because other people could not afford the time to work it all out.

What this does point to, however, is that control over the flow of information is absolutely central to the management of research. In this respect, the Secretary to a committee can play a crucial role. Most grants (including applications) are seen in detail by only a few people: the committee as a whole does not involve itself in the details. Thus, for example, the Chairman of the organisation's committee responsible for Professor A's project knew almost nothing of the dispute until it had been running for about twelve months. The academics had assumed that the Secretary or sub-committee Chairman was briefing him, and that the overall Chairman of the organisation would have consulted him. Professor A therefore had seen no need to speak to him, despite being a little surprised at his prolonged silence. The Secretary can act as gatekeeper and, as this example shows, a most efficient one.

The academics' second error was that they attempted to depersonalise the conflict by referring to the 'organisation', rather than naming names and specifically citing the Secretary or the Chairman. Therefore, any criticisms were seen as attaching equally to all staff members of the organisation, who were often individually innocent of any connection with particular events. For example, it became clear perhaps too late in the saga that, despite his early mistakes, the Secretary was at times advocating a different and more sympathetic policy from that of the Chairman (although the evidence for this is only second-hand). The two academics alienated some potential allies by mistaken efforts to protect these two from personal attack. This concern with general principles and protection of the individual is a neat parallel of their normal sociological preoccupation with moving beyond the observable act to a generalisable model of action; and with the maintenance of anonymity.

This extension of behaviour as a sociologist into behaviour as a citizen can also apply to the way in which the conflict developed. Because the priority was the completion of the research, the academics were at first patient with the market research firm. As we have seen, they treated the staff of the firm as fellow professionals whose expertise, commitment, and honesty were, within certain limits, not to be questioned. Academics often find it hard to cope with the different ethical scheme that applies in business, despite their own machinations in university politics. Equally, the two academics expected the staff of the organisation, and all the other parties who were involved, to share the same concerns with the issues of academic independence that they themselves did. When difficulties were encountered, they believed that rational discussion would identify points of difference, even if these could not be resolved by mere conversation.

When the going got really tough, the contrast in the style of the two sides is most instructive. The two academics used the traditional weapons of the liberal middle class. They involved the press, they contacted their MP, they complained to their professional body, they used existing meetings to publicise their grievance, they encouraged full and open discussion. At the core of their position, was the advice of a solicitor (a fellow 'professional') and the framework of the law on which to stand. In contrast their 'opponents' held secret meetings, used a much-edited and selective account of events, made statements which were at best misleading and at worst untrue, activated a network of acquaintances in the south east, made phone calls 'in confidence' to people in positions to bring pressure, and employed the Oxbridge Old Boy network in an attempt to fix the outcome. At the core of their position was a desire to be secretive about what had happened and to involve a network of sympathisers to exert behind-the-scenes pressures.

On reflection, this should not have been unexpected. Neither Professor A nor Ms B were Oxbridge products: they were both relatively young products of grammar schools and redbrick education, from lower-middle-class families. Their world was that of the new generation of professionals. But those in business – the entrepreneurs – and in positions of influence – the bureaucrats – were successful operators with all the right contacts.

Furthermore there is a geographical element to this. The location of the organisation's headquarters, the office of MRF Ltd, and the homes of most of the people involved, in and around London, makes a network of informal contacts possible. The academic who lives and works at a distance from the centre is restricted to occasional visits, letters and phone calls from the periphery. Gossip, when it is initiated by one party in a disagreement (who also displays a very low regard for truth), is a powerful weapon. It is a vital element in the creation and maintenance of shared understandings about the world. Interpersonal relationships are essential to the mechanisms by which new events are integrated into this understanding, and therefore the 'reality' of the MRF Ltd affair was reconstituted in the process of fuelling social relationships and cementing common assumptions about the world.

It would be wrong to say that the academics were always 'open' and the non-academics always 'secretive'. MRF Ltd had their commercial reputation to protect, and the organisation's staff felt inhibited from making public comment, whereas the academics stood to gain more by disclosure than by quietly letting the manoeuvres against them go unopposed. Indeed, the two academics concerned were somewhat unusual in that they rejected the conventional approach of the scientist by drawing attention to their problems. As we have noted elsewhere, the 'normal' way of behaving is to ignore technical difficulties, because there is the risk that the perfectly valid findings and conclusions of a study may be impugned by association with such problems. It is a mark of the very considerable strength of his case that Professor A felt able to be completely honest and open and that the risk he ran was in this instance relatively small.

As we have seen, it was their own 'common assumptions about the world' that misled the academics. In dealing with a bureaucratic organisation, they were quite prepared to encounter incompetence, poor judgment and evasion. Gossip and a lack of

candour, again, are part of the informal structure of all organisations. But the extent of all these features (which a sociology of
organisations tells one to expect) was unexpected, particularly in an
organisation concerned with social science research.

On top of the bureaucratic response, the inconsistency of advice
given, and the 'non-bureaucratic' methods of interpersonal influence (through the Oxbridge connection) were completely
beyond the academics' anticipation. Equally the disregard for the
law of contract which both entrepreneurs and bureaucrats displayed was most unexpected. The concrete elements of clause and
letter seemed to carry little weight in the face of rumour, gossip and
the fragility of reputation in a jealous profession. The dispute
followed almost classic lines of a conflict between power and
influence on one side, and an appeal to formal legitimation on the
other.

The present authors see this use of influence as illegitimate,
whereas the proper exercise of bureaucratic authority is legitimate,
in the sense that the operation of contractual obligations is also
legitimate. Openness and honesty are desirable features in all
administration as part of a democratic society. Professor A and Ms
B can be faulted for naïvely expecting a 'fair fight', but since they
were dealing with academic research, its financing, its administration, its operation – were they not entitled to demand that the
normal professional ethics should apply? Their experiences have
demonstrated that, by means of invoking the formal apparatus and
the symbols of legitimation of the sociology profession, it is possible
to protect research and research standards from the depredations of
outsiders with quite other aims.

But in recording this judgment in these terms, the present
authors are again saying, as academics, that academic values
should prevail. We are invoking precisely the same liberal symbols
of legitimation that Professor A and Ms B employed. Their
experiences equally show that these values are not shared by
hostile commercial interests and bureaucrats. At one level, it may
not matter that businesses and organisations operate with different
priorities and assumptions about the world: co-existence is possible
in a compartmentalised society. At another level, the social scientist
is part of a social system in which powerful groups regard his work
(and existence) as subversive, dangerous, and requiring at least
careful control and, at worst, complete suppression.

In the case discussed in this chapter, the control sought was not
so much over ideas or controversial evidence, but over standards of
workmanship and freedom of action for research workers. It
depended upon a peculiar coalition of interests between commercial operators and functionaries. The interpenetration of the

234

small capitalists and the bureaucrats worked through the common employment circumstances and histories of the junior staff, and through a shared class identity at the senior level. The junior staff were mobilised in the interests of the small capitalists by concerns for what they no doubt thought were valid, 'professional' goals; the senior staff were operating their own elite network as a natural response to a little localised difficulty. That this impinged so sharply on the academics is disturbing, because most social scientists have neither the contacts nor the 'skills' (nor lack of ethics) to guarantee their self-protection.

Furthermore the temptation to play dirty is a dangerous one. It is not possible to be ethical in one's research on the one hand, and unethical in dealing with administrators and businesses on the other. It is very easy for a lack of ethical conduct in one field to spread into another: the line between 'research' and its administration and financing is very thin. There can be no 'religion-is-just-for-Sundays' attitude for anybody involved. What sociologist would be slow to criticise a researcher who was caught selecting or fabricating evidence? Why should we be more generous to those who are 'associated' with social research? Most academics can only operate comfortably within their own ethical framework, and the present authors believe that as a profession, we have to insist that the non-academics play by the same sets of rules before they can be accepted as fellow professionals. Otherwise it will be our own research which will suffer.

11 Practical ethnography

As we have already remarked, there is a dearth of literature on the practical implementation of the ethnographic programme. Its most influential methods texts such as Denzin (1970), Bruyn (1966) and Glaser and Strauss (1967) present abstracted theories of method which seek to develop general principles but give little indication of the ways in which these are to be related to the actual practice of fieldwork. This omission is a strange one, given the stress which the theorists with the greatest influence on sociological ethnography, Mead and Schutz, place on the interactive nature of social life. Conventionally, ethnographic reports focus on the interchange between members of the collectivity which they are studying but have little or nothing to say about the interchange between those members and themselves. As we saw in Chapter 9 the accounts of fieldwork which do exist vary considerably in their nature and quality and in the balance which they strike between semi-autobiographical description and explicit analysis.

We have selected three case studies of ethnographic fieldwork to illustrate some of the social influences on its product. Two of these are derived from Rosalie Wax's (1971) account of her career. The first, based on her research in American internment camps for Japanese immigrants during the Second World War, is chosen for its account of the micropolitics of ethnography and the everyday bargains which fieldworkers must strike. The other is taken from an abortive study of American Indian education to illustrate the mobilisation of high-level political pressures as a parallel to our analysis in the previous chapter. Our final example is based on one of the co-author's experiences as a member of two research units, concentrating particularly on the relationship between an ethnographer and his organisational settings and the career patterns of British sociologists.

236

Wax: Japanese internees

In the spring of 1942, following a wave of public and press hysteria, the government of the USA interned all 110,000 Japanese-Americans living on its Pacific coast. Whether citizens or aliens they were shipped off to camps in isolated areas of the American West or Midwest. There had never been any evidence of treason or espionage, yet the internees had been publicly vilified and had suffered irreparable economic losses. The internment camps were torn by dissension between pro-Japanese and pro-American factions and by suspicion of the administration of the camp's heavy-handed management. Internees who were too friendly with Caucasians were likely to be branded as *inu* (dog, i.e., 'stool pigeon') and ostracised or beaten up. It was against this background that Rosalie Wax began work in July 1943, employed to conduct participant observation in one of the internment camps.

Wax observes that, although she was hired as a participant observer, she had never received any formal instruction in how this might be done. She recalls that neither Kroeber nor Lowie discussed their own fieldwork in their courses at Berkeley and that the anthropology teaching relied on relatively old-fashioned theoretical ethnology. Her pre-college experiences of poverty and slum life among Mexican Americans were eventually to prove considerably more helpful. The project which she joined had been set up independently of the government by a group of social scientists at the University of California. Most of the other fieldworkers were Japanese-American students who had themselves been interned. Wax was hired to replace a Caucasian who had resigned. Her brief was to file detailed reports to the project director of what the internees were saying and doing.

Inevitably, her initial reception in the camp was rather cool. Several months went by without her making any real contact with the internees, most of whom regarded her as some sort of spy. She came under increasing pressure for results from the project director and later discovered that she had very nearly been dismissed. Her first breakthrough came when the camp's administration decided to ship out all those who would not affirm allegiance to the USA. She obtained a copy of the list of those to be moved and went to see them. About half agreed to be interviewed and talked in great detail about their loss of faith in America. In her view, some were treating her as an 'uninvolved stranger' whom they would not see again. Others had defined their position as a moral stand which they wanted to place on record. Both of these motives are important in most projects. Some informants just like talking about themselves, others have a principled position they wish to disseminate. Shortly after this, one of the project supervisors, himself a Japanese-American, visited her and introduced her to some friends of his in the camp who began to initiate her into the etiquette of everyday life among the internees.

At last, too, she had begun to realise the importance of trust between researcher and subjects. If her subjects were going to speak and act freely she would have to give them grounds for feeling confident in her presence. She deliberately began a programme of formal interviewing, inventing questionnaires on social stratification, delinquency, child-rearing and similar peripheral topics. They provided an entrée to a cross-section of the community for repeated visits without threatening to label the respondent as an *inu*. She began to learn how to read the complicated indirect conversation used by the internees and to manage discussions in sensitive areas. This all took time, and pressure from the director continued as she submitted reports on her survey activities. Finally, however, it paid off. An internee was shot while leaving the camp. Wax immediately visited her contacts throughout the camp. The crisis, she suggests, crystallised the trust which neither she nor her informants had consciously realised existed. Where they had given her casual assistance in the past, her present need for data was obvious. They had to choose between cutting her off or accepting her as the sort of person to whom they might speak their minds. Almost all chose the latter course.

This trust was, however, an essentially personal matter. Wax does not bring this out clearly in her analysis, but she recounts, for example, how she was individually distinguished from Caucasians as a whole

> his mother, who was sitting nearby, spoke to him sharply in Japanese, warning him not to tell 'that *Keto*' too much. (*Keto* is a derogatory term for Caucasian – a rough translation being 'hairy ape'.) He replied (in Japanese) 'she is a German Nisei' (second-generation immigrant; our note).

One should also remember the role of initial personal sponsorship by the visiting supervisor, who could vouch for her as an individual to his contacts in the camp. Fieldwork is a matter of personal rapport based on the individual actions of the researcher.

The costs of this personal involvement are significant. Wax recounts her deep depression and unhappiness with the frustrations of her early days in the field when she was socially isolated from both the Caucasian camp administration and the internees. Later, after moving to an even more unstable environment at another camp for those who had refused to proclaim their allegiance to the USA, she describes some of the highs of successful fieldwork.

> I went about this task with an unflagging energy and relish that today seems rather frightening.... I knew I might be killed, and this knowledge made me feel happy and well. At the same time, I was often very much afraid; however, the thing I feared was that the administration might find out how much I was learning and order me off the project. I do not think that this manic or 'battle-mad' state hampered my fieldwork or distorted my observations. Indeed, I probably would not have been able to live and work at Tule Lake had I been entirely in my right mind (Wax, 1971: 139).

Along with this euphoria Wax began to find herself taking sides in factional arguments. She had 'naïvely ... taken the side of the "oppressed" ' (Wax, 1971: 140) and erected a melodramatic and unreal model of 'true Japanese' conduct which she used to criticise anyone who deviated. As she admits, she had lost sight of the fact that she had no business sitting in judgment on people she was trying to understand. She gradually recovered through the discipline of field observation, continuing to make a scrupulous record of all she saw and heard whether or not she liked or understood it.

Wax also had some interesting observations on fieldwork in a factionalised situation. She notes how faction leaders can see themselves as performing on the stage of history and welcome the presence of a respectful and attentive listener as a keeper of the historical record. Given this it can prove possible to maintain relationships with each faction, without coming under pressure to disclose information. Disclosing or volunteering information is, of course, a very dangerous course of action, since trust in fieldwork is indivisible. If action is inadvisable, so too is rigid neutrality. Faction leaders have nothing to gain if there is no chance that the listener will change his mind.

> Throughout, I maintained the attitude of one willing to be convinced that the person addressing me was on the side of right and justice. I assumed – as, indeed, every fieldworker should assume about every human being – that he had good justification for his position, and, following this assumption, I listened to, recorded, and tried to understand his reasoning.... I do not advise an interviewer to pretend to adopt views of which he does not approve. He will, however, do well to remember that a coquette is in a much better position to learn about men than a nun (Wax, 1971: 170-1).

While the internment camp was an extreme situation, most settings for fieldwork are likely to contain some degree of factionalisation. It is certainly not the pathological state some studies seem to imply. On the other hand, there is a problem here, namely the degree to which the sympathetic interest of the ethnographer may slide into provocation through encouraging indiscretions.

Wax: tribal elders

Following other fieldwork, Rosalie Wax and her husband, Murray, moved to a university in the Midwest in 1964. Murray Wax decided that it would be useful to his department to mount a fair-sized research project. This notion of research being 'useful to the department' is an interesting one. A feature of American sociology is the stress, partly for economic reasons, placed on holding research contracts as an indication of the vigour of a department or an individual.

An old friend who was working from a near-by university introduced the Waxes to the Six Friendly Tribes. They developed the idea of looking at Indian children in public schools to compare with their earlier work on schools run by the Bureau of Indian Affairs and on boarding schools. Having lived in the South, they were sensitive to the difficulties of coping with the local political power structure and its hostility to anything other than establishment-controlled research. At the same time, they did have more experience than many Northern sociologists in living and working with such people.

The chiefs of the Six Friendly Tribes were appointed by the US Government. The most influential chief was Bayard Mayard of the Gokachi Tribe, a major executive of a prominent industrial corporation. Rosalie and Murray Wax had met him twice before: at an Indian summer school in 1959, he had impressed them as a decent and intelligent man, but in 1960 at an American Indian conference, they had been disturbed by his nominees' use of procedural tactics, smears and insults to railroad the meeting and by his refusal to intervene.

Murray Wax submitted a proposal to the Office of Education which was informally accepted in June. He was instructed not to make this known publicly until a formal contract was signed. In consequence, no prior briefing of local agencies or personnel could begin. Months went by with nothing happening. Murray Wax was fobbed off on a visit to Washington and it was only when the university dean of research administration took the matter up in November that they heard a new procedure had been introduced which required a more detailed budget and description of project activities. This represented a difficult task. Rosalie Wax quotes her husband: ' "To prepare a detailed and itemized budget requires that one envisage a precise and predictable future, whereas the essence of good and honest ethnographic research is flexibility" ' (Wax, 1971: 285). Murray Wax created an elaborate fiction. Further administrative tangles occurred and it was not until the middle of April, two-and-a-half months after the project began, that a correct contract was received.

The tension between the requirements of successful fieldwork and the auditors' pressures on public bureaucracies have acted as an important constraint on ethnography. It is, undoubtedly, difficult to prepare a detailed timetable and breakdown of costs for a style of work so inherently unpredictable. On the other hand, those charged with the disbursement of public money are hardly likely to feel confident in a proposal which allows the investigator to 'do his own thing' for a number of years without accountability. Particularly in Britain there has been a certain amount of prejudice against such bureaucratic requirements, without considering the degree to which they can introduce a useful discipline and to which application forms based on a survey model can be renegotiated, provided that the central accounting criteria are met. Unconstrained fieldwork is the luxury of the gentleman amateur rather than the professional researcher who must balance time and resources against the practical and intellectual returns. Nevertheless, as we show in our discussion of SSRC, public bureaucracies dealing with social scientists tend to be a marginal corner of the civil service notable more for their nervous inflexibility and inefficiency than their ability to relate creatively to those whom they are commissioning.

The Waxes had made some tentative moves towards securing local co-operation, although these were constrained by the secrecy of the Office of Education. In particular, Murray Wax wrote to Bayard Mayard who expressed interest in meeting them to discuss the project. They treated this as a formal gesture and did not pursue the invitation. Approaches were also made to the local education officials. As the project got under way and the contract finally arrived, attempts were made to use local press and radio to inform the community as a whole about the project. However, the press releases were ignored and the local radio spot on a Gokachi-language broadcast appeared not to have been heard by anyone.

From the beginning, the project encountered indifference and suspicion, verging on outright hostility from local officials and tribal leaders. They were accused, among other things, of being Federal agents trying to uncover discrimination or other malpractice in the local schools and/or of being Communist agitators out to disrupt the local tribal Establishment. Eventually, Bayard Mayard wrote to the Chancellor of the Waxes' university forwarding copies of resolutions by the tribal council denouncing their activities among the Gokachi. The Chancellor still had an idealised view of Mayard, comparable to that held by the Waxes prior to their fieldwork. He asked Murray Wax to prepare an outline of events and took the matter up at a personal meeting with Mayard. In his view this meeting resolved the situtaion and he set up a further meeting between Murray Wax and Mayard. However, resistance in the field continued and Murray Wax was tipped off at the ASA annual meeting about an impending investigation by the Department of Health, Education and Welfare. HEW set this for early October and Mayard deferred his meeting with Murray Wax (yet again) until mid-October.

Both sides began to mobilise their supporters. Like the case discussed in Chapter 10, Murray Wax relied on formal academic channels. He cancelled a number of invitations to eminent researchers to act as consultants, so that they could not be excluded from the 'unbiased' HEW team. He wrote to the officers of a number of social scientific societies asking them to express to HEW their concern over the possible liquidation of competent research through political pressure. He pressed the team to complete their preliminary reports and sent copies directly to the Secretary of HEW. Finally, he also sought to get the university to involve the local congressman. Meanwhile, their opponents mounted a more overtly political campaign. They continued to stir up local hostility, denouncing the team as Communists and uttering threats against people who co-operated with them. They got the local school board to rule against their admission to any local school. In addition, they also succeeded in getting the inspection deferred to coincide with a meeting of the intertribal council, which would inevitably occupy most of the time allocated for the inspection. The Waxes were disturbed by this and immediately wrote to HEW pointing out the council's record of chicanery and insisting they would only appear at its meeting if they were guaranteed a fair hearing.

On the eve of the inspection, two curious events occurred: the grant was renewed for a further six months and one of their chief accusers appeared in an attempt to conciliate them. Rosalie Wax suggests that the tribal establishment had panicked for some reason and told this individual that he was to be left alone to appease the Waxes or take the consequences. Although Rosalie Wax does not herself make the connection it is tempting to wonder if this is a result of a decision within HEW that the allegations were specious, the grant renewal being intended as a hint, and that the tribal leaders had also received some such indication. However, this is not supported by her version of the HEW inspection. The visiting HEW official seemed convinced that the Waxes were political agitators and was astonished by the grant renewal. The details of the visit do not matter for the present account, except to note that in fact the tribal council did back off. On his return to Washington, the HEW official confirmed that the project had been re-funded and re-approved at a high level in the face of the accusations and that further monies would be available.

Rosalie Wax suggests that the would-be fieldworker has a choice of access strategies: either to appear so lowly as to invite disregard as in her experience with the Japanese relocation camps or to come in with strong political backing, as in the Thrashing Buffalo research, which we have not discussed here, or to ally oneself with the most powerful faction, a procedure which she finds distasteful. Another strategy which she does not recognise is the use of a multi-member research team where different individuals deliberately cultivate different factions, as in the Banbury re-study, for instance (Bell in Bell and Newby, 1977: 57). Put like that, such a response would be shared by many. However, in our view, Wax is skating over the central question of the political sophistication which she drew out in her account of the Japanese relocation camps. Research does not take place in a political vacuum. The lowly novice may be able to get away with a greater degree of naivete because so much less is expected. With experience, however, researchers are, understandably, expected to acquire a greater appreciation of the situation of those with whom they are dealing. One of the most important elements of any research situation is in conciliating the interests which bear upon it. This includes one's sponsors and base organisation but a central place must go to those affected directly and indirectly by fieldwork.

Only the naïve would suppose that this meant ending up in the pockets of those interests. In our experience, what matters is that their views are fairly represented. If they can be satisfied on that count any disagreements on the part of the researcher will usually be tolerated. Many of the troubles of the CDPs described earlier can be ascribed to their simple-minded stance on this point and a consequent and, seemingly, arrogant disregard of the perspectives of substantial elements of the local community leadership. The result is one-sided reports which owe more to propaganda than social science and a legacy of mistrust which is likely to dog any future investigation.

Robert Dingwall: health visitors in Britain

Since this section is transparently based on the experience of one of the co-authors, it seems perverse to write the descriptive material in anything other than the first person singular. Our consensus on the substantive issues, however, is indicated by our use of the first person plural in analytic paragraphs.

In writing any historical account, it can be difficult to identify an appropriate starting-point, especially, as in the present instance, where the aim is analysis rather than autobiography. I have, however, tried here to concentrate on two areas of my life which illustrate points of more general significance: features of my background which relate to some of our arguments in Chapter 2 and features of my experience in two research units. Unlike my co-authors I have never held a teaching job.

I am, like most of my sociological contemporaries, second-generation middle class. My family took advantage of the post-war expansion in mobility opportunities, a process continued in my generation. Few sociologists in the UK are linked by birth or upbringing to the hereditary networks of political, economic and intellectual influences which are as significant in the reformist intelligentsia as in the Conservative Party. Most British sociologists are self-made, individually mobile through grammar, direct-grant or minor public schools. Even those who have passed through elite institutions like Oxbridge have remained outsiders. The case discussed in Chapter 10 shows some of the disadvantages of this: when under attack through their opponents' ability to manipulate certain networks, that research team had no effective extra-bureaucratic response. More generally, this sense of alienation and exclusion from established networks had its influence in developing the radical character of sociologists, with their hostility to *all* discrimination, including discrimination on merit, and their thoroughgoing democratic zeal.

Second, my background is primarily an arts one. At schools which derived their values from the public school tradition, the natural, and especially the social, sciences had low prestige as subjects for able sixth formers. My own original intention was to read modern languages. Given the high 'A' level grades demanded for sociology applicants in the late 1960s, it seems fair to suppose that the preponderance of that generation of sociologists would have similar backgrounds. This would certainly provide grounds for the concern felt in some quarters about the low level of mathematical competence among British sociologists. With such backgrounds, students will have dropped mathematics at 'O' level and few university teachers seem capable of picking up from that point successfully. This bias might also go some way towards explaining the curious preference of British sociologists for textual exegesis rather than empirical research.

As an undergraduate at Cambridge, I had been actively involved in student politics and sat on both the Economics Faculty Board and, later, the Social and Political Science Management Committee. Oxford and Cambridge may be regarded as elitist universities: internally, however, one of their most important features is that of radical democracy. The difficulties of change are due as much to elaborate systems of consultation and representation as to wilful obstruction by reactionary elements. Although the inclusion of students in this system was a relatively novel element, the internal ground rules were well-established. Particularly in the disciplines I was involved with, which were also already influenced by the radicalism of the 1960s, matters appeared to get settled more by force of argument than professorial decree. In retrospect, this is a somewhat simplistic view of the internal politics of the university, particularly given the constraining role of central committees; nevertheless, redbrick professorial autocracy is not common or structurally supported at Oxbridge.

For a course which was seen by university opponents as a radical innovation, the substance of the new Social and Political Science Tripos was surprisingly traditional. While it exploited the loose connection between lectures and examinations at Cambridge to create a veritable supermarket of courses, many shared with cognate disciplines, we still concentrated on Marx, Weber and Durkheim, with the Frankfurt School as the only 'modern' work discussed in depth. Our research methods paper in the first examinations was devoted primarily to issues in the philosophy of method. (Partly because of student pressure: we all wanted to be theorists!) Through the courses on the sociology of education, however, I was introduced to the work of Bernstein and the new writing represented in Young's (1971) *Knowledge and Control* collection. From this, I developed my original thesis proposal of studying teacher training as an exercise in the reproduction of educational knowledge. My undergraduate supervisor dissuaded me on the grounds that there was already a substantial, if unimpressive, literature which would make the topic unattractive to departments with graduate places. He suggested that I look at nurses and sent me to read Olesen and Whittaker's work. I saw the possibilities and applied on that basis to every department listed in the SSRC handbook as interested in medical sociology. The only serious offer was made by the Centre for Social Studies at Aberdeen – ironically of MRC rather than SSRC funds. I accepted it.

It must be said that the competition was not exactly stiff, although I did not know that at the time. Although one would not, without sounding too immodest, want to question the quality of the appointments, it must be recognised that Aberdeen has had some difficulty in attracting staff or graduate students. In recent years, economic elements have entered into this, given the discrepancy between nationally negotiated salaries and local prices. Such a persistent feature, however, points to the metropolitanism of British sociology. It is, in part, a reflection of the limited impact of community studies and, in part, the seduction of London circles for socially ambitious young academics. The number of long-distance reverse commuters approaches scandalous proportions, particularly when allied to the attitude represented by one such individual, holding a chair at a provincial university, who remarked on radio how sorry he felt for people who were obliged to live outside the capital. Inevitably, this detracts from their ability to link local institutions to their community through research, and increases the attraction of the sort of inquiry that can be pursued on High Speed Trains or between cocktail parties.

On arrival in Aberdeen, I drifted in a state of limbo for some months. I was told that a supervisor would be negotiated when I knew the staff better, to ensure we were personally compatible, and had been given the opportunity to develop my project in more detail. Unfortunately, I received no guidance on what would count as 'more detail'. Various names came up in conversation – Schutz, Garfinkel, Freidson – so I tried to read their work. In fact, like Rosalie Wax thirty years earlier, I received virtually no specific preparation for field research. In fairness to my former colleagues, I should make it clear at this point that subsequent students had a much more structured reception. When I left the Centre at the end of 1976, new students were put through a thirteen-week coursework programme and asked to produce extended essays on aspects of this. Progress from M. Litt. to Ph.D. registration depended on satisfactory completion of these assignments. My own experience was much less structured and it was only after a period of aimlessness that it was eventually agreed that some sort of move should be made and the Deputy Director and I went to see the Principal of the adjacent nurse training school. We were turned down flat, on the ground that the Briggs Committee was expected to report shortly and everything would be changed. This was early 1972. The report itself appeared that autumn. Legislation, affecting only the accrediting bodies, was passed early in 1979. Nursing education at the level of students and tutors has continued essentially unchanged. However, at this time the possible attractions of a before and after study did not seem compelling.

We were not inclined to take this objection at face value, since the hospital authorities did not seem to regard it as a problem, although they were not in a position to overrule the Principal.

Three underlying possibilities had been suggested to me at various times. First, a similar project in the same institution had been aborted by the suicide of the researcher and this was said to have left a residue of ill-feeling. Second, it was alleged that the Centre's Director had in the past made grandiose promises of research co-operation which had never been fulfilled. Third, the school's Principal was said to have a basic prejudice against any degree of intellectualism in nursing, as evidenced later by her opposition to proposals for a degree course. The truth of the matter is unascertainable and we mention it merely to illustrate the unpredictability of the research environment. The reception a researcher gets in requesting access is influenced by factors quite out of his control, like the vagaries of central or local government policy, the legacies of other research contacts or the caprice of individuals.

It was now late July in the first year of my studentship and I was stranded without a project. Together with my colleagues and supervisors, I tried to find an alternative which would not involve me in spending time on any substantial new preparation. The idea of looking at health visitors probably originated with Derek Gill. He was the latest in a series of individual members of Centre staff who had taught sociology and social administration at a school of health visiting over a considerable number of years. It was thought that this would provide an entrée. At the time I was distinctly cool about the idea. I had no idea what a health visitor was and found that hardly anyone had ever done any research on them before. It was, however, made clear to me that this would be a neat solution, allowing me to utilise my preparation for a participant observation study of professional socialisation and being elegantly bound to twelve months' fieldwork by virtue of the length of the course. In the long run, this was a major advantage since it solved the ethnographer's perennial problem of knowing when to impose closure on fieldwork and did so at a point which left me adequate time to complete my thesis before my three years' grant expired.

Derek Gill and I met the senior health visitor tutor and one of her colleagues at the end of August. I wrote up fieldnotes on this meeting afterwards and these seem to show that the discussion was fairly superficial and no great efforts at justification were required on our part. In this instance the experience of the research gatekeepers worked in our favour and it was assumed that we were the best judges of what was worth doing and how it was to be done. I was cleared to begin fieldwork two weeks later.

One problem raised at that meeting which merits further consideration is that of individual informed consent. Most ethical codes for social science lay down that this should be sought in advance of any research. While the tutors were willing to give us a list of lecturers whom we could approach, they were reluctant to let us contact the students before their arrival. They felt that this would increase the anxiety of a group who were already under considerable stress (Dingwall, 1977a: 28-43). Instead, it was agreed that I should be given an opportunity on the first day of the course to discuss the project. The tutors' argument appeared an eminently reasonable one and this view was shared by students in later conversations.

The problem with many of these ethical codes is that they disregard the nature of the researcher's actual situation. If one is studying an organisation, then there is a hierarchy of consent. Senior personnel have to be involved, since they alone carry the authority to commit their institution. Junior personnel have to weigh the consequences of refusing involvement in a project backed by their superiors. In such a context only senior personnel can be genuinely said to be in a position to give free consent. Where the seniors are ambivalent, junior staff may be able to mobilise opposition, but, generally speaking, higher level personnel are either enthusiastically for or flatly against research proposals. In the latter case, access will be refused, in the former, junior staff must give at least apparent co-operation, though the sociology of organisations is replete with examples of the informal power of lower-status personnel to sabotage new initiatives.

Several students told me later that they realised on the first day that they were not free to say 'no' and that it would probably not make much difference if they did. Clearly if I was collecting data on group situations it was going to be impossible to omit individual objectors. The pressures were compounded by an unintentional manipulation of the group meetings to press for assent. Both here and in a subsequent meeting with fieldwork instructors, objectors were reluctant to face me down and, once one or two indicated agreement, the uncommitted rapidly swung behind them. In contrast, another researcher in the same area at a later date who approached health visitors individually by letter found that in informal conversations about the request it was the objectors who had made the running and she had a high refusal rate. When I used an individual approach on the question of accompanying students on home visits I also found them more ready to refuse.

While on the topic of consent, one other problem for the ethnographer is worth mentioning. In his conduct, he is always trying to avoid intervening in the situation he is studying. Obviously, some participation in the situations is inevitable and, indeed, necessary. However, the researcher does not want to thrust himself forward. In a study like this so many people are encountered casually that it would become impractical and totally disruptive to pointedly seek consent on each and every occasion on which a new person is seen. Obviously, the major characters will be asked but the spear-carriers in the drama may be passed over. On the other hand, critical reviews will also focus on the principals, who are thereby placing themselves most at risk.

Whether promulgated by professional associations or enshrined in statute, ethical codes are often presented as a panacea for such difficulties. They do, however, founder on the essential indeterminacy of any set of procedural rules. Ethnography is faced with particular difficulties in this respect. Where a survey questionnaire can be scrutinised for its ethical character in advance and the collection and management of identifiable data subjected to fairly precise specifications, the ethical dilemmas of the ethnographer creep up unseen and require urgent decisions. This is particularly true, given the ethnographic tradition of investigative research which can lead the researcher into legally or morally dubious environments. One instance which came up during my current research on child abuse was where a colleague observed bruising on two children, which she ascertained that the responsible health visitor had overlooked. What would be her correct action? She had to solve that problem on the spot without any possibility of discussing it with the rest of the team, although her decision could have had considerable implications for all of us.

The trouble with ethical codes is that they put a premium on research which can be policed and can make life very difficult for ethnographers, as American researchers are increasingly finding. They can also undercut the sense of personal accountability and, hence, of the importance of personal integrity. In the instance cited above, the only way our team could work was through a sufficiently close professional relationship for each of us fully to trust each other's judgment as an individual. Obviously, a certain amount can be done to protect inexperienced workers from predictably difficult encounters, but difficulties are seldom predictable.

This analysis places the personal quality of the ethnographer at the heart of the enterprise. As we saw in Rosalie Wax's account, the trust of informants is ultimately on a personal basis, although there may be an initial 'halo' effect from the researcher's home organisation. She also noted the role of the ethnographer's self-discipline in maintaining the scientific basis of research, through the emotional and interpersonal pressures. The scientific quality of social science as much as the ethical quality is a state of mind rather than a set of procedural rules.

This highly individualised mode of research sits uneasily with the organisational contexts of funding and management. We have already noted Murray Wax's problems with HEW, experiences which could be matched in Britain. The situation does, however, appear a little easier here by virtue of the comparative underdevelopment of government research management bureaucracies, which can impose their own, or their masters', criteria. There does seem to be a greater margin for negotiation. Tensions do, however, emerge in research organisations without the cushion of funding which improves teachers' ability to bargain. An analysis of these demonstrates a further set of influences on the shape of research.

The concerns of research sponsors, who put up the cash, are not very salient features of everyday research. They are, however, highly relevant for directors, who, given the short-term nature of research contracts, find themselves with continuing problems of securing a steady flow of income. This applies as much to MRC and SSRC Units which are subject to regular review or DHSS Units on medium-term rolling grants as to independent centres based on outside contracts. The director is drawn into a good deal of politicking and public relations activities which are designed to create a favourable environment for the continued flow of money. Consequently, his ability to participate in and, hence, effectively manage research is limited. At the same time, the outcome of that research is important to him, since his ability to bring in projects on time within budget and with some relevance to the original brief are factors in outside evaluation. Rosalie Wax's description of her internment camp fieldwork hints at some of these pressures. Like most investors, research sponsors prefer to back proven winners, although, paradoxically, a team which is too competent may be threatened as having been made redundant by its own success.

The director may attempt to control the uncertainty, in so far as it is within his power, by building up a stable group of trusted confederates. However, this only increases his problems in sustaining an adequate flow of cash, since the longer staff remain, the more expensive they become. In order to protect their own prospects, the staff become involved in work which will enhance their general reputation within the discipline, thereby distracting them from tasks which the director is obliged to regard as central if he is to satisfy his sponsors. Some features of Colin Bell's version of the Banbury re-study suggest such an occurrence.

An endemic conflict in research units centres on the questions of success and failure. Strong (1976) has pointed to the unsociological nature of accepted accounts of failure as an individual responsibility. From the director's point of view, it is important that success be collectivised. Credit attaches to the organisation rather than to individuals, giving a superficial appearance of continuity to support arguments for renewed funding despite individual departures. For instance, people still talk about the Chicago School although no major ethnography has been produced from that department in twenty years.

The difficulty is, of course, that outsiders do not necessarily accept this ambivalence and either applaud individuals or blame the organisation. In Aberdeen, this was an acute problem since we were very dependent on the co-operation of a few local institutions. We only had access to one each of the principal members of our society's set of health, education and welfare organisations and these were closely interlinked by the social networks of the city's professional classes. One individual failure could compromise not just that agency but the whole research programme. This, of course, can be a major source of anxiety in conceding autonomy to ethnographers. An important result is the low political profile of many publications. Controversy is a luxury researchers cannot afford. Of course, ethnographers are not in the business of exposé journalism. Nevertheless, a desire to preserve relationships with key informants or institutions can lead to an emasculating degree of self-censorship.

The alternative is for the director to make continued employment strictly contingent on compliance with his requirements. If he is to succeed, then he must adopt research modes which can readily be bureaucratised, particularly survey-type inquiries. He must also discourage staff from acquiring sufficient experience to contest his position or be distracted into career channels. Typically, the director resorts to the large-scale employment of young women graduates as 'hired hands'. Their selection orientates to conventional attitudes and modes of life. The director can, then, reasonably expect that within a few years they will retire to raise a family and will not, therefore, have particular reason to pursue career ends or seek a stake in the credit for the research. Given the convergence between these pressures and the requirements of research funding bureaucracies, the spread of this mode of research in recent years has been marked. Although Roth's (1966) criticisms of such organisations both for their ethics of recruitment and their naïve assumptions about work standards, seem to crop up in every methods reader, their practical impact appears to have been negligible.

Such developments are, however, inimical to ethnography. It is notable how surprisingly few of the major studies in Britain are produced by experienced investigators, as opposed to being the output of less tightly-regulated, graduate studentships. This constrains the scale and duration of the projects, quite apart from the hit-and-miss quality of supervision. Such restrictions limit, for instance, the degree to which empirically grounded generalisations can be made. Looking back on *The Social Organisation of Health*

Visitor Training, I am surprised at the boldness of some of the claims, although subsequent data would not impel me to make any drastic changes. Nevertheless, I am quite aware that the methodology of my present work on child abuse is much more rigorous in the way in which the project has been designed to make systematic analytic comparisons possible at all levels from individual field-workers to entire agencies. Such a design, however, reflects not just greater experience but also a larger budget and a team setting. These are relative luxuries, although they are the necessary concomitants of more solidly generalisable findings.

None of this is to discount the role of intellectual influence. The research that people want to do in any age is obviously substantially determined by the ideas available to the would-be investigator. The research that actually gets done, however, is ultimately determined by a quite different set of influences; the availability of funds, access to people and places and, most crucially, the organisational settings in which sociologists work.

12 Sociology and the Social Science Research Council

Sociological research and post-graduate training in Britain over the last fifteen years have overwhelmingly been funded by the SSRC. From the outset its performance has been a continual source of debate: each different kind of sociologist has protested that his particular branch of the discipline is not receiving fair treatment. In all this time, however, there has been little systematic study of what SSRC *as a whole* is trying to do, and what the Sociology Panel is doing. In this chapter we look at certain aspects of SSRC, particularly its basic philosophy of what sort of research needs to be done, and under what conditions. On the one hand, we find ourselves very much in agreement with SSRC's aims to improve the standards of research, and to get research done on substantive issues. On the other hand, SSRC's obsession with inter-disciplinary research, immediate pay-off, and the growing central direction of research activity, are seen as potentially serious threats to academic freedom.

Sociological research costs money, and so does training to become a sociologist by means of a higher degree. Since 1965 this money has come mainly from the SSRC which funds not only sociology but the other social sciences. In turn, its funds come from the state. It is true that other sources of research grants do exist – the large foundations both in this country and abroad, like the Nuffield, Rowntree, Leverhulme, Wolfson, Gulbenkian, Ford, Carnegie, Rockefeller and so on, together with several smaller ones – but the SSRC is the biggest, the best known, and probably the most criticised. Other sources of funding have been more demanding as clients, whether they are government departments or business organisations: they have had 'problems' and wanted direct 'solutions', an aspect of the sociological enterprise already discussed in the chapter on policy research.

While the would-be researcher can in theory choose between various sources of funding for more open-ended kinds of research, in practice this choice is somewhat limited. First, each foundation tends to have a focus of its own which directs its funds towards certain types of research and substantive topics. For example, the Rowntree Memorial Trust has been particularly active in urban sociology and race relations, the Leverhulme Trust has supported work on industry and government, while the Gulbenkian Foundation has financed a great deal of community work. Second, trusts and foundations do not have a large staff or teams of academics on hand to act as referees on applications. Like the government departments, they frequently pass over applications to the SSRC for an expert opinion. The would-be researcher therefore has relatively little room to manoeuvre, should his initial approach be turned down. And only the SSRC provides post-graduate training awards.

It follows from this that the SSRC has a central place in British sociology, and this exposed position as giver and withholder of finance inevitably leads to unpopularity. But does the SSRC have a central place in determining the subject content of sociology, its styles, its lines of new development, its fundamental nature? Given the broad thesis of this book, that the social context of the discipline is inherently bound up in what the discipline professes, the expected answer must be in the affirmative. However, the picture is not so clear-cut, since SSRC has not developed as an efficient, monolithic institution, but rather as an under-resourced and many-headed agglomeration of interests. It *has* had a basic policy, but it has not been able to maintain that policy in a consistent and forceful fashion. The social sciences have become too well entrenched in the universities to be easily directed along new paths by a governmental organisation, albeit one with considerable financial powers. SSRC's responses to this situation have been many and varied, but its own pet projects have often fallen by the wayside, undermined by a lack of skilled and experienced staff, and firm opposition often on both ideological and professional grounds from sociologists.

Some of the reasons for this state of affairs can be understood by looking firstly at the origins of government research funding since the Second World War. In 1946, the Committee on the Provision for Social and Economic Research – the Clapham Committee – reported on 'whether additional provision was necessary for research into social and economic questions' (Clapham, 1946). Clapham's view was that although more should be done to foster social research there were insufficient grounds for a research council: 'the social sciences, although rich in promise, have not yet reached the stage at which such an official body can be brought into operation' (Clapham, 1946, para. 22). They gave three reasons for this conclusion. First, because they were concerned about increasing the flow of statistical information for governmental purposes, they were interested in 'routine research', that is, the regular supply and monitoring of data. The existing research councils had not been set up with this kind of work in mind, and did not therefore encourage it. As these would be the model for a new council, the same result would ensue. Second (and with the benefit of hindsight, ironically), the committee did not wish to see 'spurious orthodoxies' overtaking the still infant social science. They feared a council would favour some orthodoxies over others. Third, they diagnosed one core problem as a shortage of social scientists, which a research council could not only not overcome, but might exacerbate by diverting the best men from practical work to co-ordination and administration.

Rather than a research council, Clapham put forward two main policy recommendations. First, the University Grants Committee (UGC) should do more to build up university staffing in social science. This could be done by earmarking funds for new posts, improved library facilities, and installing new facilities for data analysis. A UGC sub-committee should be set up to review the work done, and identify any gaps that required filling. The second recommendation was that a Standing Interdepartmental Committee on Economic and Social Research should be established to advise on research work in government departments (Clapham, 1946, para. 32). In the state of the social sciences at the time this was not unreasonable. The committee could identify only three social and political (as opposed to economic) university research institutes: LSE, with 'no continuing financial support, and small research units at Glasgow and Liverpool. Elsewhere there is nothing' (Clapham, 1946, para. 20). In the last year before the Second World War, students graduating in sociology, social administration and anthropology together made up less than one-third of 1 per cent of the graduating class.

The UGC set about implementing the Clapham Committee's report, and expanded social science provisions, for which they earmarked £1,220,000 in the 1947-52 quinquennium. The UGC also set up a sub-committee as recommended. It is not possible to be exact about what sociology gained from this, but on the basis of the Heyworth Committee's later assessment (1965) it seems likely that the discipline benefited to the tune of only about 15 to 20 extra posts (although how many would have been established in any case is a moot point). Some universities, like Southampton and LSE, merged their allocation with other funds, Cambridge used £4,800

255

for a temporary visiting Professor of Social Theory, while Oxford established one permanent lectureship in Sociology. Exeter and Hull did the same, the former also financing a permanent Research Fellowship. Several other universities set up inter-disciplinary institutes or posts in 'social studies'; Glasgow, Nottingham, Sheffield, Reading, Swansea and Manchester being the most prominent. Manchester created the Chair of Social Anthropology (which was later to nurture sociology) together with a number of research assistantships, while Glasgow acquired four teaching posts. In all, it was not a noted success for sociology, nor did it meet the intentions of the Clapham Committee to finance *research*. As Heyworth observed, 'the large majority of the posts thus created were teaching posts ... in subjects then inadequately developed, such as sociology, few of the departments for which the Clapham Committee had hoped were established' (Heyworth, 1965, para. 25). The special UGC sub-committee was disbanded in 1952 following an undertaking that UGC would treat social science on the same basis as other disciplines. The Standing Inter-Departmental Committee slowly faded out: no meetings took place after 1960, and by the time the Heyworth Committee was taking evidence from civil servants 'most ... had never heard of it' (para. 27).

In retrospect, the UGC and the universities wasted a golden opportunity to set up new departments and in particular new research posts, although of course the stimulus had come from outside, not from within the universities themselves. Clapham was primarily concerned with generating skilled professional man-power, not undergraduates, and with having a social research establishment. These permanent research organisations could have provided a career and institutional structure for social science research which would have been of immense benefit today. Instead, normal processes of academic politics took over, and after that one quinquennium sociology had little growth until public demand picked it up in the 1960s.

However, the resurgence of interest in financing social science research was not so much based on student demand, as on a revival of interest in information for policy making. A reading of the Heyworth Committee's deliberations makes this clear and, as the body which led to the setting up of the SSRC, its assumptions and approach reveal a view of government finance for social science which is quite at odds with the contemporary views of many sociologists. Its terms of reference were to review research work 'in Government departments. universities and other institutions' (note the ordering) and to advise on the arrangements 'for supporting and *co-ordinating* this research' (emphasis added, para. 1). From start, its idea of 'research' was survey research: Paragraph 2, under 'method of working' tells us that the Committee 'sent question-naires to a large number of organisations', while in defining the range of social science disciplines, the report observes that a common feature is that 'statistics and statistical method are of fundamental importance in nearly all' of these subjects entering in 'the study of social problems' (para. 7).

> Sociologists study society in the large, i.e., such topics as the
> inter-relationships of groups or classes within society, as in race
> relations; occupational mobility; attitudes of social classes to one
> another; effects of urban life. Many are concerned with demo-
> graphic material ... sociologists, although they sometimes use
> (the anthropological) method, more often make use of surveys,
> questionnaires and interviews, subjecting their findings to statis-
> tical analysis (paras 13 and 14).

In the early 1960s (the Committee was set up by R. A. Butler in June 1963) this was not an unreasonable assessment of the state of the art, even if it neglected other elements of sociological practice. To be fair, the Committee did note that the development of theory was of extreme importance (para. 13) and research should not be regarded just as 'routine fact finding, or fact finding for specific administrative purposes' (para. 9).

The Committee's view of sociology was probably influenced by the sociologists whom it consulted. In a series of seminars with social scientists which was held around the country, these sociolo-gists included most notably Halsey, MacRae, Worsley, Mays, Gittus, Williams, Sykes, Banton and Burns. There was no sociolo-gist on the small committee itself.

The central concern of Heyworth was of course not sociology, but the social sciences *in toto*, and an inter-disciplinary model was part and parcel of the Committee's work. Attention has already been drawn above to the reference to the study of social problems as a defining characteristic for social science (para. 7). In the following paragraph, the Committee goes on to say that all kinds of social and non-social sciences are also inextricably mixed 'in the kind of environmental planning that is necessary in modern society'. Several of the seminars with academics stressed the same kind of theme: 'research into problems of regional and urban develop-ment', 'fields of common interest to Government (central and local) and universities', and the final meeting at which the Committee 'assembled people from industry, local government and other fields in which the social sciences are applicable' (para. 5): 'when practitioners of different disciplines are brought together over a practical issue each finds that the other can throw light on different aspects of (the) problem ... we believe the social sciences are likely also to become more interdependent' (para. 7).

Although the BSA was consulted, and several sociologists participated in the seminars (and others like Tropp, Wedderburn and Klein gave evidence as individuals) the list of bodies giving evidence is far from dominated by sociologists or even by academics. For the academics, there were nearly forty universities and colleges of Advanced Technology, a dozen unions and educational pressure groups, twenty research institutes and as many learned societies. For the non-academics – the users of the research – there were seventeen government departments, fifteen health organisations, and the same number of charitable trusts, thirty-nine organisations concerned with welfare and penology, eight local authority associations, twenty-eight housing and planning bodies, and as many from the field of industry and commerce, three political groups and six religious bodies. A list of individuals did contain a number of senior academics but few sociologists and it also even contained a few firms like ICI, Esso, and big steel companies. The emphasis was more on the utility of research and the views of the client, than on the needs of the researcher.

While the Committee wrote that they did not attempt to identify what research was required, or should have priority, either as to topic or as to method, we have already seen the emphasis on survey method and statistical analysis. Again, in the section dealing with the need for more research, more than twice the space is given to the needs of the client than to the needs of the researcher. Although the individual 'scholar of outstanding ability and promise' is identified as a special case for support, the emphasis is quite different:

> much of the research work aimed at tackling social and
> economic problems needs teams of people trained in more than
> one discipline ... Increasingly research in the social sciences,
> particularly on practical problems, needs the co-operation of
> people trained in different disciplines (paras 94 and 95).

From the outset then, there were elements in the Committee's deliberations which were somewhat perturbing. The emphasis on client need, rather than professional autonomy is one. The frequent reference to inter-disciplinary research is another, while the status given to statistical methods is a third. These themes have been a repeated feature of the SSRC's policy over the years, and not surprisingly, the inevitable tension between autonomous professionals and state officials has crystallised around them.

It is difficult to assess how much of this concentration on certain types of research was and continues to be window-dressing. The Report came out strongly in favour of an expansion in social science research. To carry this through the political machinery required the mobilisation of support in many and varied centres, together with the presentation of a case that would be acceptable to politicians and mandarins alike. It is difficult to visualise the Committee operating without some nod in the direction of applied research, given the policy-making process. A case for funding only 'basic research' to suit the needs of the academic community was hardly likely to receive a high priority for action. The same holds true today. Indeed, there is a great deal to be said in favour of the Committee's view, apart from the success of their advocacy which helped to achieve an organisation to finance social science research. For one thing, the interest of a government department in a 'problem' does not automatically mean that it must be outside the interest of sociology. For another, although Heyworth set its face against pure or basic research *per se*, it equally rejected total and exclusive concentration on applied work:

> Basic research and applied research both have to be carried out simultaneously; neither can advance without the other.... Furthermore, the social and human factors which affect the application of research are themselves part of the subject of the research (Heyworth, 1965, para. 89).

The examples which Heyworth gives of topics suggested to the Committee, embodying their assumptions about what research is all about, cover a wide range of the concerns of that era. As Table 1 shows, many of these topics have since been researched, but most remain as pressing in the popular mind as ever.

Table 1 The Heyworth Committee's list of problems requiring more social and economic research (Heyworth, 1965, pp. 29-30)

Economic Growth and Development

Incomes policy – how do people arrive at their notion of a fair wage?

Applying Science to Industry – how can technology attract people of high ability and leadership?

Automation – what are the likely economic and social consequences of automation?

Industrial efficiency

– what are the forces maintaining restrictive practices of employers and employees?

– what are the most effective forms of organisation of industrial enterprises?

Regional Development

– what effect do developments in one region have upon those in others?

– what are the social and economic factors affecting regional migration?

Environment

Land use – how should one form of land use be compared with another?

Planning – what are the social effects of different forms of environmental planning and design?

Urban renewal – how can cities be redeveloped to form satisfactory social settings?

Education

– how does the educational system affect the social structure?
– what is the most effective form of classroom organisation? (e.g. how should 'streaming' be arranged or should we not have 'streaming'?)
– what should be the function of boarding school education in present day society

Welfare

– what special needs have old people?
– how can problem families be re-educated?
– what factors affect the success of methods of rehabilitating the handicapped and infirm?

Health

– how can the relationship between elements of the health services best be organised?
– what factors affect the rehabilitation in society of patients who have suffered from mental illness?

Delinquency

– what are the physical, psychological, genetic and social factors affecting delinquency?
– how can the most effective treatment for delinquents be determined?

Immigration

– what factors affect the integration of immigrants into society?

Law and Society

– what factors affect the relationship between police and public?
– what are the effects of legal systems, procedures and enactments upon the relationships between groups and between individuals in society?

International Relations

– what are the social and economic factors affecting the success of various methods of giving foreign aid?
– what is the legacy of colonialism in the social structures of emergent countries?

260

The list has been included in full, because it gives an excellent representation of the style of social thought which was dominant at that time, and still underpins much sociological work. The stark baldness of the questions now seems too simplistic, and not every aspect of the list is fashionable: talk of restrictive practices in industry, re-education of problem families, or genetic factors in delinquency would find few sympathetic ears in modern sociology. This is due partly to the very success of rival sociological work in demonstrating the greater power of alternative explanations. For all that, many of the other issues are still with us, and in more pressing form: automation and unemployment, in the wake of the micro-processor revolution; urban renewal, at a time when council housing stock is in physical decline; the needs of old people, with an ageing population; and even John Rex could not dissent from the need to study 'the legacy of colonialism in the social structures of emergent countries'. These problems have not, however, generally been researched on an inter-disciplinary basis, at least by sociologists. The last fifteen years have been ones of separate development for each of the social sciences, and this has resulted in a tension between SSRC and the social scientists, particularly the sociologists.

This independence of the disciplines has not been to the liking of the 'centralists' who wished to see SSRC exercising direction and influence over the scattered – and scatter-brained – academics in the country's universities. The first chairman, Michael (now Lord) Young has since lamented the way in which the organisation was set up with its 'horrific committee structure' of twelve powerful discipline committees handling the allocation of grants and post-graduate training awards: 'It was clear that the first concern of the Sociology Committee – or almost any other committee for a discipline – was going to be the advancement of sociology, rather than Heyworth's elusive benefits' (Young, 1975, 5). A similar desire to organise research effort can be found in his successor, Andrew Shonfield's, views that government departments should have more say in sponsoring research (Shonfield, 1969). If academics were left to their own devices, they would continue to do what they thought was interesting and worthwhile, rather than working in inter-disciplinary teams on practical problems. That was no way to demonstrate to the Treasury that social science research was a suitable destination for taxpayer's money.

This struggle between centralisation and academic freedom has marked SSRC's whole history. As the third chairman of SSRC acknowledged, there were and still are two camps. One sees research as problem-oriented, timely, inter-disciplinary and 'centrally-selected'. The other wishes to advance knowledge for its intrinsic value, rejects the current fads and fancies in defining what is a problem, is concerned to push out the frontiers of knowledge in its own discipline and tradition, is rigorous to the extreme, and emphasises that the researcher's job includes deciding what topic to select for research (Matthews, 1975a, 9). It was under the chairmanship of R. C. O. Matthews, the third chairman, that a major re-organisation took place, with the intention of introducing a more explicit procedure for allocating expenditure between major categories, and secondly to develop the 'research intiatives' side. In fact, while the re-organisation within SSRC may have helped administratively, the main feature of the change was to elevate the SSRC's role in commissioning – or 'initiating' – research to equal status with its research grants and post-graduate training. Only a few years before, there was little sign of this. To take one example, there is hardly a mention of the word 'initiative' in the 1972 issues of the SSRC newsletter. Initiatives did take place, but these were fewer and less grandiose. Some were handled through the unsuccessful Survey Research Unit, which for example saw to the setting up of area studies at Durham and Strathclyde, and instituted a regular opinion poll type survey to which academics could add their own questions – regardless of context! This bizarre exercise had a mercifully short life, in contrast to the Area Studies which, established in academic departments and asserting a normal academic independence, produced a great deal of competent research.

In announcing the new set-up for SSRC in the *Newsletter*, Matthews presents a strange version of the organisational structure (Matthews, 1975b). Although the new Research Initiatives Board (RIB) is included in an organisational chart, most of its supervisory functions are not drawn in. The fact that the RIB was now in charge of the SSRC Units is buried in the text, while only a footnote to the chart shows that the RIB controlled two panels (on population and energy), two working parties (pollution and transmitted deprivation) and one committee (social forecasting). While the RIB was not to be charged with generating all new initiatives, it would be responsible for *vetting* all new initiatives. Thus it could identify gaps in existing work, but also receive suggestions for work; suggestions from any source whatsoever, including: 'government departments, industry, private bodies or individuals, other research councils or components within SSRC's structure' (Matthews, 1975b, 12). Between the financial years 1976/7 and 1977/8, the RIB budget increased by £100,000. In the same period, research grants for researcher-selected projects fell by £450,000 (Mack, 1979).

What sort of thing has the RIB initiated? Its key position is shown by an examination of almost any issue of the SSRC *Newsletter*. In March 1978 for example, it was reported that £120,000 of the Council's budget would go to a joint Equal Opportunities Commission/SSRC study of women (to report to the RIB) (p. 16). A new panel 'to identify research priorities and formulate a programme of research on the relationship between central and local government' had been set up following RIB discussions (p. 17). £200,000 had been earmarked for research into accountability in education 'on the recommendation of the Research Initiatives Board' (p. 17). The Council also 'accepted the Research Initiatives Board recommendation' that a research exchange agreement with CNRS should be renewed. Other enterprises reported that year (*Newsletter* no. 38) include £750,000 for energy research, £500,000 with the Sports Council on recreation research, and £50,000 for work on accountancy. There are currently over fifteen of these projects in hand (see also *SSRC Newsletter* no. 33, 1977).

Some of the subject committees have seen the RIB as a source of extra funds, and worked closely with it. The direct consequence is that reports go through RIB to Council, not through the subject committees. The long term effect is greater central control over what research gets done. Rather than being a passive source of funding, SSRC is increasingly taking over one of the proper functions of the universities and polytechnics. Permanent officials – many with relatively little social science experience and qualification – together with a small group of academics *picked by the SSRC Council* through its own confidential system, are exercising control over a very large proportion of the total budget. Their judgments run the danger of becoming based not primarily on academic standards but on what is politically expedient at any given time.

Of course, it must be recognised that academics and research managers do sit on the RIB, and initiatives do arise in the subject panels which subsequently result in new sources of funds. However, an examination of the recent appointments to the RIB and the subject committees emphasises the status of the former and the decline of the latter. The RIB includes important people; the subject committees are important to the people in them. As one informant on the latter has commented, this compromises their ability to influence events through the awareness of their own relative insignificance. Resignations from subject committees over cuts would cause the barest ripple. If academics are not interested in the problems facing Britain today, or if they are slow to see the opportunities for research, then they create a vacuum which the RIB can fill. Much of this book has been directed to explaining why sociologists have a low research output: their lack of production makes it all the more likely that the RIB will grow in influence. Much of its work may be highly commendable, but the potential for misdirection remains, particularly in the light of SSRC's concern with projects of immediate utility.

Even in the early years, Michael Young had quite deliberately set up 'counter-committees' to balance the subject committees, out of his fear lest SSRC should come to an early demise for failing to show the benefits of applied research (Young, 1975, 5). Matthews's ploy in 1975 was a well-established one, and it reflects the obsession with political cutbacks and indeed closure which all the Chairmen including the latest, Michael Posner (Posner, 1979, 712), show, for example in the 10th Anniversary Issue of the *SSRC Newsletter* (1975, no. 29).

It is hard to evaluate their stance from the outside. Recent cutbacks by the Thatcher administration would prompt one to argue in their favour, and Shonfield in particular presents a horrifying picture of ignorance among politicians about what social science is, let alone the details of its practice. How many sociologists are going to dispute Robinson's point 'that if we want to obtain our share of public funds we are going to have to work for it much harder, and justify ourselves publicly' (Robinson, 1975, 11). Or his plea that the allocation of funds must continue to be on academic grounds as determined by academic peers? But a system of counter-balancing committees and a RIB is in danger of going too far to pacify our political masters. The pressure point of academic standards lies in the subject committees, and as professionals we have found that specialisation is the only solution to the knowledge explosion. It is not possible to reshape social science by means of the SSRC, and it is counter-productive to try.

It would be a false analysis to assume that in the subject committees all is sweetness and light, and that difficulties arise only elsewhere in the organisation. The individuals who sit on the Sociology and Social Administration Committee are inevitably a mixed bunch, as are the anonymous referees who are called upon to comment on applications for research awards. Furthermore, the committees are served by a permanent secretariat, who form (with the Committee Chairman) the link between subject committee and the rest of SSRC. The secretary holds a crucial position, although the extent of his powers has been disputed. Critics like Moore (1977b) have suggested that the secretary's role as gatekeeper is an important one: the researcher's

> relations with the committee are *mediated* by a committee
> secretary who has no formal power over applicants but whose

mediating or brokerage role gives him considerable informal power ... They choose how to edit referees' comments, or present committee views in seeking revisions of an application.... Secretaries also know the informal rules of the SSRC and may choose whether or not to make these known to applicants (Moore, 1977b, 34-5).

Although constrained by the formal rules of civil service procedure, the secretary thus has considerable *potential* for influence. In some cases this seems to have been exercised. For example, certain technical difficulties encountered in the Scottish Mobility Study (on which the research team requested advice) appear not to have been reported even to the Chairman of the Sociology and Social Administration Committee, who claimed to have found out only indirectly a year later. In the case of Aberdeen University's proposals for North Sea Oil research, Moore sees an attempt to shape even broad academic policy in the remark of one official that sociologists 'should study "the bruise and not the fist" in researching the social impact of oil' (Moore, 1977b, 35). To be fair, secretaries are constrained from entering into public debate, and their informal and conversational reactions have been protestations of innocence and loyalty. It is difficult not to harbour suspicions, however, when the secretary's job involves selecting referees for applications, and then presentation to the Committee. Since members of the Sociology and Social Administration Committee have in conversation admitted that the business, particularly in their first few meetings, is often beyond them, and that the pressure of work places great emphasis on one person's judgment – i.e., the one member of the Committee allocated a specific application to handle – then the permanent civil servant is potentially at an advantage.

Ironically, one check on potential abuse of the secretary's position is the high turnover of SSRC staff. The absence of suitable established posts within SSRC means that the typical Committee secretary must leave the research council to achieve promotion. Low establishment gradings (among other things) result in high staff turnover, and hence a shortage of practical experience and knowledge of 'case-law' on which to deal with problems. Even typing and clerical work is affected in this respect. Civil servants have informally commented that SSRC has at times been used as a dumping ground by the DES – which itself is not the brightest jewel in the civil service's crown. These features go a long way to explain the frequent delays in getting answers from SSRC on any question that is the least out of the ordinary.

A further basic problem of SSRC's operations lies in the nature of research applications. In order for peer judgment to take place, SSRC expects a formal statement of the intended project, including literature review, methodology, statement of hypotheses and so on. In general this is a sound procedure, but it is not without difficulties. First, it assumes that sociology operates in a tidy, rational fashion in which 'problems' are seen to emerge and require solution. That is, it is dictated by a model of research in which a conceptual difficulty, or some previously anomalistic finding, will provide the impetus for a controlled experiment, such that the researcher knows in advance what to expect, how to interpret it, and how it will be integrated in a wider body of theory. Second, it assumes that 'problems' are not in themselves controversial, or *urgently* in need of solution.

In fact, the sociologist may wish to explore an issue precisely because it puzzles him. He may not have a clear conception of what he will find because his work is an innovation. It may be that existing paradigms are inadequate and it is by means of doing research that the sociologist seeks to develop new theory. If it were all so cut and dried, there would be much less point in doing the research in the first place. Again, the issues may be urgent, concerning some phenomenon which will not await the convenience of the sociologist, let alone the civil service.

This seems to have been the case with Aberdeen's attempt to mount North Sea Oil research. The impact of new industries was evident to the sociologists in North East Scotland in 1972. They first applied for finance in 1973 (to the Scottish Office) and negotiated with SSRC from April 1974. The North Sea Oil Panel was set up in 1975 to co-ordinate research (in units not exceeding £10,000), but Moore was still able to write in the Spring of 1977 that 'no major sociological projects were under way' (Moore, 1977b, 1). By that time, it was a little late to monitor the social changes that the oil companies had caused.

The North Sea Oil case is a good example of what can happen when SSRC decides to handle 'initiatives'. That it is cumbersome is not the least of the worries. Many of the participants in that *cause célèbre* were convinced that a deliberate policy of obstruction was followed in order not to have SSRC associated with what might have been a politically explosive issue. This was not the only possible explanation for the lack of support. The original applications may have been unsatisfactory; the 'problem' perhaps did not really merit investigation; the Sociology Committee could have wanted to save its money by allowing the North Sea Oil Panel to pay for the research; Aberdeen had had its share of research funds and should not have had a further major grant; or perhaps other academics were not capable of filling the vacuum. As no one has seriously suggested that a topic for research did not exist, one is forced to assume *either* that the SSRC acted out of political cowardice (not inconsistent with some of the Chairmen's statements, as seen above) *or* that SSRC was incompetent in that its 'initiatives' failed, or both.

With this in mind, what is one to make of the RIB? SSRC's record of initiatives is not generally good. There is not room to deal with all of them here, but overall the balance must come down on the negative side whether one evaluates it on general criteria or adopts the test of what notable new sociology has been generated. If, then, greater resources are to be channelled into the RIB, and SSRC's tactics in its political manoeuvrings depend on the RIB's success, we could be looking to a bleak future. The best social scientists since the Second World War have generally not favoured the inter-disciplinary, problem-oriented style of work. There is surely a lesson in that: SSRC is pinning its hopes on a horse with a bad track-record, and its greater 'initiative' means greater involvement of permanent officials and further confusion of what SSRC's role should be.

There is already one example of this in SSRC's 'reviews of research' publications. These books provide a perspective on how Heyworth's ideas were carried forward in the early years of SSRC's existence, in a climate of fear of the political masters. Given that so much of SSRC's performance has been controversial, a review of some of these publications has the added advantage that the documents are there in concrete form. The sceptical reader can turn to them to make his own evaluation, should he doubt the construction that the present authors put upon them. The same cannot be said for individual decisions and personal intentions, or the other elements of policy which we will encounter later.

Written by SSRC's subject committee, or by working parties of specialists brought together under the Council's auspices, the reviews were intended to

> cover major current research schemes and possible future developments in particular areas of study. They also look at research needs in terms of men, money and organisation. The reviews will be of particular interest to research workers in each subject, but at a time of increasing specialization they will also help all social scientists and the users of their research to keep abreast of devleopments over a wider field.

This declaration of intention is carried on the cover of all the earlier editions, which consisted of two broad types of work: on the one hand there are the issue-oriented books, on social research and automation, poverty, social indicators, and comparability of data, while on the other there are the state of the discipline reports, produced by the subject panels: Political Sciences, International Organisations, Economic and Social History, Human Geography, and Social Anthropology are all represented, while the Statistics Committee chose the Census as its area of contribution, and the Comparability volume was published in co-operation with the BSA.

As Jeremy Mitchell, the series editor, notes:

> One of the SSRC's main reasons for sponsoring the preparation of these reviews is to get the views of some of the leading research workers in the field about current research developments, about likely future developments, and about the research needs of the subject in terms of men, money, other resources and research organisation.... The reviews will also provide those in industry, government, the educational world and elsewhere with information.... it should also be stressed that the reviews are in no sense formal policy statements by the SSRC – their function is to inform (Firth, 1968, vii).

However, while the reviews give a useful overview, they are severely lacking in detail or controversy. In one sense, these criticisms may be misplaced, because the intended audience is in fact not just the sociologist, but 'those in industry, government, the educational world and elsewhere' – the intelligent if ignorant layman, who lurks like some noble savage behind this enterprise, needing conversion but too immature to be given the full truth as yet. But although the series is written for non-specialists, it claims to 'be of particular interest to research workers in each subject' and 'to help all social scientists ... to keep abreast of developments over a wider field'. This claim was made (fortunately for SSRC) before the introduction of the Trades Description Act. It must be seriously doubted that the needs of the intelligent layman can be neatly matched with those of the academic from an allied field, because the latter requires a more detailed treatment of specific topics, knowing from his own experience that every discipline is marked by revealed wisdoms and heresies, and that intellectual life is built on conflict. And the same applies with even greater force to 'the research worker in each subject'.

The further notion that all social scientists should keep abreast with developments over a wider field – which presumably covers all of human geography, social anthropology, political science, economic and social history, as well as several 'problem areas' – is utopian fantasy. Most sociologists find enough difficulty in keeping abreast with the whole of their *own* subject, without setting out on a scholastic expedition. The philosophy behind the series draws excessively on the 1950s new technology era of C. P. Snow's two cultures: the reality of current professional development is inevitable specialisation, whether or not it is specialisation in a single discipline, or at the interface between two disciplines, or in a single 'problem area'. Renaissance man is dead, although the fact seems to have escaped SSRC.

What is even more ill-conceived in this endeavour is the attempt to tackle two very different problems under a single series. On the one hand there is the problem of communicating and explaining the interests and needs of each discipline, and social science as a whole, to people outside of the academic field. On the other, there is the aim of raising technical questions of social research, such as appropriate methodology ('Longitudinal Studies'), conceptual and operational clarification ('Comparability in Social Research') which do concern practitioners in the field. SSRC have confused the two, precisely because the role of the institution, and particularly its permanent staff, has not been properly specified. There has been a clear attempt to present the public relations part of the exercise as if it were a contribution to professional knowledge. This reflects a pretentiousness on the part of the officials, who have at times wished to present themselves as both the academic equals of university staff and also as their potential superiors in 'knowing how the system really works'.

As soon as this is recognised, the style of bland presentation, simplifying description (including the omission of almost all foreign work and trends) and minimal coverage of several of the books are all explained. These books have been written for the non-specialist. They are designed to introduce, explain, and justify social science activity to a basically ignorant and potentially hostile audience. That audience is not so much other social scientists who are also engaged in competition for SSRC funds, as other academics with interests in the other Research Councils: in the late 1960s SSRC was still a new outfit, seeking to establish its legitimacy. The audience also consists of the intelligent man-in-the-street, or more to the point, man-in-Whitehall. The major function of the series is not merely as part of the need for SSRC to be seen as *active* (to be exerting leadership and organisation, and so on, thereby earning its keep), but to use that activity in the production of directly relevant propaganda in the struggle for the funding of social science.

Now the activity of special pleading is often necessary and can be worthwhile: the academic who scorns the need to explain his work to the non-specialist, or to justify his demands on the public purse, suffers from the worst kind of arrogant ivory-tower mentality. But for this endeavour to masquerade as a contribution to the

269

intellectual disciplines of social science is both dishonest and dangerous, for if the series *is* taken as typical of general output, then its lack of rigour must undermine any claims the social scientist makes for academic parity.

One encouraging feature of this enterprise is that the Sociology and Social Administration Committee collaborated with the BSA to produce quite different kinds of publications (Stacey, 1969; Gittus, 1972). The BSA's professionalism shows up the superficiality of most of the other output of the SSRC's Review Series. There was, incidentally, no 'Social Research in Sociology' volume from the Sociology and Social Administration subject committee. It was not until 1979 that a reflexive style re-entered SSRC proceedings when, again with BSA collaboration, a conference on this subject was organised at Lancaster University.

The relationship between SSRC and the BSA has only in recent years been even moderately cordial. As the BSA is far from having a monopoly of membership among sociologists, the Sociology and Social Administration Committee was unlikely to have strong BSA representation on it (quite apart from the social administration and other representatives). As a result 'policy decisions' by the Committee were likely to be seen as an unwarranted intrusion in areas which the professional association might legitimately regard as its own. For example, in 1978 it appeared that the Committee wished to concentrate post-graduate awards into a small number of 'centres of excellence'. The BSA Executive organised a protest against this, only to be assured that there would be no change in the awards system. In 1980, post-graduate awards were concentrated in about fifteen 'large departments' to the exclusion of all others. It is too early to assess the actual outcome of this centres of excellence large department scheme, but the lack of initial consultation and general mistrust is not unusual.

Since 1977, there have been several meetings between members of the Committee and the Executive, and 'question and answer' sessions at the BSA Annual Conference which some current members of the Committee attend. These tend to be dominated by critics of SSRC with personal experience of long delays in dealing with problems or apparently unreasonable decisions. The allocation of studentships is the other major topic, with the perennial complaint (to which we return below) that SSRC is only concerned to promote that kind of sociology which uses survey research. The other point of collaboration is in short courses which are jointly sponsored by both organisations. These are designed for post-graduates or research assistants and normally deal with methodology and/or a substantive topic: education, and historical analysis are two recent examples.

In general, there has been little complaint about this kind of small-scale activity, which extends to financing seminars, both as series and special events, for experts working in a particular field. The ideas for these may come from outside of SSRC, or within, and usually surface through the subject committees. Some have been highly successful, like the 'Working Class Images of Society' seminar at Durham, or the 'International Occupational Mobility' seminar at Aberdeen (although this latter event nearly foundered over SSRC's initial wish to make some of the participants who had been invited to give papers pay the full cost so that the travel budget could be used to pay for *four* members of the permanent secretariat to attend!).

More controversy has surrounded the research units which SSRC has established. Of these, the Industrial Relations Unit at Warwick has had a long and productive life, the Population Unit of Cambridge has been highly innovatory, and the Socio-Legal Studies Centre at Oxford has generated some stimulating sociological research, but is still in its infancy. The Ethnic Relations Unit has not been an unqualified success, with staff problems in the early 1970s, but it has recently been re-established at Aston under John Rex. Because these units have had longer lives than the conventional research project, and also a greater output, their work has come in for criticism, particularly from those who do not share the same theoretical positions. On balance, given that there was little in the way of a model for such enterprises in British social science, the units count on the credit side of SSRC's balance sheet. Not all these units can be regarded as essentially sociological: they are in the Heyworth tradition of inter-disciplinary, problem-oriented research. They have, however, housed sociologists and provided a kind of security for researchers over a period of years during which, freed from teaching commitments, they have been able to get on with doing sociological research.

This assessment has pointedly excluded the ill-fated but little-lamented Survey Research Unit. This unit had more of the status of an in-house organisation, and its purpose was to enhance survey methodology techniques in social research. Its activities under the direction of the former Market Researcher, Mark Abrams, ranged from general proselytising by seminars, through work on social indicators, to surveys of life satisfaction. Apart from the use of a particular research tool, there seems to have been little coherence to the programme, although it did reflect concern with the issues beloved of Heyworth. The Unit's other function, as a storehouse of expertise on survey research, was probably more important, but sadly here too, it adopted a stance that few sociologists found congenial. The Survey Research Unit saw the short-term solution to a lack of technical expertise as being the employment of market research companies to do fieldwork. This doubles the cost of data collection, and can easily lead to a distortion of questionnaire design in favour of simplicity and speed of interview (to maximise company profits) and against the interests of good research design. In this way, data collection can be constrained both in breadth and depth; and what is finally produced – 'new sociology' – would be the poorer (for further discussion of this, see Payne, 1979, and associated rejoinders).

The call for market research can be attributed to two sources of inspiration. On the one hand, market research – like marxism (see above) – exists in institutional forms. The companies were there, ready to sell, and to sell hard. Given the connections between SSRC staff and the market research companies – some had previously worked in the marketing field – it was relatively easy for the firms to fill the vacuum created by the sociologists' lack of methodological expertise. Only the rigorous demands of academics and their smaller and strictly limited budgets constituted an obstacle between commerce and social science research. The other inspiration was the vacuum itself. Many sociologists were, and still are, methodologically incompetent. It is not part of their basic training to be able to run survey research. How then could decent research be mounted by those who wanted to use survey methods? How could more sociologists be persuaded by SSRC to do the kind of research which, at least in methodological terms, the rest of the civil service and the politicians recognised as 'scientific'? Market research seemed a good answer, but it could never have been more than a holding exercise. The root of the trouble lies in under-graduate and post-graduate training.

However, education and training have been generally left more or less alone by SSRC, at least in so far as they have not set up their own higher-degrees programme at the RIB. Obviously, in funding post-graduate training, SSRC can legitimately take up a position, but even here it is the university departments that have made much of the running, despite signs of the same centre/departmental struggle that has occurred in other areas. The main influence which SSRC has exerted has been in broad terms, by determining the overall levels of expenditure and in its allocations. During most of the last decade, about half of its total budget has gone in this direction, with a tendency for the annual proportion to creep up. The Council's response to the Thatcher administration's demand for a reduction in spending in 1979, in cutting out 25 per cent of promised studentships, has outraged many sociologists, principally, of course, in those departments with high quotas. The exchanges of unpleasantness in the letter columns of *New Society* during June and July of 1979 took the form that one might expect from the present analysis. On the one hand, the official line has been the need to placate hostile political masters, on the other, the academics' angry accusations of cowardice and lack of real commitment to the research enterprise. However, there is an element of window-dressing in all this: even before the cut back, there had been discussions about shifting resources from training to the direct funding of research. A strong suspicion remains that the spending cuts provided an opportunity to implement an unpopular policy in circumstances which diverted at least some of the inevitable wrath away from SSRC. It will be interesting to see by how much the RIB's budget is cut back.

Within this crude allocation of funds for post-graduate training, the system adopted for allocation of quota and pool awards has given considerable freedom to the universities and the students. From the start, SSRC rejected the DES's system of allocating studentships on an open competition basis, in favour of the Department of Science and Industrial Research's scheme. This means each university applies to SSRC on the basis of the number of eligible students who have chosen it for post-graduate study. This gives greater scope for planning and specialisation by the universities, and although there was a review in 1974, this quota system has been favoured by the departments. The mechanics of the allocation only concern us in that the *topic* of the research is not part of the decision over allocation.

The result has been a wide range of post-graduate theses, far wider than is sometimes assumed by sociologists. Perusal of the list of those working in the second year of their studentships in 1979 (*SSRC Newsletter* no. 36, 6-16) shows post-graduates interested in art history, films and poetry, linguistics and conversational analysis, ideology, Althusser, class culture, modes of capitalism and political movements, sexual deviancy of several kinds, paradigmatic science, and, of course, the Founding Fathers. At the same time there are also studies of race relations, the health and social services, the Third World, and criminology, which reflect the issues advanced fifteen years ago by Heyworth. This latter group of theses are in a marked minority, which demonstrates that SSRC has not directed the content of post-graduate training to any great degree. (Whether the academics have made a good job of organising this training on their own is an open question.)

SSRC's Summer Schools have emphasised methodology, and in recent years SSRC has modified its internal procedures so that it can be better able to 'allow committees to select between the research training areas to which they wished to give support priority' (Healey, 1975, 14). This direction of research has manifested itself in three schemes which differ from the traditional Ph. D. pattern in non-science subjects. In the first, students join one of the Area Studies, or one of the Units, and work in an inter-disciplinary team. This is the only way that SSRC has found of by-passing the departmental specialisation of the universities, apart from financing specifically inter-disciplinary courses with the natural sciences. The second innovation has been the 'Link' studentship, whereby the post-graduate joins a team already working on a project. This has been borrowed from the natural sciences and is still regarded with some suspicion. The third model – in other social sciences more than in sociology – has been to promote taught courses rather than pure research higher degrees. Despite these changes, the bulk of sociology studentships still go on traditional projects. The Post-graduate Training Board at SSRC 'considers, however, that there is also room for more direct encouragement for some new developments in approach to training which will increase the variety of provision' (SSRC, 1978, 5). Further changes must be expected, but the main thrust of the PTB so far has been towards achieving methodological competence (albeit mainly in survey methods) rather than direction towards substantive areas. How long this will last is an open question.

The short history of SSRC has been marked by tension between the centre and the researchers, and it is a history also marked by the SSRC's increased success in determining what is acceptable research – at least for financing. The balance of power has shifted to the small elite of academics 'on the inside' and to the permanent secretariat. This is even true of the conduct of research. 1975 saw the publication of a 'blacklist' in the *Newsletter* (No. 29, 21) of researchers who were late with their final reports. Subsequent outcry terminated this practice, but soon after an investigation of how research is actually conducted was initiated by Raymond Illsley (then Chairman of the Sociology and Social Administration Committee) first as a pilot, then as a larger-scale investigation under the Research Careers Exploratory Panel. At the time of going to press there is no report available. It seems that sociological research was found to differ from other social scientific research in two main ways. First, sociology is more dependent on SSRC funding, and second, sociologists seem to encounter more difficulties in doing, and completing, research.

If this is true, then the vociferousness of sociologists among SSRC's critics is perhaps explained. If the other social scientists have alternative means of funding, like government departments and private companies, they are less upset by SSRC policy decisions: they can take their custom elsewhere. Furthermore, the other social sciences are more familiar with the idea of consultancy and commissioned work, and so less suspicious of direction or initiatives. They already have learned to do only that contracted work which is congenial, and to 'add-on' their own special interest to the work that is being paid for. Thus, items like the RIB hold fewer fears for them, because they have no tradition of scholastic purity or left-wing idealism to prevent participation in a liberal democratic society.

If it is true that sociology projects are more susceptible to problems, this suggests two things. First, as SSRC and the present authors believe, too many sociologists are methodologically inept. They lack experience and training. Not surprisingly, problems occur. Second, there may be something quintessentially sociological about the discipline's troubles. Some issues *are* controversial and politically sensitive, and sociology's radicals have always found it hard to cope with those in authority. Further, sociologists committed to reflexivity are more likely to *talk* about their difficulties (as in Chapter 9). Talking about troubles is not in itself a fundamental problem; the other aspects are.

It would be wrong to portray sociologists as the sole martyrs in the cause of academic freedom. Few social scientists welcome the idea of complete central direction for their work. Research is a private activity. While teaching comes first and is central to the lecturer's working life, research is something over which he has far more control. It represents a major element in the identity of the autonomous professional. As long as the major source of research production is in Higher Education, this will remain true. It follows that there is a genuine difference of interest between researchers on the one hand and the staff and senior academics who man SSRC on the other.

Academics are here faced with a dilemma which goes beyond SSRC. Should research be done primarily by Higher Education teachers, or by full-time researchers? Provided there are opportunities for interchange of personnel, and that independence from political control is guaranteed, the latter has some attractions despite the fundamental change it would require in the role and self-image of academics. But it is hard not to harbour the suspicion that concentration of research effort could lead to increased SSRC control, given the evidence of the past. Even such champions of SSRC as Cherns and Perry (Cherns was secretary to the Heyworth Committee and the second member of staff appointed to SSRC, and Perry is a former SSRC Survey Unit employee) see that SSRC has had to work by 'somewhat devious means' (1976, 7) to bring about its control over the social sciences. Recent suggestions that the BSA contribute to priority areas in research are only another attempt to achieve the same goals.

Sociologists have in fact been less critical of SSRC than this chapter may have implied. Their opposition has been fragmented, with as much mutual criticism as concern with the Council. How often one hears the complaint that SSRC does not finance 'my' kind of sociology – usually ethnomethodological or theoretical – only survey research. Not only is this untrue (see the list of Ph. D. topics above) but it also allows for rebuttal by SSRC officials and diverts attention from the real problems. Of course SSRC spends relatively little on ethnomethodology and theoretical work: these are classically the cheap one-man scholar enterprises that require little in the way of finance.

It is not that research should never be commissioned, or that academics automatically know what is best for themselves and the world. As we have seen, sociologists can be as wrong-headed as the next man and have themselves contributed to the conditions that prompted SSRC intervention. What is at stake is a pluralism in research. Sociology is so dependent on SSRC as its major source of funding that changes affect it more than other social sciences. A healthy sociology needs independent – and preferably many independent – rival sociological enterprises (and consisting not just of grand theory or ethnomethodology). This requires an SSRC which can fund research critical of itself, its orthodoxies, its civil servants and political masters. More centralised control means more inter-disciplinary research into 'problems' as defined by someone else for the sociologist. It means more uniformity, and more conformity. It would be nice if SSRC really were a benevolent learned association doling out finance for the profession. But it has and has had no pretensions to being anything other than a governmental organisation. Unlike the MRC, SSRC has never seen itself as a buffer between government and researcher. It may be that in Posner's phrase (in reply to Mack's criticisms) 'SSRC may not be beautiful but it is useful' (Posner, 1979). But, to paraphrase the time-honoured sociological question, ' "Useful?" Useful to *whom?*'

13 A future for British sociology?

Does British sociology have a future? As we drafted this chapter in the autumn of 1979, the government was asking for a 6 per cent reduction in student numbers and indicating that this should fall disproportionately on sociology. We have already seen SSRC singled out for particular economies in the science budget and departments being obliged to rescind promised studentships. In our view, however, it is foolish merely to respond with reflex slogans about Tory butchery. As we have indicated throughout this volume, we think that there is a great deal wrong with British sociology. Given this, we may well now have a good opportunity to pause and reflect more critically on the failings of the riotous years of the 1960s. We are going to have to live with their legacy for some time yet. But if the party is truly over, we ought to learn from this nasty hangover and try to ensure that the discipline comes through in an altogether leaner and more sober condition.

We believe in sociology: this book has not been written as a hatchet-job. But when we ask the most fundamental question of them all – 'Does society owe us a living'? – the answer is very hard to provide. One can justify sociology on two grounds. It may be that we would want to say that it is worth indulging in for its own sake as an exercise of the mind. In such a case one can say that the proper level of funding is about on a par with philosophy, theology or even Sanskrit. Governments, foundations, corporations or trade unions might wish to add it to their lists of sponsored arts, sports or other entertainments. One might end up with the Benson and Hedges Chair of Althusserian Exegesis or the Gillette Reader in the Asiatic Mode of Production. A cultivated leisure class would attend periodic orations and applaud their incomprehensible elegance with their finely-sculptured, soft, white hands.

Somehow or other, we feel this vision has more in common with the fantasies of Michael Moorcock than any serious exercise in futurology. When it comes to the crunch, either sociology provides some good which the community values sufficiently to purchase, or it does not. That benefit may be of either a private or a public nature, for example, in improvements in the efficiency of some particular organisation, be it a profit-making corporation, a trades union or a public service. It may indeed relate at the most general level to the allocation of resources within a society to achieve the overall goals of that society.

Although we have chosen to assert an economic model here, we do not necessarily mean ourselves to be interpreted in a narrow sense. 'Efficiency' can mean cost-reduction in purely financial terms. Equally it can mean cost-reduction in human terms. 'Improvements' in the quality of life in an organisation can mean improvements in its decision-making, its services or its product. Improvements in the quality of life in a society do not necessarily result from increasing wealth or tinkering with its distribution. If one thing has united all the great sociologists it is an overwhelming concern for the moral nature of the society in which people live.

Let us take the example of the quality of child care. We have before us the fact that a large number of children appear to present clinical symptoms of injury or impaired development. We want, as a society, to devise programmes for improvement. What could sociologists contribute?

First, we could attempt to determine to what degree this asserted problem is a 'real' problem. What leads some social group to be concerned generally about child care? How is it possible for them to see this as a problem? What criteria are they employing? Where do they come from? What is their evidence? How has this been assembled? Do they distinguish various sub-categories like 'abuse' or 'neglect' and if so, how?

Second, if this is a 'real' problem, what is its incidence? How is it distributed through a society? To what degree is this distribution an artefact of the identification process? Under what conditions are children found to have these presenting symptoms?

Third, what patterns of family organisation are associated with these children? How do they come to be vulnerable? Do children precipitate their condition? Are there problems consequent on the positions of their parents? Does the incidence of injury or impaired development reflect intellectual deficiencies on the part of parents, failings in education for parenthood, the limited opportunities for men and women to enjoy leisure creatively, or narrow conceptions of appropriate sex roles? How is it possible, in other words, for parents to see their children in a way that precipitates damaging acts, of omission or of commission?

Fourth, suppose, as a society we wanted to design intervention programmes. If these are to have any opportunity of success, then they must be clearly articulated with the everyday lives of the target population. It is, after all, a basic principle of successful education that you begin from where the learner is, rather than where you would like him to be. There may, for instance, be limited gains from the redistribution of wealth alone. Improving family income support might reduce the undernourishment of children. It might equally increase the profits of the brewers.

Conversely, it might be possible to achieve quite significant social change without major redistribution. If one looks at preparation for parenthood, then it is clear that many parents nowadays are poorly equipped and lack confidence. In an era of small families, children get few practical lessons in child management or even any feel for what it is like to have twenty-four hour responsibility for a young baby. Intervention and monitoring systems can have the effect of further de-skilling new parents by suggesting that a child is only normal and healthy in so far as this has been professionally validated. Few people perceive any clear need to educate all prospective parents, as opposed to the lower streams of comprehensive schools. Even here, parentcraft teaching often fails because of the educators' assumptions about household organisation. Speaking very crudely, these contain an implicit middle-class bias in their conceptions of sex roles, domestic possessions and household maintenance. As such they lack realism and contribute more to the development of the fantasy childhood of advertising than to the encouragement of practical knowledge. What we would need for effective teaching would be an understanding of successful working-class models. How is it possible for some parents to raise children adequately on low incomes in an indifferent social, cultural and physical environment while others fail?

This is not to argue for a position of total cultural relativism. If we believe that the standards of the middle class in Britain represent the finest flowering of civilisation, then we are entitled, as citizens, to say so. That is a political or moral judgment, in which the sociologist has no special competence above any other citizen. But such judgments set the limits of his work inasmuch as they form the majority view expressed through the political system, however imperfect that system may be. Such a line of reasoning would apply equally in a society which valued solidarity and a spirit of social co-operation marked by relative uniformity of reward. The sociologist who disagrees and uses his professional position to campaign against that view has no automatic right to expect his fellows to provide him with a living. There might be

279

arguments for this in terms of the value of dissent and licensed disagreement for the vigour of a society, but these again are substantially moral judgments. In terms of the direction that the society took, the sociologist might advise, inform and even warn; it is not clear how far he has an unqualified right to oppose at the public expense.

With the present example, the sociologist's description of successful working-class models of parenting might enable the development of more realistic education programmes as a first step towards the dissemination of middle-class values and life-styles. One would aim to 'improve' people where they were and then to build on this. However, research might also show unsuspected strengths in alternative patterns of household organisation and question the implicit standards of success. Alternatively, it might show that successful households are in decline as a result of shifts in social policy, economic organisation or moral values.

Does all this necessarily imply that a sociologists's loyalties are determined solely by who won the last election or succeeded in the last *coup d'état?* In our view, this would not invariably be the case, except in so far as most sociologists, especially in Britain, depend on government funds for their living. Given this, it seems gratuitously stupid systematically to bite the hand that feeds us. At the same time the sociologist in a Western democracy is living in a formally pluralist society. If we think that loyal opposition is sufficiently worth having in the interests of a socially responsive political system, then it seems equally appropriate to accept a diversity of private political beliefs among sociologists. On the other hand, it also seems clear that sociologists have the same obligation to encourage diversity in their own ranks and to accept the concept of 'loyal opposition' for themselves and in their wider political action. If they refuse this obligation to avoid proselytising for the violent overthrow of the system off which they live, then it does not seem unreasonable if discrimination develops against sociologists. Where there are substantial interest groups with differing concerns to those of central government, then there is, of course, no reason why sociologists should not ally themselves to these if they provide a more sympathetic environment. One of the weaknesses of British sociology is the tendency towards monopoly in funding.

Whatever the sociologist's private beliefs, however, the justification for funding must rest in the service offered. This justification has to rest in the sociological imagination, the ability to transcend the boundaries of one particular interest. If we follow the example of injured or developmentally impaired children, then clearly many occupational groups are involved with identification and management. Most of these have occupational theorists who carry out research, often borrowing techniques, if not always in their intellectual context, from sociology.* Where these groups are limited, however, is in their ability to question their own terms of reference. Of course, it is not impossible for occupation members to do this, but it is certainly more difficult. However, some group is needed which can transcend occupational boundaries, to question the division of tasks between occupations or, indeed, between paid and unpaid workers. Similar transcendent questions arise in considering the fit between services and clients, or producers and consumers. Are the goods or service appropriate to the perceived needs of their recipients? This, of course, cannot tell us which to amend to improve the fit, although some of the options can be stated.

Sociology is not, of course, without its own blind spots. Its concentration on structural and cultural explanations omits the contribution of individual variation and tends to discount purely utilitarian considerations. The division of labour within the social sciences, however, represents an alternative way of breaking up the analysis of social organisation to that of specialised occupational theorists. One can think, metaphorically, of the latter as a vertical division, segmenting citizens by what they differ in, while the former is a horizontal division, segmenting citizens by virtue of what they have in common. The personal service occupations – medicine, nursing, social work, etc. – may seem quite distinct to their members, but social scientists see them merely as different answers to common problems. Managing a school or a hospital is very like managing any other service organisation such as a hotel or an airport, although perhaps differing from a manufacturing organisation like a car factory. Sociologists, psychologists and economists may approach from differing starting-points within social science but share this kind of generalist background. Their competition is not a weakness in the study of human life, but a sign of vigour, a check on the unnatural predominance of any single mode of explanation and a guarantee of a variety of choices for those concerned with policy formation. Again, we should perhaps emphasise that 'policy formation' does not imply an elitist vision. We are all of us, as citizens, daily making policy decisions – how we allocate our time, where we spend our money, what moral guidance we elect to adopt. Some of us make decisions which have an immediate effect on more people than others, but, cumulatively, these individual decisions have a massive, albeit slow-moving and

---

* Occupation is here and in the subsequent discussion used in a very broad sense. Unpaid workers also have theorists – in the pages of women's magazines or the writings of professional feminists, in the plethora of specialist publications and associations for every sort of hobby and pastime.

indirect, aggregate effect. Social science broadens our range of perspectives and choices and, one hopes, by so doing, improves their quality. One does not need to follow the narrower political connotations of market economics to see the advantage of enhanced consumer knowledge, whether that consumption is cultural or material. The social sciences together play a crucial role in this process and the balance of competition between them is part and parcel of the checks on tyranny in a free society.

No analysis of an academic discipline, least of all sociology, can ignore the social conditions under which it operates. For all practical purposes, it is the embodiment of ideas in occupational form which constitutes existence. Outside of Higher Education and SSRC research units and projects – both state financed – there are few jobs which generate new sociology, as opposed to providing a career outlet for graduates. While sociology is not alone in being so heavily dependent on Higher Education for its bread and butter, it is worse off than most disciplines. If the universities and polytechnics were closed tomorrow, many of the scientists and engineers could compete for jobs. Positions for sociologists, on the other hand, are few and far between. It is a fact of life with considerable relevance to the way sociology has developed in post-war Britain, and explains why the popularity or otherwise of the subject is of crucial importance.

Equally we must confront the question of how the vitality of the discipline is to be maintained. At present, the dominant mode is that university teachers do 'research' which interests them in their spare time. In this way new knowledge is gained, and translated into the body of transmitted science. The main alternatives to this pattern in sociology are SSRC Research Units, but these provide little more in the way of secure *careers* than do research projects. There are two immediate consequences. First, the quantity and quality of research depends primarily on the abilities and social conditions of lecturing staff. And second, sociology is dependent on student numbers for the resources necessary to ensure its survival.

The rapid expansion of the discipline has created a situation where few teachers have much research experience or opportunity to acquire it. Theory-writing is easily fitted around teaching commitments. Hours may happily be whiled away improvising on the thoughts of some grand master or in a search for ever more arcane and long-dead intellectual forebears. Given a gentle pressure to publish, what could be more simple than publishing one's lecture course? Publishers are attracted because, after all, every sociology student does a theory course and is a potential purchaser, while any specific area served by a research monograph is only going to attract a minority audience.

In contrast, the lack of research experience is a potent element in the apparent naivete of many sociologists when they write about empirical questions. Since theory and research are so separated, sociologists are often unaware of the limitations of their theories and the subtleties of the world they are trying to understand. If we take a field like the sociology of the professions, we can see something of the effects of this. On closer inspection writings about 'the professions' turn out to depend almost entirely on empirical work on doctors. A very large proportion of this has been done in North America against the background of a particular social organisation of health care. Several consequences follow. First, it is not clear how far doctors are typical of other groups of professional workers. They may be, but we have precious little evidence to prove or disprove it. Second, the cash nexus in American professional practice and its consequences are surprisingly ill-understood. They just seem too 'obvious' to merit interest. Third, the isolation of the study of 'the professions' can mislead us into regarding certain sorts of activity as characteristic of professionals when they may be generic to all workers. The discussion of the fantasy world of theorists of industrial society in the light of census data in Chapter 4 is another instance.

Sociology is, then, ill-equipped to face the struggles to come, struggles made keener by the arrival of the present Conservative government but predictable none the less. The discipline has acquired a reputation for ill-considered radicalism, a charge it is unable to defeat by reference to a solid body of empirical work. Paradoxically it is worth remembering that *within* sociology the orthodox view of the sociological tradition stresses its character as a conservative reaction to marxism and that Marx himself owed more to Adam Smith and Ricardo than to any sociologist.

This reputation is worth some further scrutiny. One can trace affinities between sociology and socialism as much as between economics and classical liberalism. Nevertheless, like any discipline which starts from a view of its phenomena as social products, Durkheim's reality *sui generis* is likely to be biased towards analyses and prescriptions at the level of social organisation, requiring collective rather than individual initiatives. Individualist arguments are always vulnerable to being undercut as mere epiphenomena of particular social interests. From this, one can see obvious lines of political development in terms of corporatist state planning as the embodiment of collective responses to perceived problems. Sociologists have a natural alliance with the interventionist state. This is not, however, a necessary alliance. American sociology is far more diverse politically than British, for instance. It can absorb both doctrinaire marxists and classical liberal anarchists who subscribe to many of the doctrines of *laissez-faire*. Nevertheless, any non-socialist version is likely to be a minority view while the insularity of the discipline persists. The sociologist inexperienced in empirical work finds himself with a view of the world as he would like it to be, sustained in interaction with a narrow social group, rather than dealing with the world as it is and the possibilities available within it. How many sociologists, one wonders, are Freemasons, Rotarians, or, indeed, members of any of the normal social networks of the middle classes?

As we have already shown, sociology is a young person's discipline and much of its anti-authoritarian and anti-hierarchical character can be linked to the social conditions of junior academics in a newly founded field. The young lecturer is at the bottom of both an organisational and a professional hierarchy. It is in his own interests to promote a system of rules and relationships in which his views have equal weight with those of others who happen to be more experienced than he, or who have been successful in occupying minor positions in the academic hierarchy. This tendency was compounded by the contemporary rise of student participation. The new recruits to sociology posts, working in a discipline without established traditions and career progressions, found themselves in an intellectual, emotional and political alliance with the student movement. More senior sociologists also had reason to support such a democratic thrust. There were always academic establishments to challenge, dominated by older disciplines and inevitably under-representing sociologists (Rex, 1978b).

Each institution has its own history of sociological radicalism: block signatures of petitions calling for reform; a dissenting voice at union meetings; confrontations with both departmental heads and with administrators; innovations in departmental government. Some or all of these have marked the presence of the discipline everywhere over the last twenty years. A similarly widespread feature has been the limited participation of sociologists in the formal aspects of university government. Like many radicals, those within the profession have believed themselves to be better in opposition than in government.

Why was this? We have already noted the critical position which many sociologists were able to adopt towards the academic ethic: sharing in the institution's work was therefore unattractive. Again, the young lecturer's immediate concerns are with teaching those who are still in the state which he has so recently abandoned – the students – and with getting some research done. Worries about other disciplines, or the mere mechanics of keeping the institution working, necessarily take a lesser place in his priorities.

Furthermore, to take part in committee work is to be seen to sell out. The purity of radical principles is inevitably compromised by participation in decision-making, especially when one's fellow committee men are 'reactionaries' and 'conservatives'. The great tradition of sociology has been to demystify, to expose ideology, to question, it has not been to solve problems. It would appear that the great debunkers are not people to be trapped in the minutiae of academic government. Their skills, and their interests, lie elsewhere.

The polytechnics and the universities differed only in the nature of the internal opposition. In the universities, this largely resides in elitism, conservatism and isolationism: in short, in the traditional Oxbridge values (where, incidentally, sociology was slow to develop). In the polytechnics, the conflict was between the old technical college staff and the new recruits. The former group were opposed to research as a polytechnic activity, to any discipline other than engineering and applied science, to young staff who had not served their time in the old system. The new recruits, in contrast, regard the polytechnics as only another kind of university, and are broadly cosmopolitan or professional in their outlook. In this latter climate, sociology has found itself with natural allies among students of the arts and other social sciences on one side of the in-fighting. The youthfulness of its practitioners has been disguised by the similar youthfulness of other, university-oriented, newcomers. Their radicalism has been the radicalism of a university ethic in a technical college world, which has softened some of the edge of their more fundamental opposition if only by creating confusion and dispute.

Of course, there are also structural dimensions to all this. Even if the young sociologist did wish to be active in committee work, his typical position of being junior staff, relatively new to the scene, militates against him. There will already be a system of constituencies and incumbents. He will require more electoral support than his own department can provide, and it will take time to make the contacts and friendships necessary for a successful candidature. Even then, being widely stigmatised as a sociologist, he must embark on a prolonged struggle to gain acceptance and influence on policy. This is a very slow process: where are the sociologists who hold positions of Vice-Chancellor or Polytechnic Director or even of Chairman of the key internal committees?

It should be understood that this concern with committees and entrenchment in the institutional power structure is no misguided worry about the mere trappings of professionalism. Because sociology has such a marginal existence outside the educational system, the discipline is highly dependent on a single source of employment. In a very real sense, sociology is what happens in Higher Education, and it follows that what happens in the universities, polytechnics and colleges is what happens to the discipline in this country. To protect the discipline's position, to ensure its continued flow of resources, to defend its staffing levels, to man the committees in order to promote the subject's interests, is to work directly on behalf of sociology itself. We have been extremely slow to come to terms with this hard fact, because it runs counter to our collective pre-occupation with a radical stance.

In the meantime, the other disciplines are ahead of sociology in the race. What is more, these other disciplines outrank sociology on the conventional academic criteria of qualifications and publications. Bearing in mind the state of the profession (for example, SSRC finance for post-graduate training was not available until 1967) there was no way in which the new lecturers could have had the same higher degree and early career experience as those trained in more established disciplines. The only place from which they could come was the fresh crop of graduates. At a more senior level, promotion opportunities were for a time available to people who lacked experience and, it must be said, proven ability.

This led to a confused expansion of post-graduate education in the late 1960s and early 1970s. An increase in the number of graduates, the demand for more professionals to staff expanding departments, the desire for status among university lecturers who could have post-graduates working for them, and not least the advent of SSRC to provide the finance, all combined to give the higher degree game a boost. Unfortunately, there was some confusion over what a Ph.D. in sociology was meant to be, and what kinds of training were necessary for it. Atrocity stories about higher degree supervision abounded, and the BSA felt obliged to produce a code of practice. Some sociologists began to argue that three years was too short a period to complete a Ph.D., while others implied that by judicious selection of external examiners, low grade dissertations were becoming acceptable (e.g., Rex, 1978b). It is certainly the case that even today many higher degrees still remain incompleted. Unlike students of the natural sciences, sociology candidates do not join established teams to carry out research into carefully defined subsets of the team's general work. Too many Ph.D. projects were over-ambitious in their conception, and the career opportunities of lecturing posts were too attractive, to encourage completion. Few universities even now provide formal training in research methods at post-graduate level: Wakeford (1979) reports only ten institutions in this category leaving the rest of the higher degree training either to trial and error, or, at best, a kind of apprenticeship. Both the BSA and SSRC have promoted short courses, summer schools and conferences on methodology to overcome this shortfall, but their impact has not been great. Without rigorous training in research skills, the rising generation of sociologists has consequently been in poor shape to carry out research, once embarked on their own professional careers.

The result has been the appointment of under-qualified staff and a poor record of research production. This extends both to the junior and more senior ranks of the profession. Promotions have been inhibited not just by the freeze, but by the comparative under-achievement of sociologists. Even by the profession's own standard, some senior posts have gone to most unlikely people, while some present incumbents of lecturing posts would be hard put to be short-listed in more recent years.

It may be somewhat unfair to present this argument as if it uniquely applied to sociology. After all, there has recently been the case of a lecturer in another discipline who was denied progress through the efficiency bar because in almost ten years he had published only a translation and a few book reviews. There were of course other factors in his case, but it was not encouraging to see it argued in his defence that such an output was perfectly adequate. No one would want to propose a publish-or-perish system which counted the number of publications as the sole method of evaluation but the generation of new knowledge cannot be ignored as an essential contribution to the making of a good academic.

This question of professional standards has suffered from mystification. In the first place, it is a breach of professional etiquette to probe too deeply into a colleague's productivity record, even if (unusually) one's own is good. Academics share the common belief that they are over-worked and yet struggle on as dedicated professionals. This ideology is supportive both at the individual and collective level. It manifests itself in many ways. A recent exercise in diary keeping which showed academics working in excess of sixty hours a week did not distinguish between talking to colleagues about work matters and other kinds of talk during work hours. But how much common room chat is really work-oriented? As one visiting European sociologist remarked, he had learned more during his stay from his colleagues (in one of the country's top departments) about good restaurants and the best shops than about their work.

Second, mystification has arisen out of the binary system of Higher Education. At one stage there appeared to be a big difference between the characteristics of staff in the public sector and the universities. The lower qualification levels in the former were seen as a temporary phenomenon which was inevitable and therefore not of particular interest. University staff tended to maintain a paternalistic attitude towards their public sector colleagues, who had a vested interest in keeping quiet, even if they nursed a certain sense of inferiority. The picture was complicated by those who propagated the myth that polytechnics were applied institutions which concentrated on teaching, unlike the research-centred universities. Sociologists without higher degrees or publications were, by this token, acceptable in the polytechnic, where in any case many of the old guard of technical college teachers were equally ill-equipped. The lack of research experience could be paraded as dedication to education and to one's students. The reality of separate organisations underpinned this ideological difference, and this, together with the apparent under-qualification of polytechnic staff, served to obscure the under-qualification of university sociologists.

Two factors began to undermine the dichotomy by the mid-1970s. One factor was the simple passage of time, as lecturers in the public sector completed their higher degrees, launched research projects, and had articles accepted in the leading journals. The other factor was the increased transfer of personnel between the two halves of the binary system. This started mainly as a trickle of young lecturers from the polytechnics to the universities, and then became a reverse flow, as, during the early 1970s freeze on university appointments (and later the log jam at the top of the university lecturer scale), employment opportunities and better salary levels were available in the polytechnics. The binary model is still a powerful one, but it has begun to weaken.

Where it does remain a problem is in the different teaching demands and the levels of support given to the academic. While this chapter has been critical of the young sociologists' achievements, the efforts of many in the non-university sector have been Herculean. It has not been uncommon for lecturers to teach eighteen (or, in the recent past, twenty-two or twenty-four) hours a week. Unlike university sociologists, who also tend to teach a smaller number of courses, and to work with smaller groups, the non-university sociologists will have a heavy load of general service teaching. This arises from the traditions of the college ideals of education, combined with discipline-based departments which contribute – at an introductory level – to the degree courses of many other departments. The result is bad for research. First, there can be little feedback from research into teaching if so much is done at an introductory level. Second, if teaching emphasises synthesis, simplification, and review of other authors, it is the antithesis of research in depth. Lecturers who live sociology in this way come to see the production of new knowledge as no more than further reading, criticism and review. A final difference between the two halves of the binary system is that the level of support staff in universities is much more generous. (When one of the present authors moved from a university to a polytechnic, he left a department of about fifteen staff, with six secretaries and administrative assistants, for one of nearly fifty with one part-time and three full-time secretaries.) The lecturing staff in the polytechnics must do the work that should be done by support staff, in addition to their heavier teaching loads. It is surprising that any research gets done at all. Lecturers in the former training colleges, or in Further Education, are in an even worse position.

What is equally disturbing in the light of their comparative advantage is the relatively low productivity of the university sociologists. It is this fact that the binary system has tended to obscure. The general reputation and mystique of university life has rubbed off on sociologists. There certainly are many who are well-qualified and professionally active, but the organisational development of the discipline has had its impact here as elsewhere.

We have tried to show that the work done by sociologists, most of whom are employed in the education system, has been carried out within the restrictions of their particular employment situation, in a unique historical period. The fact that sociologists, relative to other disciplines, have been younger, have had less of a formal postgraduate training, and have often spent their early careers working among others who were equally disadvantaged, must shape the way in which they approach their subject. It will influence their attitude to choice of research topics and to the place and conduct of research. It will affect their regard for established theory and the level of analysis at which they feel most comfortable. It will manifest itself in their approach to teaching, to their students and colleagues, and to departmental and institutional procedures. It will structure their sense of priorities, and shape their short-term ambitions. And just as the youthfulness of recent sociologists has been a factor in the current content of the discipline, so the next twenty years of encroaching middle age, together with the inevitable cut backs in higher education in the 1980s, will shift and change what we profess and how we study it.

What does this imply in concrete terms for sociology? What are the conditions under which the discipline may form strong and vigorous growths rather than the weedy hothouse straggle from the 1960s? The central argument of this book has been that sociology can only find a realistic base as an empirical discipline. We have, equally, sought to argue against the view that this means that it should be an empiricist discipline. Theory is important: it provides the grounds for analysing social problems and selecting appropriate modes of inquiry; it furnishes the criteria for evaluating findings and distinguishing bad work from good; and it forms the basis for generalisation which is at the heart of the sociological vision. Nevertheless, that theory cannot be separated from empirical work and must always exist in a dialectical relationship with it. Exercises in pure theory or the history of ideas may have a certain antiquarian interest. However, unless they are grounded in current practice their value is no more than that and they deserve no greater support.

Injunctions and even books like this have, however, at best a transient impact. Our second major theme has been that sociology is, itself, a social product. It is an occupation engaged in paid work in organisational contexts. These constraints affect the resulting product. Our view, then, is that the changes we have advocated are likely to be sustained only through institutional reform. The experience of the last decade has left a legacy of mistakes. The tenure system means that we shall have to live with them.

Since we have mentioned the tenure system, let us begin with that. It constitutes a nice market shelter. Frankly, it also covers up a great deal of laziness, incompetence and irresponsibility, not just in sociology. There can hardly be a department in the country which is not living with the consequences of the hasty expansion of the 1960s, viz. young men and women still twenty years off retirement and wholly unfitted for their jobs. With hindsight, many would concede that the expansion should have gone along with an extension of short contract employment, although some safeguard is obviously needed against the cruelty of an American system which can string people along well into their thirties before scrapping them. If the present government's policies are thrown into sharp reverse in 1984, or whenever the general election comes, to match Higher Education places to the demographic bulge, it is to be hoped that tenure will remain as difficult a hurdle as today.

What does one do about the dead wood? Compulsory redundancy seems some way off but there might well be advantages in improving early retirement and voluntary re-training schemes. Motivation towards this could well be enhanced by more flexible salary structures and promotions. The theory of increments is that a worker's marginal productivity improves with experience and should be rewarded accordingly. While it may be going too far to suggest that increments should be withheld from low productivity staff, it may be more appropriate to see the scale as a minimum and be willing to recognise effort by means of accelerated increments or merit awards. The personal promotion may seem in-keeping with this philosophy, but in practice it reduces competition and realistic evaluation of the merits of applicants, because there is a great deal of Buggins' turn about the whole business. If it is not to be overturned completely, we think that there is much to be said for a larger role for outside assessors and referees. Our own feeling, however, is that promoted posts should invariably be advertised and filled competitively.

Such changes might enhance the diligence of academics. One could obviously go further. In parts of Eastern Europe, academic journals pay contributors as a form of bonus on relatively low salaries. This might smack altogether too much of commerce or schoolboy bribes but it is an available option. However, such measures are not in themselves going to guarantee the shift of emphasis we have urged. If anything is to be achieved in this direction then we need to look more carefully at the way research funds are spent and graduate students trained.

One of the basic weaknesses of the British academic system has been dual financing. In their different ways, the universities and polytechnics have been expected to provide the basic infrastructure of personnel and equipment for research while research contracts top this up with funds for auxiliary staff and specific additional project-related expenditure. One can, for instance, buy a tape-recorder from a grant but seldom a filing cabinet. The implications have been that research has a secondary role, other than at the basic level of staff keeping abreast of their field. Research is the jam on this latter bread and butter. The British university or polytechnic is only marginally in the business of creating new knowledge.

In the natural sciences, these weaknesses have been less apparent. Partly because of their established practical value and partly because of their early development outside the universities, there has been a greater weight placed on freestanding research careers. One has only to look at the network of research units maintained by the natural science research councils to realise that the shape of their commitment is of an altogether different kind than that of SSRC. In addition, there are large private research groups and a substantial corps of scientists employed directly by the government for research tasks. Universities and polytechnics form one part of a network of competing institutions.

Sociology is rather differently organised. Here, there is much less private funding and relatively few sociologists in government employment as sociologists. The universities and polytechnics play a more dominant role. The consequence has been the perpetuation of a model of research which reflects the interests of teachers. SSRC runs four rather small research units. They have been under constant pressure since their inception and remained on the margins of Council's planning. Judgments are constantly being made of the units in terms of teachers' priorities; that they are elevating empirical work over theory, that they are taking on large-scale, long-term projects rather than small, quick pieces of work with instant publications, that they are not functioning solely as post-doctoral training grounds with a rapid turnover of younger staff and senior posts filled by university teachers on pleasant sabbatical secondment. These difficulties are compounded by the known lack of sympathy in some quarters for any move which would tend to the development of more secure employment, and for the establishment of research as a real alternative career line. Directors have not been recruited conspicuously for their experience in managing large research groups so much as their general academic standing, a standing determined by other teachers. SSRC's research funding has been overwhelmingly directed to grant applications, responding to teachers' initiatives, which guarantees a research system dominated by projects of less than three years' duration, directed by absentee landlords and carried out by inexperienced and disposable junior staff. As soon as a researcher acquires enough experience to be competent, he is too expensive and too threatening to the dilettante grant-holder.

The failures of British sociology can be seen in the proliferation of empiricist policy analysts, government survey researchers, whose ill thought-out questionnaires rightly irritate their respondents, and the burgeoning of rival occupational experts from management consultants to research nurses. Public policy debate becomes dominated either by particular sectional interests or by a narrow economistic/psychologistic arbitration between them.

What is needed is the deliberate creation of a more pluralistic sociology. In our view, this should entail an expansion of SSRC's support of unit or research centre based developments. The units need to be strengthened and seen as an integral part of Council's work rather than an embarrassing sideshow. The Designated Research Centre programme is to be welcomed in principle, and should be preserved in the present economic difficulties. It should however be combined with moves to promote collaboration between institutions which would bring specialists together on a local or regional basis. The general aim should be to create a structure in which the able and diligent researcher would have career prospects and continuity of employment at least comparable to his university teaching counterpart, while not eliminating the latter from the practice of research.

Within the universities and polytechnics, we think that there needs to be a substantial reconsideration of the way in which time is allocated. Frankly, the sabbatical year is probably too short to be worthwhile as anything more than a period of intellectual refreshment for someone whose main preoccupation is teaching. Its free availability is something of a luxury in the present economic climate, although most institutions have rightly become more rigorous in their scrutiny of its proposed use. Various sorts of changes could be contemplated. Could we envisage a trade-off whereby someone would spend three years doing nothing but teach with a view to being released for a similar period to work exclusively on research – at a unit or research centre? A slack period of student demand might free staffing time for this. More importantly, perhaps, we could borrow the American tradition of buying-out. Research grants could include the principal investigator's salary to free him or her to work full-time on the project. This could have a return in two directions: in terms of the quality of the research done and in expanding the number of post-doctoral contracts without making inroads into the number of tenured posts. Finally, of course, we should recognise the advantages of an organised system of staff exchange at all levels between research units and teaching departments as a way of maintaining the unity of the discipline.

We think too that the system of graduate training needs to be examined. At present this again reflects the narrow basis of funding and the dominance of teaching interests. The overwhelming majority of full time sociology postgraduates are financed by SSRC. Reflecting the theoretical bias of the discipline, many of these 'research studentships' do not in fact provide any research training but are purely secondary exercises, yet another attempt to determine what the great masters *really* said. They are more akin to medieval scholasticism than modern science.

Part of this can be attributed to the poor quality of methodology teaching at an undergraduate level. Students who are deprived of a proper understanding of empirical research cannot be expected to cope with substantive research as post-graduates; supervisor and student collude in choosing non-empirical topics. Even where data collection and so on are undertaken, the post-graduate training is frequently inadequate for the task.

In our view, research training is best provided in moderately large centres of active researchers. The distribution of quota places in ones and twos may satisfy the egos of the receiving departments and ensure that no one feels left out. It also contributes to the isolation of post-graduates: they work in groups which are too small to provide mutual support or to justify specialist coursework provision. Given the thin distribution of able and active researchers, it also makes supervision a very haphazard affair. Our experiences suggest that good supervision depends on the supervisor being an active researcher with real practical experience in the problems of research work. For this reason, the SSRC's 'Link' studentships are a promising innovation. The post-graduate groups should not, of course, be so large as to distract researchers from their prime task by the burden of supervision or to prevent a sense of personal involvement of each graduate in the group. Once again, regional or inter-institutional co-operation seems one way forward.

Post-graduate work towards a Ph. D. is best concentrated in research centres which will provide both supervision and training. We feel that mandatory coursework on the American model should be incorporated to ensure that students get a broad practical grounding. As an interim measure, we would suggest that departments with small numbers of students consider whether training could be organised on a consortia basis with a number of institutions pooling staff and resources to provide coursework, even if supervision remains a local responsibility. In our opinion SSRC studentships should be reserved solely for this task. Where students or departments want to engage in purely theoretical dissertations, this should more properly come under the humanities funding of the DES and the SED.

As far as Master's level work goes, SSRC's recent withdrawal of support is to be welcomed. There is now little case for this degree except where it is awarded as a consolation prize for someone who has not chosen, or been able to go right through for, a Ph. D., or where it forms part of an academic conversion programme for someone whose first degree is in another discipline. In our view, the Master's degree should be aimed mainly at post-experience students, often offered part-time and financed either by the students or their employers. We see such degrees as aimed at people who have taken a first degree in social science or a closely allied arts subject and gone into employment and who want to reflect more broadly on the nature of their work and its social context. They might also be useful for people teaching sociology in lower-level institutions to maintain their professional skills and awareness of current developments. This would be the main post-graduate activity of most teaching departments, particularly those without an allied research centre. It would be an important point of contact between departments and the local community and should be seen as a way of encouraging community use of the department's services on a research or consultancy basis. One hopes that it would also help to break down the insularity of many departments and their lack of knowledge of the world outside Higher Education.

Some critics may well charge that these changes will merely change the basis of academic prostitution and tie the discipline even more closely to the powerful and the rich who can buy its services. There are, obviously, dangers here. A more competitive sociology could well mean a less ethically inspired sociology, given Barber *et al.'s* 1973 data on competition in natural science. Barber does, however, conclude that competition is only inimical to ethical standards if rewards are seen to be unfairly distributed.

Nevertheless, can sociology's moral vision survive? In principle, there is no reason why not. The discipline's commitment to the holistic understanding of its subject-matter and, particularly, the renewed stress on understanding situational rationality rather than ironic evaluation could be valuable safeguards. At the end of the day, however, we come back to questions about the social context of sociology. Sociology cannot survive political tyranny. It is notable that sociologists are as suspect in Eastern European as in certain circles of the Conservative Party. Sociology depends upon social pluralism, on the willingness of a society to license dissent and alternative visions. In the evolutionary term, a society that cannot accommodate such change seems doomed. But we must be clear about what sociology can do. The arrogance of the 1960s was to claim that sociology could change the world. It cannot, for the same reason that education or health services alone cannot change society.

Experts and their institutions do not change the world: citizens do, in their use of expert knowledge and information. Sociologists alone cannot make the world a better place to live in: but without their understanding any movement of citizens to that end can be, at best, limited in its success.

Bibliography

Abrams, P. (1968), *The Origins of British Sociology 1834-1914,* University of Chicago Press, London.

Abrams, P. ed. (1978), *Work, Urbanism and Inequality,* Weidenfeld & Nicolson, London, 1978.

Althusser, L. (1969), *For Marx,* trans. B. Brewster, Allen Lane, London.

Althusser, L with E. Balibar (1970), *Reading Capital,* trans. B. Brewster, New Left Books, London.

American Sociological Review (1968), Review Symposium on *Studies in Ethnomethodology* by G. Swanson, A. F. C. Wallace and J.S. Coleman.

Amis, K. (1953), *That Uncertain Feeling,* Gollancz, London.

Andreski, S. (1974), *The Essential Comte,* trans. Margaret Clarke, Croom Helm, London.

Aron, R. (1967), *18 Lectures on Industrial Society,* Weidenfeld & Nicolson, London.

Asimov, I. (1960), *Foundation,* Panther, London.

Atkinson, J. M. (1977), 'Coroners and the Categorisation of Deaths as Suicides', in Bell and Newby (eds), *Doing Sociological Research,* Allen & Unwin, London.

Atkinson, J. M. (1978), *Discovering Suicide,* Macmillan, London.

Atkinson, J. M., and Drew, P. (1979), *Order in Court,* Macmillan, London.

Ayer, A. J. (1970), *Language, Truth and Logic,* Gollancz, London (2nd Edn).

Bain, G. *et al.* (1972), 'The Labour Force' in *Trends in British Society,* Halsey, A. M. (ed.), Macmillan, London.

Bandyopadhyay, P. (1971), 'One Sociology or Many: Some Issues in Radical Sociology', *Sociological Review,* vol. 19, no. 1.

Banks, J.A. (1967), 'The British Sociological Association – the First Fifteen Years', *Sociology,* vol. 1, no. 1.

Banks, J. A. (1971), 'Sociology as a Vocation', Inaugural Lecture, Leicester University Press.

Banks, J. A. (1974), 'The Vocational Orientations of Sociology Graduates', Research Note, *Sociology,* vol. 8 no. 2, 297-304.

Banks, J. A. (1975), 'From Scholarly Body to Professional Association', *Network*, no. 1, BSA, London.

Barber, B. and Lally, G. G., *et al.* (1973), *Research on Human Subjects: Problems of Social Control in Medical Experimentation*, Russell Sage, New York.

Barker Lunn, J. (1976), 'Streaming in the Primary School: Methods and Politics', in M. Shipman (ed.), *The Organisation and Impact of Social Research*, Routledge & Kegan Paul, London.

Barnes, J. A. (1979), *Who should know what?: Social Science, Privacy and Ethics*, Penguin, Harmondsworth.

Baumann, Z. (1978), *Hermeneutics and Social Science: Approaches to Understanding*, Hutchinson, London.

Becker, H. S. (1958), 'Problems of Inference and Proof in Participant Observation', *American Sociological Review*, vol. 23, no. 6, 652-60.

Becker, H. S. *et al.* (1961), *Boys in White*, University of Chicago Press.

Becker, H. S. (1963), *Outsiders*, Free Press, New York.

Becker, H. S. (1967), 'Whose side are we on?', *Social Problems*, vol. 14, 239-47.

Bell, C., and Newby, H. (1972), *Community Studies*, Allen & Unwin, London.

Bell, C., and Newby, H, eds (1974), *The Sociology of Community*, Frank Cass, London.

Bell, C., and Newby, H. (1977), *Doing Sociological Research*, Allen & Unwin, London.

Bell, C. (1977), 'Reflections on the Banbury Restudy' in C. Bell and H. Newby (eds), *Doing Sociological Research*, Allen & Unwin, London.

Bell, C., and Encel, S. (1978), *Inside the Whale*, Pergamon Press, London.

Benjamin, B. (1970), *The Population Census*, Heinemann, London.

Benton, T. (1977), *Philosophical Foundations of the Three Sociologies*, Routledge & Kegan Paul, London.

Bernstein, B. (1974), 'Sociology and the Sociology of Education', in J. Rex (ed.), *Approaches to Sociology*, Routledge & Kegan Paul, London.

Beynon, H. (1973), *Working for Ford*, Penguin, Harmondsworth.

Bittner, E. (1965), 'The Concept of Organisation', *Social Research*, vol. 32, no. 3, 239-55.

Bittner, E. (1967a), 'Police Discretion in Emergency Apprehension of Mentally Ill Persons', *Social Problems*, vol. 14, no. 3, 278-92.

Bittner, E. (1967b), 'The Police on Skid Row: A Study of Peace-keeping', *American Sociological Review*, vol. 32, no. 5, 699-715.

Bloor, M. (1976), 'Professional Autonomy and Client Exclusion: A study in E. N. T. Clinics', in M. Wadsworth, and D. Robinson (eds), *Studies in Everyday Medical Life*, Martin Robertson, London.

Bloor, M. (1978), 'On the Analysis of Observational Data: A Discussion of the Worth and Uses of Inductive Techniques and Respondent Validation', *Sociology*, vol. 12, no. 3, 545-52.

Bloor, M. (forthcoming, 1980), 'An Alternative to the Ethnomethodological Approach to Rule-Use? a comment on Zimmerman and Wider's comment on Denzin', *Scottish Journal of Sociology*.

Blum, A. F. (1971), 'Methods for Recognising, Formulating and

Describing Social Problems,' in E. O. Smigel (ed.) *Handbook on the Study of Social Problems,* Rand, McNally, Chicago.

Blum, A. F. (1972), 'Sociology, Wrongdoing and Akrasia: An Attempt to think Greek about the Problem of Theory and Practice', in R. A. Scott and J. D. Douglas (eds), *Theoretical Perspectives on Deviance,* Basic Books, New York.

Borgatta, E., and Bohrnstedt, G. (1969), *Sociological Methodology,* Jossey-Bass, San Francisco.

Bott, E. (1957), *Family and Social Network,* Tavistock, London (2nd edn 1971).

Bottomore, T. (1975), *Marxist Sociology,* Macmillan, London.

Bradshaw, J. (1975), 'Welfare Rights: An Experimental Approach', in R. Lees and G. Smith (eds), *Action Research in Community Development,* Routledge & Kegan Paul, London.

Brennan, M. (1978), 'S.S.R.C. Initiative on Health Policy', in *Medical Sociology News,* vol. 5, no. 3, 10-11.

Brown, C., Guillet de Monthoux, P. and McCullough, A. (1976), *The Access Case Book,* THS, Stockholm.

Brown, G. W. (1973), 'Some Thoughts on Grounded Theory', *Sociology,* vol. 7, no. 1.

Brown, R. K. (1967), 'Research and Consultancy in Industrial Enterprises: the Tavistock Studies', *Sociology,* vol. 1, no. 3, 33-60.

Brown, R. (1978), 'Work', in P. Abrams (ed.), *Work, Urbanism and Inequality,* Weidenfeld & Nicolson, London.

Bruyn, S. T. (1966), *The Human Perspective in Sociology:* Prentice Hall, Englewood Cliffs, New Jersey.

Bulmer, M., ed. (1977), *Sociological Research Methods: An introduction,* Macmillan, London.

Bulmer, M. , ed. (1978), *Social Policy Research,* Macmillan, London.

Burnham, J. (1972), *The Managerial Revolution,* Greenwood Press, Westport, Cinn. (Original 1941, John Day Co).

Byre, P. (1973), 'The Past Chairman gives his list of Objectives for SSRG', *SSRG News: Bulletin of the Social Services Research Group,* no. 2, June.

Cain, M. (1979), 'The General Practice Lawyer and the Client: Towards a Radical Conception', *International Journal of the Sociology of Law,* 7, 331-54.

Calder, A. (1971), *The People's War,* Panther, London.

Carey, J. T. (1975), *Sociology and Public Affairs: The Chicago School,* Sage, Beverly Hills.

Carlen, P. (1976), *Magistrates' Justice,* Martin Robertson, London.

Carson, W. G. and Wiles, P. (eds) (1970), *Crime and Delinquency in Britain: A Book of Readings,* Martin Robertson, London.

Cartwright, A. (1964), *Human Relations and Hospital Care,* Routledge & Kegan Paul, London.

Cartwright, A. (1967), *Patients and Their Doctors,* Routledge & Kegan Paul, London.

Castaneda, C. (1970), *The Teachings of Don Juan: a Yaqui Way of Knowledge,* Penguin, Harmondsworth.

CDP Project (1974), *Inter Project Report, 1973*, Centre for Environmental Studies, London.

Cherns, A. B. (1969), 'Social Research and its Diffusion', *Human Relations*, vol. 22, no. 3, 210-18.

Cherns, A., and Perry, N. (1976), 'The Development and Structure of Social Science Research in Britain', in N. Perry and E. Crawford (eds), *Demands for Social Knowledge*, Sage, London.

Cicourel, A. V. (1964), *Method and Measurement in Sociology*, Free Press, New York.

Cicourel, A. V., and Kitsuse, J. (1964), *The Educational Decision-Makers*, Bobbs Merrill, Indianapolis.

Cicourel, A. V. (1968), *The Social Organisation of Juvenile Justice*, Wiley, New York.

Clapham, S. J. (1946), *Report of the Committee on the Provision for Social and Economical Research*, HMSO, London, Cmnd 6868.

Clark, P. (1972), *Action Research and Organisational Change*, Harper & Row, New York.

Cohen, S., ed. (1971), *Images of Deviance*, Penguin, Harmondsworth.

Cohen, S. (1972), *Folk Devils and Moral Panics*, Paladin, London.

Cohen, S. and Taylor, L. (1972), *Psychological Survival*, Penguin, Harmondsworth.

Cohen, S., and Taylor, L. (1977), 'Talking about Prison Blues', in C. Bell and H. Newby, *Doing Sociological Research*, Allen & Unwin, London

Crewe, I. (1976), 'Marxism in University Political Studies' THES, 2 April, p. 5.

Dahrendorf, R. (1975), 'Social Institutions, Economic Forces and the Future of Sociology' Opening Address to BSA. Annual Conference, University of Kent.

Dawe, A. (1976), 'The Two Sociologies', *British Journal of Sociology*, vol. 21, no. 2, 207-18.

Dennis, N., Henriques, F. and Slaughter, C. (1956), *Coal is our Life*, Eyre & Spottiswoode, London.

Denzin, N. K., ed. (1970a), *Sociological Methods: A Sourcebook*, Butterworth, London.

Denzin, N. K. (1970b), *The Research Act*, Butterworth, London.

DES (1975), *Statistics of Education*, vol. 6, Universities, HMSO, London.

Dibble, V. K. (1975), *The Legacy of Albion Small*, University of Chicago Press.

Dingwall, R. (1978), Review of *Doing Sociological Research*, *Medical Sociology News*, vol. 5, no. 3, September/October, BSA Medical Sociology Group, London.

Dingwall, R. (1975), 'Ethnomethodology and Marxism', *Sociology*, vol. 9, no. 3, September.

Dingwall, R. (1976), *Aspects of Illness*, Martin Robertson, London.

Dingwall, R. (1977a), *The Social Organisation of Health Visitor Training*, Croom Helm, London.

Dingwall, R. (1977b), 'Atrocity Stories and Professional Relationships', *Sociology of Work and Occupations*, vol. 4, no. 4, 371-96.

Dingwall, R. (1980), 'Orchestrated Encounters', *Sociology of Health and Illness*, vol. 2, no. 2.

Dollard, J. (1937), *Caste and Class in a Southern Town*, Harper & Row, New York.

Donnison, D. (1978), 'Research for Policy' in M. Bulmer (ed.), *Social Policy Research*, Macmillan, London.

Douglas, J. D. (1974), *Understanding Everyday Life*, Routledge & Kegan Paul, London.

Dunkerley, D., and Clegg, S. (1980), *Organisation, Class and Control*, Routledge & Kegan Paul, London.

Easthope, G. (1974), *Social Research*, Longman, London.

Evans-Pritchard, E. E. (1937), *Witchcraft Oracles and Magic Among the Azande of the Anglo-Egyptian Sudan*, Clarendon Press, Oxford.

Eversley, D. (1973), *A Question of Numbers?*, Runnymede Trust, London.

Faris, R. E. L. (1967), *Chicago Sociology 1920-1932*, Chandler Publishing, San Francisco.

Festinger, L., and Katz, D., eds (1954), *Research Methods in the Behavioural Sciences*, Staples Press, London.

Filmer, P. *et al.* (1972), *New Directions in Sociological Theory*, Collier Macmillan, London.

Filstead, W. J. (1970), *Qualitative Methodology: Firsthand Involvement with the Social World*, Markham Publishing, Chicago.

Firth, R. (1968), *Research in Social Anthropology*, Heinemann, London.

Fletcher, C. (1974), *Beneath the Surface*, Routledge & Kegan Paul, London.

Floud, J., Halsey A. H. and Martin P. (1957), *Social Class and Educational Opportunity*, Heinemann, London.

Ford, J. (1969), *Social Class and the Comprehensive School*, Routledge & Kegan Paul, London.

Ford, J. (1976), 'Facts, Evidence and Rumours: A Rational Reconstruction of "Social Class and the Comprehensive School" ' in M. Shipman (ed.), *The Organisation and Impact of Social Research*, Routledge & Kegan Paul, London.

Foster, G. M. (1969), *Applied Anthropology*, Little, Brown, Boston.

Frankenberg, R. (1966), *Communities in Britain*, Penguin, Harmondsworth.

Frazer, Sir J. G. (1890), *The Golden Bough*, Macmillan, London.

Freidson, E. (1971), *Profession of Medicine*, Dodd, Mead, New York.

Freidson, E. (1976), 'The Division of Labour as Social Interaction', *Social Problems*, vol. 23, no. 3, 304-13.

Freidson, E. (1977), 'The Futures of Professionalisation', in M. Stacey, M. Reid, C. Heath and R. Dingwall (eds), *Health and the Division of Labour*, Croom Helm, London.

Friedman, N. (1967), *The Social Nature of Psychological Research*, Basic Books, New York.

Friedrichs, R. (1970), *A Sociology of Sociology*, Free Press, New York.

Furner, M. O. (1975), *Advocacy and Objectivity: A Crisis in the Professionalisation of American Social Science 1865-1905*, University of Kentucky Press, Lexington.

Garfinkel, H. (1967), *Studies in Ethnomethodology*, Prentice Hall, Englewood Cliffs, New Jersey.

Garnsey, E. (1975), 'Occupational Structure in Industrialized Societies', *Sociology,* vol. 3, September.

Gavron, H. (1966), *The Captive Wife,* Penguin, Harmondsworth.

Gee, W., ed. (1929), *Research in the Social Sciences,* Macmillan, New York.

Gerstl, J. E., and Hutton, S. P. (1966), *Engineers: the Anatomy of a Profession,* Tavistock, London.

Giddens, A. (1974), *Positivism and Sociology,* Heinemann, London.

Giddens, A. (1976), 'Classical Theory and Modern Sociology', *AJS,* vol. 81, no. 4, January.

Gittus, E., (ed.) (1972), *Key Variables in Social Research,* vol. 1, Heinemann, London.

Glaser, B. G., and Strauss, A. L. (1967), *The Discovery of Grounded Theory,* Aldine, Chicago.

Glass, D. V., ed. (1954), *Social Mobility in Britain,* Routledge & Kegan Paul, London.

Glazer, N. (1973), 'The Rise of Social Research in Europe', in D. Lerner and P. Smith (eds), *The Human Meaning of the Social Sciences,* Peter Smith, Mass.

Gluckman, M. (1963), *Custom and Conflict in Africa,* Blackwell, Oxford.

Gluckman, M. (1967), Introduction, in A. L. Epstein (ed.), *The Craft of Social Anthropology,* Tavistock, London.

Goldthorpe, J., and Llewellyn, C. (1977), 'Class Mobility in Modern Britain', *Sociology,* vol. 11, no. 3.

Goode, W. J., and Hatt, P. K. (1952), *Methods in Social Research,* McGraw-Hill, New York.

Goodenough, W. H. (1964), 'Cultural Anthropology and Linguistics', in D. Hymes (ed.), *Language in Culture and Society,* Harper & Row, New York.

Gould, J. (1977), *The Attack on Higher Education,* Institute for the Study of Conflict, London.

Gouldner, A. (1967), *Enter Plato,* Routledge & Kegan Paul, London.

Gouldner, A. (1970a), *The Coming Crisis of Western Society,* Heinemann, London, (published in Great Britain 1971).

Gouldner, A. (1970b), 'Toward the Radical Reconstruction of Sociology', *Social Policy,* vol. 1, no. 1, 18-25, May-June.

Gramsci, A. (1971), *Selections from the Prison Notebooks of Antonio Gramsci,* Lawrence & Wishart, London.

Grathoff, R. (1978), *The Theory of Social Action: The Correspondence of Alfred Schutz and Talcott Parsons,* Indiana University Press, Bloomington.

Greer, S. (1977), 'On the Selection of Problems', in M. Bulmer (ed.), *Sociological Research Methods: an Introduction,* Macmillan, London.

Habenstein, R. ed. (1970), *Pathways to Data,* Aldine, Chicago.

Habermas, J. (1972), *Knowledge and Human Interest,* Heinemann, London.

Haines, J. (1977), *The Politics of Power,* Jonathan Cape, London.

Halsey, A. H. (1972), *Educational Priority Vol 1: EPA Problems and Policies,* HMSO, London.

Halsey, A. H., ed. (1972), *Trends in British Society*, Macmillan, London.

Halsey, A. H., and Payne, J. (1972), 'The Education Priority Areas Action Research Programme', *SSRC Newsletter*, 15 June.

Halsey, A. H. (1978), 'Government Against Poverty in School and Community', in M. Bulmer (ed.), *Social Policy Research*, Macmillan, London.

Halmos, P., ed. (1964), *The Development of Industrial Societies*, Sociological Review Monograph 8, University of Keele.

Hammond, P. E., ed. (1964), *Sociologists at Work: Essays on the Craft of Social Research*, Basic Books, New York.

Harris, A. I., and Buckle, J. R. (1971), *Handicapped and Impaired in Great Britain*, HMSO, London.

Harris, M. (1968), *The Rise of Anthropological Theory*, Routledge & Kegan Paul, London.

Harrisson, T. (1947), 'The Future of Sociology', *Pilot Papers*, vol. 2, no. 1, 10-21.

Hawthorn, G. (1976), *Enlightenment and Despair*, Cambridge University Press.

Heady, B., and O'Laughlin, T. (1978), 'Transgenerational Structural Inequality', *BJS*, vol. 29, no. 1, March.

Healey, P. (1975), 'Changes in the SSRC Postgraduate Award Scheme', *SSRC Newsletter*, no. 26, February.

Hempel, C. G. (1966), *Philosophy of Natural Science*, Prentice Hall, Englewood Cliffs.

Heyworth, Lord (1965), *Report of the Committee on Social Studies*, HMSO, London, Cmnd 2660.

Hill, R. J., and Crittenden, K. S. (1968), *Proceedings of the Purdue Symposium on Ethnomethodology*, Institute for the Study of Social Change, Purdue University.

Hindess, B. (1973), *The Use of Official Statistics in Sociology*, Macmillan, London.

Hindess, B., and Hirst, P. Q. (1975), *Pre-Capitalist Modes of Production*, Routledge & Kegan Paul, London.

Hobhouse, L. T. (1907), 'The Roots of Modern Sociology', Inaugural Lecture, University of London.

Hofstadter, R., and Metzger, W. P. (1955), *The Development of Academic Freedom in the United States*, Columbia University Press, New York.

Home Office (1971), *CDP: an Official View*, HMSO, London.

Hughes, E. (1971), *The Sociological Eye*, Aldine, Chicago.

Hughes, J. A. (1976), *Sociological Analysis*, Nelson, London.

Humphreys, L. (1970), *Tearoom Trade*, Duckworth, London.

Hyman, H. H. (1954), *Interviewing in Social Research*, Chicago University Press.

Jackson, B., and Marsden, D. (1962), *Education and the Working Class*, Routledge & Kegan Paul, London.

Jacques, E. (1951), *The Changing Culture of the Factory*, Tavistock, London.

Johnson, J. M. (1975), *Doing Field Research*, Free Press, New York.

Jones, T. (1977), 'A Comment on Payne', *Sociological Review*, vol. 25, no. 2, May.

Kerr, C. *et al.* (1960), Industrialism and Industrial Mass, Harvard University Press (1st edn), (Penguin, Harmondsworth, 1973, 2nd edn).

Kolakowski, L. (1972), *Positivist Philosophy: from Hume to the Vienna Circle,* Penguin, Harmondsworth.

Korsch, K. (1971), *Three Essays on Marxism,* Pluto Press, London.

Kuhn, T. S. (1962), *Structure of Scientific Revolutions,* Chicago University Press.

Kuper, A. (1973), *Anthropologists and Anthropology: The British School 1922-1972,* Allen Lane, London.

Lazarsfeld, P. F., and Rosenberg, M., eds (1955), *The Language of Social Research,* Free Press, Chicago.

Leach, E. (1974), book review, *New York Review of Books,* 4 April.

Lee, A. M., and Lee, E. B. (1976), 'The Society for the Study of Social Problems: Parental Recollections and Hopes', *Social Problems,* vol. 24, no. 1, 1-14.

Lees, R. (1975), *Research Strategies for Social Welfare,* Routledge & Kegan Paul, London.

Lees, R., and Smith, G. (1975), *Action Research in Community Development,* Routledge & Kegan Paul, London.

Lewis, J. (1979), 'Careers in Government Research', Paper presented to SSRC Conference on Postgraduate Training, University of Sussex.

Lockwood, D. (1958), *The Black Coated Worker,* Allen & Unwin, London.

London School of Economics (1964), *Calendar 1964-1965,* LSE, London.

Lupton, T. (1963), *On the Shop Floor,* Pergamon, Oxford.

Lynd, R. S., and Lynd, H. M. (1929), *Middletown: A Study in Contemporary American Culture,* Harcourt, Brace, New York.

Lynd, R. S. and Lynd, H. M. (1937), *Middletown in Transition: A Study in Cultural Conflicts,* Harcourt, Brace, New York.

Mack, J. A. (1956), 'Social Research and the Administrator', *Sociological Review,* vol. 4, no. 1.

Mack, J. (1979), 'Should the SSRC be Shut Down', *New Society,* vol. 47, no. 48.

Madge, C., and Weinberger, B. (1973), *Art Students Observed,* Faber, London.

Madge, J. (1953), *The Tools of Social Science,* Longman, London.

Malinowski, B. (1922), *Argonauts of the Western Pacific,* George Routledge & Sons, London.

Malinowski, B. (1967), *A Diary in the Strict Sense of the Term,* Routledge & Kegan Paul, London.

Mann, F. C., and Hoffman, L. R. (1960), *Automation and the Worker,* Holt, Rinehart & Winston, New York.

Marcuse, H. (1955), *Reason and Revolution,* Routledge & Kegan Paul, London.

Marris, P. (1958), *Widows and their Families,* Routledge & Kegan Paul, London.

Marshall, T. H. (1963), 'Sociology at the Crossroads', reprinted in, *Class, Citizenship and Social Development,* Greenwood Press, Connecticut.

Marsland, D. (1979), 'Sociological Research and Social Policy: for a

Positive Programme', Paper presented to BSA/SSRC Conference on Methodology and Techniques of Sociology, University of Lancaster.

Marx, K., and Engels, F. (1962), *Selected Works (vols I and II)*, Foreign Languages Publishing House, Moscow.

Marx, K., and Engels, F. (1970), *The German Ideology*, ed C. J. Archer, Lawrence and Wishart, London.

Mass Observation (1938), *First Year's Work 1937-1938*, Lindsay Drummond, London.

Matthews, R. C. O. (1975a), 'Rothschild and After: 1972-75', *SSRC Newsletter*, no. 29, November.

Matthews, R. C. O. (1975b), 'New SSRC Structure', *SSRC Newsletter*, no. 26, February.

Matza, D. (1969), *Becoming Deviant*, Prentice Hall, Englewood Cliffs, New Jersey.

McHugh, P., Raffel, S., Foss, D. C., and Blum, A. F. (1974), *On the Beginnings of Social Enquiry*, Routledge & Kegan Paul, London.

Mayo, M. (1975), 'The History and Early Development of CDP', in R. Lees and G. Smith (eds), *Action Research in Community Development*, Routledge & Kegan Paul, London.

McGrath, M. (1975), 'Social Needs of an Immigrant Population', in R. Lees and G. Smith (eds), *Action Research in Community Development*, Routledge & Kegan Paul, London.

Merton, R. K., Fiske, M. and Kendall, P. L. (1956), *The Focused Interview*, Free Press, Illinois.

Merton R. K., Reader, G. G., and Kendall, P. L. (1957), *The Student-Physician*, Harvard University Press Cambridge, Mass.

Millerson, G. (1964), *The Qualifying Associations*, Routledge & Kegan Paul, London.

Mills, C. W. (1959), *The Sociological Imagination*, Oxford University Press, New York.

Mills, E. (1962), *Living with Mental Illness*, Routledge & Kegan Paul, London.

Mitchell, G. D. (1968), *A Dictionary of Sociology*, Routledge & Kegan Paul, London.

Mitchell, G. D. (1970), 'Sociology – An Historical Perspective', in P. Halmos (ed.), *The Sociology of Sociology*, The Sociological Review Monograph no. 16, University of Keele.

Mogey. P. (1956), *Family and Neighbourhood*, Oxford University Press.

Moore, R. (1977a), 'Becoming a Sociologist in Sparkbrook', in C. Bell and H. Newby (eds), *Doing Sociological Research*, Allen & Unwin, London.

Moore, R. (1977b), 'Sociologists Not at Work', Paper to BSA Conference, Sheffield, March.

Moore, W. E. (1974), *Social Change*, Prentice Hall, Englewood Cliffs, New Jersey (2nd edn).

Moser, C. A. (1958), *Survey Methods in Social Investigation*, Heinemann, London.

Moser, C. A., and Kalton, G. (1971), *Survey Methods in Social Investigation*, Heinemann, London.

Mullins, N. J. (1973a), 'The Development of Specialities in Social Science:

The Case of Ethnomethodology', *Science Studies*, vol. 3, no. 3, 245-73.

Mullins, N. J. (1973b), *Theories and Theory Groups in Contemporary Sociology*, Harper & ow, New York.

Neustadt, I. (1965), 'Teaching Sociology', Inaugural Lecture, Leicester University Press.

Newby, H. (1977), 'In the Field: Reflections on the Study of Suffolk Farm Workers', in C. Bell and H. Newby (eds), *Doing Sociological Research*, Allen & Unwin, London.

Newby, H., and Bell, C. (1979), 'From Epistemology to Methods', BSA/SSRC Conference on Methodology and Techniques of Sociology, Lancaster University, January.

Nicholas, A. (1978), 'Sociologists in Polytechnics', *SIP Occasional Paper*, no. 1, Hatfield Polytechnic (mimeo).

Nicolaus, M. (1969), 'Remarks at ASA Convention, Boston 1968', *Catalyst*, Spring.

Noble, T. (1975), *Modern Britain: Structure and Change*, Batsford, London.

Oberschall, A. R. (1965), *Empirical Social Research in Germany: 1848-1914*, Mouton, The Hague.

Olesen, V. L. and Whittaker, E. W. (1968), *The Silent Dialogue*, Jossey-Bass, San Francisco.

Pahl, R., and Winkler, J. (1974), 'The Economic Elite: Theory and Practice', in P. Stanworth and A. Giddens (eds), *Elites and Power in British Society*, Cambridge University Press, London.

Pahl, R. (1977), 'Playing the Rationality Game: the Sociologist as a Hired Expert', in C. Bell and H. Newby (eds), *Doing Sociological Research*, Allen & Unwin, London.

Park, R. E., and Burgess, E. W. (1921), *Introduction to the Science of Sociology*, University of Chicago Press.

Parsons, T. (1949), *Essays in Sociological Theory, Pure and Applied*, Free Press, Chicago.

Parsons, T. (1954), *Essays in Social Theory*, Free Press, Chicago.

Parsons, T. (1968), *The Structure of Social Action*, Free Press, New York, (first published 1937).

Payne, G., Ford, G., and Robertson, C. (1976), 'Changes in Occupational Mobility in Scotland', *Scottish Journal of Sociology*, vol. 1 no. 1, November.

Payne, G. (1977a), 'Occupational Transition in Advanced Industrial Society', *Sociological Review*, vol. 25, no. 1, February.

Payne, G. (1977b), 'Understanding Occupational Transition', *Sociological Review*, vol. 25, no. 2, May.

Payne, G., and Ford, G. (1977), 'A Reappraisal of Social Mobility in Britain', *Sociology*, vol. 11, no. 2, May.

Payne, G. (1979), 'Social Research and Market Research', *Sociology*, vol. 13, no. 2, May.

Peel, J. D. Y. (1978), 'Two Cheers for Empiricism', review article in *Sociology*, vol. 12, no. 2, May.

Perry, N. (1975), 'The Organisation of Social Science Research in the United Kingdom', *Occasional Papers in Survey Research*, no. 6, SSRC, London.

Phillips, D. (1971), *Knowledge from What?*, Jossey-Bass, San Francisco.

Phillipson, M. (1971), *Sociological Aspects of Crime and Delinquency*, Routledge & Kegan Paul, London.

Platt, J. (1971), *Social Research in Bethnal Green*, Macmillan, London.

Platt, J. (1976), *Realities of Social Research*, Sussex University Press, London.

Plowden Report (1967), *Children and their Primary Schools*, Central Advisory Council for Education, HMSO, London.

Popper, K. (1961), *The Poverty of Historicism*, Routledge & Kegan Paul, London.

Posner, M. (1979), 'The SSRC's Future', *New Society*, vol. 48, no. 872, 21 June.

Powdermaker, H. (1966), *Stranger and Friend: The Way of an Anthropologist*, Secker & Warburg, London.

Rapoport, R. (1970), 'Three Dilemmas in Action Research', *Human Relations*, vol. 23, no. 6, 499-514.

Rex, J. (1970), 'The Spread of the Pathology of Natural Science to the Social Sciences', in *The Sociology of Sociology*, Sociological Review Monograph no. 16, University of Keele.

Rex, J. (1974), *Sociology and the Demystification of the Modern World*, Routledge & Kegan Paul, London.

Rex, J. (1978a), 'British Sociology's Wars of Religion', *New Society*, vol. 44, no. 814, 11 May.

Rex, J. (1978b), 'The Pressures of Sociology Teaching', *New Society*, vol. 44, no. 816, 25 May.

Rex, J. and Tomlinson, S. (1979), *Colonial Immigrants in a British City*, Routledge & Kegan Paul, London.

Robbins Report (1963), *Higher Education*, Report of the Committee appointed by the Prime Minister under the Chairmanship of Lord Robbins, HMSO Cmnd 2153.

Robinson, D. (1975), 'Looking Forward from 1975', *SSRC Newsletter* no. 29, November.

Rock, P. (1973), *Deviant Behaviour*, Hutchinson, London.

Rock, P. and McIntosh, M., eds (1973), *Deviance and Social Control*, Tavistock, London.

Rock, P. (1979), *The Making of Symbolic Interactionism*, Macmillan, London.

Roth, J. (1966), 'Hired-Hand Research', *American Sociologist*, no. 1, 190-6, August.

Runciman, W. G. (1966), *Relative Deprivation and Social Justice*, Routledge & Kegan Paul, London.

Sacks, H., Schegloff, E., and Jefferson, G. (1974), 'A Simplest Systematics for the Organisation of Turntaking in Conversation', *Language*, vol. 50, no. 4, 696-735.

Schutz, A. (1972), *The Phenomenology of the Social World*, Heinemann, London (first published 1932).

Schwendinger, H., and Schwendinger, J. (1974), *The Sociologists of the Chair: A Radical Analysis of the Formative Years of North American Sociology (1883-1922)*, Basic Books, New York.

Scott, M., and Hughes, J. (1976), 'Ownership and Control in a Satellite Economy', *Sociology,* vol. 10, no. 1.

Seebohm Committee Report (1968), *Report of the Committee on Local Authority and Allied Personal Social Services,* Home Office, HMSO, London.

Sellitz, C., Jahoda, M., Deutsch, M. and Cook, S. M. (1959), *Research Method in Social Relations,* Holt, Rinehart & Winston, New York.

Sharpe, L. J. (1975), 'The Social Scientist and Policy-making in Britain and America: A Comparison', *Policy and Politics,* no. 4, 10-18.

Sharrock, W. W. (1979), 'Portraying the Professional Relationship', in D. Anderson (ed.), *Health Education in Practice,* Croom Helm, London.

Shils, E. A. (1970), 'Tradition, Ecology and Institution in the History of Sociology', *Daedalus,* no. 9, 760-825.

Shipman, M. (1972), *The Limitations of Social Research,* Longman, London.

Shipman, M., ed. (1976), *The Organisation and Impact of Social Research,* Routledge & Kegan Paul, London.

Shonfield, A. (1969), 'In the Course of Investigation', *New Society,* 24 July.

Silverman, D. (1975), *Reading Castaneda,* Routledge & Kegan Paul, London.

Simey, T. S. and Simey, M. B. (1960), *Charles Booth: Social Scientist,* Oxford University Press, London.

Simey, T. S. (1964), 'Social Purpose and Social Science', Eleanor Rathbone Memorial Lecture, University of Liverpool Press.

Skura, B. (1976), 'Constraints on a Reform Movement: Relationships between SSSP and ASA, 1951-1970', *Social Problems,* vol. 24, no. 1, 15-36.

Small, A. K., and Vincent, G. E. (1894), *Introduction to the Science of Sociology,* American Book Company, New York.

Small A. K. (1907), *Adam Smith and Modern Sociology,* University of Chicago Press.

Smith, C. S. (1975), 'The Employment of Sociologists in Research Occupations in Britain in 1973', *Sociology,* no. 9.

Smith, G. (1975), 'Action Research: Experimental Social Administration', in R. Lees and G. Smith (eds), *Action Research in Community Development,* Routledge & Kegan Paul, London.

Sprott, W. J. H. (1962), 'Sociology at the Seven Dials', L.T. Hobhouse Memorial Lecture, University of London, Athlone, London.

SSRC (1967), 'Research Review of Sociology', Unpublished Draft.

SSRC (1970), 'Conference on Action Research', York.

SSRC (1975), *SSRC Newsletter,* no. 26, February.

SSRC (1975), *SSRC Newsletter* no. 29, November.

SSRC (1975), *SSRC Newsletter,* no. 26, February.

SSRC (1977), *SSRC Newsletter,* no. 33, March.

SSRC (1978), *SSRC Newsletter,* no. 36, March.

SSRC (1978), *SSRC Newsletter,* no. 37, July.

SSRC (1978), *SSRC Newletter,* no. 38, November.

Stacey, M., ed. (1969), *Comparability in Social Research,* Heinemann, London.

Stacey, M. *et al.* (1975), *Power, Persistence and Change,* Routledge & Kegan Paul, London.

Stedman Jones, G. (1972), 'History – The Poverty of Empiricism', in R. Blackburn (ed.), *Ideology in Social Science,* Fontana, London.

Stein, M. R. (1960), *The Eclipse of Community,* Princeton University Press, New York.

Strong, P. M. (1976), 'Some Limitations on the Nature of Sociological Production', Unpublished mimeo.

Strong, P. M. (1979a), 'Sociological Imperialism and The Profession of Medicine', *Social Science and Medicine,* vol. 13, no. 2, 199-215.

Strong, P. M. (1979b), *The Ceremonial Order of the Clinic,* Routledge & Kegan Paul, London.

Sudnow, D. (1967), *Passing On: The Social Organisation of Dying,* Prentice Hall, Englewood Cliffs, New Jersey.

Taylor, I., and Taylor, L. eds (1973), *Politics and Deviance,* Penguin, Harmondsworth.

Taylor, I., Walton, P., and Young, J. (1973), *The New Criminology,* Routledge & Kegan Paul, London.

Taylor, L. (1971), *Deviance and Society,* Michael Joseph, London.

Thurley, K. (1972), 'The Organisation and Sponsorship of Action Research', *SSRC Newsletter,* no. 14, March.

Times Higher Educational Supplement (1978), 'Getting Down to the Business of Solving Real Problems', 24 November.

Town, S. W. (1973), 'Action Research, Social Policy: Some Recent British Experience', *Sociological Review,* vol. 21, no. 4, 573-98.

Townsend, P. (1957), *The Family Life of Old People,* Routledge & Kegan Paul, London.

Townsend, P. (1979), *Poverty in the United Kingdom,* Allen Lane, London.

Urry, J. (1973), 'Thomas S. Kuhn as Sociologist of Knowledge', *BJS,* vol. 24, no. 4.

Vidich, A. J., Bensman, J. and Stein, M. R., eds (1964), *Reflections on Community Studies,* Harper & Row, New York.

Vilar, P. (1973), 'Writing Marxist History', *New Left Review,* no. 80.

Wakeford, J. (1968), *The Strategy of Social Enquiry,* Macmillan, London.

Wakeford, J. (1978), Review of *Inside the Whale, Network,* no. 13, BSA, London, January.

Wakeford, J. (1979), 'Research Methods Syllabuses in Sociology Departments in the United Kingdom', BSA/SSRC Conference on Methodology and Technique of Sociology, Lancaster University.

Wall, W. D. (1968), 'The Future of Educational Research', *Educational Research,* vol. 10, no. 3.

Wall, W. D., and Williams, H. L. (1970), *Longitudinal Studies and the Social Sciences,* SSRC/Heinemann, London.

Warner, W. L., and Lunt, P. S. (1941), *The Social Life of a Modern Community,* Yale University Press, New Haven.

Wax, R. L. (1971), *Doing Fieldwork,* Chicago University Press.

Webb, B. (1926), *My Apprenticeship,* Longman, London (2nd edn 1946).

Webb, E. J. *et al.* (1966), *Unobtrusive Measures,* Rand, McNally, Chicago.

Webb, S. and Webb, B. (1932), *Methods of Social Study,* Cambridge

University Press (1975 edn).

Weinberg, I. (1969), 'The Problem of the Convergence of Industrial Society', *Comparative Studies in Society and History*, vol. 11, no. 3.

Westergaard, J., and Resler, H. (1975), *Class in a Capitalist Society*, Heinemann, London.

Westermarck, E. A. (1907), 'Sociology as a University Study', Inaugural Lecture, University of London.

Whyte, W. F. (1943), *Street Corner Society*, Chicago University Press (2nd edn 1955).

Wiles, P. (1977), *The Sociology of Crime and Delinquency in Britain: Vol 2 The New Criminologies*, Martin Robertson, London.

Willer, D., and Willer, J. (1973), *Systematic Empiricism*, Prentice Hall, New York.

Willis, P. (1977), *Learning to Labour*, Saxon House, Farnborough.

Woolf, M. (1971), *Family Intentions*, HMSO, London.

Woolf, M., and Pegdon, S. (1976), *Families Five Years On*, OPCS, HMSO, London.

Wootton, A. J. (1975), *Dilemmas of Discourse*, Allen & Unwin, London.

Worsley, P. (1974), 'The State of Theory and the Status of Theory', BSA. Presidential Address 1973, *Sociology*, vol. 8, no. 1.

Young, J. (1971), *The Drugtakers*, Paladin, London.

Young, M. and Willmott, P. (1957), *Family and Kinship in East London*, Penguin, Harmondsworth.

Young, M. and Willmott, P. (1960), *Family and Class in a London Suburb*, Penguin, Harmondsworth.

Young, M. (1975), 'The First Years: 1965-68', *SSRC Newsletter*, no. 29, November.

Young, M. F. D., ed. (1971), *Knowledge and Control*, Collier Macmillan, London.

Zelditch, M. (1962), 'Some Methodological Problems of Field Studies', *American Journal of Sociology*, no. 67, 566-76.

Zimmerman, D. H. (1969a), 'Tasks and Troubles: the practical bases of work activities in a public assistance organisation', in D. A. Hansen (ed.), *Explorations in Sociology and Counselling*, Houghton Mifflin, Boston.

Zimmerman, D. H. (1969b), 'Record-keeping and the Intake Process in a Public Welfare Agency', in S. Wheeler (ed.), *On Record: Files and Dossiers in American Life*, Russell Sage Foundation, New York.

Zimmerman, D. H. and West, C. (1975), 'Sex Roles, Interruptions and Silences in Conversations' in B. Thorne and N. Henley (eds), *Language and Sex: Differences and Dominance*, Newbury House, Rowley, Mass.

Name index

Subject Index

access, 203

action research, 163-80; action and research teams, 177, 179; Batley CDP, 169-73; CDPs as examples of, 164; continuity of, 177; co-ordination of, 175, 177; definitions of, 163-4; expectations of change in, 178; Glycorrwg CDP, 173-4; levels of intervention in, 178; local agencies and action teams, 175; personnel in, 176

American Sociological Association (ASA), 21, 55, 102, 109, 122, 242

anti-positivism, 47, 204

autobiographical accounts of research, 181

Banbury, 18, 98, 204, 207, 208

Bethnal Green, *see* Institute of Community Studies

British Sociological Association, 11-12, 44, 75; code of practice on supervision, 286; consulted by Heyworth, 258; as a professional body, 21-4; Sociology Teachers' Section of, 12, 23

British Association for the Advancement of Science, 11

capitalism, 74-5

CDP Project, 176

Centre for Contemporary Cultural Studies, 108-9

Centre for Social Studies, Aberdeen, 245; *see also* Universities (named), Aberdeen

Chicago School, 250; *see also* Universities (named), Chicago

China, 4, 72, 91

Chronically Sick and Disabled Persons Act, and social research, 143, 148

Clapham Commission Report: and criminology, 103; need for government statistics, 143; and social science research, 254, 255, 256

class, 75

Communists, 241-2, 295

Community Development Projects: alienation of community leadership, 243; as action research, 164, 168-80; assessment of, 174-9, 208; Batley, 169-73; Glyncorrwg, 173-4; and social research, 144

Community Relations Council, Batley, 170-1, 175

community studies, 95-6, 193

convergence thesis, 65, 66

conversational analysis, 116, 124, 126, 273; and democratic data, 128-9; and ethnography, 127-32, 134, 136-8

Conservative Party, 244, 272, 277, 295

Council for National Academic Awards (CNAA): BSA involvement, 23; chairman of visiting panels, 29; influence on new sociology courses, 28-30

criminology, 103-4

Cuba, 39, 72, 91; Bay of Pigs, 45

Department of Education and Science (DES), 265, 273, 294

Department of Health and Social

317